Language, Society, and N

Language, Society, and New Media uses an interdisciplinary approach, integrating frameworks from sociolinguistics and linguistic anthropology and emerging strands of research on language and new media, to demonstrate the relationship between language, society, thought, and culture to students with little to no background in linguistics. Couched in this integrative "e-sociolinguistic" approach, each chapter covers the significant topics in this area, including language structures, language and cognition, and language variation and change, to elucidate this relationship, while also extending the purview of the field to encompass forms of new media, including Facebook and Twitter. Discussions are supported by a wealth of pedagogical features, including sidebars, activities and assignments, and a comprehensive glossary. In *Language, Society, and New Media*, Marcel Danesi explores the dynamic connections between language, society, thought, and culture and how they continue to evolve in today's rapidly changing digital world, ideal for students in introductory courses in sociolinguistics, language and culture, and linguistic anthropology.

Marcel Danesi is Professor of Linguistic Anthropology and Semiotics at the University of Toronto, Canada. He has written extensively on linguistic and cultural topics and his books have been translated, overall, in to 10 languages. He is currently the editor-in-chief of *Semiotica*, the leading journal in the field of semiotics and interdisciplinary studies.

Language, Society, and New Media
Sociolinguistics Today

Marcel Danesi

Routledge
Taylor & Francis Group

NEW YORK AND LONDON

First published 2016
by Routledge
711 Third Avenue, New York, NY 10017

and by Routledge
2 Park Square, Milton Park, Abingdon, Oxon, OX14 4RN

Routledge is an imprint of the Taylor & Francis Group, an informa business

© 2016 Taylor & Francis

Library of Congress Cataloging in Publication Data
Danesi, Marcel, 1946-
Language, society, and new media : sociolinguistics today / Marcel Danesi, University of Toronto.
pages cm
Includes bibliographical references and index.
1. Mass media and language. 2. Socialization. 3. Language and culture. 4. Sociolinguistics I. Title.
P40.5.S57D36 2015
302.2301'4--dc23
2015004466

ISBN: 978-1-138-02458-8 (hbk)
ISBN: 978-1-138-02459-5 (pbk)
ISBN: 978-1-315-77565-4 (ebk)

Typeset in Goudy Old Style
by Saxon Graphics Ltd, Derby

Printed and bound by CPI Group (UK) Ltd, Croydon, CR0 4YY

Contents

Preface

Language is a truly fascinating and enigmatic phenomenon. Why did it come about in the human species? What is it? What does it allow us to do that other species cannot? The scientific discipline that aims to answer questions such as these is known as *linguistics*. The particular approach that focuses on the relation between language, society, thought, and culture is known under various rubrics—sociolinguistics, linguistic anthropology, cultural linguistics, the sociology of language, and a few others. The purpose of this book is to introduce the formal study of this relation—a study that has become increasingly more important in an age, designated the "global village" by the late communication theorist Marshall McLuhan, where languages, societies, and cultures are in constant contact and flux. Traditionally, linguists have aspired to document and examine the use of language in specific societies or by particular communities and groups, focusing on how language binds them together and on how languages vary across geographical and social spaces. Anthropologists have focused instead on how language shapes cognition and how material culture, symbols, rituals, rites, and belief systems are intertwined with it. This book will amalgamate several of these approaches, although it remains essentially an introductory text in sociolinguistics. It will also expand traditional sociolinguistics to the study of language as it is used in new media, from text messaging devices to Facebook and Twitter. This particular application of sociolinguistic theory and method will be called "e-sociolinguistics."

The underlying premise that will guide the present treatment is the idea that language varies according to individuals, situation, and media of usage. This is not a discovery of this book, of course. It has been part and parcel of sociolinguistics since its inception. The difference is that it will include topics that normally fall under different disciplines but which share a lot of ideas and practices. I believe that this type of integrative approach is necessary for two reasons: first, there is much overlap among the fields; second, I have found in my own courses that one can present a better picture of the language–society–media connection if one also deals with the language–cognition–culture connection at the same time. This might seem quite ambitious, but it is not. It really is a matter of emphasis.

I sincerely hope that readers of this book will find it useful in some way. I feel privileged to have had so many students over the years who have inspired me to bring all my experiences together and to write a book that I truly hope will be worth reading.

Marcel Danesi
University of Toronto, 2015

Features

This book will cover, as mentioned in the Preface, both traditional areas of sociolinguistics and selected themes in linguistic anthropology and e-sociolinguistics. It is intended primarily for undergraduate courses.

The chapters will have:

1   examples of classic and relevant research on the themes covered;
2   text boxes providing further information on a topic; and
3   cross-references to other chapters, so as to create an ongoing cohesive treatment.

At the end of each chapter there will be:

1   a section for reviewing technical terminology;
2   textual material for analysis; and
3   exercises and questions for discussion that can be done as assignments or as suggestions for further investigations.

At the end of the book there is a glossary of technical terms for easy reference.

Rapid Overview

Linguistics proper focuses on language as a system of rules of grammar or pronunciation; sociolinguistics, on the other hand, focuses on language as a social phenomenon and, thus, as a key to understanding how humans think, act, and behave as part of living together in groups. This book will introduce basic notions and describe key findings in this interdisciplinary area, focusing on how language mirrors social and cognitive phenomena.

Another area that this book will cover is the study of how language is used by people to interact meaningfully, systematically, and for various social functions—an area called *pragmatics*. Language is a highly adaptive and context-sensitive instrument that is shaped by forces that are largely external to it. Its forms and rules are not only intertwined with each other, but are also highly susceptible to the subtle influences that usage has on them. Geographical variation will also constitute a major topic of this book, discussing how language forms vary across physical space. If there is an abundance of differences in a specific speech area with regard to the main language of a society, they are said to constitute a version of that language called a geographical dialect or simply dialect. On the other hand, if the differences characterize how certain social groups or communities speak, the version is called a social dialect or a sociolect. Dialects develop over time as a consequence of separation of groups from a region, divisions within a society, such as those related to economic class and religion, and so on. Dialect speech is often a marker of identity. People may adopt particular pronunciations to distinguish themselves from others for varying social reasons. The related question of bilingualism, multilingualism, and ethnic speech in various communities will be discussed in detail, since these illustrate concretely how languages adapt to new situations. A special focus will be put on the case of Spanish in the United States as a marker of identity and a code for community solidarity, among other sociolinguistic functions.

In his study of American aboriginal languages, Franz Boas discovered features that suggested to him that languages served people, above all else, as cognitive tools for coming to grips with their particular environments and social realities. This can be seen in the fact that specialized vocabularies serve classificatory functions that are perceived to be critical by particular societies. For example, speakers of English have very few words for *seals*, whereas those who live in regions such as the Arctic have developed a sophisticated vocabulary to refer to them. English-speaking societies on the other hand have developed an elaborate system of color terms, probably because they are needed to refer to a different reality of English-speaking society, such as its emphasis on fashion. Thus, Boas's anthropological approach will be incorporated in this book as part of the broader sociocultural study of language. Writing as a social practice will also constitute a main theme. And, as mentioned, this book will also look at the work in the ever-expanding field of e-sociolinguistics, or the study of how language is changing in the internet age.

Illustrations

1 Sociolinguistics

> *I really do inhabit a system in which words are capable of shaking the entire structure of government, where words can prove mightier than ten military divisions.*
>
> Václav Havel (1936–2011)

From the dawn of history, humans have used a unique faculty—*language*—to think, to communicate with each other beyond the instinctual use of body signals, to transmit knowledge to subsequent generations, and to do other things that make them unique among species. Human civilization, with its legal systems and written codices of knowledge, is built on language. Altogether, the world's languages constitute humanity's collective memory system. Each word is a capsule of time-specific knowledge, an act of human consciousness, and an implicit principle of social structure. The Greek philosophers saw language as a manifestation of *lógos*, which meant both "word" and "reason or mind," and thus as the faculty that united thought and speech. The modern-day study of this manifestation is the objective of the discipline of *linguistics*; the study of language as an intrinsic part of social systems is the goal of *sociolinguistics*, a major branch of linguistics.

Humans have always been curious about how language works and what functions it plays in everyday life. Already in the 400s BCE, an Indian scholar named Pāṇini described the Sanskrit language he spoke with a set of about 4,000 rules. His work, called the *Ashtadhayayi*, is considered to be one of the first grammars of any language on Earth. Pāṇini showed that many words could be decomposed into smaller distinctive units. In English, for example, the word *incompletely* is made up of three such units: *in* + *complete* + *ly*. Two of these (*in-* and *-ly*) recur in the formation of other words and are thus intrinsic parts of grammar (the system of rules for forming words and sentences); *complete* is, instead, part of a collection of meaning-bearing forms called a *lexicon*. Pāṇini also described with precision how the words were to be pronounced, looking forward to the modern-day study of sound systems. And he argued that Sanskrit provided an indirect, yet insightful, historical record of how a particular society emerged, developed, and shaped people's worldviews, belief systems, and modes of interaction.

This chapter will provide an introductory overview of what sociolinguistics is all about. Like Pāṇini, the sociolinguist focuses on how grammar and vocabulary mirror social systems. It will present some of the main ideas in a general way. Many of these will then be discussed, developed, and illustrated in subsequent chapters.

1.1 Language

Defining language is an exercise in circular reasoning, because we need language itself to do so. The English word *language* comes from Latin *lingua*, "tongue." So, a basic definition could be the use of the tongue to create messages for human communication. But that is not all language does. It also allows us to refer to objects, states, and events in the world with sound clusters (words, phrases, sentences) and thus to record them for future reference by means of these clusters. When incorporated into the brain's memory system, these invariably affect how we perceive the world. The anecdotal proof of this is an everyday occurrence. When we see something, we respond to it in terms of distinctive sound clusters—a plant thus becomes a *tree* or a *flower*, depending on what lexicon (the collection of these clusters) we possess in order to refer to it. If we have no word for something that we feel is important, then we have several options—we can make a new one up or we can borrow a word from another language that seems to fill in the gap.

Wherever there are humans living in groups, there are languages. Animals communicate effectively with their innate signaling systems. Humans also use signals (body language and facial expression). But language is a unique faculty among species. And unlike most signaling systems, it takes on diverse forms according to place on Earth and time period of its usage. For this reason linguists distinguish between language as a faculty and diverse languages as manifestations of this faculty. The faculty is the same across time and space— what varies are the different languages that instantiate it. There is no better or worse language. All languages serve human needs equally well, no matter if the language is spoken by millions of people (like Mandarin Chinese) or a small handful (like some indigenous languages of America), and no matter if it is the main language of one or more nation states or spoken by a small community of people within a nation state. Each language is used to solve universal problems of knowledge and of social organization. In other words, languages enable people to name and reflect on the things that are relevant and meaningful to them wherever they live.

There are about 6,000 languages spoken in the world today. This number does not include dialects (local forms of a language). There are barely a little more than 200 languages with a million or more speakers. Of these, 23 have about 50 million or more speakers each. More than half of the languages spoken today are expected to disappear in the next 100 years—a tragedy that parallels the corresponding loss of natural species and resources on Earth. The

The Most Spoken Languages

1. Mandarin: 995 million
2. Spanish: 405 million
3. English: 360 million
4. Hindi: 310 million
5. Arabic: 295 million
6. Portuguese: 215 million
7. Bengali: 205 million
8. Russian: 155 million
9. Japanese: 125 million
10. Punjabi: 102 million

main languages in danger of extinction are the indigenous ones of nations like America. Understanding how all languages contribute equally to human progress can perhaps help curtail some of the language loss (known as *language attrition*). This is one of the implicit goals of sociolinguistics.

Classification is at the core of any science. This is the case in linguistics as well, which classifies languages into *families*, that is, into groups of languages related to each other historically. For example, Latin, Greek, and Sanskrit (in India) all derive from the same source, called *Indo-European*. Other language families include the Finno-Ugric (Hungarian, Finnish, Estonian), Indigenous languages of North America (Cree, Ojibwe, Na-Dene), Sino-Tibetan (Chinese, Burmese, Tibetan), and many others.

1.1.1 Features

All languages have a basic set of features in common.

1 They have a finite set of distinctive sounds used to make words or smaller units (such as *in-* and *-ly* above), ad infinitum; the sounds are called *phonemes* and the units *morphemes*. Languages might also have symbols (pictographs, alphabet characters, and so on) for imprinting the words on surfaces or other physical media (known as writing) in order to preserve messages.

2 The same set of phonemes and morphemes allows people to innovate and coin words for referring to new objects, ideas, and events. This means that languages are constantly changing and evolving along with other human expressive systems (music, drawing, art).

3 Languages have a set of rules, known as a grammar, for putting words together to form larger units of meaning (phrases, sentences, and texts).

These form the basis of dialogue, literacy, creative writing, and other communicative and expressive functions.

4 Languages make purposeful social interaction possible, providing the vocal and written means for carrying out rituals, interpersonal relations, and other social functions.

5 Languages are highly variable across time and space, splitting into variants known as dialects.

Most languages use from 20 to 60 phonemes to make their forms of speech (words, phrases, and so on). In alphabet-using societies, less than 30 characters are generally required to represent the phonemes. This feature of language is called *double articulation*—with a small set of sounds one can make words, sentences, and texts ad infinitum. This term was introduced by the French linguist André Martinet (1955). So, for example, the English word *cat* is composed of the sounds [k], [æ], and [t], in that order, which are meaningless as separate individual sounds and which can also be used to form different words with other meanings. Without double articulation, it would require an enormous inventory of sounds to create distinct words. According to the late American linguist Charles Hockett (1967), this is the key property of human language, since it allows for the expression of a potentially infinite number of messages with a small repertory of phonetic resources. This suggests a general "principle of least effort" in language, which can be characterized informally as "doing a lot with a little."

Phonetic and Phonemic Transcription

In linguistics, the symbols between square brackets represent sounds. This is called *phonetic transcription*. While spelling may vary in representing the same sound, phonetic transcription does not:

[k] = in *c*at, *k*ind, *q*uick, a*ch*e
[æ] = in c*a*t, h*a*t, m*a*te
[t] = in *t*op, caugh*t*, a*tt*ention

Some sounds function as phonemes, that is, as distinctive sound units. For example, [k] and [r] are distinctive since they cue differences in meaning in word pairs such as *cat* and *rat*. By simply changing the [k] to [r] we get a difference in meaning, as can be seen. These sounds are thus called phonemes. They are transcribed with slant lines rather than square brackets: /k/ and /r/.

Note that a sound can be transcribed in either way—phonetically or phonemically—depending on situation and need.

To distinguish between *language* itself and its uses, linguists use the term *speech* to refer to the latter. Speech can be vocal, involving the use of the vocal organs (tongue, teeth, lungs, and so on), or nonvocal, as in writing, gesturing, and the sign languages used by speech-impaired communities.

It is in using language that the need may arise to create new forms that reflect new situations, new experiences, and new needs. Every time we come up with a new word or phrase, we are acknowledging that something new has come into existence or, at least, to mind.

1.1.2 Acquiring Language

Remarkably, by simply being in regular contact with speakers of a language, children acquire it spontaneously. They listen to people, imitate them as best they can, and in short time start using words and making up sentences on their own. By the age of 5 or 6, children show a sophisticated control of the language or languages to which they have been exposed. If they control more than one language, the situation is called *primary bilingualism*. When people add another language to their linguistic repertoire, either by necessity (as in situations of immigration) or by choice (as in the learning of another language at school), it is called *secondary bilingualism*.

Vocal speech is made possible by the lowering of the larynx (the muscle and cartilage at the upper end of the throat containing the vocal cords)—a phenomenon that is unique to the human species. In early infancy the larynx is located high in the neck. During their first months of life, infants breathe, swallow, and vocalize in ways that are similar to other primates. But at some point around the third month of life, the larynx starts to descend, gradually altering how the child will breathe and swallow. This entails a few risks—food can easily lodge in the entrance to the larynx; and drinking and breathing simultaneously can lead to choking. But in compensation, the lowered larynx permits vocal speech to emerge by leaving a chamber above the vocal cords that can modify sound. Intrigued by the spontaneity with which infants acquire language, the Greek philosopher Plato asked the following question: How is it that children, whose contacts with the world are brief and limited, are able to know as much as they do about language? He concluded that this is so because much of what they know is innate, coming from earlier existence and merely reawakened in childhood. In other words, it is part of human nature to speak. But this explanation by itself does not capture the crucial importance and intricacy of the interplay between the environment in which the child is reared and the apparently instinctive knack for language. If nurturing is not present, then language simply does not emerge, as the study of "feral children"—children who have survived without normal nurturing conditions—clearly shows (Curtiss 1977). Even after a century of studying childhood language development scientifically, linguists are still unsure as to how language is acquired. In the end, all arguments are based on specific inferences about the way humans learn.

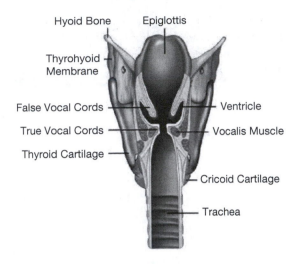

Figure 1.1 The Human Larynx

The linguist who has been the most influential in the modern debate on language acquisition is Noam Chomsky (1975, 2000, 2002), who has updated Plato's perspective by positing the presence of what he calls a Universal Grammar (UG) in the human brain in order to explain why children acquire languages so effortlessly on the basis of partial and imperfect input from speakers—known as the *poverty of stimulus*. The UG is argued to be the blueprint on which all languages are built—a blueprint composed of rule-making principles that are available to all children, hence the universality and rapidity of language acquisition. When a child learns one fact about a language, he or she can easily infer other facts without having to learn them one by one. Differences in languages are explainable as differences in rule types, or "parameters." These generate the different grammars across the world. The linguist Stephen Pinker (2007) suggests that children are born with a "language of thought" that makes them little grammarians, constantly inferring the appropriate rules from the various speech samples to which they are exposed to produce a "language of speech." Pinker also claims that the UG is present in our genes. If it is, then Plato and Chomsky may be right after all. Actually, it has been hypothesized that a gene, called FOXP2, passes on specific language impairments to one's offspring. This would suggest that language is a trait that is transmitted through genetic inheritance. But the evidence for this is specious. Moreover, as Burling (2005: 148–149) points out, FOXP2 may not even be a specifically-marked language gene:

> FOXP2 should not be considered a language gene, however. Several thousand other genes are believed to contribute to building the human brain, and a large portion of these could contribute, in one way or another,

to our ability to use language. Any one of these might interfere with language if it were to mutate in a destructive way. Nor is the influence of FOXP2 confined to language or even the brain, for it is known to play a role in the embryological development of lung, heart, and intestinal tissues.

There are other views, of course, of how language emerges in the child. An interesting view is the one that sees the ability of the child to fill conceptual gaps with words and phrases as an intrinsic form of "world-making" based on analogy (comparing things on the basis of perceived similarities). For instance, if a child does not have the concept of "moon" available to him or her, but knows the concept and word for "ball," the child will likely refer to the "moon" as a *ball*. In so doing, the child is assuming that the qualities of one object are imprinted in the word and thus that the word can be applied to any other object that shows those qualities (completely or partially). As the Russian psychologist Lev S. Vygotsky (1962) pointed out in his studies of speech development, children are essentially "little poets," using language creatively to make analogies and inferences about the world, inventing forms that are quite similar to the verbal ploys used by poets.

1.2 Sociolinguistics

Actually, children realize early on that the language they are learning is more than a means to name objects and people. They sense that they can use it as well to bring about some action, to ask for things, to express their emotions, and so on. In other words, children become increasingly aware that language is a means for interacting purposefully with others. If they are reared in English-speaking cultures, children learn, for instance, that if the person to whom they are talking is a superior or someone in a position of authority or of importance (such as a family physician or a school teacher) then using a title when addressing him or her is usually required ("Mrs. Jones," "Mr. Smith," "Dr. Brown," "Professor Green"). On the other hand, they know that it would be bizarre to address friends or close family members with titles, unless they wanted to be humorous. In a phrase, children learn that language is not only a naming tool, but also a social tool. The study of language as a social tool is the primary goal of sociolinguistics.

The first studies that are recognizable as sociolinguistic in focus, apart from early ones in general linguistics that alluded to language and its social uses, and apart from studies on dialects, can be traced to the 1930s and the work of various Indian and Japanese linguists. The American scholar Thomas Callan Hodson was likely the first to use the term *sociolinguistics* in a 1939 article titled "Sociolinguistics in India." But it was not until the late 1960s that it emerged as an autonomous field with its own methods, theories, data sets, and research agendas (Shuy 1997).

To get an initial sense of what sociolinguists study, consider the relation between biological gender and language that emerges in virtually all societies. In Japanese, the word for "stomach" is *hara* for men, but *onaka* for women. The reason for this is likely the belief that, biologically, the stomachs of men and women are different and thus that separate words are required to encode the difference. In Koasati (an indigenous language spoken in Louisiana), men say *lawawhol* to refer to "lifting," while women say *lakawhos*—a dichotomy that again suggests a differential perception (Haas 1944). Arguably, the Koasati people perceive the lifting abilities of the two genders as different and thus see the need to convey this dissimilarity routinely through lexical differentiation. In the language spoken on the Island of Carib in the West Indies women use the word *kachi* for "sun" while the men use *hueyu*. In this case, the differential vocabulary seems to acknowledge the different social roles that the men and women play; that is, when the sun is out men are probably working outside the home and women are probably working within it. Such lexical differences, called *doublets*, are markers that people within a community consider necessary in order to acknowledge perceived differences in gender roles (Taylor 1977).

An analogous pattern of linguistic encoding can be found across the whole spectrum of social relations, whereby differences in class, age, and other variables are imprinted in distinctive language forms. Using these forms constantly eventually predisposes speakers to perceive the differences as "natural," rather than merely communal (cultural). Sifting the "natural" from the "cultural" through the study of language and speech in diverse social contexts is an important goal of sociolinguistic research.

1.2.1 Historical Roots

Towards the end of the nineteenth century, language scholars started to study not only how languages changed, but also how they were structured and how they characterized specific groups of people. The Swiss philologist Ferdinand de Saussure (1916) put the finishing touches on the emerging blueprint for a science of language by making a distinction between the historical study, which he called *diachronic*, and the systematic study of languages at a specific point in time, which he called *synchronic*. He also proposed that the new science should focus on *langue* ("language"), the system of language itself (the phonemes, words, grammar, and so on), rather than on *parole* ("word"), or the ability to use the language in conversations, writing, and other social activities.

Basic to Saussure's plan for the study of *langue* was the notion of *différence* ("difference, opposition"), or the view that the forms and structures of a language do not take on meaning and function in isolation, but rather in differential relation to each other. For example, the linguist should determine the meaning of the word *cat* in English by comparing it to the word *rat*. This will show, among other things, that the initial consonants /k/ and /r/ are important in English for cuing the meaning of both words. From such *différences* we can establish what makes the word *cat* unique in English. Note that in this type of analysis phonemic transcription is required, given that spelling traditions are not always consistent or reliable in providing a key to the pronunciation of the sounds (see 1.1.1 above).

Saussure did, however, see the broader goal of linguistics as studying how language manifests itself in various kinds of speech situations. So, he did not totally exclude the study of *parole*, but he did not consider it as the main focus of the new discipline. His approach was known as *structuralism*, a term used also in psychology, a science that was coming into being at about the same time. In Europe, structuralism was adopted and elaborated by a number of linguists who congregated in the Czech city of Prague, eventually coming to be known as the Prague Circle in the 1920s. One of the techniques that the Circle established as basic to linguistic method is called the *minimal pair*—a technique that is used to this very day. The words *cat* and *rat* above constitute a minimal pair; that is, they are composed of the same combination of sounds except for the one in initial position. This allows the linguist to flesh out the differential sound cue, known as the phoneme (as we saw) that keeps these words distinct. In general, by analyzing minimal pairs, it is possible to identify all the phonemes in a language.

The Prague Circle also paid close attention to the relation between internal linguistic structures (such as phonemes) and external (social) ones, thus prefiguring the field of contemporary sociolinguistics. For example, they argued that one could distinguish speech communities on the basis of the inventory of phonemes that they possessed, since these were unique to each community. The first to apply structuralism to the study of the indigenous languages of America was the anthropologist Franz Boas (1940) at Columbia University. Boas saw the objective of linguistics as examining how different cultures used their languages for their specific purposes. He showed how languages developed specialized lexical and grammatical forms that reflected the experiences and interpretations of their speakers. This approach to language went far beyond what Saussure had envisioned for linguistics. It aimed to understand the connection between a specific language and the reality that it encodes. Evidence supporting Boas's basic perspective is everywhere. For example, the Nuer society, a herding people of eastern Africa, has developed a sophisticated vocabulary for referring to the colors and markings of cattle, but very few words to describe clothing. The reason is that cattle play a much more important role in that society than does fashion (Evans-Pritchard 1940). Modern Western societies, on the other hand, have few words for cattle but many for describing clothes. The reverse is thus true in these societies, since fashion has more value than livestock in the lifestyle schemes of common people. Languages, therefore, are traces to a society's main concerns, emphases and interpretations of the world. Boas's approach laid the foundations for *linguistic anthropology*, a branch of general linguistics that is still thriving today. Linguistic anthropology and sociolinguistics share many of the same research methods and intellectual traditions, as will be illustrated in this book (Gumperz and Cook-Gumperz 2008).

An implicit tenet of linguistic anthropology is that language, thought, and culture are intrinsically intertwined—one depends on the other (Labov 2001). This train of thought was adopted by Boas's student Edward Sapir (1921) and Sapir's own student Benjamin Lee Whorf (1956), who reworked it into the form of a hypothesis, known alternatively as *linguistic relativity* or the *Whorfian Hypothesis* (WH). Simply put, the WH posits that different societies encode specific concepts as being necessary by simply giving them specialized linguistic expression (Miller 1968; Mathiot 1979). But this specialized use does not block understanding between speakers of different languages, since analogies, metaphors, and other mental translation strategies can be used to explain linguistic specializations of every kind.

A key idea in linguistic relativity, expressed succinctly by Whorf, is that we are unaware that the categories of our language are not shared by others. In other words, we are conditioned to believe that the concepts encoded by our language are natural and universal, not specific to our historical needs. Distinguishing between universal traits and culture-specific ones has always been a goal of linguistic anthropology. For example, the linguist George Lakoff (1987) examined an interesting "Whorfian" property of the Australian language Dyirbal. Like many languages, Dyirbal has grammatical gender—each of its nouns must be assigned to one of the available grammatical genders. In European languages, the gender of the noun is many times unpredictable from its literal meaning. For instance, the word for "table" is masculine in German (*der Tisch*), feminine in French (*la table*), and neuter in Greek (*to trapézi*). Dyirbal has four genders, which are assigned instead according to the meaning of the noun. One of the four genders includes all nouns pertaining to *women*, all those referring to *fire*, and all those indicating things that are *dangerous* (snakes, stinging nettles, and the like). This way of organizing grammatical structure is clearly not arbitrary; it reflects a perception of the world that is vastly different from the perception inherent in the grammars of European languages. And it brings out the cultural emphases of Dyirbal society rather saliently.

1.2.2 Ethnography

Sapir and Whorf used the method of *ethnography*, suggested by Boas, to gather the data they needed to test their hypothesis. Since their times, it has become the main method of research in both linguistic anthropology and sociolinguistics. The ethnographer gathers the relevant information by doing *fieldwork*; that is, by living among a group of people, observing their culture and language, questioning them when appropriate, and then annotating his or her observations. Ethnography requires sensitivity to others and this entails, above all else, the ability to speak the language of others. Unlike the type of research that uses selected subjects, usually in a laboratory setting, ethnographic research attempts to maintain the spontaneity of everyday life in research projects by conducting practical work in the natural environment where the people live. Actually, to be more precise, *ethnology* is the term used to refer to the method of data-gathering itself, and *ethnography* the term used to refer to the technique of writing down one's observations. In practice, however, only the latter term is used to refer to both.

Ethnography goes right back to the origins of anthropology, defining its disciplinary character. Two classic ethnographies are Bronislaw Malinowki's *Argonauts of the Western Pacific* (1922) and E. E. Evans-Pritchard's *The Nuer* (1940). A work that has shown how powerful ethnography can be as a method in linguistics is Boas's own book on the Kwakiutl (1940), a native society on the northwestern coast of North America. As mentioned, Boas showed how the grammar and vocabulary of the Kwakiutl language served the specific needs of its speakers, providing them with the resources for talking about the world in group-significant ways and thus making social interaction fluid and meaningful. The language, Boas claimed, also revealed the worldview that the Kwakiutl espoused. The anthropological practices of ethnography and fieldwork were adopted by sociolinguists early on in the history of the discipline (Hymes 1964). They are still central to the conduct of research within sociolinguistics today.

Ethnography, Ethnology, Fieldwork

Ethnography is a research technique practiced by anthropologists and linguists whereby the researcher lives among groups of people, interacting with them and interviewing them in a systematic way, so as to gain insights about them as collectivities. Strictly speaking the method is called *ethnology*.

Ethnography refers more specifically to the writing up of such insights as a set of observations.

The actual activity of gathering information while living among a group is known as *fieldwork*.

1.2.3 Subdivisions

Sometimes, *sociolinguistics* is differentiated from the *sociology of language*, also named respectively *macro-sociolinguistics* and *micro-sociolinguistics*. The focus in the former is on the relation of a language's forms to social phenomena, while in the latter it is on the uses of the forms in common interactions. Today, the two have practically merged into the singular discipline of sociolinguistics. Like any major science, sociolinguistics is subdivided into distinct areas of investigation. These include the study of:

- *bilingualism* (the acquisition and use of two languages);
- *code-switching* (the admixture of languages in the speech of bilinguals and others);
- *communicative competence* (the rules that govern how we use language to communicate);
- *dialects and sociolects* (geographical and social variants of a language);
- *diglossia* (the social assignment of prestige to linguistic variants or dialects);
- *discourse* (language use to convey group membership and worldviews);
- *expressive uses of language* (the roles played by certain forms of language, such as poetry);
- *language and identity* (how language is used to construct and convey identity);
- *language and social variables* (how language reflects and encodes social perceptions of gender, age, class, and other variables);
- *language in digital environments* (how language is changing to serve the needs of people interacting in online media);
- *language planning* (the role of legislation and governmental policies in regulating language use);
- *language, race and power* (how language is used for reasons of power and how it is used to signal racial differences);
- *multilingualism* (the use of various languages in a particular society and the roles they play in it);
- *pragmatics and conversation* (the forms of language used in conversations and verbal interactions of all kinds);
- *registers* (the levels of language that denote meaningful social distinctions);
- *slang and jargon* (how certain forms of language are used for group solidarity or emerge in specific kinds of speech contexts);
- *style* (how language varies in socially-sensitive ways); and
- *written language and literacy* (how writing and traditions of writing impact on a society).

As is obvious, the span of sociolinguistic inquiry is vast indeed—in general, however, it can be said that it encompasses any aspect of how language varies according to social context or to use in social contexts. As mentioned, a number of its areas fall into the domain of linguistic anthropology as well. In fact, the two disciplines are sometimes combined into a general line of inquiry called *social linguistics* or *cultural linguistics*.

1.3 Methodology

Each science has its specific methods—procedures, techniques, and generic research tools that it uses to gather relevant information and data. Sociolinguistics does as well, and like other sciences, it is constantly revising and revamping them to meet new conditions in which language varies and is used. Like research in linguistic anthropology, a large part of sociolinguistic methodology is based on ethnography. But it also utilizes quantitative techniques such as inferential statistics and interviews—both of which are common methods in many social sciences and various other branches of linguistics. So, like the basic investigative purview of the discipline, sociolinguistic methodology is eclectic and wide-ranging.

William Labov is often regarded as the founder of contemporary sociolinguistic methodology, with his classic study of the social implications of pronunciation differences (1963, 1967, 1972). Labov made tape recordings of conversations of New York City residents of different ethnic and social backgrounds. One of the features that stood out in the recordings was the perceptions people had with regard to the pronunciation of /r/ after vowels in words such as *bird*, *tired*, *beer*, and *car*. An "/r/-less" pronunciation was felt to be prestigious in the past, modeled after British English. However, after World War I the prestige declined, quickly becoming old-fashioned. Labov's study confirmed this, recording the highest occurrence of the pronunciation of /r/ in young people, aged 8 to 19.

He also discovered that people aspiring to move from a lower class status to a higher one attached great prestige to the way in which the /r/ was pronounced. He chose as his subjects employees working at three stores in New York City in order of prestige: Saks Fifth Avenue, Macy's, and S. Klein. He again recorded two pronunciation strategies—one in which the final /r/ was pronounced (considered socially prestigious) and one in which it was not pronounced (considered to be non-prestigious). The rates of pronunciation of /r/ were highest in Saks, less in Macy's, and lower in S. Klein. Labov concluded that workers identified with the prestige of their employer and customers and that this identification influenced their pronunciation habits. In other words, he established that the sound system of a language is hardly an abstract one; it correlates directly with social mobility.

1.3.1 Interviews and Fieldwork

Labov's study involved both fieldwork and an analysis of the collected data with statistics. The fusion of statistical and ethnographic techniques has become a defining research characteristic of modern-day sociolinguistics (Milroy and Gordon 2003; Tagliamonte 2006; Chambers 2010). Labov's ground-breaking work was preceded by the fascinating work of John Fischer in 1958, who used a simple interview technique. Fischer interviewed a group of elementary school children noticing that they often alternated between two pronunciations of the verb suffix -*ing*: /-ing/ versus /-in/ (*reading* versus *readin'*). The choice, Fischer realized, was related to the gender, social class, personality, and mood of the speakers. If they were girls, if they came from families with an above average income, if they had dominating or assertive personalities, or if they were tense, the children tended to use the more formal /-ing/. As the interviews progressed, the children became more relaxed and were thus more likely to use the informal /-in/, no matter their sex, social class, or emotional state. Fischer's study brought out the fact that speakers of a language are sensitive both to the context in which it is used and to the perceptions associated with such use (conscious or unconscious).

Interviews, like the ones conducted by Fischer and then by Labov, continue to be primary methods in sociolinguistic research. In order to assay how a specific linguistic form is used and what it tells us about its relation to a social variable or to some social behavior the interviewer chooses subjects (also called informants) either through random-population procedures or by selecting a subgroup, called a *sample*, that is of specific interest, such as, for example, adolescents who use a certain type of slang for group solidarity purposes. There are various ways to prepare an interview. But the basic one is that the questions used should produce the information required in an unobtrusive manner. The interview may be done person-to-person, by telephone, e-mails, or through digital platforms such as social media. Sociolinguistic theories must be tested and verified empirically through fieldwork and statistical analysis before they can be considered reliable (Briggs 1986).

As in linguistic anthropology, fieldwork is an integral part of sociolinguistic research. Information is gathered primarily through observation and conversations with members of a targeted community or group of speakers. The sociolinguist may also participate in a variety of social functions and political activities during the period of study. The community's institutions and culture are studied, along with the attitudes, behavior, and interactions of its members. The sociolinguist then records his or her findings in a report called a *case study*. Case studies provide reference material for other sociolinguists who are studying similar communities.

1.3.2 Basic Statistics

As mentioned, research projects and their analyses are often guided by principles of inferential statistical design. As difficult as it may seem to those entering into this field, the basic concepts of inferential statistics are actually straightforward and, nowadays, can be easily applied to a case study with the use of appropriate software. Nonetheless, some basic understanding of these principles is required, because without a statistical aspect to it, sociolinguistic research would produce mainly a compilation of observations lacking the detection of an intrinsic pattern in it. The two main aspects of sociolinguistic research—fieldwork and statistical analysis—must inform each other in the overall design of a research project, otherwise one ends up gathering tidbits of information that may be interesting in themselves but of little overall value to the study of the relation between language and society. This two-pronged approach to research allows the sociolinguist to ask meaningful questions about features of language as they occur in context.

In the 1700s, the word *Statistik* was commonly used in German universities to describe a systematic mathematical comparison of data about different nations. Given the descriptive efficacy of the technique, statistics was quickly adopted by the emerging social sciences in the subsequent century and has since become a primary analytical tool of these sciences. The first task in statistical analysis is to organize the numerical data gathered from interviews or fieldwork. The basic procedure for doing so is to arrange the data according to frequency or recurrence. Let us assume that a sociolinguist has interviewed 25 subjects, asking them to rate, on a scale of 0 to 5, what influence they think text messaging has on the language they use offline, with 5 indicating that it has a definite effect and 0 no effect. At the end of the interview period, the sociolinguist has hypothetically collected the following ratings, in no particular order:

1, 2, 0, 4, 1, 3, 3, 1, 2, 0, 4, 5, 2, 3, 2, 3, 2, 4, 1, 2, 3, 0, 2, 3, 1

Clearly, we can surmise very little from looking at this layout of the ratings. A better idea of what they indicate can be gained by grouping them into a table that lists each different rating value (x) and its frequency (f) of occurrence. Such a table is called a *frequency distribution*:

Table 1.1 A Frequency Distribution

X	f
0	3
1	5
2	7
3	6
4	3
5	1
	25

The table tells us that there are three 0 ratings, five 1 ratings, and so on. Immediately, we can see a few things that are of interest. First and foremost, we note that most of the subjects (7 + 6 = 13) rate the influence at 2 or 3. This is called the *central tendency* or *central location* of the distribution, that is, the single rating in the set of ratings that best characterizes all the ratings. The most frequently used measure of central tendency is the simple arithmetic average, or *mean*. The *mode* and the *median* are two other measures. The mode is the value that occurs most frequently. In our data it is 2 because the number 2 occurs seven times (as we can see from the frequency distribution chart above). The median is the middle value in the data. In our example, there are 25 values. If they are laid out in sequence (in order of increasing value), the median is the thirteenth number, which is 2:

0, 0, 0, 1, 1, 1, 1, 1, 2, 2, 2, 2,	2,	2, 2, 3, 3, 3, 3, 3, 3, 3, 4, 4, 4, 5
twelve	↑	twelve
	median	

Determining the median in this case is easy to do because the total number, 25, is odd, making it possible to divide the set evenly into twelve before the middle number and twelve after. If there is an even number of values, then the median is the average of the two middle values.

The *mean* is calculated by summing all the values in the data and then dividing the sum by the number of values (25). If we do this with the set above the result is 2.16. The formula used to determine the mean is given below. It is read as follows: $\overline{X}$ = mean, N = number of scores in a set, X = an individual score, ΣX = sum of all the scores:

$$\overline{X} = \frac{\Sigma X}{N}$$

As you can see the median, mode, and mean are close to each other in value. This tends to be the case if the set of data collected is large enough or if it is truly representative. However, for most purposes the mean is probably the best method for determining the central tendency of a set.

A measure of central tendency tells us very little in itself, unless we know how it relates to the individual values in the data. Are most values clustered tightly around the mean? Are they spread out? The spread of the values in a frequency distribution is called *dispersion*. The simplest measure of dispersion is known as the *range*. This is, simply, the largest score minus the smallest one. In our sample of 25 rankings, the range is 5 – 0 = 5. This allows us to rank any one value in the set to the range and thus estimate its relative merit. A more important question is: How much dispersion is there in the data? The rating of 3 is very close in value to the mean of 2.16; more specifically, it is 3 – 2.16 = 0.84 units from the mean; on the other hand, the value of 0 is 2.16 – 0 = 2.16 units from the mean. It we add up all these "deviations from the mean," and divide them by the total number (25), we get an average value of the dispersion in the data. This is called the *standard deviation*.

It is a known fact of statistical research that the greater the dispersion, or standard deviation, the less reliable the data; the more the standard deviation clusters around the mean the more significant are the findings. Statistical tests have been developed to determine the significance level of the deviation. So, clearly being able to compute the standard deviation and then applying various other statistical tests to it is very important. Let us go through the computation method rapidly.

First, we compute how much each ranking deviates from the mean of 2.16. For example, a ranking of 3 deviates from 2.16 by 3 − 2.16 = 0.84 and the ranking of 1 deviates from 2.16 by 1 − 2.16 = −1.16. To eliminate the negative results, we can perform a clever maneuver. We simply square all the scores, which we need not do here. Next, we take the average of these deviations in the same fashion as above. This produces a "mean of deviations." Now, the reverse of squaring is taking the square root (remember that we squared the individual deviations simply to eliminate the minus signs). The result is: 1.07. To summarize, the formula for computing the standard deviation is given below: SD = standard deviation, $(X - \overline{X})^2$ = the difference between each score (X) and the mean ($\overline{X}$) squared in order to eliminate the negative signs, $\Sigma (X - \overline{X})^2$ = the sum of all the differences, $\surd$ = square root of the sum (eliminating the squaring), N = the total number of scores:

$$SD = \sqrt{\frac{\Sigma \left(x - \overline{x}\right)^2}{n}}$$

The standard deviation tells us that, on average, a ranking deviates from the mean by 1.07. Is this a high degree of dispersion or not? Since the standard deviation is a comparison measure, there are statistical tests that answer this

Basic Significance Tests

T-test: test for comparing the means of two samples, even if they have different numbers of subjects. It compares the actual difference between two means in relation to the variation in the data (the standard deviation of the difference between the means).

Chi Square: test used to compare observed or collected data with data we would expect to obtain according to a specific hypothesis.

Correlation: measure of the extent to which two or more variables collected from a research study fluctuate or vary together. A positive correlation indicates the degree to which the variables increase or decrease in parallel; a negative correlation indicates the opposite, namely the extent to which one variable increases as the other decreases.

ANOVA: technique that allows the analyst to determine significant difference between sample groups with respect to a specific variable. ANOVA permits us to break up the sample according to the variable and then see if the result is different across samples.

question precisely. These tests are called *significance tests*. Their mathematical intricacies need not be elaborated upon here, since these are available in basic handbooks of statistical methods. The main tests for the purposes of sociolinguistic analysis are the *t-test*, the *Chi square test*, *correlation analysis*, and *ANOVA* (see box). It would seem that the SD in our data is fairly low, suggesting that our findings can be explored further for significance testing. Note that the actual statistics are more complicated than what has been described here. The purpose here has been purely illustrative.

1.4 Sociolinguistics in Practice

Anything that connects language to society will potentially constitute an area of investigation for sociolinguistics. Some areas (see 1.2.3 above) have a long tradition of study, others have a more recent history. It is worthwhile taking a glimpse here into some of the factors that motivate sociolinguistic research. Essentially, sociolinguistics is an applied science, in the sense that it applies linguistic theories, techniques, and ideas to social situations. This does not mean that sociolinguistic research has had no effects on theories of language. On the contrary, sociolinguistic findings have led to many new notions, such as *communicative competence*, or the idea that it takes knowledge of how conversations and dialogues unfold in order to communicate in the language and that this kind of competence is developed in tandem with the knowledge of grammar, pronunciation, and vocabulary. This notion was already implicit in the Russian psychologist Lev Vygotsky's work on childhood development. Vygotsky (1962, 1978) showed that the employment of language for social purposes surfaces early on in life as the child tries to come to grips with his or her world. When children speak to themselves as they play, they are engaging in an internal dialogue, testing out meanings and concepts as they are imprinted in the phonic substance of words. They develop an instinctive sense that communication requires knowledge of a whole set of rules that connect them to the greater social order.

1.4.1 Language Use

Let us take as a concrete example the notion of communicative competence—a topic that we will discuss in more detail in Chapter 6. The distinction often made in linguistics is between *linguistic competence* and *linguistic performance* or, to use Saussure's terms, *langue* versus *parole*—that is, between language itself and the ability to use language for some purpose. The study of *parole* has traditionally been relegated to a subsidiary status within linguistics proper, since it was felt that the use of language for social purposes had no implications for the study of language per se. But this came to be viewed as an artificial separation early on, since research on languages within linguistic anthropology consistently revealed that as people used them in conversations, the languages themselves started changing.

By the late 1960s work on how people spoke in everyday situations led to a revision of Saussure's dichotomy (Andersch, Staats, and Bostrom 1969). This led, in turn, to the emergence of a subfield of linguistics called *pragmatics*. Research in pragmatics started showing that the ways in which people talk not only taps into a system of implicit social rules and rituals, but also shapes and changes the formal language system itself. Moreover, it revealed that knowing how to talk entailed a type of competence that was separate from linguistic competence, yet connected to it. Dell Hymes called it *communicative competence* in 1971. With this term, he wanted to suggest that knowing how to use language is as systematic as knowing the rules of the grammar of the language being employed. Hymes's pivotal notion led to a burgeoning of interest on the nature of conversations and on verbal discourse generally.

With this new research focus, sociolinguists started relating language forms to all kinds of social phenomena (Saville-Troike 1989). The sociologist Erving Goffman (1959, 1978) saw research into the pragmatic aspects of language as a key to understanding what he called the social framing of identity, whereby language is used to fit a situation deliberately to the advantage of the speaker. Another theory that has come out of the research is that conversation plays a crucial role in imparting a sense of togetherness among interlocutors as well as a sense of security. As Robin Lakoff (1975) has argued, speakers will even refrain from saying what they mean in some situations in the service of the higher goal of preserving group solidarity.

An important offshoot of this focus is the notion of *discourse*. The term refers to the unconscious use of a specific type of language that is designed to bind people or groups together in terms of shared values, worldviews, beliefs, and so on. Discourse is typically characterized by keywords that appear frequently in conversations (Stubbs 2008) and by other interlinking strategies such as jargon, conversational styles, and so on (Searle 1969; Tannen 1989, 1993a, 1993b, 1994; Fairclough 1995; Van Dijk 1997; Scollon and Wong Scollon 2001). These convey a sense of adherence to the group. Schools, corporations, universities, the media, and other collectivities all develop discourse styles that determine how members speak to each other. As the Russian scholar Mikhael Bakhtin (1981) argued, discourse styles are the products of unconscious processes of social conditioning. They are shaped by cultural presuppositions and a shared sense of solidarity during interactions. Discourse serves many social functions. Religious rites, prep rallies, political debates, formal academic lectures, among others are anchored in these styles, either traditionally worded or specifically composed for the occasion. Discourse allows speakers to maintain or indicate allegiance to the group and its causes, implicitly or explicitly.

The study of discourse has also generated implications for studying language in social context. In most societies, it would be considered rude or adversarial to address a superior at work with an informal mode of speech, unless the superior permits it ("Hey, Jack, what's up?"); on the other hand, it would be felt as aberrant or strange to carry out a conversation with a close friend using formal speech ("Hello, Mr. Smith, how are you?"). In other words, social relations such as these are mirrored in linguistic cues that sociolinguists call *registers*. In the traditional Javanese society of Indonesia, for instance, different social classes are expected to utilize specific registers according to situation. At the top of the social hierarchy are the aristocrats; in the middle the townsfolk; and at the bottom the farmers. The most formal register is used by aristocrats who do not know one another very well, but is also used by a member of the townsfolk if he or she happens to be addressing a high government official. The mid formal register is used by townsfolk who are not friends, and by farmers when addressing their social superiors. The low register is used by farmers among themselves, or by an aristocrat or town person talking to a farmer, and among friends on any social level. It is also the register used to speak to children of any class. Today the situation is a bit different, but there are still three registers: high (for formal and polite situations); mid (for many common conversations); low (for informal speech).

1.4.2 Personality

A recent work by James Pennebaker (2011) is indicative of another significant aspect of sociolinguistics—the link between language and personality. Pennebaker examined the speeches of American presidents and found, for example, that president Barack Obama emerged as the "lowest I-word user" of any of the modern presidents. Pennebaker then claimed that politicians show a tendency to use the pronoun "I" in their speeches to personalize their message, so as to convey to audiences that they are committed personally to specific causes. Obama's apparent disdain for the first-person singular pronoun does not mean, however, that he is humble or insecure; rather, it shows confidence and self-assurance. He does not need to assert himself in public with the pronoun. His assurance is implicit and thus more powerful. In effect, grammatical forms (pronouns, articles, and the like) reveal more about personality than do content words (nouns, adjectives, verbs), at least according to Pennebaker. These words have an "under-the-radar" meaning to them, constituting traces to personality.

Pennebaker started his research project by looking at thousands of diary entries written by subjects suffering through traumas and depressions of various kinds. He discovered that pronouns were indicators of improvements in mental health, claiming that recovery from a trauma or a depression requires a form of "perspective switching" that pronouns facilitate. Pennebaker also found that younger people, women, and those from lower classes seem to use pronouns and auxiliary verbs more frequently than do others. Clearly, Pennebaker's hypothesis would have to be tested much more empirically. Today, with social media sites such as Facebook and Twitter the potential sample size of diary materials has become gargantuan and can be used effectively to validate or refute Pennebaker's theory. But it is true that we all have a "personal language style," that linguists call *idiolect*. This is our particular manner of speaking that identifies us instantly, including pronunciation, tone of voice, choice of vocabulary, types of sentences used, and so on. The point to be made here is simply that work such as that by Pennebaker makes it obvious that sociolinguistics is a powerful tool for investigating the relation of language to its users.

1.4.3 Gender

Another main area of sociolinguistic research is the role played by language in social relations and how it mirrors changes in these relations. For instance, the demise of the singular pronoun *thou* in Old English and its replacement by *you* in printed documents in sixteenth-century England correlated with changes in class structure during that era. Another example concerns revisions to the use of the masculine grammatical gender in certain words and phrases, reflecting the movement towards gender equality. In the not-too-distant past, terms like *chairman* and *spokesman* revealed how the English language predisposed its users to view certain social roles in gender terms. English grammar was organized from the perspective of those at the center of the society—the men. This is why we would say in the past (and somewhat even today) that a woman married into a man's family, and why at wedding ceremonies expressions such as "I pronounce you man and wife" were used. Also, language such as "lady atheist" or "lesbian doctor" implied that atheists and doctors were not typically female or lesbian. Today, such exclusionary language has almost disappeared, as the tendency is to use more generic (gender-less) language. The general synopsis of such phenomena is that grammar and social structure are intrinsically intertwined. Investigating gender in the Iroquois language, Alpher (1987) found that the feminine gender was the default one, with masculine terms being marked by a special prefix. In other words, he found the reverse of pairs such as *waiter–waitress* or *actor–actress*, in which the special suffix *-ess* identifies the person as female. Alpher related this to the fact that Iroquois society is matrilineal. The women hold the land, pass it on to their heirs in the female line, are responsible for agricultural production, control the wealth, arrange marriages, and so on. Iroquois grammar thus reflects the social fact that in Iroquois society the women play a more central organizational role than do the men.

The gist of the foregoing discussion is that languages mirror their user's perceptions of social roles. Consider that in English the word for "general human being" was (and sometimes still is) *man*, which coincides semantically with "the male person." The word actually meant "person" or "human being" in Old English and was equally applicable to both sexes (Miller and Swift 1971, 1988). Old English had separate words to distinguish the latter: *wer* meant "adult male" and *wif* meant "adult female." The composite forms *waepman* and *wifman* meant "adult male person" and "adult female person" respectively. In time, *wifman* evolved into the modern word *woman* and *wif* narrowed its meaning to *wife*. The word *man* then: (1) replaced *wer* and *waepman* as a specific term distinguishing an adult male from an adult female, but (2) continued to be used in generalizations referring to human beings. The result of merging (1) and (2) seemed to render females invisible. Studies investigating the meanings that are elicited when *man* or *he* are used as generic forms of reference have confirmed this (Doyle 1985). Changes made to the English language over the last decades have attempted to correct this perception built into its grammar and vocabulary—*chairperson* (instead of *chairman*), *first-year student* (instead of *freshman*), and *humanity* (rather than *mankind*). But marked perceptions still exist, being more subtle. However, when the older forms are used they no longer bear within them the same gender bias they implied in the past.

1.4.4 Markedness

The feature of language that encodes sexual gender differences in terms of grammatical differences is known generally as *markedness*. Initially, the theory of markedness was applied simply to identify certain forms in a language as more common or neutral and others as more distinctive or "marked." In English the article form (1) *a* occurs before another word beginning with a consonant (*a boy, a girl*); and its complementary form (2) *an* before a word beginning with a vowel (*an apple, an egg*). Linguists refer to (1) as the *unmarked* form and (2) as the *marked* one, because the former is the more typical or representative (non-specific) of a class or system (in this case the indefinite article system); the latter is the conditioned or exceptional member. Now, when markedness features occur in the area of gender, social implications tend to emerge, as discussed above. In Italian, for example, the masculine plural form of nouns referring to people is the unmarked one, referring (non-specifically) to any person, male or female; whereas the feminine plural form is marked, referring only to females:

Table 1.2 Italian Masculine and Feminine Forms

Masculine Plural Forms	Feminine Plural Forms
i turisti = all tourists, males and females	*le turiste* = female tourists
gli amici = all friends, males and females	*le amiche* = female friends
i bambini = all children, males and females	*le bambine* = female children
gli studenti = all students, males and females	*le studentesse* = female students

The unmarked form in Italian is a cue that the males in that society were mainly the political leaders, the writers, the artists, and so on. The situation has changed, of course, but its residues are imprinted in markedness structure. In societies (or communities) where the masculine gender is the unmarked form, it is typically the men on who certain social processes depend (family lineage patterns, surnaming patterns in marriage, and so on). As King (1991: 2) aptly puts it, in societies where the masculine is the unmarked form in grammar, "men have traditionally been the political leaders, the most acclaimed writers, the grammarians, and the dictionary makers, and it is their world view that is encoded in language." In societies (or communities) where the feminine gender is the unmarked form, the reverse seems to be true, as various studies have indicated (discussed above). The close relation between markedness in language and social structure can be seen when change occurs, since it occurs simultaneously in both. Consider job designations as a case-in-point. Over the past 60 years, as women increasingly entered into traditionally male-based occupations, their job titles were marked linguistically at first by suffixes such as -ess, producing doublets: for example, *waiter*-versus-*waitress* (mentioned above). Things have since changed. Although the word *waitress* is still around, it no longer is marked socially, only biologically; that is, by and large, people use the -ess suffix mainly when they want to refer to the waiter's sex; otherwise the general term for the job category today is *waiter*, and it includes males and females.

As another case-in-point, consider feminine titles in English. The title Mrs. is a marked form, indicating a woman's marital status. So too is Miss, which implies that the woman is not married. The term Ms. was introduced in the 1970s to rectify this implicit discriminatory portrayal of women. The title was designed to provide a parallel term to Mr., thereby eliminating marital status from the semantics of the female titles. This whole social scenario indicates two things: (1) "the high premium that we put on identifying women by their relationship (past or present) to men" (King 1991: 48); and (2) the recognition that women's traditional titles no longer properly represent their current realities.

1.4.5 Variation

Sociolinguists are also interested in any regional, social or ethnic variety of a language, generally called a *dialect*. The traditional study of dialects comes under the rubric of *dialectology*, which consists of two main techniques: (1) the comparison of specific forms and structures between variants; and (2) a plausible explanation for the differences detected. Once these have been identified and catalogued, the dialectologist can then identify certain forms as "standard" and others as "dialectal," thus attempting to paint a more comprehensive picture of a given language community. Today, dialectology and sociolinguistics have merged, given that dialectal speech invariably carries with it social implications.

Deciding whether two languages are related, or whether they have changed enough to be considered distinct languages, has often proved a difficult process. Dialectologists usually rely on what they call, loosely, *mutual intelligibility* as a criterion for making such a decision. If two languages can be understood mutually by the speakers of both, at the same time that they are able to perceive differences between them as being significant, then they are likely to be dialects. If they are not intelligible, then they are different languages (or dialects of different languages). There are, however, problems with this criterion, because many levels of mutual intelligibility exist (even among unrelated languages), and dialectologists must decide at what level speech varieties should no longer be considered mutually intelligible. This has turned out, in actual fact, to be rather difficult to establish in practice. For one thing, if a speaker of one variety wants to understand a speaker of another, then intelligibility is more likely to ensue than if this were not the case. In addition, sets of speech varieties exist in which adjacent varieties are mutually intelligible, but those farther apart are not. Furthermore, one can never downplay the role of cultural and socio-political factors in shaping the perception of what constitutes a dialect and what constitutes a language. Such factors have led, in the past, to the traditional characterization of Chinese as a single language with a number of mutually intelligible dialects. But this is hardly the truth of the matter. Chinese dialects differ greatly, even though they are written with the same writing system. There are seven major dialect groups within each group. But they differ so greatly, in some cases, that someone living in one area may not be able to communicate at all with someone from another. So mutual intelligibility breaks down here as a criterion.

The study of dialect variation within the broader sociolinguistic framework involves such research questions as the following:

1   Are migrations away from tight-knit dialect-speaking communities changing the way the dialects are used and thus obliterating some of the traditional functions of dialects?
2   Are social media such as Facebook and Twitter generating new dialectal forms? If so, what are they and how do they function?
3   How do we determine today which dialect in a multidialectical society is perceived as more prestigious than others and why? This type of study comes under the rubric of *diglossia*.
4   Do dialectal differences reflect broader social tendencies, including political ones?
5   Which specific dialectal traits indicate allegiance to a group or groups?

1.4.6 Bilingualism

The questions above clearly connect traditional dialectology to the broader aims of sociolinguistic research. For example, there are many societies where more than one language or dialect of a language is used and even taught at school. The study of the social implications of bilingualism and multilingualism is now an intrinsic part of sociolinguistic research. Spanish-speaking communities in the United States, for example, tend to develop a different sense of culture with respect to the broader English-speaking culture. This produces a whole series of issues that sociolinguists study systematically. Hispanics share many of the traditional values claimed by Americans, but they are also typically proud of their own ethnic heritage. Many Hispanic Americans feel that they should not lose contact with their cultures of origin or their language, seeking to be bicultural and bilingual. And many hope that their native cultures can be accepted as being part of American culture. Studying these aspirations has become a vital component of research on bilingualism and biculturalism.

In early school bilingual programs serving Hispanics, students were taught in Spanish in such basic subjects as mathematics and science. Meanwhile, they studied English as a second language. When they were deemed to be ready, they were transferred to classes taught only in English. By the 1990s, many schools had replaced this kind of "transitional approach" with two-way bilingual education, which combined native Spanish speakers with English-speaking students in all classes. The students progressed together through the grade levels, with some school subjects taught in Spanish and others in English. The participants helped one another learn both the language and the subject being taught. Critics claimed that these programs encouraged students to rely too much on Spanish, hence the negative scholastic achievement outcomes that were being reported at the time. Supporters argued that these should not be traced to the quality of bilingual education itself but to the lack of funding and of teacher-training programs that would allow them to flourish. In 1998, California voters approved a controversial measure requiring that all public school classes be taught only in English. But bilingual classes remained available in the state to students whose parents or school boards requested them and to students with special needs. Today, most educators see bilingual education as an advantage, thanks in large part to the findings of sociolinguists, which have consistently shown that when languages receive equal social treatment they enhance school learning, not impede it.

Connected to the study of bilingualism is that of borrowing, which has traditionally fallen under the branch called *contact linguistics*. Why do languages borrow each other's words? The most common reason for this is to fill gaps present in the borrowing language. The words are called *loanwords*. In English, *naïve* (from French) and *memorandum* (from Latin) are loanwords that entered the language ostensibly because no English word existed at the time for expressing the relevant concepts (and still does not). Borrowing is thus a practical strategy. When speakers of a language do not have a word for something that they wish to identify, they can either create one for it or else borrow the word from a language that does. The latter happens more frequently than one might think. The English language has borrowed extensively from Latin and French, including affixes. The suffix /-er/, which is added to verbs to form corresponding nouns, as in the formation of *baker* (noun) from *bake* (verb), was borrowed from the Latin suffix /-arius/. The suffix reduces the effort that would otherwise be needed to come up with, and then remember, different lexical items for separate verb and noun forms.

1.4.7 Speech Communities

As these initial examples of sociolinguistic study indicate, sociolinguists do not study language in terms of its individual units and structures, but in terms of how these are used in speech communities and networks and how they mirror or affect the belief and perceptual systems of people living in these communities. A speech community is a distinct group of people who are connected by means of a common language. In the communities the variant forms used are assigned a higher or lower prestige. The high prestige forms typify official, formal, religious, and scholarly discourse, and the low prestige forms are characteristic of colloquial communication. The high forms always have behind them a strong literary and aesthetic tradition, and, thus, are reinforced as part of a prestige code through formal education and through other official channels. Therefore, understanding patterns of language prestige in society means that one also has to understand the social networks in which language is embedded. A social network is another way of describing a particular speech community in terms of relations among individual members in it. A network could be loose or tight depending on how members interact with each other. An office or factory may be considered a tight community because all members interact with each other. A large course of students, on the other hand, would be a looser community because students may only interact with the instructor and maybe a few other students.

Basil Bernstein (1971), another early founder of sociolinguistics, has distinguished between *elaborated* and *restricted* codes. Bernstein claimed that members of the upper and middle classes have various ways of organizing their speech into *codes* that are fundamentally different than how the lower classes do so. He calls the former *elaborated* and the latter *restricted*. Codes allow people in their particular network to bond and to make differentiations that are crucial to them. In Britain, for example, he found that restricted codes emphasized the "we" dimension of a social group (also called *groupthink*), whereas in elaborated codes the emphasis was on the "I" and thus on the individual. Restricted codes thus fostered greater group adhesion, and elaborated ones more individualism. This dichotomy had an effect on broader social outcomes. Bernstein found that children with a restricted code struggled at school where the elaborated code is the default form of language. The reason for this was not lack of intelligence, but the fact that the child had to learn, first, how to distinguish between the social functions of the two codes.

In certain groups, such as traditional working-class neighborhoods, the elaborated code may be considered undesirable in many situations. This is because the restricted code is a powerful in-group marker, and especially for non-mobile individuals, the use of non-standard varieties (even exaggeratedly so) expresses neighborhood pride and class solidarity. Connected to the standard (elaborated)-versus-nonstandard (restricted) dichotomy are the questions of literacy and levels of language. Literacy is essentially the ability to read and write. It is connected to social power—those who have always wielded power and influence throughout history are those who have had the highest levels of literacy. Before the 1400s, the vast majority of people were illiterate. Most had never had an opportunity to learn to read because there were few schools, and books were scarce and often expensive. Although some people at the lower levels of society could read, most literate people belonged to the upper classes. Illiterate people relied on literate people to read and write for them. Literacy spread at an uneven rate until the invention of the printing press in the late 1400s. Today, literacy is considered to be the primary means for gaining social prestige and economic wellbeing. This is why schooling has become obligatory virtually across the globe and why many organizations work to improve literacy.

1.4.8 Sociolinguistics in the Internet Age

More and more, the tools of sociolinguistics are being applied to examine the evolution of linguistic forms and their social uses in social media and on the internet generally. We are living in a truly interesting era, characterized by rapid changes brought about by an ever-expanding reliance on mass communications technologies. These include changes in social institutions, work patterns, in communicative behavior, information retrieval techniques, and, more to the point of the present book, in our perceptions and experiences of how we interact and relate to each other linguistically. The concepts of register and style, to mention but two basic notions, are being revamped by sociolinguists as they start *en masse* to study the nature and function of communication in online media. The online world has also altered the ways in which linguistic identity is created and managed, and how the sense of self is constructed, not to mention how we now go about making contact with others, constructing messages, and carrying out conversations.

Research on computer-mediated communication, or CMC, is leading to a revision of traditional sociolinguistic notions that have applied to offline and face-to-face (F2F) communication in the past. Questions that CMC is raising include the following: Is communicative competence changing or is it adapting to online forms of interaction? How are registers being determined and negotiated in online contexts? How does CMC reflect the usual dichotomies and variables such as gender, race, class, and ethnicity? Are basic conversational functions changing? These and other questions are reviving and expanding interest in sociolinguistics broadly. In this chapter, we will look only at the general implications. In subsequent chapters, relevant research findings will be discussed in more detail.

1.4.9 Studying Computer-Mediated Communication

Cyberspace

Cyberspace is the term coined by American novelist William Gibson in his 1984 novel *Neuromancer*. Gibson's description of cyberspace is worth repeating here (Gibson 1984: 67):

> Cyberspace. A consensual hallucination experienced daily by millions of legitimate operators. A graphic representation of data abstracted from the banks of every computer in the human system. Unthinkable complexity. Lines of Light ranged in the nonspace of the mind, clusters of constellations of data. Like city lights, receding.

Cyberspace now has its own communities (Facebook communities, Second Life, Multiple User Domains, and so on) and its own set of conventions for communicating and interacting.

Studies such as those by Farman (2012) on Mobile Interface Theory and Papacharissi (2011) on the construction of identity in social media are leading the way in showing the relevance of sociolinguistics to the study of CMC. Essentially, they show that communicative competence is changing in tandem with the media used to communicate. Facebook, Twitter, text messages, posts, shared links, the use of the "like" button, and the typical "post+commenting" functions all constitute new conversational spaces to which sociolinguistic theories and methods can be applied and tested. While sociolinguistics has in the past studied the use of language in traditional electronic media (radio and television), today its tools and theoretical frameworks are being applied more and more to the domain of CMC. Studying language in online contexts has implications for notions such as ethnography, fieldwork, register, speech community, and the like.

Mass communications technologies have always affected how people interact. Already in 1922, the American journalist Walter Lippmann came forward to make the claim that the mass media of his era (mass print technology, radio, and cinema) had a direct effect on people's minds. The American scholar Harold Lasswell extended Lippmann's view in 1927, arguing that propaganda delivered through mass communications technologies affected people's worldviews. Since the 1960s, the study of media and mass communications has developed its own set of theories, facts, and analytical methodologies. Although sociolinguistics had initially maintained a distance from this domain of research, it is becoming more and more obvious that it can no longer do so. Among key topics that sociolinguistics is starting to study is how people project their social and linguistic identities within the "network society." One of the more influential theorists on the importance of this type of study was not a sociolinguist, but the communication theorist Marshall McLuhan (1962, 1964). Electronic media, he claimed, have brought about an intensification, acceleration, and implosion of expansive forces. All technologies are extensions of the human body or brain, and electric circuitry is essentially an extension of the central nervous system. Under electric conditions, the world is within our grasp and perception achieves a global reach. The implications are far-reaching.

Communication in online media involves *multimodality*—the use of more than one sensory mode of communication (visual, audio, and so on)—and *hypermedia*. The latter term is used to describe any medium that involves multimodality. In contrast to *multimedia*, which refers to the amalgamation of various media into a singular text (for example, pictures and words), hypermedia refers to the linkage of different media that are external to a text. Linking the texts is done through *hypertextuality*. The best example of a hypermedium is the World Wide Web, where sites are found that provide multimedial hyperlinks. By clicking on the hyperlink, the user is immediately connected to the document specified by the link. Web pages are written in a simple computer language called HTML (hypertext markup language). A series of instruction tags are inserted into pieces of ordinary text to control the way the page looks and can be manipulated when viewed with a web browser. Tags determine the typeface and act as instructions to display images. They can be used to link with other web pages. Hypertext makes it easy for users to browse through related topics, regardless of their presented order. In internet browsers, hypertext links (hotlinks) are usually indicated by a word or phrase with a different font or color or by an underline. These create a branching structure that permits direct, unmediated jumps to related information. The first hypertext system was introduced by Apple Computer with its HyperCard software in 1987, providing users with a processing system consisting of "cards" collected together in a "stack," with each card containing text, graphics, and sound. It was Tim Berners-Lee who introduced hypertextuality to the internet in 1991, as a system that enables a user to go from one document to another by clicking words or phrases, even if the documents are found on different parts of the internet. Clicking the word brings information to the screen (information contained either on the same site or elsewhere on the internet).

Studying CMC involves two different modes of communication: *synchronous* and *asynchronous*. Asynchronous CMC occurs when the receiver or the interlocutor is not necessarily aware that a message has occurred—this characterizes e-mails, bulletin boards, blogs, and chatrooms. Synchronous CMC occurs, instead, when the interlocutor is aware of the communication as an ongoing one. F2F conversations are synchronous, dictating conversational structure. This, however, is changing in synchronous CMC, as we shall see subsequently. Offline asynchronous communication occurs mainly in written media (letters, books, and so on), which carry their own set of social values depending on the genre of writing. In CMC, the interpretation and functions of communication has changed. This is because the communication event may involve many interlocutors, as happens when an e-mail is sent to many people at once, or it may be aimed directly at someone through a text message. Thus, the value of a text and the nature of conversation are changing radically.

1.4.10 e-Sociolinguistics

The sociolinguistic study of CMC can be called *e-sociolinguistics*, that is, the sociolinguistics of electronic (online) media. How does e-sociolinguistics differ from sociolinguistics? In traditional offline contexts, politeness theory, for example, set out to determine if there were any universals in the use of styles and registers for the purposes of conveying respect during communication (Brown and Levinson 1987) or, if not, what conditions shaped politeness protocols (Wierzbicka 1991). The study of politeness became a major focus in F2F sociolinguistics because it told a compact story of how language intersected with socialness and how it was connected to communicative competence. But in CMC one may ask whether the same rules of politeness apply. Are social media platforms such as Facebook, Twitter, YouTube and Flickr changing the rules and in turn influencing politeness protocols?

Another crucial question for e-sociolinguistics is whether multimodality and hypertextuality are changing how we do things (such as gain literacy) and relate to each other in situations that required register differences in offline contexts. With the increasing range of multimedia capabilities in CMC, discourse options and choices are becoming more and more tied to these capabilities. So, as CMC platforms continue to expand and become evermore ubiquitous the targets of e-sociolinguistic inquiry will include, among many other things, the following:

1   a new focus on the *langue–parole* interface by adding new dimensions to the dichotomy, namely environment (real and virtual), multimodality, and hypertextuality;
2   a study of the new forms of literacy that are starting to characterize so-called "global societies" in cyberspace;
3   a consideration of the ways in which spoken, written and multimodal forms of language encode and allow users to construct identity and develop new forms of social power;
4   a focus on the changing face of synchronous and asynchronous communication and how this may be altering language use;
5   the study of new forms of language that are emerging online;
6   the study of social media sites and the kinds of language used on them;

7   the study of Instant Messaging (IM) and other forms of synchronous digital communications in order to determine what effect these may have on traditional literacy and social protocols. (Baron 2001)

The notions of speech community and speech network are also targets of interest for e-sociolinguistics. These have always been important ones in F2F contexts, as discussed briefly above. In his classic text on linguistics, Leonard Bloomfield (1933: 42) defined a speech community simply as "a group of people who interact by means of speech." Bloomfield pointed out that the members also were aware of what kind of speech was proper and what kind was improper. Dell Hymes (1964: 51) elaborated upon Bloomfield's definition as follows: "A speech community is defined as a community sharing knowledge of rules for the conduct and interpretation of speech. Such sharing comprises knowledge of at least one form of speech, and also knowledge of its patterns of use." Because such definitions are rather generic, Lesley Milroy and James Milroy (1978) introduced the term speech network, adding the idea of contact to Bloomfield's definition, whereby the frequency of interaction and the strength of the contact typify the nature of the network. People in "dense networks" have frequent (daily) contact with each other, and are thus likely to be linked by more than one type of bond than do those with infrequent contact, forming "weak networks." The idea of dense network is particularly applicable to CMC, since people keep in contact more than they would in physical space, given the possibility of constant contact afforded by digital technologies. As Milroy and Milroy realized, dense networks put pressure on members to conform because their values can be more readily shared. The internet has enabled people who know each other to interact so frequently that the concept of speech network seems to be either eclipsing the one of speech community or at least modifying it radically. Twitter, for example, can form the basis of interlinked personal networks—and even of a new sense of community, even though Twitter was not designed to support the development of online communities. Studying Twitter is thus useful for understanding how people use new communication technologies to form social connections and preserve existing ones.

Another major goal of e-sociolinguistics is to look at change with new theoretical eyes. For example, in CMC the second person singular pronoun in English, *you* is written typically as *u* in informal media (such as IM) reflecting the pronunciation more accurately and efficiently. But spelling patterns in CMC carry with them much more than economy of form for efficiency of delivery. They entail sociolinguistic changes that have an impact on communication generally. The form *u* is a common one in text messages and similar digital texts; and when the completely spelled form *you* is used instead to the same interlocutor, it may convey irony, anger, or some other emotion. As Coleman (2010) has written, CMC is thus leading to new forms of ethnography and fieldwork, as well as a new focus on three broad but overlapping categories of analysis: (1) the cultural politics of digital media; (2)

the vernacular cultures that are now arising because of digital media; and (3) the new pragmatics of digital media.

Terminology Review

Define or explain in your own words the following terms introduced in this chapter.

ANOVA
central tendency
correlation analysis
dialect
discourse
doublet
ethnography
fieldwork
hypermedia
idiolect
langue and *parole*
lexicon
markedness
mean
minimal pair
morpheme
multimodality
phoneme
pragmatics
register
sociolect
speech community
standard deviation
synchronous versus asynchronous
   communication
Whorfian Hypothesis

bilingualism
Chi Square
diachronic
diglossia
double articulation
elaborated versus restricted
   codes
FOXP2
hypertextuality
interview
language family
linguistic versus
   communicative competence
median
mode
multilingualism
mutual intelligibility
phonetic transcription
primary bilingualism *(had to learn)*
secondary bilingualism *(want to learn)*
speech
speech network
synchronic
T-test
Universal Grammar

Exercises and Discussion

1   This chapter mentions some features that all languages have in common. Can you think of others?

2   Why is the difference between language and speech a relevant one?

3   Each language has a system of distinctive sounds, called phonemes. These number from around 20 to 60. Sometimes, differences in phonemes may signal some social or regional difference.

Example: the *a* in *tomato*

> It can be produced by opening the mouth to the maximum, as in "bah," or else by opening it in a more lateral way, as in "pay." Both sounds are used in pronouncing *tomato* but may reflect regional differences or perhaps even individual pronunciation (idiolect).

Can you think of others? If so, explain them in your own words.

4   Each language has units known as morphemes, which bear meaning. Part of linguistic competence is being able to segment words into morphemes. Below is an anomalous word:

Example: unlegitimate

> The segment *un-* (known as a prefix) is not used with the form *legitimate*. The acceptable prefix in this case is *il-*, which produces the correct form of the word: *illegitimate*. *Un-* is used with other words, however: *unmistakable*, *unforgettable*, and so on.

What is anomalous about:

(a) uncorrect?
(b) churchs?
(c) mouses?

5   Each language has strategies for personal and social interaction. Below are English utterances that have been constructed anomalously from the standpoint of usage. Using simple explanations, indicate what is improper about them.

Example: My name is Mr. Bill.

> In polite speech, titles (known as honorifics) are used with a complete name or with a surname, not a first (or given) name (unless there is a specific reason to do so): "My name is Mr. Bill Smith" or "My name is Mr. Smith." However, the given utterance is an acceptable one if used, for example, by a speaker attempting to be humorous or facetious with friends.

(a) Glad to make your acquaintance, Mr. Jones. How the heck are you?
(b) Mother, tell your husband that I am going out!
(c) (Telephone communication) Hello, who is it? I'm Mary.
(d) (Text message) Dear Mary, how are you feeling today?

6   What do the following verbal forms indicate socially and/or culturally?

Example: Titles (Mr., Mrs., Prof., Dr.)

Some titles have the general social function of showing respect or deference when addressing certain people such as professors and doctors. Some titles reveal gender-coded differences. The *Mrs.* title indicates that a woman is married. The corresponding *Mr.* title has no similar nuance built into it. This difference reveals an unconscious differential perception of gender.

(a) Greeting protocols (Hello, Good-bye, How's it going? What's up?)
(b) Surnames or family names (Smith, Johnson)
(c) CMC forms such as *u* for *you* or *lol* for *laugh out loud.*

7   Collect data from classmates on any aspect of digital communication. Quantify it and then analyze it with simple statistics. For example, you could ask subjects if they use abbreviated forms in e-mails or if they use proper forms and why this is so.

8   The following excerpt is from Saussure's *Cours de linguistique générale* (1916):

> *A scientific study will take as its subject matter every kind of variety of human language: it will not select one period or another for its literary brilliance or for the renown of the people in question. It will pay attention to any tongue, whether obscure or famous, and likewise to any period, giving no preference, for example, to what is called a classical period, but according equal interest to so-called decadent or archaic periods. Similarly, for any given period, it will refrain from selecting the most educated language, but will concern itself at the same time with popular forms more or less in contrast with the so-called educated or literary language, as well as the forms of the so-called educated or literary language. Thus linguistics deals with language of every period and in all the guises it assumes.*

This next excerpt is from Franz Boas's article "The Methods of Ethnology" (1920):

> *At the present time, at least among certain groups of investigators in England and also in Germany, ethnological research is based on the concept of migration and dissemination rather than upon that of evolution. A critical study of these two directions of inquiry shows that each is founded on the application of one fundamental hypothesis. The evolutionary point of view presupposes that the course of historical changes in the cultural life of mankind follows definite laws which are applicable everywhere, and which bring it about that cultural development is, in its main lines, the same among all races and all peoples. Opposed to these assumptions is the modern tendency to deny the existence of a general evolutionary scheme which would represent the history of the cultural development the world over.*

Summarize each one in your own words, keeping in mind what the goals of sociolinguistic inquiry are and how you could study language in cyberspace using the method of ethnography.

9   The following excerpt is from William Labov's online article "Quantitative Reasoning in Linguistics" (2008):

> *Linguistics centers upon a common problem: variation. If every yes–no question were related to the corresponding declarative in a uniform way, no linguist would be needed to describe the system or tell new learners how to use it. But when a question is asked sometimes in one way and sometimes in another, sometimes with inversion and sometimes without, or sometimes with a final rise in pitch and sometimes a fall, a linguist is called for. Thus the central task of linguistics is to eliminate variation by discovering the exact conditions that produce one variant or the other on the surface....The study of linguistic variation requires a familiarity with both the basic tools of qualitative linguistic analysis and quantitative methods for pursuing that analysis to deeper levels. ...Given the output of quantitative analyses, we ask, what good are they? What inferences and implications can be found in these numbers that justify the time and energy needed to produce them? What are the principles of quantitative reasoning that allow us to pass from the measurement of surface fluctuations to the underlying forms and principles that produce them?*

Discuss why quantitative analysis is essential to sociolinguistic research.

10   This final excerpt is from Benjamin Lee Whorf's *Language, Thought, and Reality* (1956):

> *Every normal person in the world, past infancy in years, can and does talk. By virtue of that fact, every person—civilized or uncivilized—carries through life certain naive but deeply rooted ideas about talking and its relation to thinking. Because of their firm connection with speech habits that have become unconscious and automatic, these notions tend to be rather intolerant of opposition. They are by no means entirely personal and haphazard; their basis is definitely systematic, so that we are justified in calling them a system of natural logic—a term that seems to me preferable to the term common sense, often used for the same thing....The world is presented in a kaleidoscopic flux of impressions which has to be organized by our minds— and this means largely by the linguistic systems in our minds. We cut nature up, organize it into concepts, and ascribe significances as we do, largely because we are parties to an agreement to organize it in this way—an agreement that holds throughout our speech community and is codified in the patterns of our language. The agreement is, of course, an implicit and unstated one, but its terms are absolutely obligatory; we cannot talk at all*

except by subscribing to the organization and classification of data which the agreement decrees.

Do you think a particular language produces a specific worldview? If so, can you give concrete examples (words, grammatical categories) from any language you know?

References

Alpher, B. (1987). Feminine as the Unmarked Grammatical Gender: Buffalo Girls Are No Fools. *Australian Journal of Linguistics* 7: 169–187.

Andersch, E. G., Staats, L. C., and Bostrom, R. C. (1969). *Communication in Everyday Use*. New York: Holt, Rinehart and Winston.

Bakhtin, M. M. (1981). *The Dialogic Imagination*. Trans. C. Emerson and M. Holquist. Austin: University of Texas Press.

Baron, N. S. (2001). *Alphabet to Email: How Written English Evolved and Where It's Heading*. London: Routledge.

Bernstein, B. (1971). *Class, Codes and Control: Theoretical Studies towards a Sociology of Language*. London: Routledge.

Bloomfield, L. (1933). *Language*. New York: Holt.

Boas, F. (1920). The Methods of Ethnography. *American Anthropologist* 22: 311–322.

Boas, F. (1940). *Race, Language, and Culture*. New York: Free Press.

Briggs, C. L. (1986). *Learning How to Ask: A Sociolinguistic Appraisal of the Role of the Interview in Social Science Research*. Cambridge: Cambridge University Press.

Brown, P. and Levinson, S. C. (1987). *Politeness: Some Universals in Language Usage*. Cambridge: Cambridge University Press.

Burling, R. (2005). *The Talking Ape: How Language Evolved*. Oxford: Oxford University Press.

Chambers, J. (2010). *Sociolinguistic Theory: Linguistic Variation and Its Social Significance*. Malden: Blackwell.

Chomsky, N. (1975). *Reflections on Language*. New York: Pantheon.

Chomsky, N. (2000). *New Horizons in the Study of Language and Mind*. Cambridge: Cambridge University Press.

Chomsky, N. (2002). *On Nature and Language*. Cambridge: Cambridge University Press.

Coleman, E. C. (2010). Ethnographic Approaches to Digital Media. *Annual Review of Anthropology* 39: 487–505.

Curtiss, S. (1977). *Genie: A Psycholinguistic Study of a Modern-Day Wild Child*. New York: Academic.

Doyle, J. A. (1985). *Sex and Gender: The Human Experience*. Iowa: Wm. C. Brown Publishers.

Evans-Pritchard, E. E. (1940). *The Nuer*. Oxford: Oxford University Press.

Fairclough, N. (1995). *Critical Discourse Analysis: The Critical Study of Language*. London: Longman.

Farman, J. (2012). *Mobile Interface Theory: Embodied Space and Locative Media*. London: Routledge.

Fischer, J. L. (1958). Social Influences in the Choice of a Linguistic Variant. *Word* 14: 47–57.

Goffman, E. (1959). *The Presentation of Self in Everyday Life*. Garden City: Doubleday.

Goffman, E. (1978). Response Cries. *Language* 54: 787–815.

Gumperz, J. J. and Cook-Gumperz, J. (2008). Studying Language, Culture, and Society: Sociolinguistics or Linguistic Anthropology? *Journal of Sociolinguistics* 12: 532–545.

Haas, M. (1944). Men's and Women's Speech in Koasati. *Language* 20: 142–149.

Hockett, C. F. (1967). *Language, Mathematics and Linguistics*. The Hague: Mouton.

Hodson, T. C. (1939). Sociolinguistics in India. *Man in India* 19: 23–49.

Hymes, D. (1964). *Foundation of Sociolinguistics: An Ethnographic Approach*. Philadelphia: University of Pennsylvania Press.

Hymes, D. (1971). *On Communicative Competence*. Philadelphia: University of Pennsylvania Press.

King, R. (1991). *Talking Gender: A Nonsexist Guide to Communication*. Toronto: Copp Clark Pitman Ltd.

Labov, W. (1963). The Social Motivation of a Sound Change. *Word* 19: 273–309.

Labov, W. (1967). The Effect of Social Mobility on a Linguistic Variable. In: S. Lieberson (ed.), *Explorations in Sociolinguistics*, pp. 23–45. Bloomington: Indiana University Research Center in Anthropology, Linguistics and Folklore.

Labov, W. (1972). *Language in the Inner City*. Philadelphia: University of Pennsylvania Press.

Labov, W. (2001). *Principles of Linguistic Changes: Social Factors*. Malden: Blackwell.

Labov, W. (2008). Quantitative Reasoning in Linguistics. www.ling.upenn.edu/~wlabov/Papers/QRL.pdf (accessed 6 May 2015).

Lakoff, G. (1987). *Women, Fire, and Dangerous Things: What Categories Reveal about the Mind*. Chicago: University of Chicago Press.

Lakoff, R. (1975). *Language and Woman's Place*. New York: Harper and Row.

Lasswell, H. D. (1927). *Propaganda Techniques in World War I*. Cambridge, Mass.: MIT Press.

Lippmann, W. (1922). *Public Opinion*. New York: Macmillan.

Malinowski, B. (1922). *Argonauts of the Western Pacific*. New York: Dutton.

Martinet, A. (1955). *Économie des changements phonétiques*. Paris: Maisonneuve & Larose.

Mathiot, M. (ed.) (1979). *Ethnolinguistics: Boas, Sapir and Whorf Revisited*. The Hague: Mouton.

McLuhan, M. (1962). *The Gutenberg Galaxy: The Making of Typographic Man*. Toronto: University of Toronto Press.

McLuhan, M. (1964). *Understanding Media: The Extensions of Man*. London: Routledge.

Miller, C. and Swift, K. (1971). *Words and Women*. New York: Harper and Row.

Miller, C. and Swift, K. (1988). *The Handbook of Nonsexist Writing*. New York: Harper and Row.

Miller, R. L. (1968). *The Linguistic Relativity Principle and Humboldtian Ethnolinguistics: A History and Appraisal*. The Hague: Mouton.

Milroy, L. and Gordon, M. (2003). *Sociolinguistics: Method and Interpretation*. London: Blackwell.

Milroy, L. and Milroy, J. (1978). Belfast: Change and Variation in an Urban Vernacular. In: P. Trudgill (ed.), *Sociolinguistic Patterns in British English*, pp. 19–36. London: Edward Arnold.

Papacharissi, Z. (2011). *A Networked Self: Identity, Community and Culture on Social Network Sites*. London: Routledge.

Pennebaker, J. W. (2011). *The Secret Life of Pronouns*. London: Bloomsbury Press.

Pinker, S. (2007). *The Stuff of Thought: Language as a Window into Human Nature*. New York: Viking.

Sapir, E. (1921). *Language*. New York: Harcourt, Brace, and World.

Saussure, F. de (1916). *Cours de linguistique générale*. Paris: Payot.

Saville-Troike, M. (1989). *The Ethnography of Communication: An Introduction*, 2nd edn. Oxford: Blackwell.

Scollon, R. and Wong Scollon, S. (2001). *Intercultural Communication*. 2nd edn. Oxford: Blackwell.

Searle, J. R. (1969). *Speech Acts: An Essay in the Philosophy of Language*. Cambridge: Cambridge University Press.

Shuy, R. (1997). A Brief History of American Sociolinguistics: 1949–1989. In: C. B. Paulston and G. R. Tucke (eds.), *The Early Days of Sociolinguistics: Memories and Reflections*, pp. 11–32. Dallas: Summer Institute of Linguistics.

Stubbs, M. (2008). Three Concepts of Keywords. Paper presented to the conference on Keyness in Text, University of Siena.

Tagliamonte, S. (2006). *Analysing Sociolinguistic Variation*. Cambridge: Cambridge University Press.

Tannen, D. (1989). *Talking Voices*. Cambridge: Cambridge University Press.

Tannen, D. (1993a). *The Social Constructions of Sex, Gender, and Sexuality*. Englewood Cliffs: Prentice Hall.

Tannen, D. (1993b). *Framing in Discourse*. Oxford: Oxford University Press.

Tannen, D. (1994). *Gender and Discourse*. Oxford: Oxford University Press.

Taylor, D. M. (1977). *Languages of the West Indies*. Baltimore: Johns Hopkins.

Van Dijk, T. (ed.) (1997). *Discourse as Social Interaction*. London: Sage.

Vygotsky, L. S. (1962). *Thought and Language*. Cambridge, Mass.: MIT Press.

Vygotsky, L. S. (1978). *Mind in Society*. Cambridge, Mass.: Cambridge University Press.

Whorf, B. L. (1956). *Language, Thought, and Reality*, J. B. Carroll (ed.). Cambridge, Mass.: MIT Press.

Wierzbicka, A. (1991). *Cross-Cultural Pragmatics: The Semantics of Human Interaction*. Berlin: Mouton de Gruyter.

2 Language and Society

Of all social institutions, language is least amenable to initiative. It blends with the life of society, and the latter, inert by nature, is a prime conservative force.

Ferdinand de Saussure (1857–1913)

The Indian scholar Pāṇini, as discussed in the previous chapter, showed that a systematic study of the structure of words and phrases was not only possible, but also necessary, in order to understand the meanings imprinted in them better and in order to assess their aesthetic effects. In Greece, the philosopher Aristotle (384–322 BCE) put forward the view of language as a formal system that could be analyzed methodically by identifying the parts of a sentence. He called the main ones the *subject* and the *predicate*, and he connected the study to logical method—hence the Greek term *lógos* to refer to both "word" and "study" (section 1.1, previous chapter), thus identifying language as the means through which logical thinking manifests itself. Aristotle's ideas inspired others to look at language in a similar way, including the scholar Dionysius Thrax, who lived between 170 and 90 BCE. Thrax showed how the parts of speech related to each other systematically in the construction of sentences. He named them *nouns*, *verbs*, *articles*, *pronouns*, *prepositions*, *conjunctions*, *adverbs*, and *participles*—categories adopted by the Roman Priscian, in the sixth century CE, becoming subsequently the basis for writing the grammars of vernacular (non-Latin) languages in the medieval and Renaissance periods in Europe, even if the fit between Thrax's categories and the languages was not always perfect. The same sentence divisions are used to this day.

Already in antiquity the notion that "good grammar" mirrored elegance and literacy became part of social ideology—a notion that exists to this very day. Behind it is the idea that certain forms of language constitute a *norm*, from which others can deviate in one of two directions—upwards or downwards. The former is a sign of a cultured (literate) language user, the latter of an uncultured (lower class or illiterate) user. Grammar was thus seen as a metric of social achievement and mobility, and still is. This meaning of "grammar" was modified in the sixteenth and seventeenth centuries, when the first scientific surveys of languages were carried out. A group of French scholars, called collectively the Port-Royal Circle, started examining grammar as a cognitive, rather than social, phenomenon, aiming to determine which of its features were universal and which were specific to various languages. They put forward in tentative form the idea of a "universal grammar," showing how certain sentences were, essentially, derivatives of more basic ones and that people (no matter what their social background) possessed a set of principles of basic sentence-formation that they used unconsciously to construct sentences. The linguist Noam Chomsky has always acknowledged his debt to the Port-Royal grammarians, admitting that it was strikingly similar to his 1957 framework for describing linguistic competence early on in his career (see section 1.1.2, previous chapter).

At around the same time, the German scholar Wilhelm von Humboldt (1767–1835) took a different view, foreshadowing contemporary linguistic anthropology and sociolinguistics. Rather than focusing on grammar as based on universal principles of construction, he maintained that each grammar reflects the differential experiences of different people. The use of a particular language thus led to an *innere Sprachform* (internal speech form) that conditioned how particular speakers came to view reality. He put it as follows (Humboldt 1836 [1988]: 43):

> The central fact of language is that speakers can make infinite use of the finite resources provided by their language. Though the capacity for language is universal, the individuality of each language is a property of the people who speak it. Every language has its *innere Sprachform*, or internal structure, which determines its outer form and which is a reflection of its speakers' minds. The language and the thought of a people are thus inseparable.

Humboldt's claim continues to be debated today and is often juxtaposed against the universalist claim of linguists such as Chomsky. We will return to this topic in Chapter 8. This chapter will look at the relation of the *innere Sprachform*—the vocabulary, grammar, and sound system of a language—to the social constructs (gender, race, class, and so on) that it reflects. This topic is perhaps the most fundamental one in sociolinguistics (and e-sociolinguistics), since it brings out saliently how language, speech, and society are intrinsically intertwined.

2.1 Vocabulary

Making a link between the words people speak and the social realities they reflect is something we all do instinctively. For example, we typically evaluate others in terms of specific native words they use, categorizing them (and sometimes stereotyping them) in the process: *spaghetti* (Italians), *Wiener*

The Lexicon

In linguistics, the term *lexicon* is used to refer to the set of *lexemes*, a technical term for words or word constructions. For example, the word *broadcast* consists of two lexemes: *broad* and *cast*.

The lexicon is, more specifically, the potential stock of all lexemes in a language; while *vocabulary* refers to the particular lexemes used in specific ways by given languages.

Schnitzel (Germans), *junk food* (Americans), and so on. Clearly, even at an intuitive level vocabulary bears socially coded meanings, existing in what can be called a "social space" that characterizes its users. The notion of *core vocabulary* is of particular relevance to this whole line of inquiry. This is the basic set of words referring to things and concepts that languages across the world purportedly (and most likely) encode because they refer to commonly-shared experiences that play a universal role in human life—words for *mother*, *father*, *sun*, *moon*, and so on. Early scientific work on core vocabularies can be traced to the Indo-European scholars of the nineteenth century who used cognates to determine if languages were related. Cognates are words that are derived from the same linguistic source or root. For example, *domicile* ("residence," "home") in English and *domicilio* ("residence") in Italian derive ultimately from the Latin word *domicilium* ("dwelling"). Continuing in this tradition, the American linguist Morris Swadesh (1951, 1959, 1971) saw the use of core vocabularies as an empirical tool for reconstructing early societies by determining which words united them and which words set them apart.

As the work on core vocabularies has shown, words and word classes can be examined to determine what cultural differences and diverse cognitive emphases exist in a given society. The *lexicon* is thus a key to understanding social systems, both in their origins and in their current constitution. This suggests a general principle—changes in the lexicon mirror changes in society. Vocabulary thus provides a key to understanding how social systems have evolved, what values they espouse, and what institutions are relevant to them. Below is an example of a core vocabulary of 11 items in eight different Bantu languages, spoken in parts of Africa:

Table 2.1 Core Vocabulary Items in the Bantu Family (from: Werner 1919)

	Zulu	Chwana	Herero	Nyanja	Swahili	Ganda	Giau	Kongo
human	umuntu	motho	omundu	muntu	mtu	omuntu	umundu	muntu
humans	abantu	vatho	ovandu	antu	watu	abantu	babandu	antu
tree	umuti	more	omuti	mtengo	mti	omuti	—	—
trees	imiti	mere	omiti	mitengo	miti	emiti	—	—
tooth	ilizinyo	leino	eyo	dzino	jino	erinyo	lisino	dinu
teeth	amazinyo	maino	omayo	mano	meno	amanyo	kamasino	menu
chest	isifuba	sehuba	—	chifua	kifua	ekifuba	—	—
chests	izifuba	lihuba	—	zifua	vifua	ebifuba	—	—
elephant	indhlovu	tlou	ondyou	njobvu	ndovu	enjovu	itsofu	nzau
elephants	izindhlovu	litlou	ozondyou	njonvu	ndovu	enjovu	tsitsofu	nzau
wand	uluti	lore	oruti	—	uti	—	—	—

Such inventories allow linguists to compare languages with the social realities they reflect. For instance, the lack of a word for *wand* in several of the languages may mean various things—the languages have other ways of conveying the idea (such as through metaphor or paraphrase); the speakers of those languages may not use wands for social practices; and so on. Core vocabularies can also be used to estimate the relative length of time that might have elapsed—known as *time depth*—since two languages in a family began to diverge into independent languages. The method of calculating time depth is known as *glottochronology*. It starts by counting the number of cognates among the languages being compared. The lower the number, the longer the languages are deemed to have been separated. Two languages that can be shown to have 60 percent of cognates in common are said to have diverged before two which have, instead, 80 percent (Lees 1953).

2.1.1 The Lexicon

In order to establish a direct link between the lexicon of a language and the society that uses it, the linguist must at times delve into the history and evolution of core vocabularies in order to understand why some have undergone changes in meaning. Consider how some Latin words changed in meaning after they developed into Italian forms—Latin is the source language of modern Italian:

Table 2.2 Changes in Meaning in Italian Words

Latin Word	Original Meaning	Italian Form	New Meaning
DOMU(S)	house	*duomo*	dome
CASA(M)	shack	*casa*	house

This table shows how the words used by common people to designate certain things reflect their social conditions. Most speakers of early vernacular Italian lived in homes that were "shacks." Thus, the fact that the word for "shack" (*casa*), and not the official word for "house" in Latin (*domus*) and its Italian derivative *duomo*, became the source for "house in general" reflects the social status of most of the first speakers of Italian.

The linguist can also use vocabulary to examine social variables such as gender. Recall from the previous chapter (section 1.2) that the study of lexical doublets in various languages, whereby pairs of lexemes—one for the men and one for the women—shows how vocabulary is used to convey different perceptions of gender. A well-known example of this usage comes from Japanese, where lexical doublets are intrinsic to the language. Below is a small list of the words used by the men and those by the women to refer to the same referents:

Table 2.3 Lexical Doublets in Japanese

Meaning	Men Use...	Women Use...
I	boku	watashi
to eat	kuu	taberu
water	mizu	ohiya
delicious	umai	oisii
mother	ohukuro	okasan

In searching for and documenting gendered differences such as these, sociolinguists present their data and then draw general inferences from them. Various hypotheses have in fact been put forward to explain these doublets. But in all of these there is a sense that they emerge from the perception that men and women play different social roles or have different biological capacities. Many times it is hard to draw conclusions from the data because the informants themselves may be unaware of the effects of social conditioning that are involved. Also, gender may not be the only factor for lexical differentiation in the data—the real variable that induces it might be class, ethnicity, or some other variable. Sifting out the relevant factors is a difficult problem. All that can be said here is that it is part of how sociolinguistic research is conducted and then how the findings are debated and assessed. Actually, it is useful to reproduce here Jennifer Coates' (1986) list of four approaches to the study of the linguistic encoding of gender roles:

1 the *deficit approach*, which assumes that the adult male language is the standard or unmarked form of language, and thus that women's language is a deviation from the male benchmark;

2 the *dominance approach*, whereby women's speech is seen as subordinate given the patriarchal system in which it occurs;

3   the *social difference approach*, which analyzes differences in men's and women's speech as a result of socialization; working within this paradigm aims to show that language is used differentially by men and women because their societies require them to do so;

4   the *social constructionist approach*, which looks at the multiple factors that bring about gendered language; thus, certain speech forms may be affiliated with a specific gender, but they can be utilized by speakers of any gender as the situation requires it.

The last approach is the one that has become the most common one in contemporary sociolinguistic research methodology. However, the others may also surface in the data, depending on who conducts the research and what his or her aims are.

2.1.2 Group-Coded Vocabulary

Vocabulary often defines group identity thus constituting a "code," which for the present purposes can be defined as a set of lexical forms that reflect the values and beliefs of a group and which thus set the group apart from others. So-called *argots* and *cants* are perfect examples of how vocabularies are coded for specific social functions. The distinction between the two is negligible—both refer to the codes of criminals or marginal groups that are designed to prevent outsiders from understanding conversations among group members and to reinforce group solidarity. *Argot* designates more specifically the linguistic code of street gangs and *cant* that of organized gangs. Thus, argot is likely to be more comprehensible to outsiders, since deviation from the norm is not as drastic among speakers. Cant is usually less comprehensible, being marked by a highly specialized (secret) vocabulary.

The first dictionary of criminal cant was published in 1819. It was compiled by an English nobleman, James Hardy Vaux, who had spent his early life in London and Liverpool and who had become a thief to support his addiction to gambling (Nicaso and Danesi 2013). Vaux recorded the cant spoken by English criminals and wrote the dictionary probably to gain a pardon, which he in fact received in 1820. Historical documents show that various criminal cants were spoken centuries prior to Vaux's book, many going back to the medieval period. Members of organized criminal groups are expected to develop fluency in their particular type of cant, because it is crucial in allowing them both to keep group operations secret and to express group unity through the "insider savvy" imprinted in the words. A classic example is the cant used by the Russian Mafia (Lunde 2004), which is a trace to the gang's social structure, activities, and mindset. For example, *akademiya* (literally "academy") refers to the prison where the gangster (*vory v zakone*) learns his trade; *dan* stands for extortion money; *krysha* (literally "root") refers to the protection provided after someone has paid the extortion money; *Panama* is the descriptive English name given to the dummy company set up to launder extortion money; *khoda* refers to a gang meeting. Likewise, the Yakuza, the Triads, and other criminal organizations have developed their own cants that allow members to speak about people and events in specific group-based ways.

Lexical codes are also typical of subcultures. As a specific example, take the case of hip-hop slang, also known as urban slang or African American Vernacular English (AAVE). AAVE vocabulary is replete with social nuances that convey the particular worldviews of African American youths. As Darren Garratt (1977: 144) puts it, this type of code allows adolescents "to express their independence from adult society," and, as Janice Rahn (2002) suggests, to take control of their own lives through linguistic empowerment. AAVE, as Geneva Smitherman (2000: 34) also points out, connotes attitudes of "rebelliousness against societal constraints" and the "fierce determination to live on one's own terms." Part of this "fierce determination" is imprinted even in the names assumed by rap artists. LL Cool J, Sista Souljah, Jay-Z, Snoop Dogg, Busta Rhymes, Lil Jon, Puff Daddy, and Missy Elliott, to mention just a handful, are imbued with social subtexts, from an obvious facetious sexual one in Snoop Dogg, to a descriptive one in Lil Jon. Rap artists also spell their performance names differently—*Dogg* instead of *Dog*, *Sista* instead of *Sister*, and so on. The subtext in this case is perhaps an allusion to the fact that "correct" spelling is a sign of imposition from the past. The differential spelling code thus allows Black youths to break from their social past.

Poverty and urban decay in many inner urban places have produced, as Marcus Reeves (2008: 23) puts it, "an environment that had become comparable to the one in 'Lord of the Flies,' where children stranded on an island with no adult guidance create a new, brutal social order of their own." AAVE is in part a response to this environment, bespeaking of a sassy and satirical attitude that blurts out "I'll speak and write English in my own way," not the way of the mainstream. Phrases such as *BIB* or *boyz in blue* (police), *off the hook* (great), and *government cheese* (welfare) are defiant descriptors of how Black youths living in a Lord of the Flies environment perceive certain people, institutions, and ideas in white culture. This makes AAVE an anti-hegemonic code. By flying in the face of the orthographic and grammatical traditions of Standard American English (SAE), AAVE indirectly alludes to the association between language and social conditions. Correct grammar and spelling are more than a sign of a person's education—they reflect a social system that has historically excluded Blacks from the mainstream.

Samy Alim (2004) characterizes AAVE as "Hip-Hop Nation Language." Alim may be right in using the term "Nation," since AAVE also involves declaring a form of independence from white America, in an analogous way, incidentally, that American English allowed Americans to declare their own independence from Britain. The American spelling of certain English words— *color* instead of *colour*, *program* instead of *programme*, and so on—is not much different as an identity-construction tactic than how AAVE spelling reflects

Black identity. As rap artists know, to speak and write the language of a society correctly is to validate the ideological biases of that society. AAVE promotes a subtle, yet powerful, rejection of those biases. Needless to say, questions of the use of AAVE in the broader social system have come up consistently in educational and workplace circles. Studies, such as the one by Alim, suggest that upwardly-mobile young Blacks use AAVE in a contextualized fashion— among peers or for in-group purposes—and SAE for broader social purposes. This situation can be described as diglossic (Chapter 3), whereby one of the codes has group functions and the other more official ones. A distinction is also made between AAVE and AAE, or African American English in general (Thomas 2007). AAE is the speech of many African Americans and is not coded in the same way as AAVE. It is basically SAE with a few modifications. Speakers may employ the different versions for social reasons. AAE is more common in the workplace, for example. Moreover, with increasing social mobility, younger professional Blacks now use SAE increasingly, given their experiences, which are now vastly different from that of many of their predecessors.

2.1.3 Semantic Phenomena

The study of the meanings of words and other structures (phrases, sentences) comes under the rubric of *semantics*. In sociolinguistics the relevant aspect of semantic analysis is how meaning reflects social roles, attitudes, beliefs, and values. The most common technique for identifying those semantically-coded differences that imply specific social perceptions is to do exactly what the core vocabulary scholars did, that is, collect core semantic data or information that allows the researcher to detect social features in it.

Semantics

Semantics is basically the study of meaning as exhibited by words, phrases, and sentences.

It is now divided into several branches, including:

- formal semantics, which studies the logical structure of meaning;

- lexical semantics, which studies word meanings and word relations; and

- conceptual semantics, which studies how linguistic meaning reflects the structure of concepts.

The technical term for what a word or phrase encodes is *referent*. So, for example, the referent of the word *cat* is an animal with recognizable features (a tail, body hair, whiskers, retractile claws, and so on). This type of meaning is called *literal* or *denotative*. If cats play certain roles in a given society, then usage of the word *cat* takes on different *senses*. For example, in some societies a cat is perceived to be a household companion, while in others it is considered to be a sacred animal, and so on. The senses (also called *connotations*) are of particular relevance to sociolinguists, because they indicate the relevance of a certain word in social terms. Where the word for *cat* does not exist, the implication is that this kind of mammal either does not exist in the territory where the language is spoken or that it plays few, if any, social roles.

Since the senses of a word are keys to unraveling certain social ideas or beliefs, the sociolinguist will always have to keep in mind the contextual conditions that hold between native speakers and their words. Technically, this feature of words is called *polysemy*, that is, "many meanings." The distinction between literal reference and polysemy is the key principle used in the making of dictionaries—known as the science of *lexicography*. The primary task in the latter is to unravel all the meanings, including senses, of a word or phrase.

A common notion in semantics is the *lexical field*. This is defined as a set of lexemes that share the same basic referential range. For instance, included in the lexical field of words in English referring to "colors" are *red*, *blue*, *green*, *yellow*, *brown*, among others. Within the field further distinctions can be made with figurative terms such as *crimson*, *navy blue*, *pea green*. The topic of color is actually one that has generated much debate in linguistics, sociolinguistics, and linguistic anthropology. It is worth discussing it briefly here. At a denotative level, we use color terms to indicate gradations of hue on the light spectrum. The terms are not universal. Each language segments the spectrum in different ways. A simple example is the word *blue* in English. The same hue gradation is covered by three different terms in Italian—*azzurro*, *celeste*, and *blu*. These are not just shades of *blue*; they are different words for different color referents, even though they seem to fall, more or less, into the same category. Experts estimate that we can distinguish perhaps as many as 10 million hues. Obviously, then, our limited number of color terms is far too inexact to describe all the colors we are potentially capable of distinguishing. The restrictions imposed on color perception by color vocabularies are the reason why people often have difficulty trying to describe or match a certain color. To overcome problems of this kind, experts have developed various systems of classifying colors. Two widely used ones are: the Munsell Color System and the CIE System of Color Specification. The former was developed in the early 1900s by Albert H. Munsell, an American portrait painter; the latter is used by manufacturers of such products as foods, paints, paper, plastics, and textiles who must often name colors precisely. But because of the indeterminate nature of color, the systems turn out to be highly limited. The CIE System simply provides a more refined color nomenclature that is based on metaphorical language.

Consider what you would see if you were to put a finger at any point on the color spectrum. You would perceive only a negligible difference in hue immediately adjacent to your finger at either side. Depending on where you put it, however, you might name the difference in a specific way. This is because you have become accustomed to "seeing" the spectrum in terms of English color terms. But there is nothing inherently "natural" about the lexical naming system used in English. By contrast, speakers of other languages are predisposed to see other color categories on the very same spectrum, because of the terms used in their languages. Speakers of Shona, an indigenous African language, for instance, divide the color spectrum up into *cipswuka*, *citema*, and *cicena*, and speakers of Bassa, a language of Liberia, segment it into two categories, *hui* and *ziza*. So, when an English speaker refers to something as *blue*, a Shona speaker might refer to it as either *cipswuka* or *citema*, and a Bassa speaker as *hui*. If we refer to something as *yellow*, *orange*, or *red*, the Bassa speaker would see it as *ziza*; and so on. The relative (and approximate) proportional widths of the gradations that these color names represent vis-à-vis the English categories are shown graphically below:

Table 2.4 Color Terms in Different Languages

English	purple	blue	green	yellow	orange	red
Shona	cipswuka	citema		cicena	cipswuka	
Bassa	hui			ziza		

But the above analysis does not mean that the use of a specific set of color terms blocks people from perceiving color reality as others do. The specific color names one has acquired in cultural context in no way preclude the ability to perceive how other cultures recognize color. Perception is shaped by language; not blocked by it. This is, indeed, what a learner of another language ends up doing when he or she studies the color terms of the new language. The student must learn how to reclassify the content of the spectrum via the new terms.

In 1969, the linguists Berlin and Kay argued that differences in color terms are only superficial matters that conceal universal principles of color perception. Using the judgments of the native speakers of twenty widely divergent languages, they came to the conclusion that there were "focal points" in basic or "focal" (single-term) color systems which clustered in certain predictable ways. They identified eleven focal points, which corresponded to the English words *red*, *pink*, *orange*, *yellow*, *brown*, *green*, *blue*, *purple*, *black*, *white*, and *gray*. Not all the languages they investigated had separate words for each of these colors, but they detected a pattern in the naming practices of the languages. If a language had two focal colors, then they were equivalents of English *black* and *white*. If it had three, then the third one corresponded to *red*. A four-term system had either *yellow* or *green*; while a five-term system had both of these. A six-term system included *blue*; a seven-term one had *brown*. Finally, terms for *purple*, *pink*, *orange*, and *gray* were found to occur in any combination in languages which had the previous focal colors. Berlin and Kay thus discovered, remarkably, that languages with, say, a four-term system consisting of *black*, *white*, *red*, and *brown* did not exist.

Examples of languages possessing from two to eleven focal terms are given in the following chart:

Table 2.5 Focal Color Terms

Number	Terms (English Equivalents)	Example of Language
Two	white, black	Jale (New Guinea), Ngombe (Africa)
Three	white, black, red	Arawak (Caribbean), Swahili (eastern Africa)
Four	white, black, red, yellow/green	Ibo (Nigeria), Tongan (Polynesia)
Five	white, black, red, yellow, green	Tarascan (Mexico), !Kung (southern Africa)
Six	white, black, red, yellow, green, blue	Tamil (India, Sri Lanka), Mandarin (China)
Seven	white, black, red, yellow, green, blue, brown	Nez Percé (Montana), Javanese
Eight–Eleven	white, black, red, yellow, green, blue, brown, purple/pink/orange/gray	English, Zuñi (New Mexico), Dinka (Sudan), Tagalog (Philippines)

In 1975, Kay revised the sequence in order to account for the fact that certain languages—such as Japanese—encoded a color that can only be paraphrased in English as "green-blue." He gave it a name though, GRUE, and placed it both preceding or following *yellow* in the original sequence. Since then it has been found that further modification is required because Russian and Italian do not have a single color for *blue*, but rather distinguish "light blue" and "dark blue" as focal colors.

The main implication of Berlin and Kay's study is that color terminology follows a universal sequence (explicated above) and this means that some hues are perceived as more fundamental across the world than others, which are added to the sequence in a predictable way. One problem remains with these conclusions—the problem of figurative terms. For example, Swahili is basically a three-color-term language, but its color vocabulary is bolstered by figurative reference to objects (for example, yellow = *manjano* "turmeric") and through borrowing (blue = *buluu*). The archeological record strongly suggests in fact that metaphor may be the source for the color terms themselves (Wescott 1980). In Hittite, for instance, the words for colors initially designated plant and tree names corresponding to English *poplar, elm, cherry, oak*, and so on. But despite the fact that metaphor was not taken into account, the study by Berlin and Kay is still a solid one. Above all else, it has brought out how crucial vocabulary is in the study of variation across languages and in the search for semantic features that transcend the socially specific but reflect universal human experiences.

The study of such semantic phenomena comes under the rubric of *ethnosemantics*, which looks at how semantic systems reflect particular social and cultural experiences. Cultures where color plays a productive social role will develop larger color vocabularies than those where it does not. This is a practical strategy on two counts: first, the color terms allow speakers to refer to their realities in a specialized way; and second, the encoding is efficient for this purpose.

2.1.4 Contextualized Meaning

In everyday life, the required or intended meaning of a lexical item is determined by the *context* in which it is used. What does the linguist mean by this term? Basically, it is the situation in which speech is used, affecting the meanings of the forms uttered. Consider a sentence such as *The chicken is ready to eat*. The word *chicken* has several meanings according to the social situation in which it occurs. If it is spoken by a farmer during feeding time, then the utterance has a literal meaning: "There is an animal called a chicken which is ready to eat." If it is uttered by a cook who is announcing the fact that he or she has finished cooking chicken meat that has become available for consumption, then the utterance has a different meaning: "The cooked chicken is ready for people to eat." If expressed critically by a person to describe someone who is afraid to eat something, then the utterance has metaphorical meaning: "The person who appears to be afraid of eating [something] is now ready to eat it."

All this suggests that language is an adaptive instrument as well as a tool for helping us understand the value of specific situations (Goodwin and Duranti 1992; Kay 1997). The anthropologist Bronislaw Malinowski (1923) argued that all languages create words to make sense of situations and to solve problems that might arise from them. For example, making contact in communities where the people know each other involves a formulaic and routine form of speech, which he called *phatic*. If you meet someone you know in English, invariably you will make contact with a formula such as "Hi, how are you?" This simply acknowledges the presence of the other. It is not meant to ask about the other's health. However, if the interlocutor is a medical doctor and it involves a physical examination then it would take on that meaning. The branch in sociolinguistics that studies the role of context on speech is called *pragmatics* (as mentioned already), a term coined by the American philosopher Charles S. Peirce (1931) and adopted in the 1930s by another American philosopher, Charles Morris (1938). Pragmatics analyzes meaning as varying according to the contexts in which language is used.

In an era of mobile communications, the notion of context will need to be expanded or at least modified. The concept of "contextual mobility," for example, has emerged to capture the fact that social relations and phatic formulas may "move about" during interaction on mobile devices. This has led to the notion of "shifting contexts" and research is starting to show that these also have effects on communicative and social processes. As Bruhn Jensen (2010: 109) puts it: "Communication transports contexts of meaningful interaction across space and time, and communicators bring contexts with them from place to place, as virtually present in their minds." This new view of context is discussed in subsequent chapters.

2.2 Figurative Language

Research on figurative language over the last five to six decades has led to a revised view of traditional semantics. We hardly realize how prevalent such language is in everyday conversations. When asked how we feel about something, we might say that we are "*cool* about it," or that we are "*lukewarm* about it." These expressions reveal that we perceive feeling in terms of the sensations we experience in response to physical conditions that we have named *cool* and *lukewarm*.

The approach to the study of language as a system of concepts grounded in figurative language is known today as *cognitive semantics* or *cognitive linguistics*. But, there really is no need to distinguish cognitive linguistics from linguistic anthropology or sociolinguistics, since they share the same goals. Boas, Sapir, and Whorf (section 1.2.1, Chapter 1), among other early anthropological linguists, would have been called cognitive linguists today, since they too saw figurative language as a basic strategy in human discourse.

2.2.1 Linguistic Versus Conceptual Metaphors

A metaphor is a figure of speech that connects two seemingly dissimilar entities conceptually so that we can understand one in terms of the other. So, when we say something like "That linguist is a snake" the probable reason for correlating two seemingly unrelated referents—*linguist* and *snake*—is an unconscious sense of a connection between people and animals. In this case, the perceived qualities associated with snakes in English-speaking culture (treachery, deceit) come from a long tradition that attributes them to snakes, including canonical narratives such as the Bible. These are projected onto the linguist, becoming elements of a conceptual portrait of his or her personality.

Modern-day scientific interest in metaphor is due to the pivotal work of the early experimental psychologists in the latter part of the nineteenth century. The founders of the new discipline—the German physicist Gustav Theodor

Fechner and the German physiologist Wilhelm Wundt—were the first to conduct experiments on how people processed figurative language (Wundt 1901). A little later, the German linguist Karl Bühler (1908, 1951) collected some truly intriguing data on how subjects paraphrased and recalled proverbs. He found that the recall of a given proverb or idiomatic expression by people was excellent if it was linked to a second proverb; otherwise it was easily forgotten. So, an expression such as "You're playing with fire" would be better recalled if followed by a semantically connected one such as "You're throwing caution to the wind." Bühler concluded that metaphorical-associative thinking produced an effective retrieval form of memory and was, therefore, something to be investigated further by linguists. Shortly after, I. A. Richards (1936) argued that the meaning implications in a metaphorical expression such as "The linguist is a snake" cannot be completely captured by literal paraphrases such as "The linguist is sneaky," "The linguist is deceptive," and so on. The philosopher Max Black (1962) expanded Richards' theory by suggesting that such an utterance is part of a conceptualization, which can be seen manifesting itself further in expressions such as "That man is a gorilla" and "My friend is a tiger." These are linked conceptually because they are perceived to imply that the people's personalities are perceived in animal features. In 1977, a study by Pollio, Barlow, Fine, and Pollio showed that figurative language pervades common everyday speech. They found that speakers of English uttered, on average, an astounding 3,000 novel metaphors and 7,000 idioms per week. Conclusion? Figurative language could hardly be construed to be a mere stylistic accessory to literal language. This became even more convincing after the publication of several collections of studies (Ortony 1979; Honeck and Hoffman 1980) and a highly popular 1980 book by George Lakoff and Mark Johnson, *Metaphors We Live By*. These set the groundwork for a new approach to the study of meaning that came to be known as *Conceptual Metaphor Theory* (CMT).

Lakoff (1979) elaborated Max Black's distinction between a *linguistic* and a *conceptual metaphor* (above). In "The linguist is a snake" the *linguist* could have been linked metaphorically to any other animal or insect. We could have labeled him or her a *gorilla*, a *pig*, a *puppy*, and so on. The result would have been a different assessment of his or her personality with each new animal term. The set of these *linguistic* metaphors is the concept *people are animals*, which is a *conceptual* metaphor. "People" is called the *target domain* and "animals" the *source domain*. Research within CMT has become widespread. The main findings that are of relevance here relate to the fact that common discourse is not only replete with conceptual metaphors, but also guided by them through further connections among the concepts (Lakoff and Johnson 1980, 1999; Johnson 1987, 2007). As target domains are associated through usage with many kinds of source domains, the concepts become increasingly more unconscious and intertwined, leading to what Lakoff and Johnson call *idealized cognitive models* (ICMs). To see what this means, consider the target domain of *ideas* and its related notion of *theories*. The following source domains, among many others, shape a large portion of talk about ideas and theories:

sight
(1) I can't *see* the point of your idea.
(2) *Seeing* is believing.

geometry
(3) Her ideas are *parallel* to ours.
(4) Instead, his idea is *diametrically* opposite to ours.

plants
(5) That idea has deep *roots* in Cartesian philosophy.
(6) Hers is a *budding* new theory about the atom.

buildings
(7) Quantum theories today are *constructed* on mathematical notions.
(8) The *cornerstone* of that theory goes back considerably in time.

food
(9) It is difficult to *digest* those ideas easily.
(10) That is an *appetizing* thought.

fashion
(11) Those ideas went *out of style* years ago.
(12) That theory is in *fashion* nowadays.

commodities
(13) I don't *buy* your ideas.
(14) She must *package* her ideas differently.

The constant juxtaposition of such source domains in common discourse produces, cumulatively, an ICM. This allows us to navigate mentally through the source domains as we speak. So, if the topic of a conversation is ideas then it is typical to hear statements such as:

Speaker A: I just couldn't *digest* what he said
Speaker B: Yeah, I didn't *buy* it either. I don't *see* the point.

Before CMT, the study of metaphor fell within the field of *rhetoric*, where it was viewed as one of various *tropes* (figures of speech). But since the early 1980s the practice has been to consider tropes as revealing particular kinds of figurative concepts. Thus, *personification* ("My cat speaks Italian") would be classified as a particular kind of conceptual metaphor, one in which the target domain is an animal or inanimate object and the source domain a set of vehicles that are normally associated with human beings. Two tropes, however, are considered to be conceptually different—metonymy and irony. *Metonymy* entails the use of an entity within a domain to represent the entire domain:

1   She loves *South Park* (= the sitcom with that name).
2   There are too many new *faces* around here (= people).
3   They bought a *FIAT* (= car named FIAT).
4   The *buses* are on strike (= bus drivers).
5   The *Church* does not condone that act (= theologians, priests).
6   The *White House* made another announcement today (= the president, the American government).

Irony in CMT constitutes a strategy whereby words are used to convey a meaning contrary to their literal sense—for example "I love being tortured" uttered by someone in excruciating pain. Of course, context is crucial in gleaning ironic meaning. If the sentence is uttered by a masochist, then it would hardly have ironic meaning (Winner 1988).

2.2.2 Figurative Language and Society

In the language spoken by the Batammaliba people who live in the border region between the West African states of Togo and the Benin Republic the parts of the house are named with body terms (Tilley 1999: 41–49). Known as anthropomorphism, this strategy suggests that we project our bodies metaphorically onto the referents that make up our lives in order to, perhaps, connect conceptually with them. This type of conceptualization abounds across cultures. As a concrete example, take the Western Apache language of east-central Arizona, which names the parts of the automobile as if they were body parts (Basso 1990: 15–24):

Table 2.6 Metaphorical Terms for Car Referents in Apache

English Equivalent of Apache Term	Auto Part
fat	grease
chin and jaw	front bumper
shoulder	front fender
hand and arm	front wheel
thigh and buttock	rear fender
mouth	gas pipe opening
foot	rear wheel
back	bed of truck
eye	headlight
face	area from top of windshield to bumper
nose	hood

English Equivalent of Apache Term	Auto Part
forehead	top, front of cab
entrails	machinery under hood
vein	electrical wiring
liver	battery
stomach	gas tank
intestine	radiator hose
heart	distributor
lung	radiator

Basso (1990) explains the use of such metaphors in two ways. First, there is the fact that cars have replaced horses in Apache life and, thus, the terms used to describe the horse have been applied to describe the car. Second, since vehicles can generate and sustain locomotion by themselves, they are likely to be perceived as extensions of human locomotion and, thus, as having imaginary body parts.

The gist of the foregoing discussion is that figurative language is intertwined with social and cultural phenomena of all kinds; in other words, conceptual metaphors reflect social emphases and perceptions, and are often a key to understanding symbols and rituals. Take, for instance, the *love is a sweet taste* conceptual metaphor in English, which can be seen manifesting itself in such common linguistic metaphors as "She's my sweetheart," "They went on a honeymoon," and so on. But the manifestations of this conceptual metaphor do not stop at the level of language. Giving sweets to a loved one on St. Valentine's day, symbolizing matrimonial love at a wedding ceremony with a cake, sweetening the breath with candy before kissing a paramour, and so on are all ritualistic correlates of the same conceptual metaphor. Incidentally, in Chagga, a Bantu language of Tanzania, similar cultural practices exist. It is no coincidence that the language possesses the same conceptual metaphor. In Chagga the man is perceived to be the *eater* and the woman his *sweet food*, as can be detected in expressions that mean, in translated form, "Does she taste sweet?" "She tastes sweet as sugar honey" (Emantian 1995: 168). Ongoing research on CMT is showing that material, symbolic, and ritualistic culture is itself a nonverbal metaphorical language that mirrors verbal language.

Figurative language, also, is a trace to the unconscious knowledge and wisdom of a society. A proverb such as "He has fallen from grace" refers in its origin to the Adam and Eve story in the Bible. Today, we continue to use it with only a dim awareness (if any) of its Biblical origins. Conceptual metaphors that portray life as a journey—"I'm still a *long way* from my goal," "There is no *end* in sight"—are similarly rooted in Biblical narrative. As the Canadian literary critic Northrop Frye (1981) pointed out, one cannot penetrate such expressions without having been exposed, directly or indirectly, to the original Biblical stories. These are the source domains for many of the conceptual metaphors we use today in English for judging human actions and offering advice, bestowing upon everyday life an unconscious metaphysical meaning and value. When we say "An eye for an eye and a tooth for a tooth" we are invoking imagery that reverberates with religious meaning in an unconscious way. Every culture has similar proverbs, aphorisms, and sayings. They constitute a remarkable code of practical knowledge that anthropologists call "folk wisdom." Indeed, the very concept of *wisdom* implies the ability to apply proverbial language insightfully to a situation.

2.3 Grammar

The word *grammar* has had many meanings over the centuries, as pointed out at the start of this chapter. In theoretical linguistics, however, it means something specific—knowledge of how lexemes and morphemes are constructed and then combined according to rules of organization allowing speakers to create sentences and entire utterances. The study of grammar is divided traditionally into two main areas—*morphology* and *syntax*. The former is the study of how words and other structures are put together from smaller units (morphemes), and the latter of how these are organized into phrases and sentences. Sociolinguistics does not focus on grammar per se, but on what it might tell us about social phenomena. To make it clear that we are studying grammar from a sociolinguistic, rather than purely theoretical, perspective, the terms *sociomorphology* and *sociosyntax* are sometimes used.

2.3.1 Sociomorphology

Describing and analyzing grammatical systems in themselves starts with how words are formed and what word-construction principles are involved. This falls under the category of morphology.

As discussed, the units that make up single words are called *morphemes* (section 1.1.1, Chapter 1). The word *cats*, for instance, consists of two morphemes: *cat*, whose meaning can be roughly rendered as "feline animal," and *-s*, whose meaning is "more than one." If the meaning of the morpheme is lexical (*cat*), then it is called a root morpheme or lexeme (as we have seen); if it is grammatical or has recurrence in other words (*-s*) it is called a grammatical morpheme. The process of identifying morphemes is known as *segmentation*. It entails breaking up a word into segments (units) that cannot be split any further. The word *friend* cannot be segmented any further, but the word *unfriendly* can be broken down into three segments: *un-*, *friend*, and *-ly*.

Morphology

Morphology is the study of how words are composed of lexemes and morphemes.

For example, in the word *unceremoniously*, there are four units: *un-*, *ceremony*, *-ous*, and *-ly*. Each one has a meaning and function. *Ceremony* is the lexeme (or lexical morpheme) and thus is excluded from analysis by morphology proper. It falls under semantics, as we saw above.

The other three are morphemes proper and have specific functions: *un-* is a prefix that denotes absence or contrariness; *-ous* is an affix meaning "characterized by;" and *-ly* is a suffix that changes an adjective into an adverb.

Morphological structure often encodes differences in social roles. In the Koasati language of Louisiana, verb endings identify the sex of the speaker (Haas 1944). The native words are given in English-spelling transcription, which only approximates their pronunciation. Actual pronunciation features of Koasati can be found on the following website: www.omniglot.com/writing/koasati.htm.

The addition of /-s/ indicates a male speaker. In terms of markedness theory, this suggests that the masculine gender in Koasati is the marked one (recall section 1.4.4, Chapter 1), which in turn suggests that the society is matrilineal. And this turns out to be the case. Koasati is part of a native civilization called *Muscogee* in which clan membership is matrilineal and authority over the clan is ascribed to the women (mainly elderly). Thus, the distinction in the morphology of words in Koasati is a reflection of a distinction in social structure based on matrilineage. In Kuruk, a Dravidian language spoken in northern India, the verb suffixes are similarly gender-coded (Ekka 1972), but have a different social meaning—one set for the men speaking to women and another for the women speaking to women. When the men and women interact the masculine suffixes are the default (or unmarked) forms. In contrast to Koasati, these features reflect the fact that the society is patriarchal.

Table 2.7 Gendered Differences in the Verbs of the Koasati Language

English Gloss	Women say...	Men say...
lift it	lakawohl	lakawohs
he is saying	ka	kas
don't sing	taalawan	taalawas
he is building a fire	ot	os

In American culture, there are no equivalent verb morphemes for how men and women are expected to speak. But, as we saw (section 1.4.3, Chapter 1), the English language has lexical doublets, such as *waiter–waitress*, that indicate a markedness relation with respect to gender roles (Adler 1978). With the advent of gender equality movements, the relation shifted and was lost, so that today the suffix /-ess/ as in *actress* has specialized meaning—if the *actor* (as the role is now designated in general) is a woman and we wish to indicate this for some reason, then *actress* might be used. Thus, unlike the past, the term *actor* includes males and females; *actress* is specialized in its reference but does not bear with it a markedness quality. Such changes in grammar suggest that American society today is no longer rigidly patrilineal.

2.3.2 Sociosyntax

Syntax

Syntax is the study of how morphemes and lexemes are combined into phrases, clauses, sentences and other larger structures (such as texts).

There are various general theories of syntax, a prominent one being called *generative grammar*, associated with the ideas and work of Noam Chomsky. This describes a language in terms of a set of logical rules that are used to generate an infinite number of possible sentences and providing them with the correct structural description.

The approach known as *cognitive syntax* is a derivative of conceptual metaphor theory and, contrary to generative grammar, connects the rules of syntax to conceptual structures such as metaphors.

In many languages, word order is involved in how the individual words that compose it relate semantically to each other. If the words in (1) "Alex teased Sarah" are reversed to (2) "Sarah teased Alex," the meanings are also reversed. The words in the sentence mirror an actor–action–receiver relationship. The actor functions as the subject of an English sentence, the action as its verb, and the receiver as its aim (or object). The latter two together make up the predicate of a sentence. In (1) *Alex* is the actor while in (2) it is *Sarah*. In (1) *Sarah* is the receiver of the *teasing* action, while in (2) the receiver is *Alex*. This is why the meanings are also reversed.

But word order is not just a matter of internal grammatical principles that allow for literal meaning to be conveyed. In 1921, Edward Sapir argued that a change in the order of words in a sentence such as "The farmer kills the duckling" ("Kills the farmer the duckling"), or omitting any of its words

("Farmer, kill the duckling") from it, reflects different concepts. He showed that thirteen distinct concepts could be expressed with the same words. As he put it (Sapir 1921: 87): "The sentence is the outgrowth of historical and of unreasoning psychological forces rather than of a logical synthesis of elements that have been clearly grasped in their individuality."

As Sapir also argued, syntax is often a guide to various social differentiations. Gender-based grammar, as we saw above, is hardly ever recognized as such at a conscious level because of frequency of usage of the grammar in conversations and in discourse generally (Crawford 1995; Hall and Bucholtz 1996). Psychologist Cheris Kramer noted in 1974 that the speech of American men and women was differentiated by a distinctive blend of characteristics, such as tone, profanities, and the use of tag questions ("Don't you think?" "Isn't it?"). Kramer presented captions of cartoons taken from a number of magazines to a group of college students (25 men, 25 women), asking them to guess the sex of the speakers in the cartoons. The subjects classified the captions according to male and female speech characteristics, as instructed to do, with no hesitation. As expected, cartoons with tag questions were assigned to the female gender more often than not; those with profanities to men. Although the situation has changed since then, gendered linguistic differences such as tags still persist in English (Macaulay 2009).

Follow-up work on tags and women's speech has indicated that it might indicate social power relations, reflecting how women themselves perceive their social roles (Lakoff 1975; Holmes 1984). But when social power is equilibrated, as when men and women professionals (doctors, lawyers, and so on) speak to each other, tags no longer emerge in female talk to any significant degree (Cameron, McAlinden, and O'Leary 1988).

Gender is not the only area that is mirrored in syntactic forms. In 1969, Jacqueline Lindenfeld found a correlation between syntactic complexity, degree of formality of conversations, and class membership. Using notions such as sentence length and embedded clauses (clauses starting with *that*, *which*, or *who*), she discovered that the greater the length and the degree of embedding in certain contexts the more the syntax was associated with educated and higher class speech. Similar findings have been reported across the world, including in Belgium (van de Broek 1977) and the Netherlands (Huls 1989). In AAVE, there are various syntactic features that differentiate it from SAE. One explanation is that AAVE has many affinities with Creole languages of the Caribbean (described in Chapter 3). Whatever the reason, the point is that differences in grammar indicate differences in speech community. A few examples will suffice:

- "Why they ain't goin?" lacks the inversion of words that characterizes SAE ("Why aren't they going?")
- "He my brother," "She my friend," show the dropping of the copula verb ("He is my brother," "She is my friend").

- "He write great songs," "She go every day" lack the third personal morpheme /-s/ of SAE verbs in the present tense ("He writes great songs," "She goes every day").
- "My momma sister" lacks the genitive marker *'s* of SAE ("My mother's sister").

2.4 Phonology

Phonology and Phonetics

Phonology is the systematic study of sound systems, while *phonetics* is the science of classifying vocal sounds according to their physical features.

An example of the latter would be the difference between the sound *p* in *pin* and the sound *b* in *bin*. The phonetician would note three critical features:

- Both sounds involve the two lips coming together, called a *bilabial* feature.
- Both sounds involve a sudden emission of the air that builds up behind the lips, called occlusion.
- The difference is that in the case of *b* the vocal cords in the larynx are vibrating; whereas they are not in the case of *p*. Thus, *b* is called a *voiced* sound, and *p* a *voiceless* sound.

Since the two sounds are used distinctively, as the minimal pairs *pat–bat* and *pin–bin* show, they would be considered phonemes.

As we saw, William Labov connected the pronunciation of a phoneme in final position, /-r/, to social identity and upward mobility in a specific situation (section 1.3, Chapter 1). The study of the relation of phonology (sound system) to society is sometimes called *sociophonology*. Essentially, it involves determining which phonemes or pronunciation features relate to social processes, including the forging of social identities.

Sociophonological analysis starts with a phonetic description and inventory of the vocal sounds in a language. The symbols commonly used to represent sounds are those found in the International Phonetic Association (IPA), founded in 1886. The IPA was established for consistency in phonetic representation, given that the world's spelling systems vary so widely and are often unreliable for representing sounds. For example, the [f] sound in words

Table 2.8 The International Phonetic Alphabet

THE INTERNATIONAL PHONETIC ALPHABET (revised to 2005)

CONSONANTS (PULMONIC)

© 2005 IPA

	Bilabial	Labiodental	Dental	Alveolar	Post alveolar	Retroflex	Palatal	Velar	Uvular	Pharyngeal	Glottal
Plosive	p b			t d		ʈ ɖ	c ɟ	k ɡ	q ɢ		ʔ
Nasal	m	ɱ		n		ɳ	ɲ	ŋ	N		
Trill	ʙ			r					R		
Tap or Flap		ⱱ		ɾ		ɽ					
Fricative	ɸ β	f v	θ ð	s z	ʃ ʒ	ʂ ʐ	ç ʝ	x ɣ	χ ʁ	ħ ʕ	h ɦ
Lateral fricative				ɬ ɮ							
Approximant		ʋ		ɹ		ɻ	j	ɰ			
Lateral approximant				l		ɭ	ʎ	ʟ			

Where symbols appear in pairs, the one to the right represents a voiced consonant. Shaded areas denote articulations judged impossible.

CONSONANTS (NON-PULMONIC)

Clicks		Voiced implosives		Ejectives	
ʘ	Bilabial	ɓ	Bilabial	ʼ	Examples:
ǀ	Dental	ɗ	Dental/alveolar	pʼ	Bilabial
ǃ	(Post)alveolar	ʄ	Palatal	tʼ	Dental/alveolar
ǂ	Palatoalveolar	ɠ	Velar	kʼ	Velar
ǁ	Alveolar lateral	ʛ	Uvular	sʼ	Alveolar fricative

OTHER SYMBOLS

ʍ	Voiceless labial-velar fricative	ɕ ʑ	Alveolo-palatal fricatives
w	Voiced labial-velar approximant	ɺ	Voiced alveolar lateral flap
ɥ	Voiced labial-palatal approximant	ɧ	Simultaneous ʃ and x
ʜ	Voiceless epiglottal fricative		
ʢ	Voiced epiglottal fricative	Affricates and double articulations can be represented by two symbols joined by a tie bar if necessary.	k͡p t͡s
ʡ	Epiglottal plosive		

VOWELS

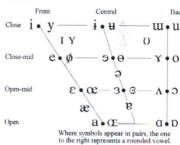

Where symbols appear in pairs, the one to the right represents a rounded vowel.

SUPRASEGMENTALS

ˈ	Primary stress	ˌfoʊnəˈtɪʃən
ˌ	Secondary stress	
ː	Long	eː
ˑ	Half-long	eˑ
̆	Extra-short	ĕ
ǀ	Minor (foot) group	
ǁ	Major (intonation) group	
.	Syllable break	ɹi.ækt
‿	Linking (absence of a break)	

DIACRITICS   Diacritics may be placed above a symbol with a descender, e.g. ŋ̊

̥	Voiceless	n̥ d̥	̤	Breathy voiced	b̤ a̤	̪	Dental	t̪ d̪
̬	Voiced	s̬ t̬	̰	Creaky voiced	b̰ a̰	̺	Apical	t̺ d̺
ʰ	Aspirated	tʰ dʰ	̼	Linguolabial	t̼ d̼	̻	Laminal	t̻ d̻
̹	More rounded	ɔ̹	ʷ	Labialized	tʷ dʷ	̃	Nasalized	ẽ
̜	Less rounded	ɔ̜	ʲ	Palatalized	tʲ dʲ	ⁿ	Nasal release	dⁿ
̟	Advanced	u̟	ˠ	Velarized	tˠ dˠ	ˡ	Lateral release	dˡ
̠	Retracted	e̠	ˤ	Pharyngealized	tˤ dˤ	̚	No audible release	d̚
̈	Centralized	ë	̴	Velarized or pharyngealized	ɫ			
̽	Mid-centralized	e̽	̝	Raised	e̝	(ɹ̝ = voiced alveolar fricative)		
̩	Syllabic	n̩	̞	Lowered	e̞	(β̞ = voiced bilabial approximant)		
̯	Non-syllabic	e̯	̘	Advanced Tongue Root	e̘			
˞	Rhoticity	ɚ a˞	̙	Retracted Tongue Root	e̙			

TONES AND WORD ACCENTS

LEVEL				CONTOUR			
e̋ or	˥	Extra high	ě or	˩˥	Rising		
é	˦	High	ê	˥˩	Falling		
ē	˧	Mid	e᷄	˦˥	High rising		
è	˨	Low	e᷅	˩˨	Low rising		
ȅ	˩	Extra low	e᷈	˧˦˧	Rising-falling		
↓	Downstep			↗	Global rise		
↑	Upstep			↘	Global fall		

such as *fun*, *pharmacy*, and *tough* is phonetically the same one, even though it is spelled differently. The sound has the following main phonetic features:

1   the lower lip touches the upper teeth;
2   the airstream emanating from the lungs is expelled in a constricted fashion through the slit formed in (1);
3   the vocal cords (in the larynx) are kept taut (non-vibrating).

These are labeled as follows: (1) *labiodental*; (2) *fricative*; and (3) *voiceless*. Thus, the phonetic symbol [f] stands for a *voiceless labiodental fricative*. The terms are self-explanatory. *Labiodental* refers to the lower lip (the *labio* part) and the upper teeth (*dental*); *fricative* refers to the manner in which the sound is articulated; and *voiceless* to the fact that the cords are not vibrating. This is, in a nutshell, how phonetic description is carried out. We will not go into a detailed discussion of phonetics here. The interested reader can consult any basic phonetics manual. Technical terminology will be explained in boxes as the case arises. The IPA chart is reproduced here for the sake of convenience.

2.4.1 Phonemes, Allophones, and Tones

Certain sounds can take on slightly different articulations in certain positions within words. For example, in English the voiceless bilabial stop [p] is aspirated— that is, pronounced with a slight puff of air (represented as [pʰ])—when it occurs in word-initial position followed by a vowel, as readers can confirm for themselves by pronouncing the following words while keeping the palm of one hand near the mouth. Note that if [s] is put before, the aspiration is blocked.

Table 2.9 Allophones of the phoneme /p/ in English

[pʰ]	[s] + [p]
pit	spit
pill	spill
punk	spunk
pat	spat

The pronunciation of /p/ as [pʰ] is a predictable feature of English phonology— when /p/ occurs in word-initial position followed by a vowel it is aspirated as [pʰ]. So, the actual pronunciations or variants of the phoneme /p/, [p] and [pʰ], are called its *allophones*. The phoneme is defined as the minimal unit of sound that can distinguish the meaning of words. This implies in practice that /p/ can replace other consonants, such as /w/ and /b/, to make English words—*pin* vs. *win* vs. *bin*. The pronunciation of the phoneme /p/ as either unaspirated ([p]) or aspirated ([pʰ]) is due to the fact that the articulation of a sound is conditioned by its position within words. The allophones of a phoneme are said to *complement* each other; that is, where one occurs the other does not.

Another key technical concept is *tone*. Tone is defined as the relative pitch with which a syllable, a word, phrase, or sentence is pronounced. In some languages, such as North Mandarin Chinese, tone has phonemic value. The single syllable [ma], for example, can have various meanings according to whether the tone is high level, high rising, rising, or falling:

1   [high level]   =   *mother*
2   [high rising]   =   *hemp*
3   [rising]   =   *horse*
4   [falling]   =   *scold*

In Bini, an indigenous language of Nigeria, tone marks a grammatical function—verb tense. For instance, the morpheme [ima] varies as shown:

1   [high-low]   =   *I am showing*
2   [low-high]   =   *I showed*
3   [low]   =   *I show*

In English, tone is used primarily to signal differences in the intent or function of sentences. This use of tone is known more specifically as *intonation*. Raising or lowering the tone often changes the meaning of words in English as well. Take, for example, the word *Yes*. If uttered with a level tone it indicates affirmation. If uttered with a rising tone (*Yes?*) it indicates "Can I help you?" If uttered with an emphatic tone (*Yes!*) it indicates assertion and satisfaction.

2.4.2 Sociophonology

As we have seen (section 1.3, Chapter 1), social mobility (or stratification) is often tied to phonological features. Peter Trudgill discussed in 1974 how this general principle applies to the speech community in Norwich, England. He showed that pronunciation signaled class structure in the community. The more people became educated, the more they aspired to use "proper" or standard forms of pronunciation. And he discovered that it was the women who most used standard pronunciation and grammar—for example they were more inclined to use the /-ing/ verb ending instead of the informal /-in/ one in words such as *walking*-versus-*walkin'*. These differences were particularly noticeable for the highest and lowest of the classes. In the middle classes, women always used the standard /-ing/, while the men used /-in/ in casual speech for about one-third of the time. Even in the lowest class, women used casual pronunciation only sporadically, using the standard one in formal contexts. Trudgill's study suggested that women tend to be more sensitive to the social value of phonological cues, whereas men prefer to speak in a manner that connects them to their communities.

More Terms

Palatal: sound produced at the palate (such as the *ch* in *church*).

Velar: sound produced towards the back of the mouth (such as the *k* in *kite*).

Dental: sound produced when the tongue touches the upper teeth (such as the *t* in *tooth*).

Diphthong: sound produced by combining two vowels into a single sound (such as *ou* in *bout*).

Gender-based differentiations in pronunciation abound across the globe. In Atsina, an Algonquin language once spoken in Montana, women used palatalized velar stops (such as *ky* rather than *k*) and men palatalized dental stops (such as *dy* rather than *d*). So, for example, the word for *bread* was pronounced as *kjatsa* = /kyatsa/ by the women and as *djatsa* = /dyatsa/ by the men. This was intended to keep the genders distinct. In 1922, Bogaras documented similar doublets in the Chukchee language of Siberia, where the consonants /č/ (pronounced like the *ch* in *change*) and /r/ in male speech are replaced with /s/ or /š/ (pronounced like *sh* in *shore*) in female speech. So, for instance, the word for the phrase "by a buck" would be pronounced as /čumñata/ by the men, but as /šumñata/ by the women, and "people" as /ramkičin/ by the men and as /šamkiššin/ by the women.

Similar patterns are found in various societies. Levine and Crockett (1967) found that white women speakers in North Carolina would tend to use standard pronunciation more than men if the situation required formal speech. Wolfram (1969) found that in AAVE-speaking communities in Detroit, the women tended to use the more prestigious /-r/ in words such as *far* and *car* more than the men when the occasion called for standard language. Overall, sociophonological research has shown that women tend to be more conscious of prestige forms of pronunciation because, it is argued, they are socialized to behave more politely than men. Trudgill called this "covert prestige." For women the prestige is towards the norm, for the men it is away from the norm, likely reflecting the social roles assigned to men and women in various societies.

In a northern Indian village called Khalapur pronunciation differences in the local Hindi dialect signal caste differences (Gumperz 1971). The lower castes use the single vowels /a/, /u/, /o/ before consonants, whereas the higher castes use the more standard Hindi diphthongs /ai/, /ui/, /oi/. So, the word for "ear of corn" would be pronounced as /bal/ by the lower castes and as /bail/ or just /bai/ by the higher castes. Contrasts of this type characterize virtually the entire vowel system of Khari Boli, as the local Hindi dialect is called. It is relevant to note that the lower caste pronunciation is evaluated as "backward" by the higher castes, indicating that the members of their society are very sensitive to phonological variants as socially significant.

There are three general things to note with regard to the relation between phonology and society. First, actual pronunciation can vary from speaker to speaker, which may be due to various factors. Speakers of English living in Alabama, for instance, pronounce vowel sounds differently from those living in Newfoundland. The differences are dialectal (and will be discussed in more detail in the next chapter). Second, sociophonological research has introduced an important distinction into general linguistics—the difference between *etic* and *emic* structure. Native speakers process words unconsciously in terms of its "phonemics," or simply *emics*; that is, in terms of the distinctive cues signaled by sounds in the chain of speech; non-native speakers, on the other hand, tend to hear the "phonetics" of words, that is, the actual sounds or allophones that make up the chain of speech. So, they have a harder time processing meaning. This notion was put forward by Kenneth Pike in his monumental 1954 book *Language in Relation to a Unified Theory of the Structure of Human Behavior*. As subsequent research has shown, this distinction applies not only to the phonological level, but to all levels of language. Third, phonology, like vocabulary and grammar, reveals power dynamics in a society. For example, women might employ intonation more frequently, while men tend to keep pitch levels neutral (Lakoff 1975; McConnell-Ginet 1983; Fishman 1983) in order to secure a response in a conversation. Intonation might thus reveal who has the power in a specific context.

Pronunciation also characterizes how social groups or communities keep themselves distinct. The inhabitants of Martha's Vineyard, in Massachusetts, for example, have adopted particular vowel pronunciations to distinguish themselves from people vacationing on the island (Labov 1963). As we have seen, AAVE features are symbolic of identity. The omission of the final consonant in words like *past* (*pas*) and *hand* (*han*), the pronunciation of the *th* in *bath* as *t* (*bat*) and the pronunciation of the vowel in words like *my* as a long *ah* (*mah*), some of which occur in vernacular southern white English, too, bespeak nonetheless of group identity and solidarity (Smitherman 2000). Interestingly, in Black communities across the US, social mobility is sometimes tied to the acquisition of SAE pronunciation, while AAVE phonology is relegated to use for the purposes of community allegiances, in-group entendres, and the like. AAVE is close to the everyday thoughts and feelings of the speakers, constituting a more effective tool of communication within communities, while SAE is a key to social mobility.

2.5 E-sociolinguistics in Practice

The purpose of e-sociolinguistics, as discussed (section 1.5, Chapter 1), is to document and analyze language use in online contexts and then compare the findings to offline research findings.

The starting point is to take a look at the kind of language that characterizes CMC. The term *netlingo* was coined by David Crystal (2006) to describe CMC in its various forms. A conspicuous characteristic of netlingo is its compactness, allowing interlocutors to increase the speed at which their messages can be inputted and received. So, a series of common abbreviations, acronyms, and other compact forms have become "standardized." These are generally easy to explain: for example, removing vowels in frequently-used words and expressions does not impact comprehension in any significant way, and using single letters for entire words also requires little effort to decode the message: "How r u?" ("How are you?").

In netlingo, punctuation and apostrophes are often eliminated (*im, dont, isnt, didnt*). In so doing, time is saved overall in the hand actions performed on keyboards. Crystal (2006: 87) calls this the "save a keystroke principle." Most of netlingo is thus not case-sensitive, which motivates the random use of capitals or no capitals at all. Or else, it involves the use of capitals for expressive purposes: "I LUV U!" conveys more emphasis than "i luv u."

Netlingo		
b4	=	before
bf/gf	=	boyfriend/girlfriend
f2f	=	face-to-face
gr8	=	great
h2cus	=	hope to see you soon
idk	=	I don't know
j4f	=	just for fun
lol	=	laughing out loud
cm	=	call me
2dA	=	today
wan2	=	want to
ruok	=	Are you OK?
2moro	=	tomorrow
g2g	=	gotta go

2.5.1 Abbreviated Language

Abbreviated writing was used by the Greeks as early as the fourth century BCE, gradually evolving into a true shorthand code, known as *tachygraphy*. The Roman slave Tyro also developed shorthand writing around 60 BCE, apparently for recording the speeches of Cicero. Scholars and scientists have always used abbreviations of various kinds to facilitate technical communications among themselves, making them precise (*etc., et al., op. cit. N.B.*). In this case, abbreviation implies a high level of literacy. Also, we abbreviate the names of friends and family members (*Alex* for *Alexander*), common phrases (*TGIF* for *Thank God it's Friday*), and anything else that refers to something or someone familiar.

But what sets the abbreviation tendencies in netlingo apart from the past is the speed and extent to which they are spreading and becoming part of communicative behavior throughout the internet and also migrating to the offline world. There is an expectation in the internet universe that responses to e-mails, text messages, and the like must be rapid, whether the medium is synchronous or asynchronous (section 1.5.1, Chapter 1). Logically, abbreviation helps people meet this expectation by making it possible to "get back" to the sender more quickly. This is creating new types of literacy and communicative practices. CMC bespeaks of much more than a contemporary manifestation of abbreviation tendencies in human communication. It has led to new literary genres, and writing practices, among other things. Internet citizens are becoming constantly more influential in determining the evolution of linguistic practices.

Some work has shown that register (level of formality) is determined by whether or not abbreviations are used. In formal CMC, such as in e-mails to authority figures or strangers, words tend to be spelled out completely and traditional grammar and punctuation also tend to be used. In text messages (to friends), however, the reverse is true. Actually, if a word is spelled out completely in a text message it is either because the software used by the mobile device is a corrective one or because it adds meaning to the message: "How are you?" versus "How r u?" The latter is the normally expected one; the former is not and thus can be interpreted in various ways, including as conveying subtle anger or irony.

With the proliferation of Web 2.0 technologies—a term used to distinguish contemporary social media from their immediate predecessors, the static Web pages and message forums that had characterized what was retroactively dubbed Web 1.0—there has been an increase in communicative interactivity, flexibility, social connectivity, user-generated content, and textual creativity, facilitating more participation than did previous digital platforms and greater interaction among larger swaths of the global population. Although CMC usage may initially seem resistant to ethnographic analysis, the ongoing study of digital media has shown that fieldwork in cyberspace is as realizable as it is in real space. Sociolinguists now must distinguish among various modalities of communication in order to conduct ethnographic work, including:

1   Face-to-Face (F2F) communication which occurs in real time and in real space; this includes common conversations and public speaking.
2   Pen-to-Paper (P2P) communication refers to traditional print communication, including letters, newspapers, books, and so on.
3   Pen-to-Ear (P2E) communication, such as the previous use of telegraphs with the Morse code, which made written communication available through the electronic transmission of dots and lines.
4   Ear-to-Ear (E2E) communication, such as phone conversations and radio broadcasts.
5   Eye and Ear-to-Eye and Ear (E^2E^2) communication, such as Skype and FaceTime modes of communication, which are essentially visual phone conversations. This is also called Visual Computer Mediated Communication or VCMC.
6   Finger-to-Keyboard (F2K) communication, such as e-mail, text messaging, and writing on social media sites.

Clearly, the study of linguistic communication, which has traditionally focused on F2F and P2P interactions, is now broadened to cover other forms of communication and their effects on users. Speech protocols and conventions are changing or morphing. Typically, people initiate an e-mail or text message simply with the salutation *Hey* or nothing, rather than *Dear So and So*. Streamlining is the strategy of zeroing in on key content at the expense of traditional word and sentence structure and message contents. For example, the sentence "Do you have any books on phonology, because I need them quickly?" can be streamlined to: "Any books on phon? Need them quick."

Text Messaging

Text messaging (TM) is the term used to describe the act of transmitting and receiving an electronic message by cellular phone or other mobile device.

The message is sent over the internet or some other computer network. It occurs in real time, since both users can conduct a back-and-forth exchange.

Text messages involving mobile phones and personal digital assistants are said to use short message service (SMS). The actual texts are called both text messages and SMS.

The term *textspeak* is now the general term used to refer to the writing practices evident in text messages (Crystal 2008). Textspeak is an "e-dialect," so to say, of netlingo manifesting itself across languages. In languages across the world, from English to Mandarin Chinese, numbers that sound like words are used in place of the words. And there is now software that attempts to infer what words are being typed so that text messaging can occur even more quickly. Websites such as *transl8it* ("translate it") have standardized textspeak so that it can be used more broadly for CMC. As a consequence, there are now dictionaries and glossaries of textspeak available online.

Some observers are decrying textspeak as a product of modern-day inertia and laziness-inducing technologies. Helprin (2009), for instance, cautions that such forms of communication, and the internet generally, produce an addictive effect on how people process information, rendering them much less pensive and less inclined to appreciate artistic and literary greatness. Others respond that textspeak is no more than an efficient way to create written messages for informal communication. People use textspeak, not to generate thoughtfulness and literary communication, but to keep in contact and to facilitate communication. In no way does this imply that people have lost the desire to read and reflect upon the world.

TM has become an everyday medium of communication, as studies such as the one by Lenhart (2010, 2011) make clear. She found that teens (12 to 17 years of age) contacting their friends used the following methods:

- Text messaging: 54%
- Cell phone: 38%
- Face-to-face: 33%
- Social network site: 25%
- Instant messaging: 24%
- Landline phone: 30%
- E-mail: 11%.

Similar statistics have been found for adult users of mobile devices. A Pew Research Internet study in 2011 (www.pwerinternet.org/category/publications/reports/) discovered that around 83 percent of American adults own cell phones and three-quarters of them are text message users. The researchers asked texters how they preferred to be contacted: 31 percent said they preferred texts to talking on the phone, while 53 percent said they favored a voice call. Another 14 percent said that the contact method used depends on the situation. Heavy text users are much more likely to prefer texting to talking. Around 55 percent of those who exchange more than 50 text messages a day said that they would rather get a text than a voice call. Those between the ages of 18 and 24 exchange an average of 109.5 text messages per day. Overall, however, the survey found that both text messaging and cell phone use is leveling off for the adult population as a whole.

It is relevant to note that no less an authority on language trends than the *Oxford English Dictionary* has listed items from textspeak into the dictionary (*lol*, *24/7*, *g2g*, and many more). This is an affirmation of the plasticity and adaptability of language.

2.5.2 Relevant Findings

Topics such as textspeak and its uses are raising new questions for sociolinguists to address and leading to interesting new findings. In F2F contexts, the data collected is governed by *in situ* (in a specific social situation) and *in locu* (in a particular form of contact) situations. As Nazir (2012) has shown, the internet has not changed this situation radically, since it presents analogous types of contexts and thus the same pattern of sociolinguistic relations characteristic of F2F communication. She found, for instance, that the way in which males and females use Facebook reflects the same gendered relations that characterize F2F interactions. Also, women tend to use Facebook in order to maintain existing relationships, while men are more likely to use it for new relations.

Other findings of relevance that are emerging from e-sociolinguistic research are listed below:

- A study by Tossell, Kortum, Shepard, Barg-Walkow, Rahmati, and Zhong (2012) found that females sent more messages with emoticons, arguably to display emotion more overtly than males; however, surprisingly, males unexpectedly used a diverse range of emoticons as well, suggesting that they were more inclined to convey more emotional content in digital contexts than they do in offline contexts. This might imply that technology is closing the gender gap.
- A study by Vandergriff (2013) showed that emoticons, nonstandard punctuation, and lexical surrogates ("hmmm") have brought about new ways of interpreting the same type of language used in offline contexts. In Italian (Danesi 2013), for example, the textspeak form *tvb* ("I love you") has a meaning of love, but when the complete form is used, *ti voglio bene*, it is interpreted ironically or as a sign that romance has altered for the worse. Such studies are accumulating and starting to show that CMC and F2F may intersect, overlap, or diverge—depending on situation and context.
- Lewis and Fabos (2005) examined the functions of IM in the interactions of seven youths who used it regularly in their daily lives. They found that the participants manipulated the word choice and subject matter of their messages to fit their needs. Again, this situation parallels the F2F one. Interestingly, the participants moved back and forth between traditional spelling practices and IM ones. They were neither absorbed by nor reliant on textspeak; in fact, they often preferred using conventional spelling and punctuation and were acutely aware of the various audiences they were addressing.

In a comprehensive study of Facebook, Schwartz et al. (2013) analyzed 700 million words, phrases, and utterances collected from the Facebook messages of 75,000 volunteers, who also took standard personality tests. The researchers found conspicuous variations in language forms and use with respect to personality, gender, and age. Some of the findings were highly predictable—subjects living in regions of high elevation talked about the mountains, neurotic individuals disproportionately used the expressions "sick of" and "depressed," and so on. But they also discovered that Facebook is simply a new locus for the same kinds of social distinctions that characterize offline language. For example, males used the possessive *my* when mentioning their *wife* or *girlfriend* more often than females used it with *husband* or *boyfriend*, indicating that males still unconsciously perceive their relationships as under their governance. Females used more emotion words and expressions ("excited," "I love you" and so on). Males used more swear words and object references ("Xbox").

Terminology Review

Define or explain in your own words the following terms introduced in this chapter.

AAVE
anthropomorphism
cant
complementary distribution
conceptual semantics
contextualized meaning
denotative
figurative
formal semantics
ICM
intonation
irony
lexical field
lexicography
metonymy
netlingo
phonology
referent
syntax
textspeak
tone

allophone
argot
cognate
conceptual metaphor
connotative
core vocabulary
emic versus etic
focal color
grammar
IM
IPA
lexeme
lexical semantics
lexicon
morpheme
phonetics
polysemy
semantics
text messaging
time depth
vocabulary

Exercises and Discussion

1   Explain the implications in social terms that each title entails.

(a) Miss
(b) Ms.
(c) Professor
(d) Doctor
(e) Reverend
(f) Madam
(g) Sir

2   In many societies, men and women are expected to use different forms of speech. In English, too, certain mannerisms of speech appear to be gender-coded. If so, how might women and men intentionally differentiate themselves (if they so desire) to communicate the following things in English?

(a) politeness with a stranger
(b) excusing oneself among friends
(c) inviting a new romantic partner out for a date
(d) telling a "dirty" joke among friends

3   The following terms and expressions use *man* to indicate or imply that the masculine gender is the unmarked one. What terms are currently used (or should be used if there are none) in their place to eliminate the markedness bias implicit in them?

(a) fireman
(b) postman
(c) mankind
(d) manpower
(e) man and wife
(f) men of letters
(g) man-made

4   Can you give examples of different vocabulary between any variant of English (such as AAVE) and Standard English that signal differences in class or gender?

5   Can you now give examples of different features of pronunciation that signal differences in class or gender?

6   Create a short message in textspeak and then discuss it with others to see if they can decipher it. Together identify and analyze linguistically the characteristics of the language used.

7   Provide the denotative meaning of each of the following words and then use each one in a sentence that exemplifies a connotative meaning. For

example, the denotative meaning of the word *cat* is "small feline with retractile claws, whiskers, and emits sounds known as purring, hissing, and meowing." A connotative use of the word can be seen in "They always play cat and mouse," where the sentence implies a series of cunning strategies designed to thwart an opponent.

(a) dog
(b) blue
(c) way
(d) right
(e) ground

8 The following excerpt is from: P. Eckert and S. McConnell-Ginet, *Language and Gender* (2003):

> *We are surrounded by gender lore from the time we are very small. It is ever-present in conversation, humor, and conflict, and it is called upon to explain everything from driving styles to food preferences. Gender is embedded so thoroughly in our institutions, our actions, our beliefs, and our desires, that it appears to us to be completely natural. The world swarms with ideas about gender—and these ideas are so commonplace that we take it for granted that they are true, accepting common adage as scientific fact. As scholars and researchers, though, it is our job to look beyond what appears to be common sense to find not simply what truth might be behind it, but how it came to be common sense. It is precisely because gender seems natural, and beliefs about gender seem to be obvious truths, that we need to step back and examine gender from a new perspective. Doing this requires that we suspend what we are used to and what feels comfortable, and question some of our most fundamental beliefs. This is not easy, for gender is so central to our understanding of ourselves and of the world that it is difficult to pull back and examine it from new perspectives. But it is precisely the fact that gender seems self-evident that makes the study of gender interesting.*

Do you think gender differences are based primarily in biology or in culture? Explain your position.

9 The following excerpt is from: G. Lakoff, *The Contemporary Theory of Metaphor* (1979):

> *Imagine a love relationship described as follows: Our relationship has hit a dead-end street. Here love is being conceptualized as a journey, with the implication that the relationship is stalled, that the lovers cannot keep going the way they've been going, that they must turn back, or abandon the relationship altogether. This is not an isolated case. English has many everyday expressions that are based on a conceptualization of love as a journey, and they are used not just for talking about love, but for reasoning about it as well. Some are necessarily about love; others can be understood*

that way: Look how far we've come. It's been a long, bumpy road. We can't turn back now. We're at a crossroads. We may have to go our separate ways. The relationship isn't going anywhere. We're spinning our wheels. Our relationship is off the track. The marriage is on the rocks. We may have to bail out of this relationship. These are ordinary, everyday English expressions. They are not poetic, nor are they necessarily used for special rhetorical effect. Those like Look how far we've come, which aren't necessarily about love, can readily be understood as being about love.

Can you give other examples of conceptual metaphors connected with love. For example, another one could use expressions such as "She's my sweetheart," "We are going on a honeymoon," "Our love has become very bitter," which reveal that we think of love as a taste.

10   The following excerpt is from R. Hudson, *Sociolinguistics and the Theory of Grammar* (1986):

The choice of forms depends inter alia [among other things] *on the speaker's "social knowledge," which includes their classification of the speaker according to social categories. This classification need not be categorical—indeed, there is now ample evidence that people often classify themselves and others as members of some group to varying degrees… It also depends on the speaker's intentions, which include such questions as how badly they want to be classified as a member of some social group, or how much they want the hearer to like them. This too is clearly a matter of degree and can influence the quantitative distribution of sociolinguistic variants in speech.*

Is there a difference between social knowledge and communicative competence? If so, how so; if not, why not?

11   The following excerpt is from E. R. Thomas, *Phonological and Phonetic Characteristics of African American Vernacular English* (2007):

Some special considerations relate to AAVE. First, AAVE is often distinguished from African American English (AAE). AAVE relates specifically to a vernacular form, spoken principally by working-class African Americans. AAE refers to the speech of all African Americans, including middle-class African Americans. Middle-class AAE most often lacks the more stigmatized morphosyntactic variants, although some middle-class speakers may employ them for stylistic effect or to express solidarity. Most pronunciation variables are not as stigmatized, however, and, for many of them, there may be no meaningful distinction between AAVE forms and AAE forms… Third, AAVE (and AAE) have a unique migration history. They originated in the South, and specifically in the Coastal Plain and Piedmont sections of the South, and were at first tied to a rural lifestyle. However, beginning before World War I and continuing through World War II, the Great Migration occurred in which large numbers of African

Americans migrated to cities outside the South in order to find work and to escape Jim Crow laws. A result was that the focus of African American culture shifted to urban life.

What social functions do you think AAVE encompasses? Is pronunciation an index of class, race, or ethnicity? Provide examples.

12 The following excerpt is from S. M. Wilson and L. C. Peterson, *The Anthropology of Online Communities* (2002):

Analyzed through the lens of contemporary approaches in ethnographies of communication, research in multilingual, multisited internet experiences would contribute to debates in the literature which seeks to position studies of mediated communication and technology in local social and communicative practices. Such research might help our understanding of the ways in which speakers incorporate new technologies of communication from existing communicative repertoires, and these technologies influence new and emerging cultural practices. In this sort of investigation, researchers must ask: Where do community members situate computers and other communication and information technologies in their daily lives? How are the tools of new media changing the contexts and frames of communicative practices? Are new forms of communicative competence developing as a consequence of new media tools in offline speech communities? How does technology enhance or displace discourses and practices of tradition? How might new technologies alter novice–expert relations? How do linguistic structures of online interactions affect offline practice?

Design an online study accessing social media sites to determine if there are differences in the language used by males and females, paying special attention to vocabulary and grammar.

References

Adler, M. K. (1978). *Sex Differences in Human Speech: A Sociolinguistic Study*. Hamburg: Helmut Buske.

Alim, S. (2004). Hip-hop Nation Language. In: E. Finegan and J. Rickford (eds.), *Language in the USA*. New York: Cambridge University Press.

Basso, K. H. (1990). *Western Apache Language and Culture: Essays in Linguistic Anthropology*. Tucson: University of Arizona Press.

Berlin, B. and Kay, P. (1969). *Basic Color Terms*. Berkeley: University of California Press.

Black, M. (1962). *Models and Metaphors*. Ithaca: Cornell University Press.

Bogaras, W. (1922). Chukchee. *Handbook of American Indian Languages*, pp. 631–903. Washington, DC: Bureau of American Ethnology.

Bruhn Jensen, K. (2010). *Media Convergence*. London: Routledge.

Bühler, K. (1908/1951). On Thought Connection. In: D. Rapaport (ed.), *Organization and Pathology of Thought*, pp. 81–92. New York: Columbia University Press.

Bühler, K. (1934). *Sprachtheorie. Die Darstellungsfunktion der Sprache*. Stuttgart/New York: Gustav Fischer.

Cameron, D., McAlinden, F., and O'Leary, K. (1988). Lakoff in Context: The Social and Linguistic Functions of Tag Questions. In: J. Coates and D. Cameron, *Women in Their Speech Communities*, pp. 74–93. London: Longman.

Chomsky, N. (1957). *Syntactic Structures*. The Hague: Mouton.

Coates, J. (1986). *Men, Women, and Language: A Sociolinguistic Account of Gender Differences in Language*. London: Longman.

Crawford, M. (1995). *Talking Difference: On Gender and Language*. Thousand Oaks: Sage.

Crystal, D. (2006). *Language and the Internet*, 2nd edn. Cambridge: Cambridge University Press.

Crystal, D. (2008). *txtng: the gr8 db8*. Oxford: Oxford University Press.

Danesi, M. (2013). *La comunicazione verbale al tempo di Internet*. Bari: Progedit.

Duranti, A. (2003). Language as Culture in U.S. Anthropology: Three Paradigms. *Current Anthropology* 44(3): 323–348.

Eckert, P. and McConnell-Ginet, S. (2003). *Language and Gender*. Cambridge: Cambridge University Press.

Ekka, F. (1972). Men's and Women's Speech in Kurux. *Linguistics* 81: 25–31.

Emantian, M. (1995). Metaphor and the Expression of Emotion: The Value of Cross-Cultural Perspectives. *Metaphor and Symbolic Activity* 10: 163–182.

Fishman, P. (1983). Interaction: The Work That Women Do. In: B. Thorne, C. Lamarae, and N. Henley (eds.), *Language, Gender, and Society*, pp. 89–101. Rowley, Mass: Newbury House.

Frye, N. (1981). *The Great Code: The Bible and Literature*. Toronto: Academic Press.

Garratt, D. (1977). *Youth in Society*. London: Sage.

Goodwin, C. and Duranti, A. (1992). Rethinking Context: An Introduction. In: A. Duranti and C. Goodwin (eds.), *Rethinking Context: Language as an Interactive Phenomenon*, pp. 1–13. Cambridge: Cambridge University Press.

Gumperz, J. (1971). Dialect Differences and Social Stratification in a North Indian Village. *American Anthropologist* 60: 668–681.

Haas, M. (1944). Men's and Women's Speech in Koasati. *Language* 20: 142–149.

Hall, K. and Bucholtz, M. (1996). *Gender Articulated: Language and the Socially Constructed Self*. London: Routledge.

Helprin, M. (2009). *Digital Barbarism: A Writer's Manifesto*. New York: Harper Collins.

Holmes, J. (1984). Hedging Your Bets on Sitting on the Fence: Some Evidence for Hedges as Support Structures. *Te Reo* 27: 47–62.

Honeck, R. P. and Hoffman, R. R. (eds.) (1980). *Cognition and Figurative Language*. Hillsdale, NJ: Lawrence Erlbaum Associates.

Hudson, R. (1986). Sociolinguistics and the Theory of Grammar. *Linguistics* 24: 1073–1078.

Huls, E. (1989). Turkse gezinnen als startpunt voor een schoolloopbaan [Turkish families as a point of take-off for a school career]. In: Batenburg, M. et al. (Eds.), *Conferentie-bundel voor de Achtste Onderwijssociologische Conferentie 'Onderwijs en Gezin'*. SISWO publication 345, Amsterdam, pp. 1–21.

Humboldt, W. von (1836 [1988]). *On Language: The Diversity of Human Language-Structure and Its Influence on the Mental Development of Mankind*, trans. by P. Heath. Cambridge: Cambridge University Press.

Johnson, M. (1987). *The Body in the Mind: The Bodily Basis of Meaning, Imagination and Reason*. Chicago: University of Chicago Press.

Johnson, M. (2007). *The Meaning of the Body: Aesthetics of Human Understanding*. Chicago: University of Chicago Press.

Kay, P. (1975). Synchronic Variability and Diachronic Change in Basic Color Terms. *Language in Society* 4: 257–270.

Kay, P. (1997). *Words and the Grammar of Context*. Cambridge: Cambridge University Press.

Kramer, C. (1974). Folk Linguistics: Wishy-Washy Mommy Talk. *Psychology Today* 8: 82–85.

Labov, W. (1963). The Social Motivation of a Sound Change. *Word* 19: 273–309.

Lakoff, G. (1979). The Contemporary Theory of Metaphor. In: A. Ortony (ed.), *Metaphor and Thought*, pp. 203–251. Cambridge: Cambridge University Press.

Lakoff, G. (1987). *Women, Fire, and Dangerous Things: What Categories Reveal about the Mind*. Chicago: University of Chicago Press.

Lakoff, G. and Johnson, M. (1980). *Metaphors We Live By*. Chicago: Chicago University Press.

Lakoff, G. and Johnson, M. (1999). *Philosophy in the Flesh: The Embodied Mind and Its Challenge to Western Thought*. New York: Basic.

Lakoff, R. (1975). *Language and Woman's Place*. New York: Harper and Row.

Lees, R. (1953). The Basis of Glottochronology. *Language* 29: 113–127.

Lenhart, A. (2010). More and More Teens on Cell Phones. Pew Internet & American Life Project. http://pewresearch.org/pubs/1315/teens-use-of-cell-phones (accessed September 1, 2011).

Lenhart, A. (2011) More and More Teens on Cell Phones. Pew Internet & American Life Project. http://pewresearch.org/pubs/1315/teens-use-of-cell-phones (accessed September 1, 2011).

Levine, L. and Crockett, H. (1967). Speech Variation in a Piedmont Community: Postvocalic r. In S. Lieberson (ed.), *Explorations in Sociolinguistics*, pp. 76–98. Bloomington: Indiana University Press.

Lewis, C. and Fabos, B. (2005). Instant Messaging, Literacies, and Social Identities. *Reading Research Quarterly* 40: 470–501.

Lindenfeld, J. (1969). The Social Conditioning of Syntactic Variation in French. *American Anthropologist* 71: 890–898.

Lunde, P. (2004). *Organized Crime: An Inside Guide to the World's Most Successful Industry*. London: Dorling Kindersley.

Macaulay, R. (2009). *Quantitative Methods in Sociolinguistics*. New York: Palgrave-Macmillan.

Malinowski, B. (1923). The Problem of Meaning in Primitive Languages. In: C. K. Ogden and I. A. Richards (eds.), *The Meaning of Meaning*, pp. 296–336. New York: Harcourt, Brace and World.

McConnell-Ginet, S. (1983). Intonation in a Man's World. In: B. Thorne, C. Larmarae, and N. Henley (eds.), *Language, Gender, and Society*, pp. 69–88. Rowley, Mass: Newbury House.

Morris, C. W. (1938). *Foundations of the Theory of Signs*. Chicago: University of Chicago Press.

Nazir, B. (2012). Gender Patterns on Facebook: A Sociolinguistic Perspective. *International Journal of Linguistics* 4: 252–265.

Nicaso, A. and Danesi, M. (2013). *Made Men: Mafia Culture and the Power of Symbols, Rituals, and Myth*. Lanham: Rowman & Littlefield.

Ortony, A. (1979) (ed.). *Metaphor and Thought*. Cambridge: Cambridge University Press.

Peirce, C. S. (1931–1958). *Collected Papers*. Cambridge, Mass.: Harvard University Press.

Pike, K. (1954). *Language in Relation to a Unified Theory of the Structure of Human Behavior*. The Hague: Mouton.

Pollio, H., Barlow, J., Fine, H. and Pollio, M. (1977). *The Poetics of Growth: Figurative Language in Psychology, Psychotherapy, and Education*. Hillsdale, N. J.: Lawrence Erlbaum Associates.

Rahn, J. (2002). *Painting without Permission*. Connecticut: Bergin and Garvey.

Reeves, M. (2008). *Somebody Scream: Rap Music's Rise to Prominence in the Aftershock of Black Power*. London: Faber & Faber.

Richards, I. A. (1936). *The Philosophy of Rhetoric*. Oxford: Oxford University Press.

Sapir, E. (1921). *Language*. New York: Harcourt, Brace, and World.

Schwartz, H. A., et al. (2013). Personality, Gender, and Age in the Language of Social Media: The Open-Vocabulary Approach. *PLOS ONE* 8: 1–15.

Smitherman, G. (2000). *Black Talk: Words and Phrases from the Hood to the Amen Corner*. Boston: Houghton Mifflin.

Swadesh, M. (1951). Diffusional Cumulation and Archaic Residue as Historical Explanations. *Southwestern Journal of Anthropology* 7: 1–21.

Swadesh, M. (1959). Linguistics as an Instrument of Prehistory. *Southwestern Journal of Anthropology* 15: 20–35.

Swadesh, M. (1971). *The Origins and Diversification of Language*. Chicago: Aldine-Atherton.

Thomas. E. R. (2007). Phonological and Phonetic Characteristics of African American Vernacular English. *Language and Linguistics Compass* 1: 450–475.

Tilley, C. (1999). *Metaphor and Material Culture*. Oxford: Blackwell.

Tossell, C. C., Kortum, P., Shepard, C., Barg-Walkow, L. H., Rahmati, A., and Zhong, L. (2012). A Longitudinal Study of Emoticon Use in Text Messaging from Smartphones. *Computers in Human Behavior* 28: 659–663.

Trudgill, P. (1974). *The Social Differentiation of English in Norwich*. Cambridge: Cambridge University Press.

Van de Broek, J. (1977). Class Differences in Syntactic Complexity in the Flemish Town of Maaseik. *Language and Society* 6: 149–181.

Vandergriff, I. (2013). Emotive Communication Online: A Contextual Analysis of Computer-Mediated Communication (CMC) Cues. *Journal of Pragmatics* 51: 1–12.

Werner, A. (1919). *Introductory Sketch of the Bantu Languages*. New York: Dutton.

Wescott, R. (1980). *Sound and Sense*. Lake Bluff, Ill.: Jupiter Press.

Wilson, S. M. and Peterson, L. C. (2002). The Anthropology of Online Communities. *Annual Reviews in Anthropology* 31: 449–467.

Winner, E. (1988). *The Point of Words: Children's Understanding of Metaphor and Irony*. Cambridge, Mass.: Harvard University Press.

Wolfram, W. (1969). *A Sociolinguistic Description of Detroit Negro Speech*. Washington, DC: Center for Applied Linguistics.

Wundt, W. (1901). *Sprachgeschichte und Sprachpsychologie*. Leipzig: Eugelmann.

3 Variation in Geographical Space

You can be a little ungrammatical if you come from the right part of the country.
Robert Frost (1874–1963)

Fundamentally, sociolinguistics studies language variation in all kinds of spaces—geographical, social, cultural, pragmatic. Traditionally, the study of *variation* came under two branches of linguistics: (1) *dialectology*, or the study of dialects; and (2) *contact linguistics*, or the investigation of languages in contact (such as Spanish in contact with English in the US, producing what is commonly called "Spanglish," a mixture of Spanish and English). The study of dialects and contact phenomena is becoming especially relevant in the current internet age, since these notions are changing and evolving in online media. A dialect is defined as a variant of a language, showing different features (phonological, grammatical, lexical, pragmatic) according to where it is spoken and who speaks it. But the line between a "language" and a "dialect" is rarely clear-cut. What we call English turns out to be a complex term, since English varies not only across nations (British English, American English, Canadian English, Australian English, and so on), but also within a nation—Southern English, Midwestern English, and so on. In effect, English is made up of dialects, spoken in territories that achieved nationhood at some point after British colonization, but we do not call them dialects any longer. American, Canadian, and Australian English are called *national languages*, because they are spoken in territories that have political autonomy. Only variants within each are now called dialects (Cajun American, Newfoundland Canadian, and so on).

This chapter will look at various aspects of geographical-dialectal variation and its sociolinguistic implications. In the final section it will look at how this type of variation is unfolding in online contexts. The themes studied by dialectologists include not only geographical variation and contact phenomena, but also bilingualism, diglossia, language maintenance, language planning, and other related topics.

3.1 Dialects

The term *dialect* comes from the Greek word *dialektos* meaning "speech." It referred to the actual ways in which people spoke in everyday informal conversations—ways that differed from a grammatical (usually written) "norm" or "standard" that was established for formal or official speech. Actually, it is often the case that the standard language is itself historically a dialectal variant that became the norm at some point in time for various social, literary, or political reasons. For example, in France the language spoken in Paris, known as Parisian French, is considered today to be the standard language. Speech communities which do not use it or differ from it in specific ways, having historically lived away from Paris, are said to speak a regional variant or dialect of French. The reasons why Parisian French became the official (national) standard are connected with the social, political, and economic prestige and dominance of Paris. Initially, there was no perception of the Parisian variant as being the standard. But the instant that it became so, the other variants took on dialect status. This historical pattern applies to the linguistic situations of most other nations. The emergence of Florentine Tuscan as the basis for the standard language of Italy, for instance, had nothing to do with the quality of its phonology, grammar, or lexicon, but rather, with the fact that several great medieval writers (Dante, Petrarch, and Boccaccio) used it as part of an incipient literary style that people from all over Italy wanted to emulate. Also, Florence had become a major political and economic force in Italy and, thus, the language of the Florentines was perceived as influential, becoming, over time, the basis for a national standard.

As discussed in the opening chapter (section 1.4.5), determining whether two variants are dialects or distinct languages is guided by the notion of mutual intelligibility. To reiterate it here, this means essentially that if speakers of the variants understand each other, then they likely speak dialects of the same language, if they do not, then they are probably speaking distinct languages. As Chambers and Trudgill (1998: 3) state, this view "has the benefit of characterizing dialects as subparts of a language and of providing a criterion for distinguishing between one language and another." There are, however, problems with this criterion, because many levels of mutual intelligibility exist (even among unrelated languages), and dialectologists must decide when speech varieties should no longer be considered mutually intelligible. In practice, though, it is a useful notion because most people can tell whether or not two variants are related or not. As a trivial example, Canadians recognize the language spoken by Americans as English, and vice versa. Historically, both are dialects of British English. Canadian English is more conservative of its British heritage than is American English, although the two are becoming more and more alike given the many daily interactions between the two nations and, of course, the influence of the internet in leveling off linguistic differences. However, we do not consider these dialects of British English or of each other any longer because they have evolved into standard languages because of political reasons. Note the spelling differences below as an illustration of how American and British English vary:

American	British
color	colour
odor	odour
center	centre
program	programme
analyze	analyse
recognize	recognise

In the area of vocabulary, Canadian and American English show an affinity and, thus, a differentiation from their British predecessor:

American and Canadian	British
mail	post
gasoline	petrol
TV	telly
friend	mate
elevator	lift
subway	underground

In the US, there are three major dialects of English: (1) Northern, also called Eastern or New England; (2) Southern; and (3) Midland, also known as Western or Midwestern. Many local variants exist within these main ones. The Northern dialect is spoken mainly in New York and New England. Some of its characteristics include dropping the /-r/ sound at the end of words (*car* pronounced /kah/), and using a short close /o/ instead of an open /ɔ/ (*fog* = /fog/ rather than /fɔg/). The Southern dialect is spoken, logically, in the southern states. Some of its features include the complete loss of the /-r/ sound, the use of a broad /a/ (*time* = /taʰm/), and of a short /ɨ/ for /e/ before a nasal sound (*pen* = /pɨʰn/). The Midland dialect is spoken in Pennsylvania, West Virginia, and states west of the Appalachian Mountains. This is sometimes considered the standard form because it is spoken over the largest geographic region. Pronunciation characteristics include the use of the /r/ sound in all word positions, the use of the open /ɔ/ for short /o/, and of a long /ay/ in the word *time* (/taym/ not /taʰm/). Documenting differences in pronunciation, grammar, and vocabulary is the basic task of dialectology.

The notion of *dialect continuum* is also used by dialectologists to explain why some dialects may be perceived as separate languages. This is an interconnected group of geographically adjacent or historically associated variants that were initially mutually comprehensible to speakers, but which, over time, became less comprehensible as distance between the speakers increased through migration or as some of the dialects started to assume different social functions. For example, the Romance languages—Portuguese, Spanish, Catalan, Provençal, French, Romanian, Italian, and others—originally formed a continuum. Over time most of these became national languages, evolving along different lines and leading to more and more incomprehensibility. Although there still is some mutual intelligibility between speakers of Italian and Spanish today, distance and historical events have separated them enough so that it has become increasingly more tenuous.

Social factors, such as level of education, socioeconomic status, and so on, can also lead to the formation of separate dialects in geographically-defined areas. Isolation from the center of prestige is what fosters differentiation from the norm in such cases, as communities tend to adopt the linguistic features of the group rather than those of the standard. The various dialects of American English are examples of this type of dialect formation.

Vowels

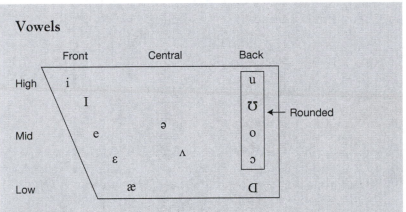

Vowels are described in terms of the position of the tongue on its vertical (high, mid, low) or horizontal axis (front, central, back).

For example, the front of the tongue is moved from low to high in pronouncing the vowel in the word *beet*, and the back of the tongue is raised in pronouncing the vowel in *boot*.

The quality of a vowel depends on whether the lips are rounded or unrounded, close together or open, or the tip of the tongue flat or curled up (retroflex). In some languages, vowels can take on the quality of any nasal consonant that surrounds them in words.

For instance, in French the vowel [a] becomes nasalized, shown with the symbol [ã], before a nasal consonant—for example, the word *gant* ("glove") is pronounced [gã].

Dialects are essentially versions of the same basic linguistic template, showing differences that locate them in geographically-specific communities. Like any science, dialectology is based on observation, data-collection, description, and the theoretical explanation of the data. It does not make blanket statements about what is "good language," or negative comments about "dialectal speech," as do the many kinds of grammatical texts that were once used in schools. It does not espouse a normative, or prescriptive, approach to the study of dialects, but a descriptive one.

3.1.1 Dialect Atlases

To study dialects, a number of specific empirical tools have been developed by dialectologists. One of these is the *dialect atlas*. This is, as its name indicates, a collection of maps of specific regions showing the actual pronunciation, morphology and other structural features that a word or phrase takes on in them. The first to construct a dialect map was a German school teacher named Georg Wenker in 1876. Wenker sent a list of sentences written in Standard German to other school teachers in northern Germany, asking them to return the list transcribed into the local dialect. By the end of the project, he had compiled over 45,000 questionnaires. Each questionnaire contained 40 sentences. Wenker then produced two sets of maps, highlighting the main differential features. The maps were bound together under the title *Sprachatlas des Deutschen Reichs* (1881).

Questionnaires remain the main tool for conducting dialect surveys to this day. Dialectologists send trained observers into the designated region(s) to conduct and record interviews. The Swiss linguist Jules Gilliéron, in the last decade of the nineteenth century, devised a questionnaire for eliciting 1,500 common vocabulary items, constituting a kind of core vocabulary for dialect research. He then chose a fieldworker, named Edmond Edmont, to compile the relevant data in the designated parts of France. From 1896 to 1900, Edmont recorded 700 interviews at 639 sites. Known as the *Atlas linguistique de la France*, publication of the atlas got under way in 1902 and was completed in 1910. It became the model for all subsequent atlases.

There has been some criticism of traditional dialect atlases, from a social perspective. First, there was an implicit belief that the "real speakers" of a dialect lived in rural areas, untainted by the global (exterior) influences of urban speech. A second presupposition was that older male speakers were the authentic bearers of the language forms, since younger speakers and female speakers might in some way contaminate the data. This male-centered view of speakers reflected the biases inherent in the early stages of linguistic science. The situation has changed today, given especially that older males are in the minority and are not necessarily the bearers of the traditional forms of a variant. Today, the majority population includes mobile, younger, and urban subjects of both genders. Phone surveys and the internet provide the primary means for gathering relevant data. Labov, Ash, and Boberg in 2005 used a telephone survey of 762 local speakers as the means to compile their authoritative *Atlas of North American English: Phonetics, phonology and sound change*, which has recast the distribution of regional dialects on the basis of sound changes active in the 1990s.

Maps allow for a relatively precise basis upon which to describe dialectal variation and to examine changes in the dialect continuum. Today, dialectologists have at their disposal a wide array of research tools, including computer software that allows them to analyze large amounts of data quickly and to produce linguistic maps with a great degree of accuracy. These tell us a lot about how languages have spread and, potentially, what linguistic markers are crucial to group identity.

As an example of how a linguistic map can accomplish this, consider a differential lexical pattern for expressing "now" in the three main dialect regions of Italy—northern, central, and southern. There are three lexical items for this concept, *adesso, ora, mo*, that are distributed geographically as shown in the map below. Note that *adesso* is found in areas of central Italy, alongside the form *ora*. *Adesso* was embraced instead by most of the northern dialects, but not *ora*. By the way, *ora* is common in the dialects clustered around Rome. However, in the south, the form *mo* is widespread. This tripartite dialectal distribution can be shown on a map simply as follows:

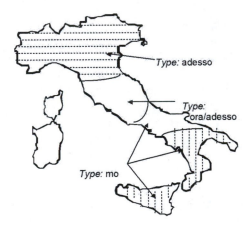

Figure 3.1 Distribution of Lexical Forms for "Now" in Italy

Now, this simple dialect map provides us with some rather interesting insights into how Italians perceive their language and themselves. If one were to hear *mo* spoken in a conversation, then it is highly probable that the speaker comes from southern Italy; if a speaker uses *ora* then we can usually exclude him or her as speaking a northern version of the language; and so on. In addition to containing geographical information related to the speaker, these differential forms also have historical value as markers of social identity. If a southern speaker were to be conversing with a northern one and desires to indicate his or her identity, consciously or unconsciously, the use of *mo* would do the trick rather well.

3.1.2 Pidgins and Creoles

Not all geographical variants are dialects. The *Pidgin* and *Creole* tongues spoken in various parts of the world are examples of non-dialectal variants (Holm 1989). They are forms of language that arise spontaneously to make communication possible between two or more groups that speak different mother tongues. Examples include the Melanesian Pidgin English of the Solomon Islands and New Guinea, and Haitian Creole, based on French. Pidgins result, in a phrase, when people of different linguistic backgrounds have been brought together in specific situations, with no common language to use. This happened, for example, to Africans brought as slaves to the Americas; it has happened to the people of Papua New Guinea, recently united in a new nation with a new focus on the use of indigenous languages (Bruce 1984). In such situations, people respond in a similar way—they construct a rudimentary language with a circumscribed vocabulary and grammar, so that they can communicate effectively and efficiently for everyday social purposes. But this does not imply a loss of linguistic sophistication. On the contrary, pidgins restructure the grammars and vocabularies of their source languages to produce new versions of them.

There are several possible outcomes for a pidgin. It may eventually disappear, if it loses its original purpose, which is what happened to Hawaiian pidgin, now

Examples of Pidgin English

The following examples are from the pidgin spoken along the West African coast between Sierra Leone and Cameroon, which has developed into a Creole (Obilade 1993; Sebba 1997; McArthur 2005).

Meri bin lef (Mary left, Mary had left)

Meri de it (Mary is eating)

Why I go kill my master? (Why would I kill my master?)

And even if to say I de craze why I no go jump for inside lagoon? (And even if I become crazy, why would I not jump inside the lagoon instead?)

almost entirely replaced by English, the common language of Hawaiians. It can remain in use for generations, or even centuries, as has happened with some West African pidgins, but then gradually drop out of use. It can evolve into a mother tongue. When people in a pidgin-using community get married and have children, the pidgin develops into a new language. The children of such people are its first native speakers. This new language is called a *Creole*. The word comes from the Spanish word *criollo*, meaning "native to the place." Creole speakers develop their own cultures and narrative traditions, some of which can become renowned beyond the Creole-speaking territory. The Creole music of Louisiana, for example, is now viewed as an important artistic musical form. Creoles are testimony to the powerful instinct in humans to create language on the basis of need.

Linguists classify Creoles according to the source language that has most contributed to the formation of its lexicon. The main parent language is called the *lexifier language*. Currently, there are over seventy languages that are classified as Creoles based on the following nine lexifier languages—a distribution that reflects to some degree the scope of colonization pursuits that each corresponding society has carried out over history:

- English (31)
- French (14)
- Portuguese (11)
- Malay (8)
- Arabic (5)
- German (2)
- Spanish (2)
- Mandarin (1)
- Ngbandi (1)

3.1.3 Lingua Francas

The geographical documentation and study of dialects, pidgins, and Creoles has many sociolinguistic implications. The investigation of these sometimes comes under the category of "sociolinguistic dialectology," which may study, for example, the global forces that are changing the very nature of dialects, including increasing urbanization, geographical mobility and diaspora, mass education policies, and the like.

As we saw, the criterion of mutual intelligibility implies the existence of a norm, that is, of an abstract idealization of a language against which variation can be defined or construed. In today's global village it is becoming increasingly difficult to identify what the norms are. On the internet, the tendency is to use English as the "default" form of communication among speakers of different national backgrounds but also among those who have learned English as a second language. English is thus what linguists call a *lingua franca*, a language systematically, rather than casually, used to make communication possible between people not sharing a native language. Lingua francas have arisen throughout human history, often for commercial, scientific, or other official reasons. Thus the question of what kind of characteristics English is developing as a lingua franca and the social roles the new "Englishes" play in peoples lives is becoming evermore critical. However, in the case of "global English" the problem is determining which is the standard for the language, since it functions as a lingua franca in online contexts and this, as we shall see below, entails a different view of lingua franca and literacy generally.

Another pertinent sociolinguistic problem is that of the awareness of native speakers of English with respect to the emerging lingua franca speakers, given that they often assume that if someone speaks their language they instinctively understand their cultural presuppositions. This is often called "linguistic imperialism," which can have very negative effects on interpersonal communications between two speakers of English who come from different backgrounds. But this situation may be as old as history. Latin and Greek were the lingua francas of the Roman Empire and Aramaic of a large part of Western Asia through several empires. From writings of the Romans, for example, it is easy to detect that they believed that those who were forced to adopt Latin after conquest would understand the world like they did. Thus, military imperialism and linguistic imperialism seem to go hand in hand. But, of course, this is not always the case. There are many lingua francas in existence today in particular regions. In a few countries the lingua franca is also the national language, as is the case of Urdu, which is both the lingua franca of Pakistan and its national language.

3.2 Diglossia and Related Topics

People do not react neutrally to dialectal variation. They evaluate it socially and assign dialect speech to different social strata. Typically, speakers of dialects are considered to be in lower classes than those who speak more standard forms of a language—whether this is true or not. Some dialects are considered to be more prestigious than others. The term *diglossia* is used to refer to such differential social perceptions related to dialect speech (Ferguson 1959). Sometimes, in a diglossic speech community, a bilingual code emerges, whereby one of the variants is used for writing and one for speaking. This has happened in various Semitic-based language areas. For reasons such as these, the notion of diglossia has received considerable attention from sociolinguists (Fishman, Cooper, and Ma 1971; Haugen 1972; Hudson and Fishman 2002). Such research has shaped to a significant degree how studies of bilingualism, such as the use of Spanish in speech communities throughout the US, have been approached.

Ferguson (1959) came to the notion of diglossia by researching speech communities where two markedly divergent varieties of a language, each employed in specific social ways, were characteristic of everyday speech situations. He noted that one of the varieties was invariably the basic code for ordinary conversations; the other was the code instead for formal communications and writing. He designated the former Low (L) and the latter High (H) variants. Some widely known examples of this dichotomy are found in Modern Greek, Arabic, and Swiss German:

Table 3.1 Examples of Diglossia

	High	*Low*
Greek	Katharévousa	Dhimotiki (Demotic)
Arabic	'al-fush (Classical)	'al-'ammiyah (Colloquial)
Swiss German	Hochdeutsch (High German)	Schweizerdeutsch (Low German)

In these speech communities, the distinction between H and L forms is clear-cut and socially significant; in others it is not as clear-cut. It all depends on where one lives in these countries. H forms are used typically for writing, sermons, lectures, newscasts on television, poetry, science, and so on; L forms are used instead for everyday talk and in informal texts (including humor, folk events, and the like). Essentially, H and L forms of speech have specific functions in societies where diglossia is an intrinsic feature of the language(s) spoken. For example, in Greece, there are word pairs having H or L function, such as *ínos* (H) and *krasí* (L) for referring to "wine." In restaurants, only the H form is written on menus, while diners would ask for wine with the L word (Trudgill 1983). Thus, topic, situation, level of formality, and other factors are involved in diglossia. Using the inappropriate variety in the wrong context would be socially incorrect or incongruous.

Typically in diglossic societies, children learn the low variety as a native language, since it is the language of the family, the marketplace, of friendship, and of solidarity. In contrast, the high variety is spoken by few or none as a first language. It is taught in school and used for public speaking, formal lectures, media broadcasts, sermons, and formal writing practices. Ferguson noted as well that the H form always had a strong literary tradition behind it. But this does not mean that the tradition itself will guarantee an H status. The history of Italian dialects is replete with examples of diglossic differentiation. The Florentine dialect became a norm early on, as mentioned, because it had an emerging important literary tradition (through the writings of Dante, Petrarch, and Boccaccio), being perceived as a *volgare illustre* (an illustrious vernacular), and thus a high dialect, by many throughout the Peninsula early on. Other regions also have had great literary traditions. It is within them that the diglossia criterion can be applied. So, within the Neapolitan dialect area, some forms of the language are considered to be higher than others, but only with respect to the dialect, not to Standard Italian.

3.2.1 High and Low Speech

The H and L forms of language reveal differences in phonology, grammar, and vocabulary. For instance, there is a noticeable difference in the pronunciation of *Hochdeutsch* and *Schweizerdeutsch*, each one evoking social perceptions associated with the differential pronunciations. There are three noun cases in Classical Arabic, whereas Colloquial Arabic does not have any. In Greece, only the H form is written, for example, on menus, while diners would typically use L forms with the waiter (according to social level of restaurant).

The H and L dichotomy is a functional one even in areas where situations such as those described above do not exist. In English-speaking countries, an H form of English is used for official written texts such as academic books, government legislation, and the like. Written English also boasts illustrious literary traditions, which extend beyond the specific dialect communities from which they emanated. A measure of highness or lowness would be the ability of a dialect to migrate beyond its community borders and be read and even spoken in other areas. It is a fact that the poetry, prose, and music written in some dialects are read and performed in their original languages by any and all speakers. This was the case of Florentine Italian in the medieval period (Clivio, Danesi, and Maida-Nicol 2011), which eventually became the standard language of the entire nation. Often, the survival of a dialect is determinable in terms of its diglossic value—the higher it is the more likely it is to survive.

The table below summarizes the main differentiated social functions of diglossic speech:

Table 3.2 High and Low Dialects

Low Dialect	High Dialect
Low prestige	High prestige
Intimate communication	Formal communication
Group solidarity	Social authority and power
Mainly spoken	Part of literacy traditions
Informal	Formal
Usually a native language	Usually a learned language
Passed on in community	Passed on through schooling

In dialect speech communities, H and L forms are indexes of identity and group membership. Florentines continue to feel fiercely proud about their vernacular speech, perceiving phonological and lexical characteristics as signs of group solidarity and personal pride in their heritage. This is true in Naples and Venice and a few other places in Italy, where the historical dialect has an H value. Indeed, in Florence and Naples, using Standard Italian in ordinary conversations might even be considered to be snobbish or artificial. In the context of a political debate, it could even raise questions of loyalty to the tribe. These dialects are believed by their speakers to be more beautiful and logical and thus more appropriate for aesthetic and various other social purposes than the artificial national norm.

As the above discussion alludes, allegiance to the dialect seems to reveal an unconscious need to preserve tradition and social identity, in the face of globalizing and standardizing movements and tendencies. Dialects that have historically had an L prestige attached to them remain in use mainly in localized areas or in areas where little immigration has occurred. To this day, being unable to speak Standard Italian carries various social stigmas in such areas, and thus the use of dialects is rarely found in formal speech situations. Similarly, a speaker of Midwestern English would never try to modify indigenous pronunciation habits in interactions with speakers of an L version of American English, whereas those who use an L form might attempt to attenuate their pronunciation habits in such instances. In effect, dialect variation is, and always has been, diglossic in its social implicature. Members of certain dialect areas often adopt a particular pronunciation as a way of distinguishing themselves from other social groups.

For such reasons, L forms of speech persist, since they have "community value," allowing people in specific geographic areas to come together for ritualistic purposes. The dialect allows them to feel comfortable about themselves. To quote Michael Adams (2009: 59–60):

> Speech is not merely a tool of communication but a fundamental human characteristic implicated in social and personal identity. Humans are social animals; if you don't belong to at least one group, then you aren't a fully realized person. Inevitably, you identify with a group and its speech; in turn, you will be identified by that speech, until someone outside the group successfully appropriates it.

Dialect allows people to be part of communal life, no matter what outsiders think. It is a code that bonds specific groups of people together, conveying a sense of identity different from that of the mainstream language. It is something that one feels, rather than understands rationally. It constitutes a form of *sprezzatura*—an Italian word, which can be defined as "studied carelessness." It was coined by Baldassare Castiglione in his 1528 *Book of the Courtier*. Although Castiglione used it to describe "cultivated language," it is, paradoxically, the force behind the maintenance of dialects.

3.2.2 Code-Switching

The practice of moving back and forth between two languages or dialects, including between H and L forms of a language, is called *code-switching*. It occurs more typically during oral conversations rather than in writing, but it crosses all media and modes of communication (Zentella 1997).

Examples of Code-Switching in Spanglish

(From Stavans 2004)

"What is *esa cosa* (this thing) in Spanish?"

"Hey, *chica* (girl), you have a bad *mancha* (spot) on your *camiseta* (blouse)."

"My *padrito* (dad) likes to watch *el beisból* (baseball)."

"Hey, *amigo* (friend, dude) *dónde* (where) are you going?"

"He is really *loco* (crazy)."

Bilinguals may code-switch simply because of fluency problems in their weaker (or other) language. Code-switching can also mark a switch from informal to formal situations. Gumperz and Cook-Gumperz (1982) found, for example, that in a small Puerto Rican community in New Jersey, some of the members would code-switch in casual and formal gatherings, depending on situation, topics, and the like. Others were hesitant about using Spanglish, restricting it to the home and especially to conversations with children. As the researchers also discovered, code-switching between parents and children in bilingual homes is a strategy of endearment and of pride in one's heritage. It is thus an index of group identity (Das 2011).

Code-switching has many functions in AAVE (African American Vernacular English), with the switch occurring during conversations in SAE (Standard American English) or AAE (African American English). If the interlocutors are young, it is likely to be a sign of identity-differentiation from the mainstream or other groups. It has also been documented in employment interviews (Hopper and Williams 1973; Akkinaso and Ajiritutu 1982), in a range of educational settings (Smitherman 2003), in legal discourse (Ray 2009), and various other contexts, where it seemingly is advantageous especially in the presence of SAE speakers—for instance, it reminds the speakers of their African American background; it is a sign of upward social mobility, given that the switch back and forth between formality and informality is often perceived as an advantage in certain situations; and so on. In all such situations, the crux of the question has always centered around what the ideal speech is in that situation.

Linguists sometimes distinguish between code-switching and code-mixing. A fluent bilingual speaker addressing another bilingual speaker might engage in code-switching as we saw. There are two main types of code-switching: *intersentential* and *intrasentential*. The first refers to code-switching between sentences and the second refers to code-switching within sentences. The former normally manifests itself in spoken dialogue and the latter in writing.

Many researchers believe that intrasentential code-switching is more elaborate and involves a bilingual individual who is proficient in both languages, as switching within sentences requires a high level of efficiency to avoid violating grammatical rules of either language. Code-mixing occurs when a bilingual will start a message in one language (say English) and end it in the other (Spanish) (Romaine and Kachru 1992). This occurs especially when a new topic is introduced. The distinction between the two is, however, a fuzzy one. And indeed, many sociolinguists prefer to use simply the term code-switching broadly to indicate any form of switching from one code to the other.

Code-switching and code-mixing serve several functions:

1   They allow bilinguals to fill in conceptual gaps in one language from the other one.
2   They show allegiance to the group, as, for example, when an Hispanic switches to or mixes in Spanglish when speaking to other Hispanics in English or even to monolingual English speakers.
3   They indicate that certain topics are felt to be more appropriately articulated in one or the other language.

In the middle part of the twentieth century, researchers tended to see code-switching as a substandard form of dialogue, characteristic of contact situations (see below). However, since then research has shown it to be characteristic of specific kinds of bilingual and multilingual speech communities, bearing functions such as the ones mentioned here (Goldstein and Kohnert 2005; Brice and Brice 2009). Code-switching also manifests itself in dialects and registers, constituting a means of organizing speech strategically in conversational settings. Code-switchers choose a language that marks their rights and obligations during conversations (Wei 1998; Sebba and Wooton 1998; Cromdal 2001). According to Carol Myers-Scotton (1993), when there is no unmarked language choice, speakers employ code-switching to explore possible choices. On the other hand, Peter Auer (1984) has suggested that code-switching does not simply mirror social situations in conversational settings, but rather that it is a factor in creating them. So, when the code-switcher chooses to use one or the other language for a conversational turn, the switching influences the subsequent choices of all interlocutors. Rather than the social values inherent in the code chosen, the speaker concentrates on the meaning that the act of code-switching itself creates.

Research has also shown that code-switching is a strategy to minimize social distances and differences during speech. Bilinguals seek approval by adapting their speech choices to accommodate the interlocutor. This can include not only vocabulary switches, but phonological and grammatical ones that designate the accommodation. In contrast, speakers might also engage in a divergent speech, whereby the code-switching is meant to emphasize the social distance between the code-switchers and other speakers.

3.2.3 Bilingualism and Multilingualism

The discussion of diglossia and code-switching leads directly to the topic of *bilingualism*. Bilingualism is defined essentially as the ability to speak and use two languages. When more than two are involved it is called *multilingualism*. Bilingual competence may be acquired early by children in regions where two languages (or dialects) are in contact socially (for example, French and dialectal German in Alsace, German and Italian in the Dolomite valleys). Children may also become bilingual by acquiring two languages in different social settings; this is often the case in immigrant communities, where the native language (or ancestral language) is spoken in the home and the language of the host society outside of the home. It can also be a characteristic of upbringing—for example, British children in India learned an indigenous language from their nurses and family servants. A second language can also be acquired in school. The term also refers to a school system, whereby models of bilingual education allow children to maintain the home language and gradually acquire the host language.

The main forms of bilingualism are summarized below:

1 *Individual and social bilingualism*. The former indicates that individuals can be reared or become bilingual users; the latter indicates that a society can be bilingual, wherein many speakers are themselves bilinguals and the society uses more than one language as part of discourse practices and (typically) for legal reasons. An example is Canada, where English and French are official languages.

2 *Productive and receptive bilingualism*. This former refers to an individual who can speak (and of course understand) two languages and the latter to one who mainly understands just one of the two. Immigrant children of the second or third generation raised in a bilingual situation, for example, typically understand (to varying degrees) the language of origin or ancestry because of exposure, but do not use it functionally in the home. They are receptive or passive bilinguals.

3 *Primary and secondary bilingualism*. The former refers to an individual who was reared functionally in two languages and the latter to one who acquires a second language outside of his or her rearing and typically later in life.

4 *Additive and subtractive bilingualism*. The former refers to a society that allows the bilingual child to maintain the home language in some formal way at school, adding on the school language; the latter refers instead to a social situation that does not allow (and may even discourage) the use of the home language at school.

From a sociolinguistic standpoint, the broader study of bilingualism and multilingualism involves several themes, including how bilingual communities form social networks which sometimes makes them keep to themselves and thus to resist acculturation. In such instances, people can live next door to one another and not participate in the same network. In the United States, English became the mainstream language from coast to coast, largely replacing colonial French and Spanish and the languages of Native Americans. In the Caribbean and perhaps in British North America where slavery was practiced, Africans learned the English of their masters as best they could, creating a pidgin for immediate and limited communication. When Africans forgot or were forbidden to use their African languages to communicate with one another, they developed a pidgin and later a Creole. African American Vernacular English may have originated this way.

As we have seen, Bernstein (1971) distinguished between elaborated and restricted codes in reference to the ways in which speech varieties reflect, and are classified, as patterns in different social classes. He also studied how children with a restricted code struggled at school where the elaborated code is the official language. In immigrant bilingualism situations, the restricted code (the native tongue) expresses community pride and class solidarity, but it might present problems for children entering monolingual schools. This has been the most persuasive argument for bilingual education, which allows a restricted code to become a basis upon which to develop the elaborated one (see, for example, Cummins and Danesi 1990).

In today's global village, bilingualism and multilingualism have become increasingly common. And this new situation has the power to transform the entire world socially (Tuan 1991). Wherever multilingualism is a fact of life, diversity in social practices seems to be the norm, enhancing social life for many, given the transformative power of language to shape the public sphere (Vertovec 2007). This area of sociolinguistics is becoming more and more crucial, given global processes of urbanization.

Code-switching and code-mixing are typical of bilingual and multilingual situations. A speaker who has a positive attitude towards both languages, will tend to switch and mix frequently. Bilingual interaction can take place without the speakers switching of course; this means usually that the two languages do not play similar social roles, with one having a lower prestige. This is the case of ethnic dialect speakers of a language in communities abroad (Danesi 1985). For example, educated speakers in immigrant Italian communities in Canada and the US, will hardly switch to Italese (the Italian equivalent of Spanglish) when speaking to native Italian speakers since it is marked stigmatically as L speech, unless humor is intended or a certain focus on the uniqueness of the ethnic's situation. Spanglish speakers on the other hand perceive their code as prestigious and so may switch to Spanglish within the same conversation constantly. Speakers of Swedish and Norwegian and of Danish can communicate with each other speaking their respective languages because of mutual intelligibility, but few can speak all three languages. So, rather than call the situation code-switching, it is called "non-convergent discourse." This occurs as well in Argentina where Italian and Spanish are both widely spoken.

3.3 Languages in Contact

In bilingual communities and in situations of diglossia the languages involved are said to be in contact (Weinreich 1953, 1954). As an early branch of sociolinguistics and dialectology, contact linguistics aimed (and continues) to document the influences languages in contact have on each other and, consequently, on their speech communities. Among the most interesting of the contact phenomena studied by linguists is the kind of "mixed language" that emerges when languages borrow from each other for socio-communicative reasons. Usually it is a host language that influences an immigrant language, although there are cases of mutual influence on record.

A term often used for the mixed language is *koiné*. This was the word used in Ancient Greece to describe the speech based on the Attic language that became the common vernacular of the Hellenistic world, and from which later stages of Greek are descended. A koiné loses those indigenous features that have a community-specific function, so that it can be used as a more generic medium of communication between peoples of different backgrounds. Koinés show what are called interference phenomena. A case-in-point is Spanglish, which is characterized by American English words that have been "Hispanized," that is, rendered to reflect the phonology and morphology of native Spanish words. This is called *nativization* and will be discussed below.

3.3.1 Borrowing

The term *borrowing* refers to the fact that languages in contact will tend to borrow words from each other. The term "contact" here covers a wide range of phenomena: languages in physical proximity (Spanish and English in the US), languages in intellectual proximity (such as Latin and English), and languages used for varying purposes, such as science and technology.

Borrowing is particularly prominent in the languages spoken by immigrant communities, which are in contact with the language(s) of the host society. In such cases, speakers tend to borrow extensively from the host language, since these allow the speakers to carry out the routine tasks and activities of everyday life (Betz 1949; Haugen 1950; Weinreich 1953, 1954; Scotton, Myers, and Okeju 1973; Poplack, Sankoff, and Miller 1988). Borrowing is, in other words, the strategy used to fill gaps present in the native language or else unknown to the native speaker. The words that are borrowed are called *loanwords*. But borrowing is not just a phenomenon that is characteristic of immigrant speech. In English, loanwords such as *naïve* (from French) and *memorandum* (from Latin) entered the language because there were no ways to express the concepts in it. Borrowing allows speakers to say something for which they have no resources in their own language, but which they want to identify just the same.

If conceptual gap-filling is the reason behind a loanword, then it is called a *necessary loan*; if the reason is social, such as the use of a foreign word in place of a native one then the loanword is called a *luxury loan*. Whereas luxury loans retain their original structure, necessary loans are typically adapted to the structure of the borrowing language as they gradually gain currency—a process referred to as *nativization*. Among the words that English has nativized from Italian, one can mention *alarm* (from *allarme*), *bandit* (from *bandito*), *bankrupt* (from *bancarotta*), *carnival* (from *carnevale*), *gazette* (from *gazzetta*), and *sonnet* (from *sonetto*). These now have English word-structure and are pronounced according to English rules of phonology. The nativization of these loanwords can be seen especially in the dropping of final vowels. In Italian final vowels have morphemic value, indicating the gender and number of the noun. This is not a feature of English morphology. So during nativization they are dropped.

In addition to loanwords, borrowing can also lead to *calquing*. Calques are phrases that have been translated literally. They are also called *loan translations*. Here are some examples from North American Italese (the Italian spoken in immigrant communities in English societies) (Danesi 1985):

Table 3.3 Calques in Italese

English Source	Calque	Standard Italian Form
it looks good	*guarda bene*	*gli/le sta bene*
downtown	*bassa città*	*centro*
to make a call	*fare il telefono*	*telefonare*

The primary reason why loanwords and calques are so plentiful in immigrant communities is, as mentioned, need. They are forms that people require in order to refer to the objects and ideas in their new physical and social environment with facility. Lacking an appropriate native word for *mortgage*, for instance, the immigrant is forced to adopt the English word and make it his or her own linguistically. The result in Italese is *morgheggio*.

Loans and calques exist in all languages. A classic example of a calque in English is the translated title by which the novel written by Fyodor Dostoyevsky, *The Brothers Karamazov*, is known. We no longer realize that this is a calque from the Russian title, in which the adjectival name (*Karamazov*) follows the noun (*Brothers*). In English it should be *The Karamazov Brothers*, a word order that is reflected commonly in such parallel phrases as the *Smith brothers*, the *Carpenter brothers* and so on. Changing the order—the *brothers Smith*, the *brothers Carpenter*—brings out the fact that the Dostoyevskian translated title is wrong syntactically.

3.3.2 Nativization

English is a language with an extensive loanword component to its lexicon. In fact, on almost every page of a dictionary of the English language one finds evidence of borrowing. If one were to remove only the words borrowed from Latin and its descendants (Italian, French, Spanish, and so on) from the English lexicon everyday speech would become rather impoverished. One cannot handle an object, talk about some abstract concept, or praise the personality of another person without recourse to some word or expression derived from Latin: for example, *disc* traces its origin to the Latin word *discus* (itself derived from the Greek *diskos*); nouns ending in -*tion* (*attention, education, nation*) also have their roots in the Latin lexicon, as do most of the nouns ending in -*ty* (*morality, sobriety, triviality*); and the list could go on and on. Why did this happen?

About 1,500 years ago three closely related tribes (the Angles, the Saxons and the Jutes) lived beside each other on the north shore of what is now northern Germany and southern Denmark. They spoke a language that was similar to the current West German dialects. Known as Old English, it allowed the tribes to establish social autonomy from their Germanic ancestry. Old English had inflections that resemble those of modern German, and it formed the new words it needed largely by rearranging and recombining those present in its lexical stock. It borrowed infrequently from other languages.

However, the situation changed drastically after the invasion and conquest of England by the Normans from northwestern France in 1066. Although they were originally of Viking extraction, by the middle of the eleventh century the Normans had adopted French as their language. They imposed their French-speaking ways upon the Anglo-Saxons. As a consequence, English became saturated with Latin-based words, which have survived in common speech to this day. Their French origin is no longer consciously recognized because of the fact that they have become completely nativized in pronunciation and spelling.

In many instances, English came to adopt Latin-based synonyms even when they were not imposed by the Normans. There are several reasons for this, but perhaps the most important was the fact that Latin was a prestige language in the medieval world. To borrow its words was perceived as a means of enriching the lexicon of any emerging vernacular. This is, in fact, one of the reasons for the coexistence of such synonymous pairs in English as *clap* and *applaud*, *fair* and *candid*, *wedding* and *matrimony*, of which the second item is of Latin descent.

Loanwords are nativized in predictable ways. Thus, for example, in Italese the borrowed nouns are assigned a gender through the addition of final vowels: garbage → *garbiccio*, mortgage → *morgheggio*, switch → *suiccia*, fence → *fenza* (Danesi 1985); verbs are all assigned to the first conjugation, the most regular of the three conjugations of Italian: push → *pusciare*, squeeze → *squizare*, smash → *smesciare*. The latter example illustrates a common feature of nativization—only regular forms are involved in the process, that is, the nativization process does not produce so-called irregular nouns, verbs, and the like, only regular ones. Once the loanword has been restructured phonologically and morphologically, it enters the native speakers' lexicon and is perceived to be an item like any other native item. Research has shown that in gender-using languages, over 80 percent of nativized loans are common nouns (Danesi 1985). Of these, around 60 percent are typically assigned to the masculine gender, 35 percent to the feminine one, and the remainder to forms displaying fluctuating gender. These statistics reflect markedness features of languages with morphological gender

If the social prestige of immigrant languages increases, so too does the likelihood that they will rise above the ethnic communities to become generic codes. To speak with a Spanish accent is to claim that "I am what I am and I am proud of it," as a subtext of each word used, whether the speaker intends this or not. It is a social fact in the US, not a personal one. Spanglish is particularly marked in young people who use it typically in everyday interactions and acquire it through unconscious imitation in their native speech environments. This code is particularly noticeable on social networking sites such as Facebook among speakers of Spanglish, as the relevant research has shown.

Examples of Nativized Loanwords in Spanglish

chequear = to check

parquear = to park

troca = truck

caro = car

sinco = sink

flora = floor

3.4 Standard Languages

In territories that achieve political and cultural autonomy at some point, one of the language variants within them often evolves into a standard language. Without doubt, it is the medium of the *written word* that has always had the greatest influence on this outcome. Modeling the standard language after writers and grammarians has, until recently, always been the greatest factor in shaping language norms. Although this is not completely the case today in the age of electronic mass communications, there are still linguistic authority structures and institutions, such as schools that dictate, or at least continue to influence, linguistic norms and literacy practices.

How does standardization come about? In the past, varieties such as the Florentine vernacular in Italy became a national norm by undergoing a process of standardization, which is accomplished by writing an official grammar for the vernacular and compiling a dictionary, and other linguistic reference works. This process is governed by authoritative institutions, producing a standardized spelling and grammar. In France that institute is the *Académie française* and in Spain the *Real Academia Española*. This standardized language then becomes the official, literary norm to be used in governmental interactions, legislatures, schools, writing practices, and other institutions. In Italy, Florentine became the foundation for the standard language because of the literary prestige of writers born in Florence, as well as the central position of the city within Italy and its aggressive commerce. Before the 1200s the "literary language" of Italy was Latin. The earliest poetry written in *volgare* (language of the people) emerged in Sicily, and this had a profound impact on the development of linguistic trends within the emerging Italian nation and on the practices of writing generally. At the same time, the dialects flourished, being used for regional and local purposes. Many of these became popular throughout the Peninsula. Prose works in native dialects also added to the rich linguistic heritage of Italian as a national code. The writings of explorers throughout Italy in native dialects bear this out. But the first grammars of Italian were based on the Florentine dialect and the *Accademia della Crusca*, the first language academy, was built in Florence to establish norms for the rest of Italy. Today, Standard Italian is different from its Florentine predecessor in having undergone modifications to its spelling, grammar, and vocabulary that reflect a broader use of the language in areas of prestige such as in Genoa, Turin, and Milan in northern Italy.

As the above example shows, a standard language becomes the norm through the process of *language spread*. The reasons for this spread are aesthetic, political, and economic. So, in many communities a kind of diglossia emerges, with the dialect remaining the language of the community and the standard language the code for official communications. There is, in other words, a *language shift* in the community as one variety, having become a standard, assumes social prestige. Until recently, the print medium has been the primary source for initiating shifts towards standardization. With the advent of electronic media since the mid-1950s, it has become saliently obvious—even to a casual observer—that the "medium of influence" in the modern-day evolution of languages is hardly the traditional print one, but the electronic one. Standards are being modified and made in online environments. Although the ones that have social prestige, such as blogs written by journalists, tend to follow the standard form of a language, subtle changes in style, grammar, and vocabulary are bound to occur; over time these will accumulate to redefine standard languages and literacy practices.

3.4.1 Language Loyalty

If dialects are to survive, they actually owe their debt to the new media, which allow for greater use of individual expression and thus a linguistic space for promoting personal and local identities through varieties of language. For instance, there is strong evidence that dialects such as the Neapolitan one in Italy are making a comeback on Facebook and Twitter among young people. For example, Clivio, Danesi, and Maida-Nicol (2011) found that the "handles" or cybernames of young people in Italy have dialectal forms, such as *scugnizzo223* (a Neapolitan handle), *beddamadre* (a Sicilian name), and so on. The first handle refers to a "street savvy lad" and the second to a Sicilian expression meaning literally "good mother." The researchers found, in effect, that the dialects are taking on more and more symbolic value as identity-preserving codes, with young people in particular in centers such as Venice, Naples, Florence, Rome, and a few other places adopting particular pronunciations, lexical items and phraseology, in order to distinguish themselves from others.

People tend to be loyal to their community codes, becoming loyal to the standard through aspirations of social mobility, as a result of education, or for various personal reasons. Linguists refer to the tendency to remain loyal to the community language as, simply, *language loyalty* and to the tendency to maintain that language as *language maintenance*. As Stoessel (2002) has shown, in multilingual language-contact situations, these two factors become critical for the survival of a minority language, since the selection and conversational use of that language are determined by a variety of factors that are difficult to characterize as group-based or as norm-based. The term *language shift* (above) has thus been applied to the process whereby minority populations switch from the mother tongue to another language in everyday use "whether or not at the same time they also give up a language or variety that they had previously used" (Fishman 1972: 107). This process thus includes developing different degrees of bilingualism without simultaneously losing mother-tongue skills. The existence of support from within a group is thus a critical factor for language maintenance. First generation immigrants who live in their ethnic communities tend to be native-language maintainers for the simple reason that they live in a native-language community environment, and they need to learn the host language to get by in their everyday lives, especially if they enter the workforce. During the process of assimilation to the mainstream society, the immigrants, mostly as children, learn a particular way of behaving that renders them bilingual and bicultural for a period of time, until assimilation becomes complete in subsequent generations and migration away from the ethnic community becomes common because of intermarriages, schooling, job mobility, and the like.

But degrees of language loyalty persist even in subsequent generations, who may hardly be fluent in the native language any longer. This is particularly true in multilingual societies where immigrants tend to preserve their linguistic heritage at the same time that they desire to participate in the broader society. Immigrants tend initially to settle into specific areas producing collectivities known as ethnic communities ("Little Italy," "Chicano district," and so on). Language loyalty among the immigrants tends to be stronger among refugees who may have left their countries of origin for various political or ideological reasons. If they emigrate for economic reasons they may attempt to give up their loyalty to the native language more easily, even though they may have a hard time learning the language of the host society. When the children of first generation immigrants start going to school and developing acquaintances outside the ethnic community, they tend to develop forms of bilingualism consisting of the home and host languages with diminishing competence in the former as time goes by. In some nations, such as Canada, governments provide schooling in the native language in areas where it is requested. However, obtaining public funds and pedagogical support becomes less and less likely as the immigrant community assimilates to the larger society.

3.4.2 Language Planning

The term *language planning* refers to the kinds of measures taken by official (usually governmental) agencies to maintain or preserve the forms and hegemony of the standard language or languages of a particular speech community. Sociolinguist Joshua Fishman (1987: 49) has defined language planning as "the authoritative allocation of resources to the attainment of language status and corpus goals, whether in connection with new functions that are aspired to, or in connection with old functions that need to be discharged more adequately." There are four main varieties of planning:

1   Status planning, whereby the government takes measures (such as legislation) to guarantee that the status of a language remains stable.
2   Corpus planning, whereby official institutions (such as academies and authoritative dictionary makers) assign social prestige to a language.
3   Language-in-education planning, which is designed to privilege a certain language through education.
4   Prestige planning, which involves getting all communities to accept the standard as the prestige code through the use of a language for literacy practices and for mainstream media transmissions.

Language planning arises sometimes when speakers of different languages compete for resources or where a linguistic minority is denied access to basic rights. An example is the Court Interpreters Act of 1978, which provides an interpreter to any victim, witness, or defendant whose native language is not English. A common language planning strategy in multilingual or diglossic regions is simply for the government to autocratically declare one of the languages as the standard or official language, in order to promote linguistic unity.

Some countries set up language academies which dictate what is authentic and what is in good taste when it comes to official language norms. The French Academy is a classic example of this kind of language planning which, to this day, emits edicts of what is good grammar and acceptable vocabulary, putting these in its official dictionaries and encyclopedias. Academies of this type exist in various European countries (Italy and Spain, for instance). Another form of language planning is called *language revitalization and maintenance*, which occurs in countries that were colonized and then subsequently achieved independence. Such nations have faced decisions as to what indigenous language(s) to designate as the standard for use in the official political and social arenas. In such cases, language planning is often closely aligned with the desire of new nations to symbolize their newfound identity by giving official status to the indigenous language(s). Today, in many multilingual societies, language planning issues often revolve around attempts to balance the language diversity that exists within a nation's borders with traditional literacy and education practices brought about by immigration rather than by colonization.

There are four general ideologies that motivate language planning (Nahir 2003). The first is *linguistic assimilation*, which is the belief that every member of a society should learn to use the standard language and shed their bilingual heritage. In the US, this is known as the "English-only" movement; the movement espouses the belief that only English reflects the historical and social ethos of the country, ignoring the role that indigenous languages and Hispanic culture have played in the linguistic history of the US. In contrast, the second ideology is called *linguistic pluralism*, which espouses the use and institutionalization of multiple languages within one society. Examples include the coexistence of German, French, Italian, and Romansh in Switzerland, and English, Tamil, Malay, and Chinese in Singapore. In such areas, however, one of the languages is still perceived to be the standard one for all language speakers. A third ideology, called *vernacularization*, supports the restoration or development of an indigenous language along with its institutionalization as the standard language. Examples include Quechua in Peru and Hebrew in Israel. A fourth ideology, known as *internationalization*, is the adoption of a non-indigenous language as the official one in order to connect a country to the global village. Examples are the use of English in countries such as India, Singapore, the Philippines, and Papua New Guinea.

3.4.3 Literacy

Basic literacy is the ability to read and write with the writing system of a language. Literacy also refers to the possession of enough knowledge and skill to function intellectually in a society. This is called *functional literacy*. Literacy is embedded in the standard language of a nation, although the term is often used to refer to different kinds of competencies involving other languages. In the case of bilingualism, the degrees of literacy in one language and the other constitute what linguists call levels of *biliteracy*.

The role of writing and reading in the definition of literacy cannot be overstated. Before the fifteenth century and the advent of cheap print technology, most people in Europe were illiterate, never having had the opportunity to learn to read and write. Not only were there few schools, but literacy was not required to carry out work in farming villages and in the trades of the medieval towns. Most literate people belonged to the nobility, the upper classes, or the clergy. But the printing press changed this. The late Marshall McLuhan (1962, 1964) characterized the new world order brought about by the advent of the printing press as the "Gutenberg Galaxy," after the European inventor of the printing press, the German printer Johannes Gutenberg. Through cheap books and other materials, the printed word became the chief means for the propagation and recording of knowledge and ideas. And because books could cross national boundaries, the printing press set in motion the globalization of knowledge and especially science, thus encouraging literacy across the globe and paving the way for such events and movements as the European Renaissance, the Protestant Reformation, and the Enlightenment. With the spread of literacy and with industry becoming a dominant part of economic life during the eighteenth and nineteenth centuries, great numbers of people started migrating to cities. In order to find employment they had to learn how to read instructions and perform other tasks that required literacy. Governments began to value education more, and systems of public schooling cropped up everywhere. By the late 1800s, formal elementary education had become a virtual necessity.

Today, literacy is considered to be the chief means for gaining prestige and economic well-being. In the 1960s, the United States government set up a federal program called Adult Basic Education to provide basic instruction in reading and writing for illiterate or undereducated adults. In 1970, the Office of Education (now the Department of Education) initiated the "Right to read" movement in order to improve how literacy is imparted in schools and to encourage private organizations to offer instruction to illiterate adults. Countries across the world have similar literacy programs and legislation. In the 1960s, China hired 30 million volunteer teachers with the slogan "You Who Can Read, Teach an Illiterate." In 1961, Cuba sent many of its teachers to rural areas to instruct illiterate people, increasing the country's literacy rate from 75 to 96 percent. However, functional illiteracy remains a major problem in all countries. A 2003 US Department of Education survey discovered that many Americans lacked functional literacy skills—about 15 percent of Americans aged sixteen and older were unable to find and understand information in short texts. As a consequence, some states now require students to pass standardized reading and writing tests before they graduate from high school.

Literacy has become a virtual necessity in the contemporary world. This is reflected in the relevant statistics. By 2000, 79 percent of people were literate. Today, there are new forms of literacy that have emerged because of the digital revolution. Digital and media literacy have entered the common lexicon to characterize this new situation. Literacy is changing, but its basic functions have not, since most media texts, digital and otherwise, still require the ability to read and write.

3.5 Online Variation

The influence of electronic media on language and communicative behavior generally may have started as early as the 1930s, when radio and early television services were in place in several Western countries. So, it should come as no surprise to find that writing practices are changing all the time, inducing changes in the spoken language and in traditional literacy. A new kind of biliteracy has emerged, whereby there now seems to be one way to write a language in the online medium and another to write it offline (Varnhagen, Mcfall, and Pugh 2010). Netlingo forms such as *g2g* and *lol* are now part and parcel of an online literacy, which can be called e-literacy, that is often in conflict with offline literacy, but also a source of influence on the latter. Some would even say that e-literacy is not a full language, but simply a shorthand form of a language that is adapted to the digital medium. In the Internet Age the notions of diglossia, bilingualism, multilingualism, code-switching, standardization, and literacy, therefore, are morphing into different constructs of linguistic diversity (Ivkovic and Lotherington 2009). With the increasing scope of multilingual capabilities in CMC, multilingual voices and choices are becoming more prevalent in e-literacy practices. These voices are important forces in the ever-broadening globalism movement.

The intersection of mobile people and mobile texts has thus led to a reassessment of the traditional sociolinguistic notions of variation. Some warn of the dangers of a new kind of internet linguistic imperialism, whereby English has become a lingua franca of the global village, thus endangering other languages. But the English-based lingua franca is hardly the traditional type of lingua franca. It consists of what can be called linguistic hybridization whereby it incorporates features from other languages. Susan Cook (2004) has argued that the impact of global English on the non-English-speaking world is hardly a hegemonic one, since it actually reproduces the social, political, and economic relations that exist in the real world. She also points out that there is growing evidence that the new electronic landscape, unlike the real landscape, is not playing by the expected sociolinguistic rules.

3.5.1 e-Literacy

Twitter

Twitter was founded in 2006.

It is an information and social network with specific user practices that distinguish it from other social media.

These include:

- follower structure

- link-sharing

- use of "hashtags"

- real-time searching.

Twitter users convey their specific interests, professional affiliations, and tweet history on a Profile page. Followers are other Twitter users who subscribe to the tweets. Twitter allows for links to other Web content.

Common practices on Twitter include:

- the use of @ plus the user name (@mdanesimus) at the beginning of the tweet to indicate a message or a reply;

- the hashtag (#) to label and organize tweets, classifying them as part of a particular category or conversation, such as #SCL2015 (to designate a 2015 conference in sociolinguistics) or #lingchat (displaying a stream of tweets about a specific subject, linguistics in this instance);

- the letters RT are used to signify a "retweet," that is, forwarding someone else's tweet to a specific group of people.

Prominent on the agenda of e-sociolinguistics is the focus on global English—that is, the spread of English throughout the world, often at the expense of other languages. Although non-English language websites exist in large numbers, most of the web's contents are in English. Also prominent are the new forms of literacy that are evolving online. One such form of e-literacy, called *Twitteracy*, involves the linguistic and textual practices that now characterize Twitter communications. In a relevant study, Greenhow and Gleason (2012) explored tweeting as a literacy practice, combining or amalgamating traditional and new digital literacies, and impacting both informal and formal norms and registers. In effect, Twitter has become a prevalent way to write language and to communicate (Verhejjen 2013). Since social media are often used interchangeably with Web 2.0, such e-literacy practices have become a major source of general literacy in the online and offline worlds.

There are over 200 million active users of Twitter, of all demographics, who send and receive approximately 180 million tweets per day. People use Twitter for a variety of reasons: conversing with friends and acquaintances, making new contacts in a specific social domain, connecting to public figures, sharing information, exploring job opportunities, and mobilizing support for social and political issues. The tweets share many features of netlingo and textspeak, but have also introduced new linguistic phenomena such as hashtags and established new types of speech networks based on interests rather than geography and historical traditions.

Twitteracy is an ever-growing phenomenon (Coiro, Knobel, Lankshear, and Leu 2008; Livingstone, Van Couvering, and Thumim 2008). It combines aspects of traditional print-based literacy with the efficiency of writing principle associated with CMC, leading to a new conceptualization of the nature and role of literacy. Twitteracy involves a broad, situation-specific, multimodal, and socially mediated practice (Kress 2003; Hull and Nelson 2005; Lankshear and Knobel 2006). In the online world, literacy entails not only control of language forms and styles but also knowledge of how and when to use specific technologies and which forms and functions of language are strategic for supporting one's communicative purposes. Changes in the medium, from the page to the screen, now make it easy to use a variety of communicative modes (images, video, music, sounds, and so on) to convey a message. Multimodality is thus becoming an integral component of e-literacy. Multimodal texts can also be interactive as recipients can "write back," thus blending authorship, readership, production, and consumption.

Black (2008) examined the e-literacy practices of adolescent immigrant and English-language learners in online fan fiction communities—communities that used tweets to write about popular culture. The same population also frequently participated in other technology-mediated environments such as Facebook. Black conducted a longitudinal ethnographic study, finding that they adopted a form of "global literacy" that cuts across national borders, including the manipulation of popular cultural artifacts, turning out unique pastiches of text, image, and sound that expressed their responses to these artifacts. Davies (2012) examined the e-literacy practices of British teenagers on Facebook, via semi-structured interviews, talk-alouds of Facebook profiles, and screenshots of Facebook pages. She found that self-presentation and friendship management were the primary concerns of the Facebook users. The photos helped the subjects construct "pictorial narratives" whereby friends could comment, add nuance, or generate tags as a means of interaction (Davies 2012: 27). She also determined that Facebook's automatic self-publishing capabilities allowed the young people to create a new literacy context based on collaboration. Overall, they used multimodality in order to communicate effectively.

Other work has corroborated these findings. Perkel (2008: 1), for instance, suggested that social media have brought about new shared literacy practices, made possible by the "cut-and-paste" capabilities of CMC: "The expressive power found in the creation of a MySpace profile concerns a technically simple but socially complex practice: the copying and pasting of code as a way to appropriate and reuse other people's media products." The process of finding and re-using resources of others can be called "bidirectional literacy," which amalgamates analysis (reading) and production (writing), as well as interactive sharing (video-sharing, blog-sharing, photo-sharing, and so on). Cumulatively, such studies are showing that communication practices on social network sites are leading to new literacy practices. Authorship of a text is now neither individualistic nor completely original, since remixing is fundamental to how people create texts (Alvermann 2008).

As James Gee (1999: 601) has aptly pointed out, literacy is tied to specific changes in social emphases. Effective communication on Twitter now requires understanding how to self-present oneself, participate (*mentions*), distribute information (*retweets*), and organize conversations (*hashtags*). These e-literacy practices dovetail with traditional, print-based literacy skills. As Carter, Weerkamp, and Tsagkias (2013) have noted, e-literacy involves using a lot of ingenuity in order to overcome the limitations of short, unedited and idiomatic texts. Haas and Takayoshi (2011) distinguish, in fact, between "standard literacies" found in formal offline contexts and online "everyday literacies" which entail knowledge of text messaging style. Actually, Twitteracy and e-literacy generally may be catalysts for imparting basic (ability-to-read) literacy to larger populations. Barden (2012) noticed an increase in literacy competence in dyslexic middle school subjects, explaining this unexpected outcome with the fact that the dyslexics had to engage in text structures that presented the relationship of letters-to-phonemes in bare outline form. This led to a better understanding of sequence and relation in linear texts. In other words, the medium improved in dyslexics the ability to read or interpret words, letters, and other symbols.

3.5.2 e-Dialects

The compression of language evidenced in netlingo, textspeak, and other e-literacies is in line with a general principle of communication called the Principle of Least Effort. The Harvard linguist George Kingsley Zipf (1929, 1932, 1935, 1949) was among the first to show that there is a mathematical correlation between the frequency of a form (such as a word or sentence) and its size (as measured in number of phonemes, words, and so on). Practically, this means that there is a tendency in language towards efficiency and economy, which manifests itself in compressed forms (abbreviations of words and phrases, acronyms).

This principle is the force behind the new e-literacies and it is also the force behind the evolution of what can be called e-dialects, which attest to a new form of diglossia. Indeed, an H form of language is used to write e-mails and most blogs, whereas tweets and text messages are perceived to have an L status. Tweets are inserted on a user's profile page and delivered to followers. Twitter is essentially an SMS (short message service) on the internet, since it allows for text messaging to take place without text messaging devices. Most tweets are purely conversational—exchanges between friends, associates, colleagues, and acquaintances. Despite what the company says, information is not the main attraction of Twitter—indeed, only around 10 percent of its contents can be considered to be purely informational. It is psychological and social. Some have designated such sites as venues for "social grooming," that is, for presenting oneself in a favorable way to others in order to gain attention and to gather followers. Institutions of various kinds, from NASA to universities, now use Twitter as a source of contact with clients and colleagues. Tweeting is thus an e-dialect, requiring knowledge of its forms and how they differ from the standard ones. It is suggested that the limited length of each tweet, the desire for followers, and the constant flow of tweets are all leading to a withdrawal from reflective communication and to an engagement in superficial exchanges. While this may be somewhat true, the critics may be missing the historical point that informal daily interaction has probably always been this way, as the Principle of Least Effort suggests. Twitter has simply made it possible for people to enlarge the range of the informal communication, not introduce it into social life.

Perhaps the most important notion to be explored by e-sociolinguistics in this domain is the reconceptualization of speech community. A speech community is a group of people sharing a common language or dialect. What is the speech community in the case of Twitter? In a relevant study, Gruzd, Wellman, and Takhteyev (2011) approached this notion, indicating that even in its F2F origins it has "often been caught between concrete social relationships and imagined sets of people perceived to be similar" (Gruzd, Wellman, and Takhteyev 2011: 1294). The internet has enabled people who belong to a speech community to interact without meeting physically. This means that "connections on Twitter depend less on in-person contact, as many users have more followers than they know" (Gruzd, Weilman, and Takhteyev 2011: 1294). The study showed that Twitter now forms the basis of interlinked communities—and even provides a sense of community that was typical of F2F speech communities. They summarize this as follows (Gruzd, Wellman, and Takhteyev 2011: 1313):

> An "imagined" community on Twitter is dual-faceted. It is at once both collective and personal. It is collective in the sense that all tweeps belong to the worldwide set of tweeps who understand Twitter's norms, language, techniques, and governing structure. Moreover, almost all tweeps' pages and messages are reachable—and hence readable—except for a small number of partially locked private pages. Yet community on Twitter is also

personal because tweeps imagine they are following and talking to unique and identifiable tweeps. The collective Twitter community forms around high centers that are popular individuals, celebrities, or organizations such as media companies. Yet even less popular individuals on Twitter can play the role of local high centers of predominantly mutual networks. The high centers in personal Twitter networks are often characterized by high betweenness centrality: a social network analysis measure that indicates how many times an individual appears on the shortest path between all possible pairs of people in the network. Because tweeps with high betweenness centrality link different social circles, they play a critical role in community building and information gate-keeping on Twitter.

Tweeps (Twitter users) are essentially e-dialect users who communicate within an imaginary dialect community. Gouws, Metzler, Cai, and Hovy (2011) found that a kind of "meta-dialectal" world in the Twitterverse has surfaced, whereby, for example, British English speakers differ markedly from American ones in the use of compressed forms. For instance, they found that British tweeps were more likely to use contractions and suffixes, but far less likely to drop final letters, all the vowels, or to repeat a given letter multiple times. This implies that British tweeps tend to write more along the lines of standard literacy and make use of different styles for abbreviating words as compared to American tweeps, who tend to be less formal. This might be related to the differences in the linguistic heritage and perceptions between the two "Englishes." They also found that real-world dialects influence e-dialects. Inhabitants of southwestern regions in the US drop the /-g/ in forms such as *running = runnin'*, which manifests itself as well in digital contexts. It would seem that dialectal fragmentations now occur across digital media paralleling real-world speech communities.

Overall, the online world is developing its own new hierarchy of communities. The frequencies of words used within those communities along with the transformation patterns (abbreviations, acronymy, and so on) are tokens of (virtual) community membership.

Z-Score

Also known as *standard score*. This is the number of standard deviations an observation or datum is above the mean. Thus, a positive Z-score represents a datum above the mean, while a negative one represents a datum below the mean.

Recall from the first chapter that the standard deviation is a quantity calculated to indicate the extent of deviation for a group as a whole.

Bryden, Funk, and Jansen (2013) used such patterns to determine how Twitter communities were formed. They found that specific words characterized each of the communities according to the words used in messages sent by the tweeps. They ranked words in each community by the Z-score of their usage so as to identify the words most representative of that community. Some communities used relatively common words (*chillin, forever, foodies*), while others used much rarer words (*singtei, kstew, sxsw*).

The relation between community structure in an online social network and language use in messages within that network was determined by considering words, word fragments or word lengths. This was, of course, done implicitly in traditional dialectology, where the lexicon and grammar were examined differentially as indicators of dialect speech community. The language people use bears the signature of social or speech community structure, and can be used to identify cultural groups. Online interlocutors expect to have some language in common. When groups share language, and also converse with each other, then the language emerges to identify communities.

As Wilson and Peterson (2002) have written, the internet has created new kinds of communities, bringing together dispersed groups of people with shared interests, but with different linguistic and social backgrounds. These new communities might be mobilized to further particular political agendas, to bring together dispersed members of familial or ethnic groups, or they might be organized around commodity consumption or corporate interests. In traditional dialectological and sociolinguistic study, a community is a delimitable entity which is complete and self-contained. And thus it is often isolated from other communities. But this situation does not hold up in the online world. A more fluid concept of speech community is thus emerging.

The internet has also put a new focus on bilingualism and multilingualism. Cunliffe, Morris, and Prys (2013) found that young bilinguals (Welsh–English) on Facebook used code-switching and code-mixing strategically to garner empathy for ethnic individualism, which, of course, goes back considerably in time in that region. In other words, bilingualism online is not there for the survival reasons that characterize bilingual communities; nor is it a part of community-based solidarity speech. It constitutes a form of pride in one's past and one's distinctive personality in an age of globalism (Danet and Herring 2007).

In effect, multilingualism online has ascribed great value to code-switching. It is relevant to note that recently National Public Radio (NPR) in the US established a blog called Code Switch to examine the "frontiers of race, culture and ethnicity." The site points out that on a daily basis, young people confront the challenges and opportunities of code-switching in digital spaces, at home and at school. The rules of the code-switching game in digital environments vary from one space to the next. Through mash-ups, cutscenes, YouTube, reality TV, and gaming, the code-switching occurs not so much within a language as it occurs across media. The new digital code is multimedial and so too is the code-switching. But some patterns remain the same, no matter what media are involved. Paolillo (2011) examined the use of English, Hindi, and Punjabi in four internet communication contexts that differ on the dimensions of ethnic homogeneity. The traditional sociolinguistic theory of code-switching predicts that code-mixing of English and Hindi or English and Punjabi would occur primarily in ethnically homogenous conversational contexts. Paolillo's quantitative analysis of the four contexts supported this prediction and led to the suggestion that synchronous communication is an important part of what it means for a communication mode to be "conversational."

In sum, while there is change to literacy, dialect status, diglossia, and code-switching in cyberspace, there is also much retention of the same rules of the variation game in offline contexts. This suggests that communication in both online and offline environments is rooted in an understanding of shared context.

Terminology Review

Define or explain in your own words the following terms introduced in this chapter. Some of these have already been introduced, but are elaborated in this chapter and thus are reviewed here.

bilingualism
calque
code-switching
dialect
dialect continuum
diglossia
e-literacy
koiné
language contact
language maintenance
language shift
lingua franca
literacy
multilingualism
nativization
standard language
Z-score

borrowing
code-mixing
Creole
dialect atlas
dialectology
e-dialect
functional literacy
language assimilation
language loyalty
language planning
language spread
linguistic pluralism
loanword
mutual intelligibility
pidgin
vernacularization

Exercises and Discussion

1   Below are some spelling and vocabulary differences between American and British English.

American Spelling	*British Spelling*
favor	favour
realize	realise
defense	defence
axe	ax
meter	metre
connection	connexion

American Vocabulary	*British Vocabulary*
hood (of a car)	bonnet
trunk (of a car)	boot
truck	lorry
attorney	barrister
tube	subway
public toilet	restroom

Can you provide other examples of differences, not only in spelling and vocabulary but also in other areas of language, such as pronunciation or grammar?

2   Now, conduct a similar kind of comparison between Standard American English and any regional dialect of which you may be aware. In this case compare pronunciation and vocabulary only.

3   A pidgin is the simplified language that results when people of different linguistic backgrounds have been brought together in specific situations, with no common language to use. Pidginization is the process of simplifying utterances for communicative purposes, such as when speaking to people who are not native speakers, children, and the like. In English, this involves mainly elimination of morphological detail. For example, the sentence "She is going to the store tomorrow" can be pidginized to "She go store tomorrow" without any loss of meaning. How would you pidginize the following sentences?

(a) They will be going to the mall this afternoon.
(b) I had already arrived yesterday when you called.
(c) I don't know where I put the book that you had given me yesterday.
(d) Your friends had already been taking that subject at school.

4   Each of the following English words was borrowed. Using an etymological dictionary, indicate the source language and explain the nativization process involved.

Borrowed Word	Source Language	Nativization Process
cipher		
algorithm		
education		
puissant		
naïve		
cinema		

5   Read the following excerpt from *The Economist* (How a Dialect Differs from a Language, 2013):

> *Two kinds of criteria distinguish languages from dialects. The first are social and political: in this view, "languages" are typically prestigious, official and written, whereas "dialects" are mostly spoken, unofficial and looked down upon. In a famous formulation of this view, "a language is a dialect with an army and a navy". Speakers of mere "dialects" often refer to their speech as "slang", "patois" or the like. (The Mandarin Chinese term for Cantonese, Shanghaiese and others is fangyan, or "place-speech".) Linguists have a different criterion: if two related kinds of speech are so close that speakers can have a conversation and understand each other, they are dialects of a single language. If comprehension is difficult to impossible, they are distinct languages. Of course, comprehensibility is not either–or, but a continuum—and it may even be asymmetrical. Nonetheless, mutual comprehensibility is the most objective basis for saying whether two kinds of speech are languages or dialects. By the comprehensibility criterion, Cantonese is not a dialect of Chinese. Rather it is a language, as are Shanghaiese, Mandarin and other kinds of Chinese. Although the languages are obviously related, a Mandarin-speaker cannot understand Cantonese or Shanghaiese without having learned it as a foreign language (and vice-versa, though most Chinese do learn Mandarin today). Most Western linguists classify them as "Sinitic languages", not "dialects of Chinese".*

Can you give examples of languages that are mutually intelligible yet belong to different nations and thus not usually considered to be dialects of each other? Why do you think they are mutually intelligible?

6   Read the following excerpt from A. Hudson (Outline of a Theory of Diglossia, 2002):

> *Diglossia, in its ideal form, may be conceived of as the quintessential example of linguistic variation where linguistic realization as opposed to language acquisition—here, grossly oversimplified, the use of H or L—is a function solely of social context, and not of social identity of the speaker. In diglossia, it is context, not class, or other group membership, that controls use. Sociolinguistic situations therefore may be compared to each other in terms of*

> the degree to which the variation between two or more alternants in their respective code matrices is determined by social context, as opposed to the social identity of the speaker, and in situations such as those described for Switzerland, Greece, most Arabic-speaking countries, and numerous other cases, the bulk, if not all, of the variance in the use of H and L appears to be explained by situational context.

Does diglossia exist in the US? If so, how so? Would you consider Spanglish-versus-Standard Spanish to be a diglossic dichotomy? What about Standard American English-versus-African American Vernacular English?

7   Read the following excerpt from J. Cummins (*Bilingualism and Minority-Language Children*, 1981):

> Minority language children pick up L2 in much the same way in the street and/or in school. First, there is a period which can range from several days to several months when the child says very little in L2 but tries to decipher the L2 utterances of others through linking up the utterance with the meaning of the situation. Then words and phrases will be tried out and the effects of these utterances will be observed. Utterances which are not appropriate or don't have the expected effects will be modified until gradually the words and the rules for combining them (grammar) begin to fit together into an organized system that gradually approximates that of a native-speaker of L2. The amount of time necessary to acquire mastery of a second (or first) language will depend on the extent to which individuals have the opportunity and inclination to interact with competent users of the language. It is thus not surprising that immigrant children usually learn the second language more rapidly than their parents since, typically, they have much more exposure to the language than their parents.

How would you define a minority language? What minority languages are there in the US?

8   Read the following excerpt from A. Hudson (Outline of a Theory of Diglossia, 2002):

> The association between diglossia and literacy, in the sense of both the incidence of individual literacy skills and the existence of a literary tradition, is not an accidental one, since social stratification of literacy may give rise to the independent development of two or more increasingly divergent language varieties. As the linguistic varieties become more divergent, more extensive training is required for the mastery of the literary variety, a development that in turn confers additional prestige upon it: "With the development of writing and a complex and introspective literature, the language variety so employed will often be accorded such high value because of the recorded nature of the medium and the need to be trained to read and write it" (Abrahams 1972: 15).

How would you define literacy today? What about online literacy?

9   Read the following excerpt from R. Page (The Linguistics of Self-Branding and Micro-Celebrity in Twitter: The Role of Hashtags, 2012):

> *Within the linguistic marketplace of Twitter, hashtags are a crucial currency which enables visibility and projects potential interaction with other members of the site. Hashtags can be used to make a term searchable and therefore visible to others who are interested in tweets written about the same topic. When a hashtag is used with sufficient frequency, it may be listed in the 'trending topics' sidebar of the Twitter site, hence promoting a topic or term (and hence the tweets and their authors) to an audience which extends far beyond the follower list of the person who used the hashtag. For a hashtag to achieve a rank in the trending topics list is taken as a signal of status and influence. For example, fans of the pop star Justin Bieber notoriously manipulated Twitter's trending topics in order to demonstrate the popularity of the singer and the influence of his fan base.*

Do you have a hashtag? Explain its characteristics using some of the insights found in this reading. Why do you think hashtags have become so crucial?

10   In your own words explain the difference between a dialect and a standard language.

References

Adams, M. (2009). *Slang: The People's Poetry*. Oxford: Oxford University Press.

Akkinaso, F. N. and Ajiritutu, C. S. (1982). Performance and Ethnic Styles in Job Interviews. In: J. J. Gumperz (ed.), *Language and Social Identity*. Cambridge: Cambridge University Press.

Alvermann, D. E. (2008). Why Bother Theorizing Adolescents' Online Literacies for Classroom Practice and Research? *Journal of Adolescent and Adult Literacy* 52(1): 8–19.

Auer, P. (1984). *Bilingual Conversation*. Amsterdam: John Benjamins.

Barden, O. (2012). If We Were Cavemen We'd Be Fine. Facebook as a Catalyst for Critical Literacy Learning by Dyslexic Sixth-Form Students. *Literacy* 46(3): 123–132.

Bernstein, B. (1971). *Class, Codes and Control: Theoretical Studies towards a Sociology of Language*. London: Routledge.

Betz, W. (1949) *Deutsch und Lateinisch: Die Lehnbildungen der althochdeutschen Benediktinerregel*. Bonn: Bouvier.

Black, R. W. (2008). Just Don't Call Them Cartoons: The New Literacy Spaces of Anime, Manga and Fanfiction. In: J. Coiro, M. Knobel, C. Lankshear, and D. Leu (eds.), *Handbook of Research on New Literacies*, 538–610. New York: Lawrence Erlbaum Associates.

Brice, A. and Brice, R. (eds.) (2009). *Language Development: Monolingual and Bilingual Acquisition*. Old Tappan, N. J.: Prentice Hall.

Bruce, L. (1984). *The Alamblak Language of Papua New Guinea (East Sepik)*. Canberra: Australian National University.

Bryden, J., Funk, S., and Jansen, V. (2013). Word Usage Mirrors Community Structure in the Online Social Network Twitter. *EPJ Data Science* 2013, 2:3, www.epjdatascience.com/content/2/1/3 (accessed 6 May 2015).

Carter, S., Weerkamp, W., and Tsagkias, M. (2013). Microblog Language Identification: Overcoming the Limitations of Short, Unedited and Idiomatic Text. *Language Resources and Evaluation* 47(1): 195–215.

Chambers, J. K. and Trudgill, P. (1998). *Dialectology*, 2nd edn. Cambridge: Cambridge University Press.

Clivio, G. P., Danesi, M., and Maida-Nicol, S. (2011). *Introduction to Italian Dialectology*. Munich: Lincom Europa.

Coiro, J., Knobel, M., Lankshear, C., and Leu, D. (2008). Central Issues in New Literacies and New Literacies Research. In: J. Coiro, M. Knobel, C. Lankshear, and D. Leu (eds.), *Handbook of Research on New Literacies*, pp. 1–21. New York: Lawrence Erlbaum Associates.

Cook, S. E. (2004). New Technologies and Language Change: Toward an Anthropology of Linguistic Frontiers. *Annual Review of Anthropology* 33: 103–115.

Cromdal, J. (2001). Overlap in Bilingual Play: Some Implications of Code-Switching for Overlap Resolution. *Research on Language and Social Interaction* 34 (4): 421–451.

Cummins, J. (1981). *Bilingualism and Minority-Language Children*. Toronto: OISE Press.

Cummins, J. and Danesi, M. (1990). *Heritage Languages: The Development and Denial of Canada's Linguistic Resources*. Toronto: Garamond Press.

Cunliffe, D., Morris, D., and Prys, C. (2013). Young Bilinguals' Language Behaviour in Social Networking Sites: The Use of Welsh on Facebook. *Journal of Computer-Mediated Communication* 18(3): 339–361.

Danesi, M. (1985). *Loanwords and Phonological Methodology*. Montreal: Didier.

Danet, B. and Herring, S. C. (eds.) (2007). *The Multilingual Internet: Language, Culture, and Communication Online*. Oxford: Oxford University Press.

Das, S. (2011). Rewriting the Past and Reimagining the Future: The Social Life of a Tamil Heritage Language Industry. *American Ethnologist* 38: 774–789.

Davies, J. (2012). Facework on Facebook as a New Literacy Practice. *Computers & Education* 59: 19–29.

Ferguson, C. (1959). Diglossia. *Word* 15: 325–340.

Fishman, J. (1972). *The Sociology of Language. An Interdisciplinary Social Science Approach to Language in Society*. Rowley, MA: Newbury House.

Fishman, J. (1987). *Ideology, Society and Language: The Odyssey of Nathan Birnbaum*. Ann Arbor: Karoma.

Fishman, J. A., Cooper, R. L., and Ma, R. (1971). *Bilingualism in the Barrio*. Bloomington: Indiana University Press.

Gee, J. (1999). *An Introduction to Discourse Analysis: Theory and Method*. London: Routledge.

Goldstein, B. and Kohnert, K. (2005). Speech, Language and Hearing in Developing Bilingual Children: Current Findings and Future Directions. *Language, Speech and Hearing Services in Schools* 36 (3): 264–267.

Gouws, S., Metzler, D., Cai, C., and Hovy, E. (2011). Contextual Bearing on Linguistic Variation in Social Media. In: *Proceedings of the Workshop on Language in Social Media*, pp. 20–29. Portland: Association for Computational Linguistics.

Greenhow, C. and Gleason, B. (2012). Twitteracy: Tweeting as a New Literary Practice. *The Educational Forum* 76: 464–478.

Gruzd, A., Wellman, B., and Takhteyev, Y. (2011). Imagining Twitter as an Imagined Community. *American Behavioral Scientist* 55 (10): 1294–1318.

Gumperz, J. J. and Cook-Gumperz, J. (1982). Language and the Communication of Social Identity. In: J. J. Gumperz (ed.), *Language and Social Identity*. Cambridge: Cambridge University Press.

Haas, C. and Takayoshi, P. (2011). Young People's Everyday Literacies: The Language Features of Instant Messaging. *Research in the Teaching of English* 45: 378–414.

Haugen, E. (1950). The Analysis of Linguistic Borrowing. *Language* 26: 210–231.

Haugen, E. (1972). The Stigmata of Bilingualism. In: S. A. Dil (ed.), *The Ecology of Language: Essays by Einar Haugen*, pp. 307–324. Stanford: Stanford University Press.

Holm, J. A. (1989). *Pidgins and Creoles*. Cambridge: Cambridge University Press.

Hopper, R. and Williams, F. (1973). Speech Characteristics and Employability. *Speech Monographs* 40: 296–302.

Hudson, A. (2002). Outline of a Theory of Diglossia. *International Journal of the Sociology of Language* 157: 1–48.

Hudson, A. and Fishman, J. (2002). Focus on Diglossia. *International Journal of the Sociology of Language* 157: entire issue.

Hull, G., and Nelson, M. E. (2005). Locating the Semiotic Power of Multimodality. *Written Communication* 22(2): 224–262.

Ivkovic, D. and Lotherington, H. (2009). Multilingualism in Cyberspace: Conceptualising the Virtual Linguistic Landscape. *International Journal of Multilingualism* 6: 17–30.

Kress, G. (2003). *Literacy in the New Media Age*. New York: Routledge.

Lankshear, C., and Knobel, M. (2006). *New Literacies: Everyday Practices and Classroom Learning*, 2nd edn. New York: Open University Press.

Livingstone, S., Van Couvering, E., and Thumim, N. (2008). Converging Traditions of Research on Media and Information Literacies: Disciplinary, Critical, and Methodological Issues. In: J. Coiro, M. Knobel, C. Lankshear, and D. Leu (eds.), *Handbook of Research on New Literacies*, pp. 103–132 New York: Lawrence Erlbaum Associates.

McArthur, T. (2005). *Concise Oxford Companion to the English Language*. Oxford: Oxford University Press.

McLuhan, M. (1962). *The Gutenberg Galaxy: The Making of Typographic Man*. Toronto: University of Toronto Press.

McLuhan, M. (1964). *Understanding Media: The Extensions of Man*. London: Routledge.

Myers-Scotton, C. (1993). *Social Motivations for Codeswitching: Evidence from Africa*. Oxford: Clarendon.

Nahir, M. (2003). Language Planning Goals: A Classification. In. C. Paulston, C. Bratt, and R. Tucker (eds.), *Sociolinguistics: The Essential Readings*. Oxford: Blackwell.

Obilade, T. (1993). The Stylistic Function of Pidgin English in African Literature: Achebe and Soyinka. In: B. Lindfors and J. Gibbs (eds.), *Research on Wole Soyinka*. Africa World Press.

Page, R. (2012). The Linguistics of Self-Branding and Micro-Celebrity in Twitter: The Role of Hashtags. *Discourse & Communication* 6: 181–201.

Paolillo, J. C. (2011). Conversational Codeswitching on Usenet and Internet Relay Chat. *Language@Internet*, 8, article 3.

Perkel, D. (2008). Copy and Paste Literacy? Literacy Practices in the Production of a MySpace Profile. In: K. Drotner, H. S. Jensen, and K. C. Schroeder (eds.), *Informal Learning and Digital Media: Constructions, Contexts, and Consequences*, pp. 203–224. Newcastle, UK: Cambridge Scholars Publishing.

Poplack, S., Sankoff, D., and Miller, C. (1988). The Social Correlates and Linguistic Processes of Lexical Borrowing and Assimilation. *Linguistics* 26: 47–104.

Ray, G. B. (2009). *Language and Interracial Communication in the United States: Speaking in Black and White*. New York: Peter Lang.

Romaine, S. and Kachru, B. (1992). Code-mixing and Code-switching. In: T. McArthur (ed.), , *The Oxford Companion to the English Language*, pp. 228–229 Oxford: Oxford University Press.

Scotton, C., Myers, M., and Okeju, J. (1973). Neighbors and Lexical Borrowing. *Language* 49: 871–889.

Sebba, M. (1997). *Contact Languages: Pidgins and Creoles*. Palgrave-Macmillan.

Sebba, M. and Wooton, T. (1998). We, They and Identity: Sequential Versus Identity-Related Explanation in Code Switching. In: P. Auer (ed.), *Code-Switching in Conversation: Language, Interaction, and Identity*, pp. 263–286. London: Routledge.

Smitherman, G. (2003). *Talkin That Talk: Language, Culture, and Education in African America*. London: Taylor & Francis.

Stavans, I. (2004). *Spanglish: The Making of a New American Language*. New York: HarperCollins.

Stoessel, S. (2002). Investigating the Role of Social Networks in Language Maintenance and Shift. *International Journal of the Sociology of Language* 153: 93–131.

Trudgill, P. (1983). *Sociolinguistics*. Harmondsworth: Penguin.

Tuan, Y. F. (1991). Language and the Making of Place: A Narrative-Descriptive Approach. *Annals of the Association of American Geographers* 81: 684–696.

Varnhagen, C., Mcfall, P., and Pugh, N. (2010). lol: New Language and Spelling in Instant Messaging. *Reading and Writing* 23(6): 719–733.

Verhejjen, L. (2013). The Effects of Text Messaging and Instant Messaging on Literacy. *English Studies* 94(5): 582–602.

Vertovec, S. (2007). Super-Diversity and Its Implications. *Ethnic and Racial Studies* 30: 1024–1054.

Wei, Li (1998). The 'Why' and 'How' Questions in the Analysis of Conversational Codeswitching. In: P. Auer (ed.), *Code-Switching in Conversation: Language, Interaction, and Identity*, pp. 156–176. London: Routledge.

Weinreich, U. (1953). *Languages in Contact*. New York: Linguistic Circle of New York.

Weinreich, U. (1954). Is a Structural Dialectology Possible? *Word* 10: 388–400.

Wenker, G. (1881). *Sprachatlas des Deutschen Reichs*. MS folio. Marburg University.

Wilson, S. M. and Peterson, L. C. (2002). The Anthropology of Online Communities. *Annual Reviews in Anthropology* 31: 449–467.

Zentella, A. C. (1997). *Growing Up Bilingual*. Malden, MA: Blackwell.

Zipf, G. K. (1929). Relative Frequency as a Determinant of Phonetic Change. *Harvard Studies in Classical Philology* 40: 1–95.

Zipf, G. K. (1932). *Selected Studies of the Principle of Relative Frequency in Language.* Cambridge, MA: Harvard University Press.

Zipf, G. K. (1935). *The Psycho-Biology of Language: An Introduction to Dynamic Philology.* Boston: Houghton-Mifflin.

Zipf, G. K. (1949). *Human Behavior and the Principle of Least Effort.* Boston: Addison-Wesley.

4   Variation in Social Space

Language is a part of our organism and no less complicated than it.
Ludwig Wittgenstein (1889–1951)

The previous chapter dealt with the sociolinguistic study of variation in geographical space and in cyberspace. Starting with studies such as the one by Labov (mentioned several times already), a primary target of sociolinguistic investigation has been also to study variation in social spaces through research on how human interaction unfolds in specific ways in such spaces. The variant forms of speech are called *social dialects*, extending the traditional geographical notion of *dialect* to encompass variation in the social domain. They are now also commonly called *sociolects*.

The purpose of this chapter is to look at various aspects of sociolectal variation in F2F and CMC spaces. It will deal with such sociolinguistic phenomena as slang, jargon, cants, registers, styles, and language codes. The distinction between geographical and social dialects is frequently hard to make when it comes to their perceived roles in society. Those who speak the standard variety of a language have a head start on others who do not in many social situations, from career opportunities to financial achievement. Linguists call this *social alignment*. Those who "talk the talk" will have privileges, while others tend to be marginalized or excluded, being limited to largely in-group interactions. Paradoxically, therefore, language fosters both alignment and exclusion. It works somewhat as follows:

- Dialect speakers, or speakers of some non-dominant variety, are more likely to be less educated and thus work in less skilled jobs.
- They are more likely to be under-represented in the mainstream media and in politics; but tend to be over-represented in negative ways.
- Speakers of the standard variety are more likely to be educated and possess higher job skills.
- They are more likely to be represented in the mainstream media and in politics.

Dialect speakers and others who speak a non-standard variety can also exclude outsiders on the basis of language, as we saw with cant and argot in the second chapter. In a phrase, language is the means to create alignments, exclusions, and reinforce group identity within a speech community or network.

4.1 Sociolects

In his founding textbook of 1916 (Chapter 1), Saussure was the first to use the term *speech community* to indicate a group of people sharing a common language or dialect; it has been extended by contemporary sociolinguists to include sociolectal variation, that is, the use of socially-significant variants of language within socially-specific boundaries. To be considered part of a speech community an individual needs to have communicative competence, that is, the ability to use a language (or dialect) in a way that fits the situation. Speech communities are based on specific forms of language, indicating that people use language to convey their connection to distinct groups, from professional organizations, who speak what is called a *jargon*, to groups such as school cliques, families, and gangs, which often speak *slang*. Slang can also arise from popular culture and mass communications language. This is why a slang expression may be a new word, such as *glitzy* (gaudy) or *hype* (advertising that relies on gimmicks or tricks), or it may be an old word with a new meaning, such as *fly* (stylish) or *cool* (sophisticated). People use slang more often in speaking than in writing, and more often with friends than with strangers. Slang bespeaks of friendliness and commonality; jargon does not. This is why many slang expressions become *colloquialisms*, that is, expressions used in everyday conversation that are not considered appropriate for formal speech or writing.

The study of how language varies in social spaces starts with a consideration of slang and jargon. These are examples of sociolects—variants of a language that are produced by social variation not variation connected to the geographical distance between speakers. There is overlap between the use of these terms, as we have seen. Basically, if the main identifiers of a speech variant are regional then the variant is a dialect; if they are social (based on differences in class, age, gender, ethnicity, and so on) then the variant is a sociolect.

4.1.1 Slang

Slang is a version of a language that crystallizes in certain periods of a society's history, typically arising within certain groups or communities for reasons of group solidarity or allegiance. There are two forms of slang—*general* and *group-based*. Features of the former usually emerge in special situations and, then, spread to society at large through expressive activities. For example, the word *scuffle* used as a noun designating a fight comes from Shakespeare's play *Antony and Cleopatra* (Act I, Scene I). A change in grammatical category of a common word is one of the mechanisms through which a slang form often arises. Now, this particular word (*scuffle*) started out as slang, but given the influence of Shakespeare on English and English society generally, it gained currency, becoming over time a *colloquialism*, defined as a word or phrase that is not part of the standard vocabulary but used as part of ordinary or familiar conversation. If it does not, it remains restricted to the context from which it sprang. This is why we call certain forms of language "theater slang," "musical slang," "adolescent slang," and so on. These are part of group slang. As such, they are for showing allegiance to a group. Cants and argots are also group-based slangs, showing allegiance to the criminal group, at the same time that they allow messages to be secretive and undecipherable by the authorities.

We hardly ever realize that vocabulary items such as *scuffle* often trace their source to slang. Colloquialisms such as *jock, cool, loony, chick, dude, sloshed, chill out, 24/7*, among many others, have become so much a part of our everyday lexicon that we no longer realize that they originated in slang: the word *jock*, referring to a "macho man," goes back to the 1950s and the adolescent slang of that era. All the above words actually were, at some point in time, part of adolescent slang. The fact that they have remained as colloquialisms to this day bespeaks of the influence of the mass media to divulge and reinforce slang items, showing at the same time a social emphasis on youth themes and behaviors.

The distinctive features of slang are not restricted to vocabulary. Slang involves the deployment of other systems, from phonology to pragmatics. An example of how these might coalesce is in adolescent slang, an area that has received much attention from sociolinguists. One feature of adolescent slang in general is that it tends to be highly emotive, in the sense of the word used by the linguist Roman Jakobson (1960), namely as based on emotional qualities, rather than rational or purely information-exchanging purposes. This manifests itself in such features as tag expressions—"Right?" "You follow?" "Got it?" (or their equivalents)—which show a need to secure consensus and, thus, indirectly, to assure solidarity, especially if the speaker has a high status within the adolescent clique or group. Emotivity also manifests itself in the abundant use of *fillers* and *hedges* (words and expressions that allow speakers to keep the flow of conversations moving)—"Uhmmm," "Like…"—and in the frequent use of *profane* language, that is, of vulgarisms and swear words of various kinds.

Needless to say, these are common speech features; but they seem to be particularly prevalent in slang. Tagging ensures the full participation of interlocutors in what speakers are saying: "You're coming tomorrow, aren't you?" "You did it, right?" Fillers and hedges have various social functions. For example, "duh" is a term that allows speakers to undercut mindless talk or insulting repetition. With its perfectly paired linguistic partner, "yeah-right," it constitutes a means for conveying savvy and sarcasm. "Like" surfaced in the 1980s as a common hedge and filler of adolescent slang: "I, like, wanna come but, like, I'm a little busy now."

Tags, hedges, fillers

Tag question:

A question that ends with a "tagged on" phrase that is designed to seek approval, agreement, or consent:

"You agree with me, *don't you?*"

"This is the truth, *isn't it?*"

"This is how to do it, *right?*"

Hedge:

A word or phrase that makes utterances less forceful:

"It's *kinda* good to say this."

"She *sort of* said that."

Filler:

A sound or word that indicates to other interlocutors that the speaker has not finished speaking, but has simply paused to gather his or her thoughts. Common fillers are:

"like"

"you know"

"well"

"so"

Quotative:

A word or expression that introduces a quotation:

He's *like*: "I didn't say that."

And she's *like*: "Oh yes, you did."

As often happens in societies where slang is used and even glorified by the media (especially movies), these features have now become common and have taken on various other functions, such as indirect citation, known as a *quotative* replacing expressions such as "she said" or "he repeated" followed by a quotation (Romaine and Lange 1991; Blyth et al. 2000). For example, the slang version of "Mike said: 'What are you doing'?" would be "Mike was like: 'What are you doing'?" A third common function of "like" that has surfaced through the same channels of usage is that of a quantifier, replacing such expressions as "nearly," "approximately," and "very:" "The ticket's, like, 20 dollars;" "It's, like, late, ya know;" and so on. A fourth function is as an exemplifier word: "They're, like, OK!" (Siegel 2002). Some of these features predate contemporary slang. In fact, "like" as a slang item surfaced in the 1950s, as evidenced by a 1954 *Time* magazine article—*You Wanna Hear Some Jazz, Like?*—that descried the use of this term in this way.

Slang that is diffused through the media has social appeal and is often used as a symbol of social trends. The use of "like" as a quotative was satirized in 1982 by the late rock musician Frank Zappa with his song *Valley Girl*, using it to parody the "Valley Girl" slang that was in vogue at the time. It was also used as a hedge in the Scooby-Doo comics and cartoons of the late 1960s, functioning as an indirect comedic comment on human foibles. The story of "like" is a case-in-point of how slang terms and emotive features become part of everyday language. Many of these would have remained part of slang—the language of restricted groups—if it were not for the media's appropriation of slang, spreading it broadly. Laroche (2007: 48) provides the following relevant commentary:

> The media not only help spread new language from all quarters, they also produce it when they coin terms to describe themselves and their activities. Media-related words are especially interesting because they often have social resonance. They're not just appropriate or imaginative describers of a certain medium, but also say something important about our larger world. The hybrid "infotainment," for example, merges information and entertainment, just as some media increasingly do. The hybrid word not only reflects the fact, but it also tells us something about our society and our society's values, pressures, trends.

Slang is often transgressive of norms and standard language distinctions. A word such as "guys," is a case-in-point; it is now used by both males and females to refer to their gender peers equally, going contrary to its standard meaning. This does not mean that slang is egalitarian. While females may now use "guys" among themselves, no group of heterosexual males would normally refer to each other as "gals," unless irony was intended. Of course, in non-heterosexual communities these words may reverse their meanings and social functions. There are several interpretations of the heterosexual usage. First, it shows that women have achieved a different social status from the past that allows them to use unmarked (masculine) forms without any social repercussion. Second, it shows that males still see themselves as different from females and thus continue to use markedness features from the past. In other words, slang is a gauge of change in social roles and ideologies.

Slang is also a trace to how people modify speech in accordance with social changes. For instance, "dude," referring to a generic male person with no distinctive qualities, is now used in greetings ("What's up, dude?"), in exclamations ("Whoa, dude!"), as a means to convey commiseration ("Dude, I'm so sorry."), and to one-up someone ("That's so lame, dude."). Historically, *dude* meant "old rags"—a "dudesman" was a scarecrow. In the late 1800s, a dude was a dandy, a meticulously dressed man, in contrast to the "cowboy" image of a male as a virile man. Dude began its rise in English colloquial vocabulary with the 1981 movie *Fast Times at Ridgemont High*, spreading to other fictitious and real contexts, including the adolescent slang of the 1980s and 1990s. The same kind of sociolinguistic story can be found in many of our current slang/colloquial forms. The word "cool" (meaning "nice, attractive," and so on) was used in the fifteenth century as a term of approval, suggesting calm and refrain. But its modern meaning comes from jazz slang. In the 1920s and 1930s jazz was "hot," fast, passionate and free of intellectual intent. In the late 1940s, a new type of jazz emerged that was controlled and overtly intellectual, starting with Charlie Parker's 1947 *Cool Blues*; it was designated as "cool." Cool became the attitude associated with the jazz scene, spreading in the 1960s and 1970s to hippie culture as a sign of defiance against the stress-filled world of mainstream society (Danesi 1994).

Below is an etymological (historical) sketch of some terms that were born as slang evolving over time as colloquialisms (Morrish 1999):

- *Geek:* today it includes fantasy gamers, trekkies, neo-pagans and other self-proclaimed geeks; they relate with other geeks, not others. The word is defined as referring to a person with an odd personality. In Victorian times it meant a fool or dupe. Shakespeare used it in *Twelfth Night* and *Cymbeline* with this sense.
- *Gross:* meaning disgusting, is an American coinage from the Valley Girl talk of the 1980s, actually coming into prominence, according to the *Saturday Review*, in the early 1970s from teen talk to express a dislike of daily life. It derives from Latin *grossus* "big." In the fifteenth century it was used in English, in fact, to refer to large people who stand out and were thus perceived to be disgusting. It is used in this way by Shakespeare, Hobbes, and Boswell.
- *Icon:* as in pop icon. The term is of religious origin and used for the first time in pop culture to describe the American pop singer Madonna. At first, people probably were aware of the sacrilegious irony of this use of the term, given that the name Madonna refers to the Virgin Mary in Christian tradition. But that soon faded and is now used broadly.

- *Nerd*: has no connection originally to computer users; it started as an insult by teens in the 1980s against the unfashionable. It may be a euphemistic modification of *turd*, or it may come from a Dr. Seuss rhyme of 1950: "And then I'll show them, I'll sail a Ka-Troo,/And bring back an It-Kutch, a Preep and a Proo,/A Nerkle, a Nerd, and a Seersucker, too! In the 1957 issue of the Glasgow *Sunday Mail* there is an intriguing reference to the teen meaning of this word: "Nerd—a square." As part of adolescent slang it goes back to the 1960s.

As these examples reveal, we are often unaware of the long-standing history behind some slang forms. Take, as another example, the use of the word "hip" that is found throughout popular culture and colloquial English today. John Leland (2004) has dated the origin of the word to 1619 when the first Blacks arrived off the coast of Virginia. Without Black culture, Leland maintains, there would be no hip American pop culture. Hip is all about a smooth and subtle transgressive attitude, similar to the one exemplified by rock musicians and rap artists. It is something that one feels, rather than understands, and that is why it has always been associated with musical styles—the blues, jazz, swing, hip-hop. In a 1973 tune, the funk group Tower of Power defined *hip* as follows: "Hipness is—What it is! And sometimes hipness is, what it ain't." Hip is about a distinct social identity that people wish to convey. It is about a flight from mainstream conformity, a way to put oneself in contrast to it, to stand out, to look and be different. In the history of this one word, one can discern a mini-history of social trends in American society.

As mentioned above, slang is often profane. Terms like "hottie," "babe," "player," among many others, are sexual metaphors. Each coinage is comparable, essentially, to a one-word or one-phrase ironic sketch of some sexual theme. As a semantic strategy, irony is an unconscious part of slang (Winner 1988). Urban slang items such as "epic" (a long ride), "fly girl" (party girl), and "sperm donor" (a father who's never around) are really ironic jokes, satirical sketches that allow speakers to poke fun at specific aspects of everyday life, in much the same way that a satirist would. Other slang coinages show a coded social savvy about certain topics—for example, "chick flick" (sentimental movie, indicating that it is a genre watched by females), "crib" (home, emphasizing the childish treatment young people tend to receive at home), and "issues" (personal problems). These allow speakers to make indirect assessments of common things and people, without elaboration or justification.

Interestingly, many slang items have made their way into standard dictionaries of the English language. Even expressions such as "easy" (see you later), "floss" (to show off, brag), "mad" (anything to its extreme), and "tight" (to be broke), have been added to no less an authoritative dictionary than the *Random House* dictionary. The spread of slang, or more accurately colloquialisms derived from slang, is no doubt due to the media culture in which we live.

Criminal slang, known as argot or cant, rarely spreads to society at large, given its in-group coded functions. Such slang emerges in groups to whom secrecy is of utmost importance. Facing unique dilemmas of whom to trust, and of how to make themselves trusted without being detected, many criminals develop their own type of speech to communicate among themselves. The subtlety and ingenuity of each cant is truly remarkable. Starting in the late 1800s, Italian criminal gangs communicated with a truly inventive method, using *pizzini*, little pieces of paper on which they wrote their messages (Nicaso and Danesi 2013). Many times the messages were encrypted with special words that could only be decoded by the intended receivers. Over time, these became increasingly sophisticated, and continue to be used today because, unlike electronic forms of communication, the *pizzini* are hand delivered and thus less likely to be intercepted.

The use of so-called "thieves' cant" was particularly popular in the sixteenth century when the leading Elizabethan playwrights and pamphleteers of the day, such as Thomas Harman, Thomas Dekker, and Christopher Marlowe, invented a literary genre known as the "Literature of Roguery," writing about the "underworld" and incorporating underworld slang in plays and other publications (Chandler 1907). Thomas Harman, for instance, included samples

Thieves' Cant

Examples of the cant used by pickpockets in England are found below (from Lunde 2012: 129):

- *bung*: the targeted purse
- *cuttle-bung*: the knife used to cut the purse
- *drawing*: taking the purse
- *figging*: pickpocketing
- *foin*: a pickpocket
- *nip*: someone who cuts the strings of the victim's purse
- *shells*: the money in the purse
- *smoking*: spying on the victim
- *snap*: a pickpocket's accomplice
- *stale*: an accomplice who distracts the victim
- *striking*: the act of pickpocketing.

of thieves' cant in his *Caveat for Common Cursitors* (1566). He claimed that he collected his information from vagabonds that he had interrogated at his home in Essex. If so, then this might be the first study of slang in history. In 1591 Robert Greene produced a series of five pamphlets on various aspects of the criminal underworld, followed by pamphlets by Thomas Middleton (*The Black Book*, 1604) and Thomas Dekker (*The Bellman of London*, 1608 and *Lantern and Candlelight*, 1608). Cant was included in these works together with (alleged) descriptions of the social structure of beggars, the techniques of thieves, and descriptions of the underworld, making them quite popular. Many of these pamphlets borrowed from earlier works. Shakespeare used cant in his *As You Like It* (1623) and *The Winter's Tale* (1623), bringing realism into his plays through the language he crafted for his lowlife characters.

Because of its secretive nature, cant is also known as a *cryptolect*, a type of slang that, like cryptographic writing in general, aims to disguise communication. In excluding others, cant creates a sense of unity among its speakers. Knowing the cant of gang members can allow investigators to effectively understand and communicate with them. It has been shown that those who can speak the cant are more likely to gather more information about the criminals or about gang activities. Criminal organizations like the Mafia, the Japanese Yakuza, the Chinese Triads, as well as street gangs of various kinds, all have their own form of cant and accompanying (or even substitutive) gesture language. In such situations, the language conveys prestige, denoting group membership or distinguishing group members from those who are not a part of the group. Using Michael Silverstein's (1976) notion of different orders of *indexicality*, or terms that refer implicitly to specific referents or contexts, a slang item in group-based situations is an index of identity vis-à-vis the group. It also allows the speaker to allude to desired qualities within the group.

Indexicality permeates all slang. As Mattiello (2008) has argued, a word like "foxy" is not just a simple slang synonym of "sexy." Rather, it allows young men to index their social status as "hunters" of women and thus connects them to their age or peer group, thus excluding others. Hip-hop slang, as we saw previously, flies in the face of standard grammatical and lexical traditions, which bespeak of a past based on slavery. With their own form of language, Black youths are declaring a kind of sociopolitical autonomy from the hegemony of white culture, revealing how they feel about traditions that have historically excluded them from the mainstream. Some of the features of hip-hop talk are actually corrective ones, conveying a sense of satire towards linguistic imperialism. For example, the spelling of *was* as *wuz* shows the correct spelling of the /z/ phoneme. The noncompliance attitude built into hip-hop slang, in sum, exudes linguistic empowerment, giving speakers control over their lives.

The driving force that attracted hundreds of inner city ghetto African American youths to rap music was, in fact, its anti-hegemonic attitude and its ability to give expression to socially powerless voices. Rapper Chuck D boldly articulated rap's anti-hegemonic stance clearly in a 1992 interview with *XXL* (a popular rap magazine): "This is our voice, this is the voice of our lifestyle, this is the voice of our people. We're not going to take the cookie cutter they give us let them mold us." But, as rap continued to grow and influence the lifestyle of many city youths in the late 1990s, its audiences also became broader. As a consequence, its original subversive speech forms started to evanesce or become colloquialisms. Today, hip-hop language has infiltrated mainstream (white) language. This does not mean that rap's original anti-hegemonic subtext has been completely obliterated. Like other trends, it can and often does serve as a voice for dispossessed people. But it no longer has the broad impact in this regard that it once had.

4.1.2 Jargon

Jargon is a form of slang, even though it is not always recognized as such. It has all the social features of slang—it is part of in-group behavior, it signals group membership, and it has a highly specialized vocabulary. To use an analogy to diglossia studies, common slang is an L sociolect, whereas jargon is an H sociolect; that is to say, common slang is part of familiar, everyday speech, marked for group membership initially but spreading to the population (in some part) as colloquial speech, while jargon is part of specialized speech generally of professionals or those with a high class status.

The primary characteristic that distinguishes jargon from all other sociolects is specialized vocabulary, usually (but not necessarily) connected to occupational groups. Jargon allows its speakers to communicate with each other effectively and unambiguously, as well as to convey their social identities to others. As a case-in-point, consider medical jargon:

Table 4.1 Medical Jargon

Medical Term	Common Term
hematoma	blood clot
coronary thrombosis	heart attack
pruritis	itchiness
verruca	wart
furuncle	boil, pimple
rectum	bum
pustule	pus
varicella	chickenpox
posology	dosage
hemeralopia	impaired vision
strabismus	squinting
contusion	bruise

Denotation Versus Connotation

Denotation:

This is the referential meaning of a word; that is, when used by itself, it points out a referent that can be separated from any other use.

The word *cat* when used in this way means (and only means) "mammal with four legs, long tail, whiskers, and retractile claws."

Connotation:

This is one of the senses that a word takes on in social context. The connotative meaning manifests itself when the word is used in phrases or sentences: "He's a cool cat" (an attractive person); "You let the cat out of the bag" (secret); and so on.

Although jargon can always be converted to standard lexemes, the latter are never completely synonymous with the jargon terms. The difference lies in the subtle semantics of the two modes of speaking. Recall that denotation is the primary (literal) meaning of a word, while connotation is the set of meanings that accrue from its uses in social contexts. In other words, denotation does not vary, connotation does, adding a socially-significant component to the semantics of a word. Jargon is denotative, when used among the members of the group—it is precise and invariable as to what it designates.

For example, a *coronary thrombosis* indicates a condition resulting from a blockage of a coronary artery by a blood clot, which in turn obstructs the blood supply to the heart muscle, resulting in death of the muscle. The end result is a "heart attack," in colloquial terms, that is, an "attack on the heart." The term *infarction* refers to the actual heart attack itself. As this example shows, denotation is crucial in medical terminology. The colloquial term "heart attack," however takes on various social nuances, as can be seen in common expressions such as "You almost gave me a heart attack," "If you go out with her, she will give you a heart attack," and so on.

Some jargon makes it into the common lexicon, either because a paraphrase or a colloquialism has never been created for it or because it is too cumbersome to do so. Medical terms like *arthritis* and *eczema* have made their way into everyday vocabulary. But in so doing, they acquire connotative meanings—*arthritis* has connotations of aging, while *eczema* in common usage may evoke images of incessant scratching. In all cases, the technical term indexes the speaker as authoritative and it also allows the professional to elaborate on a situation in "lay person's terms," thus implicitly assigning an H value to the speech.

In her widely-quoted book, *Illness As Metaphor* (1978), the late writer Susan Sontag cogently argued it is society that predisposes people to think of specific illnesses in certain ways, rather than as medical practitioners (in principle) would. Using the example of cancer, Sontag showed how in the not-too-distant past the very word *cancer* was perceived as an emotionally unsettling death sentence, not just a dangerous physical disease (Sontag 1978: 7): "As long as a particular disease is treated as an evil, invincible predator, not just a disease, most people with cancer will indeed be demoralized by learning what disease they have." Later, she argued the same for AIDS. In other words, it is connotation that turns jargon into a language of admonition or reprimand for lifestyle choices. In a similar vein, Jacalyn Duffin (2005) has argued that diseases are often interpreted culturally or even constructed for various reasons. "Lovesickness," for instance, was once considered a true disease, even though it originated in the poetry of antiquity. Its demise as a disease is due to twentieth-century skepticism. At any given point in time, concepts of disease crystallize from sociocultural factors, not just from any scientific study of disease. The ways in which a culture defines and represents health will largely determine how it views and treats disease, what life expectancy it sees as normal, and what features of body image it considers to be attractive, ugly, normal, or abnormal. Some cultures view a healthy body as being a lean and muscular one, others a plump and rotund one. Certain cultures perceive a healthy lifestyle as one that is based on rigorous physical activity, while others perceive it as one that is based on a more leisurely and sedentary style of living.

Jargon, like slang, is a sociolect. But jargon can be used by anyone, even if he or she does not belong to a specified social group. The reason can be practical. For instance, the vocabulary needed to describe tools is an example of practical or popular jargon. Terms such as *hammer*, *pliers*, *wrench*, *screwdriver*, and *tweezers* have achieved a broad diffusion, outside of their use by construction workers and other specialized workers; but other ones, such as *vise*, have not. The same applies to musical jargon, which comes largely from the Italian language. Anyone desiring to study music will have to master this jargon, since it is the basis for pedagogical communication between teacher and student and part of the professional practice of music.

All areas of specialized skill and knowledge require jargon, from the sphere of auto mechanics to software programming. It allows for denotation to guide work, to allow users to make appropriate choices, and for various other specialized purposes. It also is a sign of belonging to some group or, even, of level of education or intellect. Think of mathematics, which everybody studies from elementary school on. Like any discipline, it has its particular jargon. However, since we are all expected to learn it, we hardly perceive terms such as *equation*, *coordinate*, *factoring*, and *prime number* as jargon. Only terms with a lower frequency in educational contexts are perceived to be part of math jargon: for example, *matrix*, *fractal*, *parameter*, *imaginary number*. The line between jargon and common vocabulary is obviously a thin one, given the fact that most people have had some degree of formal education, which is based on jargon, and given the technological nature of modern societies.

Table 4.2 Musical Jargon

Musical Term	Meaning
a piacere	freely
a tempo	with the original tempo
adagio	slowly
allegro	quickly, brightly
andante	slowly, but not too slowly
cadenza	a virtuosic solo passage
coda	tail-end of a part or piece
da capo	from the beginning
forte	loud
largo	very slow, deliberate
moderato	at a moderate pace
presto	fast
vivace	vivacious, lively
cantabile	in a singing manner

4.2 Register

The use of various linguistic forms (lexical, grammatical, phonological) relates also to *register*, discussed briefly in the opening chapter. A register is a level of usage, determined by the degree of formality required by a social situation. It manifests itself through linguistic forms that are adapted to communicative purpose, social context, and the social status of the users. A trivial, yet insightful observation with regard to register, applies to the language that academics and scientists use, when speaking formally, which has more technical words in it, more passive than active sentences, which eliminate the need to use personal pronouns, and so on. This type of register gives a sense of objectivity to the speech event. To say "Yesterday, I conducted an experiment that didn't work out" is at a lower register and, thus perceived to be less objective than, "The experiment conducted yesterday did not produce the anticipated results."

Registers involve the selection of specific kinds of speech acts and verbal protocols. Take, for example, saying goodbye to another person in English. This might vary somewhat as follows:

Highly Formal:	Good-bye!
Mid Formal:	Bye!
Informal:	See ya'!

The choice of one expression or the other is not random or optional. The highly formal one is considered to be polite and is used with strangers, superiors, and so on. The mid formal expression is used basically with those whom we see frequently and with whom we have developed a degree of familiarity (co-workers, peers, and so on). The informal expression is used with those with whom we are in the friendliest or intimate of terms. The misuse of one or the other is perceived as a breach of social etiquette or as a sign of anomalous communication. It would be considered rude to address a superior at work with an informal mode of speech (unless the superior permits it); and it would be considered to be aberrant or strange to address a close friend with a highly formal register. This type of speech variation is found throughout the world.

The term *register* was first used with this sense in 1956 by Thomas Bertram Reid in order to distinguish among language variants on the part of the speaker determined by variables such as age, gender, class, and geography. Halliday and Hasan (1956) subsequently defined register as the linguistic features associated with these social variables as situated in a field of discourse that required control over the mode. They define field is the total event in which speech functions together with the purposeful activities of the speakers. Mode is the function of the speech act in a context—it could be narrative, rhetorical, humorous, ironic, and so on. They also indicated that register is governed by tenor—the type of social roles at play in the interaction.

4.2.1 Features

We instantly recognize a register as formal or informal through the specific linguistic forms (phonological, grammatical, lexical) used. An example showing how this distinction is maintained lexically is the list below:

formal	*Informal*
abode	house, place
alcoholic beverage	drink, booze
offspring	children, kids
dollars	bucks

The formal items typify government forms to be filled out, academic periodical articles, communication with people in high authority, and so on. The informal items typify common everyday speech among friends, family members, colleagues, and acquaintances.

In formal registers, clipped or abbreviated words also tend to be avoided, including in online communications (such as e-mails to people in authority):

Formal	Informal
laboratory	lab
advertisement	ad
newspaper	paper
goodbye	bye
hello	hi

We all use registers unconsciously at different times of the day, as the linguist Martin Joos cleverly argued in his classic 1967 book titled *The Five Clocks of English*. To grasp this, consider the different kinds of speech used during a typical day in a North American city by an average individual who works in, say, an office environment. How would she speak in the morning when she gets up with family members? How would she speak at a place of work with co-workers? How would she speak at a place of work with superiors? How would she converse with friends at a bar after hours? How would she communicate late at night with a romantic partner? Answers to these questions would show how registers are synchronized with daily life routines and interpersonal interactions. Although there is much leeway in the grammatical and lexical choices that can be made to carry out conversations successfully, these are nonetheless constrained by factors such as situation and social relationship. For example, the utterances below convey anger, but in different socially-sensitive ways:

1   Don't say that, idiot!
2   It is best that you not say that!

The first one might be uttered by someone who is on close or intimate terms with an interlocutor; the second one by someone who is on formal terms, or else is intended to be ironic. The two choices are constrained by situation and social relationship.

Rather than *register*, the term *diatype* is sometimes used to describe socially-based language variation (Gregory 1967). In this framework, dialect is defined as a variant according to user and diatype as a variant according to use (such as specialized academic language). This brings the notion of register closer to that of diglossia. But register continues to be the main term used because it allows the sociolinguist to zero efficiently in on a specific sociolect and how it is used, rather than analyze all aspects of the usage.

4.2.2 Politeness

The greeting rituals mentioned above lead to the notion of *politeness*, which is a primary register within language usage. The choice of one or the other cue is conditioned by a simple politeness rule: the formal register is used with social superiors or strangers and the informal register with close friends and intimates; otherwise the mid formal register is appropriate. In some societies, such as in Java (as already discussed in Chapter 1), politeness registers are tied much more strictly to a hierarchy of social distinctions: the aristocrats (at the top); the townsfolk (in the middle); and the farmers (at the bottom). Politeness forms are obligatory when those at lower levels address those at higher levels; informal ones are operative among social peers.

We all use politeness registers unconsciously. They allow us to indicate class, education level, type of relation with an interlocutor, and so on. Needless to say, having no access to the system of cues that imply politeness can lead potentially to conflict situations. If speaker A (a non-native speaker of English) were to use a register or a style that is highly formal with a friend, then he or she might be misconstrued by B (a native speaker) as attempting to be ironic or emotionally distant. On the other hand, if A uses a highly intimate form of speech with a superior, miscommunication based on various modes of interpretation would tend to surface. If the speech act does not match the politeness register, then misunderstanding or confusion between speakers is a distinct possibility. Using the *tu* (familiar) forms with a stranger in Italy, rather than the *Lei* (polite) forms, will be considered to constitute an act of impoliteness or downright rudeness, unless the speaker reveals that he or she is a foreigner either directly or indirectly through an accent. Saying *ciao* ("hi"), rather than *scusi* ("excuse me") to a policeman in order to get his attention will tend, initially at least, to prompt a negative response (if any). Breaking this rule of discourse is perceived as a break in social manners, not a lack of linguistic knowledge.

Politeness will be taken up in more depth in Chapter 6 as part of conversational strategy. Suffice it to say here that there are various modes that are deployed to convey politeness, such as using hedges to express uncertainty and ambiguity rather than directness ("I think that, maybe, this can be interpreted, hmm, in a different way"), with euphemisms ("She has passed on"), and with tags ("This is what you mean, isn't it?"). Previous studies showed that women used politeness strategies more than men, but current research shows that the situation is more complex, since it also involves class and age variables. Nevertheless, there still seems to be an expectation that women be more polite in mixed company than men, as will be discussed (Holmes 1995).

4.2.3 Honorifics

Politeness is operative in the use of titles and other forms of respect, known as *honorifics*. These include the use of first names and/or last names, of titles either accompanying names (like *Mr.*, *Ms.*, *Miss*) or used in isolation (like *Sir* or *Madam*), but also, in languages like French, Italian or German, the choice of the personal pronouns used to refer to the social status of the interlocutor.

In some languages, such as Korean, there exist complex systems of honorifics. Korean honorifics combine the lexical choice between plain and honorific nouns (for example, "meal" *pap* vs. *cinci*) and verbs ("eat" *mek-* vs. *tusi-*) and different grammatical morphemes for marking the same grammatical function according to the honorific status of the person being addressed. The subject of a sentence, for instance, can be marked either by the plain nominative case *–ka* or by its honorific variant *–kkeyse*. Compare the following two Korean sentences (the lexemes and morphemes marked for honorific status are in bold—from Lee 2007):

1   *Minho-ka pap-ul mek-ess-ta* (Minho had a meal)
2   *Minho halapeci-**kkeyse** **cinci**-lul **tusi**-ess-ta* (Minho's grandfather had a meal)

In some societies, the key factor in determining who is to be treated as superior is the relative age of the participants. The social power of the participants is taken into account but only as a secondary factor. In their use of the honorific system in speech, Koreans continuously attend to age differences between the speakers, even very young ones. It is not surprising, therefore, that Korean speakers will try to learn the age of a new acquaintance as soon as possible or at least to estimate it as accurately as possible: this is necessary in order to be able to choose the proper speech register and honorifics to address the interlocutor.

Overall, honorifics are used to convey social distance, politeness, humility, deference, or respect. There are three main types of honorifics. The first is the *addressee honorific* which is designed to allude to the social status of the person addressed. In Javanese, there are three different words for "house," to be used in accordance to the social level of the addressee. If the person has social superiority then the word for "house" will reflect this—it is analogous to using the word "domicile" rather than "house" in English. If the addressee has lower social status then the speaker would use a different form for "house" analogous, more or less, to English "hut." A second type of honorific is called *referent* because it references the level of formality of the speakers. In French this can be seen in the use of *tu* or *vous* (both meaning "you") on the basis of both level of familiarity and formality. A third type is called *bystander* because the honorific is designed to express the status of an interlocutor who is a bystander, not a participant in the conversation. This involves changing one's speech patterns in the presence of the bystander thus indirectly acknowledging his or her presence.

4.3 Style

Style is a way of using language that shows sensitivity to, or understanding of, specific situations, levels of formality, modes of speech that are appropriate, and so on. Style is not simply a matter of personal taste. In many instances, it is governed by the situation or by the kind of utterance that is required. A simple example of this is the difference between active and passive sentences. They are not alternatives; they are stylistic variants in some instances. Consider the sentences below:

1   The apple was eaten by Rebecca. It was not eaten by me, nor was it my intention to do so. The eating action was accomplished quickly. The apple was devoured by her.
2   I put sodium together with chlorine. I knew I was going to get a reaction. I thought I would get salt. But it didn't work out for some reason.

If told that (1) was written by one friend to another and (2) by a scientist in a professional journal, we would immediately think that something is amiss. The reason for this is that stylistic practices dictate that (1) should be phrased mainly in active sentences and (2) in passive ones, along with other adjustments. Active sentences are used to emphasize the speaker as the actor in a direct relation with the goal (the person spoken to or the object involved), whereas passive ones are used to de-emphasize the speaker as actor and highlight the goal as the "object" of interest. The requirement of "objectivity" in scientific writing, in effect, translates into the linguistic practice of using passive sentences, where the "goal-object" is highlighted over the "subject-actor." Reformulating both sentences by reversing their voice rectifies the stylistic anomalies:

1   Rebecca ate the apple. I didn't eat it, nor did I intend to do so. She ate it quickly. She devoured the apple.
2   Sodium and chlorine were mixed, in order to attain the expected reaction. The anticipated outcome was salt. However, this outcome was not achieved for some reason.

4.3.1 A Typology

One of the most analyzed areas of style is the *mode* of language as determined by the situation on a formality scale. In the study mentioned above, Martin Joos (1967) identified five styles in English. First, there is *frozen* or *static* style. This is a form of language that is formulaic and is passed on as such; it includes archaisms, aphorisms, Biblical quotations, and so on. Examples of frozen style are the oaths taken in court or the Pledge of Allegiance ("I solemnly swear to tell the truth, the whole truth, so help me God"). The main characteristic of this style is that the wording is exactly the same every time it is spoken or written. Second, *formal* style manifests itself in all kinds of formal situations, from dictionary style where exact definitions are crucial to the kinds of introductions that are common between strangers ("Hello. My name is Ms. Smith. Glad to make your acquaintance"). Third, *consultative* style involves two-way interaction; in this case background information is provided and prior knowledge is not assumed. Interruptions are allowed. Examples of such style include teacher and student dialogues, doctor and patient consultations, expert and apprentice talk, and the like. Fourth, *casual* style is used with friends and acquaintances. Incomplete sentences, slang, and colloquialisms are frequent and interruptions common in this style of talking. Finally, there is *intimate* style, which is private and involves increased intonation more than wording or grammar and special vocabulary. This is most common among family members, close friends, and paramours.

The ability to recognize and use different style modes of language according to situation is an essential component of communicative competence, enabling people in a speech community to recognize meaningful differences in grammar and vocabulary and what they entail. For instance, when someone receives a card sent by a friend, rather than one sent by a dentist, in the mail, one immediately can formulate specific hypotheses as to the nature of the card's content even before reading it. The friend might have sent it to wish the receiver a happy birthday, to congratulate him or her for having achieved something, and so on. A card from a dentist would hardly have a similar function, unless the dentist is a friend or family member. Its purpose is to remind a patient about an appointment or to request payment for some service. One will also be able to predict what style will be used. In the former it will be casual; in the latter it will be formal.

Style also has many sociopolitical functions. In communist Poland, for example, the *podanie* form of Polish flourished for a specific reason—it allowed common people to write their requests to the authorities in a strategic fashion (Wierzbicka 1991). In a *podanie*, petitioners were expected to ask the authorities for "favors" and to portray themselves as highly dependent on their "good will." The word *podanie* and the style it designates have no equivalent in English, because the practice of asking favors from authorities has never had the same significance in English-speaking societies that it had in communist Poland, where people's lives "were dominated, to a considerable degree, by their dependence on the arbitrary decisions of bureaucratic despots" (Wierzbicka 1991: 193). The socially strategic significance of this discourse practice was corroborated by the term used in Polish to designate the A4 paper format, *papier podaniowy*, which means "paper for writing *podanie*." If we compare the *podanie* genre to an English bureaucratic genre, such as an application form, we can easily flesh out socially significant differences from them. As Wierzbicka (1991: 195) puts it: "a person who is writing an *application* is *applying*, not *asking for* or *requesting*" and thus an application in an English-speaking country can be unsuccessful, but not refused or rejected. This was never the case with *podanie*.

4.3.2 Genre

Style involves control of speech genres (Bakhtin 1981), which are modes of speaking or writing that people learn to imitate or emulate and then weave together into specific utterances—letters, grocery lists, lectures, and so on (Fairclough 2003). As Charaudeau and Maingueneau (2002: 278–280) have indicated, an utterance's genre can be determined by the particular wording and choice of vocabulary, in addition to its social function. Lack of the ability to distinguish among genres is a major cause of interactional breakdowns. As Bakhtin (1983: 80) observed, "many people who have an excellent command of a language often feel quite helpless in certain spheres of communication because they do not have a practical command of the generic forms used in the given spheres." A native speaker of English, who is perfectly fluent in the language, might still not be able to write an academic paper according to the proper conventions of that speech genre. Conversely, someone may well be able to write such a paper, but be strikingly awkward when it comes to face-to-face conversation.

"Genre competence" is a subcategory of communicative competence. Knowing how to recognize or realize speeches, job interviews, university lectures, medical consultations, courtroom dialogue, and the like are all speech genres, characterized by specific stylistic features. Finally, stylistic or genre competence also serves many performative functions, being the basis of most social rituals. Religious rites, sermons, prep rallies, political debates, and other ceremonial gatherings are anchored in discourse genres, either in frozen (formulaic) style or specifically adapted to the occasion. The use of language in ritual is not to create new meanings, but to assert communal sense-making and to ensure cultural cohesion. People typically love to hear the same speeches, songs, and stories at specific times during the year (at Christmas, at Passover, and so on) in order to feel united with the other members of the group. In their origin, words were probably perceived to be sacred messages. Those who possessed knowledge of words were thought to possess supernatural or magical powers. In many early cultures, just knowing the name of a deity, for example, was purported to give the knower great power—in Egyptian mythology, the sorceress Isis tricked the sun god, Ra, into revealing his name and, thus, gained power over him and all other gods. In most societies, ancestral names given to children are perceived to weave a sort of magical protective aura around the child. In some traditional Inuit tribes, an individual will not pronounce his or her ancestral name, fearing that this senseless act could break the magical spell of protection that it brings with it.

Genre-based communication tends to be formulaic and rely upon widely known and accepted conventions and linguistic structures. These conventions help interlocutors understand what happens in texts and help speakers enunciate these texts, since they can rely upon expectations on the part of interlocutors and can use formulas to satisfy these expectations. In essence, we classify texts according to their genres. At the opposite pole to genres are texts that follow no formulas and are highly inventive, such as Joyce's novels *Ulysses* and *Finnegan's Wake*.

4.4 Language and Social Variables

The department store study by Labov, mentioned several times, is a perfect example of how a specific linguistic feature—the pronunciation of final /-r/—is perceived by people to relate to social stratification and how it can be used to gain social mobility. In effect, it showed how perceptions of class are embedded in particular speech characteristics. In this book we have already discussed several aspects of the relation between language and social variables. In Chapters 1 and 2, studies relating language to gender roles were examined. In this section the focus will be on the relation of language to class, ethnicity, and race.

In effect, each social class or ethnic community forms a speech community, which is characterized by specific forms or registers of language (slang, jargon), styles, and other characteristics that render it identifiable. The term *community of practice* is sometimes used, putting the focus on everyday language practices that relate to socialization and identity. Speech communities may exist within a larger community of practice. Crucial to sociolinguistic analysis in this domain of inquiry is the concept of *prestige*. Certain speech features are seen as having a positive or negative value. In the case of /-r/ the positive value assigned to its pronunciation meant working at a more prestigious place. And there is also the notion of code, as already discussed, which allows speakers in communities to relate to each other in specific ways and then map these against community practices.

4.4.1 Class

A classic study on the relation between social class and language is the one by Basil Bernstein (1971), mentioned briefly in the first chapter, in which he elaborated an interesting theory of *language codes*, which he divided into elaborated and restricted, as we saw. The code is a "set of organizing principles behind the language employed by members of a social group" (Littlejohn 2002: 278). Bernstein used this notion to show how the language people use in everyday life both reflects and influences the social expectations and assumptions of a certain speech community. The personal relationships established by the code also affect the ways in which language is used. Bernstein wanted to find a rationale for the relatively poor performance of working-class students in language-based subjects, at the same time that they scored as high as their middle-class counterparts in mathematics. He found that the restricted code excluded the students from the learning process. It was only when they realized that the elaborated code was required did they improve their grades. As he (Bernstein 1971: 76) puts it, "Forms of spoken language in the process of their learning initiate, generalize and reinforce special types of relationship with the environment and thus create for the individual particular forms of significance." The forms of a specific language code and how it is used within a speech community affects the way people assign meaning to the things about which they are speaking. In a phrase, the code that an individual uses symbolizes and enacts his or her social identity.

The terms restricted and elaborated refer to contexts of use and what each type of code is specialized to do for its speakers. The restricted code is better suited for "in-group" situations, which involve a great deal of shared and embedded knowledge. It is economical and to the point, conveying a vast amount of information and meaning with minimal linguistic resources. These function like an index finger, pointing implicitly to a whole set of social nuances, background knowledge, and shared beliefs to which only the group members have access. This is why the restricted code is often called *indexical*. It creates a sense of belonging and inclusion.

Conversely, the elaborated code uses a more complicated lexicon and grammar that allow interlocutors to spell out their intentions and meanings explicitly, not assume them as in the restricted code. Whereas the latter is strictly for insider use, the elaborated one is for outsider use and works better in situations where there is no prior or shared knowledge system and, thus, where more detailed explanation is needed. As Bernstein (1971: 135) puts it, "Clearly one code is not better than another; each possesses its own aesthetic, its own possibilities. Society, however, may place different values on the orders of experience elicited, maintained and progressively strengthened through the different coding systems."

The learning and adoption of one code or the other, or both, depends on the nature of socializing agencies (family, special group, school, work) present in a society or community. When these involve small speech communities, a restricted code tends to emerge as the default form of language. When they involve the broader community of practice, an elaborated code arises. In a society that values individuality elaborated codes tend to be the crucial ones for advancement, while in a community that values conformity, restricted codes are the rule. In his research, Bernstein found that restricted codes are typical of working classes, while the use of both codes typifies middle class language. The restricted code is less formal with shorter sentences and an abundant use of tag questions and hedges: "you know," "you know what I mean," "right?" and "don't you think?" Elaborated codes have a longer, more complicated sentence structure that incorporates uncommon vocabulary and turns of phrase. There are fewer fillers or hedges ("ummm," "well," "you know").

A working class person uses the restricted code as a result of the particular socialization process into which he or she was born. The same is true for the middle class person who uses the elaborated code in tandem. This, Bernstein claims, explains the poor performance in language-based subjects by working-class students at school. Bernstein's and Labov's work, in sum, has made it obvious that class and occupation are reflected in language and that social aspirations influence the use of various linguistic forms and styles. Those from a lower class who aspire to move up the social ladder will adopt the speech style of the upper classes, adjusting their own speech habits to mimic them.

It is generally assumed that non-standard language is low-prestige language. However, in certain groups, such as those living in traditional working-class neighborhoods, the standard language may be considered undesirable in many contexts. This is because the working-class dialect is a powerful in-group marker, and especially for non-mobile individuals, the use of specific dialects or slangs expresses group pride and solidarity.

The looseness or tightness of a speech community may thus affect speech patterns adopted by a speaker. For instance, Dubois and Horvath (1998) found that speakers of English in one Cajun Louisiana community were more likely to pronounce English "th" [θ] as [t] (or [ð] as [d]) if they participated in what they called "a relatively dense social network" (that is, a speech community that demonstrated strong local ties among the members and interacted with many other speakers in the community), and less likely if the networks were looser (that is, had fewer local ties). This is because not only class, but class aspirations, are important.

Dentals and Interdentals

A *dental* consonant is produced when the tongue touches the upper teeth.

- /t/ is a voiceless dental consonant: that is, produced without the vibration of the vocal cords: "ten," "tot," "two."

- /d/ is a voiced dental consonant: that is, produced with the vibration of the vocal cords: "den," "dad," "do."

An *interdental* consonant is produced by putting the tongue between the teeth.

- /θ/ is a voiceless interdental consonant: "thing," "thought," "think."

- /ð/ is a voiced interdental consonant: "that," "though," "they."

4.4.2 Race and Ethnicity

The terms *race* and *ethnicity* always come up when talking about society and language. Human beings the world over typically classify and think of themselves as members of *races* or *ethnic* groups, that is, as belonging to groups of people with whom they have a common genetic-historical link. But racial or ethnic classifications are often misleading. No two human beings, not even twins, are identical genetically. The proportions of traits are distributed differently from one part of the world to another; but, as it turns out, these proportions are quantitatively negligible. Geneticists have yet to turn up a single group of people who can be distinguished from others by their chromosomes. There is no genetic test that can be used to determine race or ethnicity. Moreover, since people have always engaged in interbreeding, it should come as no surprise to find that 99.9 per cent of DNA sequences are common to all humans (Sagan and Druyan 1992: 415). So, from a purely biological standpoint, human beings defy classification into types. Nevertheless, the historical record shows that from ancient times people have, for some reason or other, always felt it necessary to classify themselves in terms of racial or ethnic categories. Paintings and sculptures from the past show human beings with physical traits that were thought to distinguish them racially and ethnically.

The systematic study and classification of races and ethnic groups was a consequence of the worldwide explorations of the sixteenth and seventeenth centuries, which piqued the interest of Europeans in the peoples of other lands. A century later, the Swedish botanist Carolus Linnaeus (1707–1778) was among the first to consider categorizing the apparent varieties of human beings. The German scholar Johann Friedrich Blumenbach (1752–1840) then gave the world its first racial typology. After examining the skulls and comparing the physical characteristics of the different peoples of the world, Blumenbach concluded that humanity had five races: Caucasians (West Asians, north Africans, and Europeans except the Finns and the Saami), Mongolians (other Asian peoples, the Finns and the Saami, and the Inuit of America), Ethiopians (the people of Africa except those of the north), Americans (all aboriginal New World peoples except the Inuit), and Malayans (peoples of the Pacific islands). These divisions remained the basis of most racial classifications well into the twentieth century and continue to be commonly accepted in some quarters even today. But population scientists now recognize the indefiniteness and arbitrariness of any such demarcations. Indeed, many individuals can be classified into more than one of Blumenbach's racial categories or into none. All that can be said is that the concept of race or ethnic group makes sense, if at all, only in terms of lineage: that is, people can be said to belong to the same ethnicity if they share the same pool of ancestors. But, as it turns out, even this seemingly simple criterion is insufficient for rationalizing a truly scientific classification of humans into discrete racial or ethnic groups in such a way that everybody belongs to one and only one because, except for brothers and sisters, no individuals have precisely the same array of ancestors. This is why, rather than using genetic, anatomical, or physiological traits to study human variability, anthropologists today prefer to study them in terms of geographic or social criteria. Race and ethnicity are now viewed by social scientists fundamentally as historical or cultural notions, not biological ones.

Sociolinguistic research has shown that we sense someone's race or ethnicity through language features in situations where physical features are not available. This is the case of AAVE, which we assume is spoken by young African Americans and when it is not we detect an anomaly. In this sense language is racially coded. This includes phonological characteristics as well as grammatical and lexical ones. Psychological experiments have shown that participants exposed to voice recordings will identify the speaker according to race. In one such experiment (Purnell, Idsardi, and Baugh 1999), subjects were exposed to only the word "hello" and asked to identify the speaker's race. The subjects were surprisingly accurate at identifying the race of the speaker as Chicano or White, although a sizable portion was not able to classify the African American English (AAE) speaker correctly as the chart below shows:

Table 4.3 Racial Classification Via Accent (from: Purnell, T., Idsardi, W., and Baugh, J. 1999)

Subject's Guesses	Speaker's Accent		
	AAE	Chicano	White
AAE	15%	5%	3%
Chicano English	4%	27%	1%
White English	13%	2%	29%

In another study the researchers had 50 African American men and 50 White men record a single vowel. Subjects then heard two vowels pronounced. They were told that one vowel was articulated by a White man and the other by an African American man and that they had to decide which was which. On average, they did it about 60 percent of the time. Such studies suggest that we can make reasonably accurate judgments about people's races based on features of language.

The problem with associating language and race is that it may result in *linguistic profiling*, which is the practice of identifying the social characteristics of an individual on the basis of his or her speech (accent, dialect, and so on). The notion was first developed by John Baugh (2003) to describe discriminatory practices in the housing market influenced by the language spoken by clients. Linguistic profiling has been found in employment areas, education, and the like. It is the auditory equivalent of racial profiling. One interesting insight of this line of inquiry is that we even experience fictional and non-human characters in media as members of different races. Lippi-Green (1997) examined the characters in some of Disney's animated films, concluding that Disney casted voice actors with linguistic features that marked them as belonging to a particular race in order to draw on stereotypes, whether negative or positive, about racial groups. In *The Lion King* (1994), for example, clear linguistic lines are drawn between the positive lion characters (Simba and Nala) and the villains (Scar and the hyenas). The former speak with a Standard American English accent, even if the voices were African American; the latter display linguistic diversity (Scar, for instance, speaks with a British accent). The hyena Shenzu is voiced by Whoopi Goldberg who speaks with an AAE accent; and the hyena Banzai, voiced by the Latino Cheech Marin, has a decided Latino-American accent and occasionally code-switches ("¿Qué pasa?"). Lippi-Green suggests that the character voices accentuate their similarities to racial minorities. Lippi-Green (1997: 122) puts it as follows: "The message is a familiar one: AAVE [African American Vernacular English] speakers occupy the dark and frightening places, where Simba does not belong and should not be; he belongs on the sunny savannah where SAE [Standard American English] speakers like his father live."

Linguistic profiling occurs beyond the domains of race and ethnicity to geographic origin. Clopper and Pisoni (2004) found that the perception of phonological differences between regional dialects of American English by naïve listeners involved stereotyping. In one experiment, they used acoustic techniques to identify sentences that revealed different dialectal features. Then, recordings of the sentences were played back to naïve listeners who were asked to categorize speakers into one of six geographical dialect regions. Results showed that listeners were able to categorize speakers using three broad dialect clusters (New England, South, North/West), but that they had more difficulty categorizing speakers into six smaller regions. Taken together, the results confirmed that listeners have unconscious knowledge of phonological differences between dialects and can use this knowledge to categorize talkers by region.

4.5 e-Sociolects

CMC variation is now connected to different virtual speech communities, some of which are like the offline ones and some of which are different. Twitter communities, for instance, have come together because the people who populate them have a common occupation or interest. As a result, they have developed their own distinctive languages, or more accurately, e-sociolects (as they can be called). In other words, the language someone uses in such media makes it possible to predict to which community he or she is likely to belong.

So, just as people have varying regional accents or outright dialects, social media communities can be said to speak particular kinds of e-dialects and e-sociolects. Twitterlect is one such e-sociolect. A Twitterlect that came about from a Twitter community that was formed to follow the pop singer Justin Bieber made many of its words end in "ee," in reference to the vowel pronunciation of "ie" in "Bieber" as a long /i/: "Hi-ee, how are you-ee." Such e-communities now show differences in register and style with respect to traditional offline ones. Studying e-sociolects is becoming more and more crucial since the use of social media has become extensive. The following facts are taken from Phew Internet and other Google sources to show how extensive the use of one social medium, Twitter, has become:

1   There are over 500 million Twitter users.

2   Twitter is the fastest growing social network in the world, by active users, meaning that 21 percent of the world's internet population is using Twitter every month.
3   Twitter's fastest growing age demographic is 55 to 64 year olds.
4   Fifty-three percent of Twitter users never post any updates but watch and click.
5   One-third of Twitter users use Twitter daily.
6   Sixty-three percent of American Twitter users have a college degree.
7   The average user has 208 followers.
8   Four hundred million tweets are sent daily.
9   One-third of American Twitter users update their social networks daily.
10   Females tweet more than males.
11   Fifty-three percent of American Twitter users use it to consume and not create content.

4.5.1 Style and Register

Because of word-count limitations, Twitter constitutes a perfect field laboratory for studying how registers and styles emerge in constrained-usage contexts. Participants in F2F conversations tend to converge to one another's communicative behavior, by synchronizing their style (choice of words, syntax, utterance length, pitch and gestures) to the situation at hand—known as *accommodation theory*. The question of how this theory applies to Twitter conversations is clearly a crucial one, since the setting is unlike any other in which accommodation has been observed. To investigate this, Danescu-Niculescu-Mizil, Gamon, and Dumais (2011) developed a probabilistic framework that could model accommodation and measure its effects, applying it to a large Twitter conversational dataset specifically developed for this task. While investigating accommodation, they discovered a complexity of stylistic options that was never observed before.

In F2F environments, stylistic accommodation involves choices in grammar, vocabulary, and even phonology. One would thus expect style to be compromised in the Twitter environment. But studies such as the one above have found that style is still central in Twitterlects. In Twitter, as in F2F, there is still a desire to gain the other's social approval and to maintain a positive social identity with the interlocutor. Danescu-Niculescu-Mizil, Gamon, and Dumais (2011) used a system to measure word use in psychologically meaningful categories (articles, auxiliary verbs, positive emotions, and so on). They found that a tweet exhibits a given style if it contains words from these categories. Their research is part of more general research on the connection between language and thought, which will be discussed in a later chapter. A tweet can exhibit multiple styles and, in fact, the vast majority of tweets do. They also found that tweets belonging to the same conversation are closer stylistically than tweets that do not. Tweeps who converse regularly are likely to employ a similar linguistic style simply because they know each other or are similar to each other.

As research such as this shows, a connection between the social status of Twitter users and language is established through new forms of style. By comparing #followers, #followees, #posts, #days on Twitter, #posts per day and ownership of a personal website the above researchers also found that stylistic features appear to be only weakly connected to the traditional social stratification of offline speech. But this might mean that the social status of the interlocutors may not be known, and thus a generic form of style and register is adopted. Paolillo (2001) also documented weak ties between the two in chat relays, and Gilbert and Karahalios (2009) noted a weak correlation in Facebook sites. In such cases the reason would seem to be that unlike F2F, where physical contact is a factor in style adjustments, social media treats all users the same, whether they are trusted friends or total strangers, with little or nothing in between. But Gilbert and Karahalios also noted that certain features, such as intimacy words, did fall onto a social knowledge scale that paralleled F2F communication. Strangely, it would seem, people use two sets of sociolinguistic registers and styles depending on whether they communicate online or offline.

Ramage, Dumais, and Liebling (2010) looked at millions of Twitter posts, identifying four general registers, which they characterized as being based on *substance*, *status*, *social* and *style* variables: that is, on events, ideas, things, or people (substance), on some social goal (social), related to personal updates (status), or indicative of broader trends of language use (style). A primary factor in changing the sociolinguistic rules (or at least modifying them) is frequency of interaction. Twitter conversations can occur constantly, unlike F2F ones, and thus make it necessary to streamline conversations making them more likely to be open, rather than dyadic (two-person). This affects the nature of speech acts, making them more likely to be audience-based rather than inter-subjective (between two people). The gist of all this is that register and style, along with the sociolectal parameters that they entail, still exist in cyberspace, but they are adapting to its new requirements.

4.5.2 Social Variables

In a comprehensive study of Twitter, Rao, Yarowsky, Shreevats, and Gupta (2010) looked at how gender, age, regional origin, and political orientation played out in Twitter conversations. The task they put to themselves was to determine if it was possible to detect if a Twitter user was male or female simply by the content and behavior of the postings. While many Twitter users use their real name, which can reveal their gender, many choose fictitious nicknames that do not convey gender. So, the researchers concentrated on whether or not it was possible to infer gender exclusively from the content and style of the writing. A similar approach was used to identify age and regional origin variables. Age is also a difficult variable to analyze in such environments.

Not only does it change constantly, but also age-sensitive communication behavior differs according to socioeconomic variables, and there is no known indicator for age on Twitter. The regional origin of a user often correlates with a user's dialect, such as whether they are from the South or Northeastern US. The researchers looked at these as well as speakers of English by their national origin, such as someone writing in English from India.

The absence of prosodic cues in Twitter, the fixed utterance size limitations, and nature of tweeting versus F2F conversation were examined as well by the above researchers, who found that the cues were substantially different. For instance, a very peculiar cue is the presence of a sequence of exclamation marks, which they discovered was indicative of a female user in the dataset. Certain kinds of emoticons were also strong indicators of female users. The genders laugh differently on Twitter as well. While women LOL, men tend to LMFAO. They also discovered that age can be determined by lexical choices. The use of terms like "dude" and "bro" almost certainly indicates a younger user. The older users tend to be more articulate, using fully formed sentences within character limits as opposed to the more inarticulate choice of using ellipses among many younger users.

Alphabetic character repetition refers to the "pumping" of identical characters in sequence in informal communication to emphasize an emotional content. Some examples of character repetition include *niceeeee*, *gawwwd*, and *noooo waaaay*. Again, female users were found to employ character repetition 1.4 times more often than male users. The following features also were found to be more characteristic of female tweeps:

- *Repeated Exclamation* such as a string of !'s.
- *Puzzled Punctuation* such as a combination of any number of ! and ? in any order.
- OMG ("oh my god").

Research such as the one described here shows that gender, age, class, and other social variables continue to be in play in cyberspace, but their forms and uses have changed somewhat. So, in some ways, e-sociolects parallel offline sociolects in terms of their social functions, but their forms (styles and registers) have changed considerably.

4.5.3 e-Slang

One final area of online e-sociolects can be called e-slang study, or the study of slangs that emerge in online communities. A perfect example of this is among video-gamers.

To keep themselves apart from others, gamer cliques also have their own language, known as l33t or leetspeak. The original version of this language was developed for usage on forums to prevent outsiders from barging into discussions. Over time it has been modified, fusing with other kinds of e-dialects. Examples are:

- GG = Good Game
- gl hf = good luck, have fun
- newb = new player to the game
- noob = you play like a novice
- leik = like
- J00 = you
- hack0r = hacker
- teh = the
- sux = sucks

The term *leetspeak* itself is indicative of the built-in social connotations that the code embodies. It comes from the word *elite* referring to a hierarchy among early so-called BBS (bulletin board system) users. Elite users were allowed special board privileges, such as access to pirated software or to hidden discussion sites. The essence of the leet code is concealment to outsiders, in line with the overall geek code of separation from the mainstream and in-group symbolism. One technique of the code is to substitute numbers for letters: *hacker* becomes *h4acker* or *hack0r*, and *leet* becomes *l33t*. Other techniques include intentional misspellings (*teh* instead of *the*), substituting sound-alike letters (*h4xx* for *hacks*), using other characters in place of letters (/ \ / in place of *N*).

E-slangs are springing up all the time. However, it remains to be seen how widespread they become, since the purpose of these slangs is in-group solidarity, by and large.

Terminology Review

Define or explain in your own words the following terms introduced in this chapter, some of which were introduced earlier but elaborated here.

argot	cant
colloquialism	fillers
genre	hedges
honorific	indexicality
jargon	linguistic profiling
quotative	register
restricted versus elaborated code	slang
sociolect	style
tags	

Exercises and Discussion

1   Variation occurs constantly on a social level. As you have seen throughout this textbook, a distinction between *formal* and *informal* speech is found in all languages. The former is used to show deference and politeness. The latter is used to show friendliness and a feeling of closeness. Change each word, expression, or protocol from formal to informal speech.

   (a) residence
   (b) advertisement
   (c) soft drink
   (d) adhesive
   (e) greetings
   (f) hello
   (g) goodbye

2   Give examples of current adolescent or urban slang, explaining what linguistic process is involved (hedging, tagging, and so on).

3   The type of vocabulary used by specific occupational groups is known as jargon. How much jargon do you know from the various professions?

   (a) lawyer talk
   (b) professor talk
   (c) doctor talk

4   Correct the following utterances in a stylistically appropriate fashion.

   (a) The journey was taken by Bob. It was not taken by me, nor was it my intention to do so. The journey preparations were accomplished quickly. The journey was taken by Bob for several reasons. These reasons were necessitated by stressful situations.
   (b) The experiment was, like, good. I knew I was going to get a chemical reaction. I thought I would get salt. But I got something else instead. I will try the experiment again.

5   From Twitter sites, collect markers (emoticons, abbreviations, and so on) that you can associate with some social variable (gender, age, class, and so on). Do you think that the findings compare to those in F2F speech, or do you think they are quite different? Why?

6   Read the following excerpt from D. Hymes (*On Communicative Competence*, 1971):

   The internalization of attitudes towards a language and its uses is particularly important (Labov, 1965, pp. 84–5, on priority of subjective evaluation in social dialect and processes of change), as is internalization of attitudes toward use of language itself (e.g. attentiveness to it) and the relative place that language comes to play in a pattern of mental abilities (Cazden, 1966), and in strategies—what language is considered available, reliable, suitable for, vis-à-vis other kinds of code. The acquisition of such competency is of course fed by social experience, needs, and motives, and issues in action that is itself a renewed source of motives, needs, experience. We break irrevocably with the model that restricts the design of language to one face toward referential meaning, one toward sound, and that defines the organization of language as solely consisting of rules for linking the two. Such a model implies naming to be the sole use of speech, as if languages were never organized to lament, rejoice, beseech, admonish, aphorize, inveigh (Burke, 1966, p. 13), for the many varied forms of persuasion, direction, expression and symbolic play. A model of language must design it with a face toward communicative conduct and social life.

Explain in your own words why social cues are embedded in language and how these can be used to detect social variables in online messages.

7   Read the following excerpt from D. W. Lee (Genres, Registers, Text Types, Domains, and Styles: Clarifying The Concepts and Navigating a Path through the BNC Jungle, 2001):

One way of making a distinction between genre and text type is to say that the former is based on external, non-linguistic, "traditional" criteria while the latter is based on the internal, linguistic characteristics of texts themselves (Biber, 1988, pp. 70 & 170; EAGLES, 1996). A genre, in this view, is defined as a category assigned on the basis of external criteria such as intended audience, purpose, and activity type, that is, it refers to a conventional, culturally recognised grouping of texts based on properties other than lexical or grammatical (co-)occurrence features, which are, instead, the internal (linguistic) criteria forming the basis of text type categories. Biber (1988) has this to say about external criteria. Genre categories are determined on the basis of external criteria relating to the speaker's purpose and topic; they are assigned on the basis of use rather than on the basis of form (p. 170). However, the EAGLES (1996) authors would quibble somewhat with the inclusion of the word topic above and argue that one should not think of topic as being something to be established a priori, but rather as something determined on the basis of internal criteria (i.e., linguistic characteristics of the text).

Classifying texts is a difficult process. How would you classify the following texts, using simple distinctions such as formal-versus-informal, slang-versus-standard, and so on?

(a) An email to a teacher
(b) A tweet to a follower
(c) A text message to a friend
(d) An essay in sociolinguistics

8   Read the following excerpt from J. B. Walther (Interaction through Technological Lenses: Computer-Mediated Communication and Language, 2012):

> *In remarking on communication technology, social psychology, and language since the appearance of our special issue, I wish to frame certain observations in light of an issue that has remained central throughout the evolution and diffusion of this field: the influence of different communication systems on the restriction or provision of non-verbal cue systems that may accompany language in online interaction. Certainly there are other meta-constructs in the field of communication technology research. Yet some, if not most, of the field's most enduring issues have concerned the psychological and communication effects that occur on and through language when people do or do not see or hear one another, without the nonverbal elements of communication on which so much otherwise often relies. Research alternatively describes the restriction of technology-mediated communication to language as a constraint or a liberation.*

Summarize the argument made in your own words. Then, indicate what features of CMC differ from F2F communication in terms of technology.

9   Read the following excerpt from C. Danescu-Niculescu-Mizil, M. Gamon, and S. Dumais (Mark My Words! Linguistic Style Accommodation in Social Media, 2011):

> *Twitter conversations are unlike those used in previous studies of accommodation. One of the main differences is that these conversations are not face-to-face and do not happen in real-time. Like with email, a user does not need to immediately reply to another user's message; this might affect the incentive to use accommodation as a way to increase communication efficiency. Another difference is the (famous) restriction of 140 characters per message, which might constrain the freedom one user has to accommodate the other. It is not a priori clear whether accommodation is robust enough to occur under these new constraints.*

Indicate what style differences there might be among the three kinds of communication environments.

(a) Text messaging
(b) Twitter
(c) Facebook

10   Read the following excerpt from J. Gillen and G. Merchant (Contact Calls: Twitter as a Dialogic Social and Linguistic Practice, 2013):

> *Twitter is currently achieving a new level of institutionalisation as it features in legal cases, debates about privacy, and political intrigue. It is, like the social networking site Facebook, a commercial success, a triumph of*

marketing that was fortunate in striking a complementary note with other applications, software and hardware innovations, so that it quickly captured the public imagination. In the first few years after its launch in 2006 it spawned more than 50,000 third-party applications (Potts and Jones, 2011). The microblogging tool Twitter is in some ways a "conversation" – at once democratic, in that everybody can join, ostensibly on equal footing, and a powerful, way of communicating one's message in an age of "networked individualism" (Wellman, 2001). It will not, we think, be difficult to argue that "tweeting" is a significant social practice worthy of attention: even if some people wholly shun participation themselves, they will, in a variety of contexts, have become aware that Twitter is impinging on many areas of life that touch upon the mass media. The use of Twitter is clearly more than peripheral in diverse social spheres, including revolutionary movements, the dalliances of celebrities, government, industrial disputes and international sporting events (Attia et al., 2011; Cottle, 2011; Jones and Salter, 2011; Zappavigna, 2012).

What do you think the term "dialogic" in the title of the article means? How would you characterize socially based dialogue online?

References

Bakhtin, M. M. (1981). *The Dialogic Imagination*. Trans. C. Emerson and M. Holquist. Austin: University of Texas Press.

Baugh, J. (2003). Linguistic Profiling. *Black Linguistics: Language, Society, and Politics in Africa and the Americas* 155: 155–163.

Bernstein, B. (1971). *Class, Codes and Control: Theoretical Studies towards a Sociology of Language*. London: Routledge.

Blyth, C. et al. (2000). I'm like, Say What? A New Quotative in American Oral Narrative. *Journal of American Speech* 65: 215–227.

Chandler, F. W. (1907). *The Literature of Roguery*. Boston: Houghton Mifflin.

Charaudeau, P. and Maingueneau, D. (2002). *Dictionnaire d'analyse du discours*. Paris: Seuil.

Clopper, C. G. and Pisoni, D. (2004). Some Acoustic Cues for the Perceptual Categorization of American English Regional Dialects. *Journal of Phonetics* 32: 111–140.

Danescu-Niculescu-Mizil, C., Gamon, M., and Dumais, S. (2011). Mark My Words! Linguistic Style Accommodation in Social Media. *International World Wide Web Conference Committee*, ACM 978-1-4503-0632-4/11/03.

Danesi, M. (1994). *Cool: The Signs and Meanings of Adolescence*. Toronto: University of Toronto Press.

Dubois, S. and Horvath, B. (1998). Let's tink about dat: Interdental Fricatives in Cajun English. *Language Variation and Change* 10 (3): 245–261.

Duffin, J. (2005). *Disease Concepts in History*. Toronto: University of Toronto Press.

Fairclough, N. (2003). *Analysing Discourse: Textual Analysis for Social Research*. London: Routledge.

Gilbert, E. and Karahalios, K. (2009). Predicting Tie Strength with Social Media. *Proceedings of the SIGCHI Conference on Human Factors in Computing Systems*, pp. 211–220. New York: ACM.

Gillen, J. and Merchant, G. (2013). Contact Calls: Twitter as a Dialogic Social and Linguistic Practice. *Language Sciences* 35: 47–58.

Gregory, M. (1967). Aspects of Varieties Differentiation. *Journal of Linguistics* 3: 177–197.

Halliday, M. A. K. and Hasan, R. (1976). *Cohesion in English*. London: Longman.

Holmes, J. (1995). *Women, Men and Language*. London: Longman.

Hymes, D. (1971). *On Communicative Competence*. Philadelphia: University of Pennsylvania Press.

Jakobson, R. (1960). Linguistics and Poetics. In: T. Sebeok (ed.), *Style and Language*. Cambridge, Mass.: MIT Press.

Joos, M. (1967). *The Five Clocks*. New York: Harcourt, Brace and World.

Laroche, P. (2007). *On Words: Insight into How our Words Work and Don't*. Oak Park, Ill.: Marion Street Press.

Lee, D. W. (2001). Genres, Registers, Text Types, Domains, and Styles: Clarifying the Concepts and Navigating a Path through the BNC Jungle. *Language Learning & Technology* 5: 37–72.

Lee, E. (2007). A Semantic Restriction on Scrambling in Korean. *LSO Working Papers in Linguistics 7: Proceedings of WIGL*, pp. 109–123.

Leland, J. (2004). *Hip: The History*. New York: Harper Collins.

Lippi-Green, R. (1997). *English with an Accent: Language, Ideology, and Discrimination in the United States*. London: Routledge.

Littlejohn, S. (2002). *Theories of Human Communication*. Albuquerque: Wadsworth.

Lunde, P. (2012). *The Secrets of Codes*. San Francisco: Weldonowen.

Mattiello, E. (2008). *An Introduction to English Slang: A Description of Its Morphology, Semantics and Sociology*. Milano: Polimetrica.

Morrish, J. (1999). *Frantic Semantics: Snapshots of Our Changing Language*. London: Macmillan.

Nicaso, A. and Danesi, M. (2013). *Made Men: Mafia Culture and the Power of Symbols, Rituals, and Myth*. Lanham: Rowman & Littlefield.

Paolillo, J. (2001). Language Variation on Internet Relay Chat: A Social Network Approach. *Journal of Sociolinguistics* 5: 180–213.

Purnell, T., Idsardi, W., and Baugh, J. (1999). Perceptual and Phonetic Experiments on American English Dialect Identification. *Journal of Social Psychology* 18: 10–30.

Ramage, D. Dumais, S. and Liebling, D. (2010). Characterizing Microblogs with Topic Models. *International AAAI Conference on Weblogs and Social Media*. Association for the Advancement of Artificial Intelligence, pp. 130–137.

Rao, D., Yarowsky, D., Shreevats, A., and Gupta, M. (2010). Classifying Latent User Attributes in Twitter. In: *Proceedings of the 2nd International Workshop on Search and Mining User-Generated Contents*, pp. 37–54. New York: ACM.

Reid, T. B. (1956). Linguistics, Structuralism, Philology. *Archivum Linguisticum* 8: 28–37

Romaine, S. and Lange, D. (1991). The Use of Like as a Marker of Reported Speech and Thought: A Case of Grammaticalization in Process. *American Speech* 66: 227–279.

Sagan, C. and Druyan, A. (1992). *Shadows of Forgotten Ancestors: A Search for Who We Are*. New York: Random House.

Saussure, F. de (1916). *Cours de linguistique générale*. Paris: Payot.

Siegel, M. E. A. (2002). Like: The Discourse Particle and Semantics. *Journal of Semantics*, 19: 35–71.

Silverstein, M. (1976). Shifters, Linguistic Categories, and Cultural Description. In: K. Basso and H. A. Selby (eds.), *Meaning in Anthropology*, pp. 11–56. Albuquerque: University of New Mexico Press.

Sontag, S. (1978). *Illness as Metaphor*. New York: Farrar, Straus & Giroux.

Walther, J. B. (2012). Interaction through Technological Lenses: Computer-Mediated Communication and Language. *Journal of Language and Social Psychology* 31: 397–414.

Wierzbicka, A. (1991). *Cross-Cultural Pragmatics: The Semantics of Human Interaction*. Berlin: Mouton de Gruyter.

Winner, E. (1988). *The Point of Words: Children's Understanding of Metaphor and Irony*. Cambridge, Mass.: Harvard University Press.

5 Language, Personality, and Identity

Trying to define yourself is like trying to bite your own teeth.
Alan Watts (1915–1973)

Language varies not only in geographical and social spaces, but also personally. The personal style that identifies speakers, as mentioned previously, is called *idiolect* by linguists. The topic of language, personality, and identity constitutes a broad area of sociolinguistic research, especially since identity-construction in online contexts is revealing itself very much to be a creation of individuals in conjunction with models of identity acquired in real social and cultural contexts.

Throughout life, one's sense of identity—which can be defined simply as the awareness of one's distinctiveness both personally and as part of a group or of groups—changes according to age and situation, but remains largely embedded in the linguistic and cultural realities of one's rearing experiences. Some theorists see identity as a genetic endowment, a fixed quality of Selfhood and character that is modified only superficially by environmental factors. On the other hand, many others argue that it is largely constructed (modified, adapted) by individuals throughout life in response to the experiences they have. James Baldwin (1985: 23) encapsulates this perspective perfectly as follows: "An identity would seem to be arrived at by the way in which the person faces and uses his/her experience." Although the debate has never been resolved one way or the other, the research in sociolinguistics has left little doubt that the language (or languages) one acquires in childhood is a major factor in shaping one's sense of identity.

Needless to say, there is more to identity than language. Identity is influenced as well by ethnic, national, religious, gender, and other influences on a person's life. For this reason, the term *linguistic identity* is preferred when alluding to the impact of language on identity. This is defined loosely as the patterns of linguistic behavior that are felt as meaningful to the speaker both because they are consistent with those of the group or groups with which he or she wishes to be associated or because he or she believes that they have special qualities. As sociolinguists now concur, this is largely a constructed dimension of human personality (Bucholtz 1999; Bucholtz and Hall 2005). In this sense, linguistic identity is a system, composed of the linguistic forms that we absorb in childhood and adapt to our own particular life experiences.

5.1 Personality

The study of the relation between language and personality, or how the language we use reveals who we are or what we think, crosses disciplinary lines, involving both psycholinguistics and sociolinguistics—the former focusing on the relation between language and the construction of the Self and the latter, of course, between language and social identity. Research has been showing since at least the 1950s that language and personality are interconnected. As discussed in Chapter 1 (Pennebaker 2011), the specific ways in which personal pronouns are used may show assurance and confidence or in some cases the opposite. Grammatical morphemes appear to reveal more about personality than do content words (nouns, adjectives, verbs). The method used to collect data consists in assembling personal writing texts (speeches, diaries, letters, and so on) and in interviewing subjects. As described in Chapter 1, the data can then be submitted to statistical analysis.

Today, with social media sites the potential sample size of diaries and personality profiles has become gargantuan and can be used to validate or refute research findings. Studies have started to show that some grammatical morphemes are indicators of improvements in mental health, revealing the inner life of the psyche, as well as correlating with age, gender, and class differences. People who lack power seem to require a more direct engagement with the thoughts of others, perhaps to validate themselves socially. But this does not really answer the question of why certain morphemes are more prevalent in certain people than in others. We all have an idiolect, which is our particular manner of speaking that identifies us instantly, including pronunciation, tone of voice, choice of vocabulary, types of sentences used, and so on. Correlating linguistic features with personality, however, is always tricky, since people and circumstances of language use change constantly. However, patterns do emerge. Starting with the work of J. R. Firth (1950), sociolinguists have found that various marked features of language generally give away our gender, social background, regional origin (if dialect is involved), and other constituents of our personalities. This can be called, for the sake of convenience, a language profile, or L-profile.

5.1.1 Age

One of the more obvious areas where the L-profile manifests itself and becomes a marker of identity is during the various stages of life. People speak differently in childhood, adolescence, and old age, for example, for various physical, psychological, and social reasons.

The role of age on linguistic personality can be seen conspicuously in adolescent talk. Since the middle part of the twentieth century, a solid tradition in sociolinguistics of investigating adolescent speech patterns has been established (Gusdorf 1965; Labov 1972; Eble 1989, 1996; Rampton 1995); these show that language in adolescence is more than slang. It is a means of asserting or constructing an identity often different from the one inherited from childhood—especially in societies where adolescence is marked as a specific stage of development. Identity-construction in this period of development is implanted in various ways, from lifestyle to speech. The latter is the one that most reveals how age and language intersect, since the discourse styles and the language features of adolescents reflect those established in peer groups or else those emanating from various media sources. In the sense used by Bernstein (previous chapters), adolescent talk is a restricted code intended to convey allegiance to the group while declaring independence from both childhood and the mainstream society.

Young people in Western societies have typically resorted to coded words since the Medieval Ages in order to strengthen group identity and to set themselves apart from others. Medieval university students, for instance, used the word *lupi* "wolves" to refer to spies who reported other students for using the vernacular instead of Latin (Eble 1989). If adolescent talk has a specific social function, then it can hardly be considered a form of aberrant communicative behavior. It is a kind of sociolect that can be defined simply as "the social dialect of adolescence." Hudson (1984), too, sees a difference between slang in general and what he calls more specifically teenage slang. The latter is a code "used by teenagers to signal the important difference they see between themselves and older people" (Hudson 1984: 46). Adults too frequently resort to slang to color or emphasize their messages. But for adolescents coded language typically becomes a key for gaining access to meaningful social interaction with specific groups of peers. So, it can be said that slang is a speech option available to the population at large; but the adolescent form of slang, on the other hand, is a social dialect of the standard language that is shaped by an age-based L-profile.

The whole gamut of emotional responses that teenagers have to their immediate context, as well as the creative strategies they employ to handle specific social situations, are reflected in the ways in which they program their discourse, in the kinds of words they coin, and generally in the highly emotive style of delivery they manifest. As discussed, emotivity is a feature of slang sociolects. It varies according to type of message: poetic texts, for example, tend to be more emotive than information-transfer ones, such as science textbooks. Among features that reveal emotivity are increased or decreased rates of speech delivery for emphasis, overwrought intonation contours, expressive voice modulations, and so on. For instance, utterances such as "He's sooooo cute!" "She's faaaaar out!" "That's amaaaazing!" exemplify the common emotive pattern of overstressing highly emotional words by a prolongation of the tonic vowel (Danesi 1994; Eble 1996).

Examples of Teen Slang (2013–2014)

affluential: someone with money and power ("affluence" + "influence")

all emo: drama queen (from emo subculture)

awesomity: highest degree of "awesome"

bro-tox: males getting botox

busted: ugly

flamed: taken something too seriously

frenemy: duplicitous person ("friend" + "enemy")

greycation: grandparents on vacation

iceman: friend with nerves of steel

my bad: my mistake

The tendency to coin descriptive words, or to extend the meaning of existing words, in highly connotative ways is also a salient feature of adolescent sociolects. Connotation is at the core of the adolescent's L-profile. Words such as *vomatose* (a combination of *vomit* + *comatose*), *thicko* (slow-brained), *burgerbrain* (version of *thicko*), *knob* (hard-headed) of a few years ago are cases-in-point. They are graphic descriptors of social and emotional experiences and evaluator terms of others. But no matter from what generation of teens the words come, the creative mechanism is the same—it is grounded in connotation that is aimed at the description of others or the evaluation of a specific social situation.

Research on adolescent sociolects throughout the world shows that such phenomena have a very short lifespan. As Eble (1989: 12) aptly points out, "by comparison with vocabulary change in the language as a whole, which sometimes takes centuries, the rate of change in slang vocabularies is greatly accelerated." Research also shows that there are actually adolescent terms that gain general currency, cutting across regional and dialectal boundaries. Words such as *cool, jock, nerd, chill out, busted,* and others, which come out of a specific generation of adolescent talk, have made their way into the mainstream as colloquialisms. Overall, adolescent talk reveals rather conspicuously that young people are keenly sensitive to bodily appearance and image, as well as to the perceived sociability of peers. At puberty the changes in physical appearance, and the emotional changes that accompany them, are perceived as significant. To offset this preoccupation with Self-image, they talk deflectively, that is, about how others act, behave, and appear so as to deflect attention away from themselves.

During childhood the individual's modes of interaction with the environment are centered upon a constantly developing consciousness of Self. The child is typically concerned about how he or she fits into the scheme of things. At puberty, however, the child's social consciousness comes to dominate his or her thinking and actions. While human beings of all ages are influenced by their relation to others, and tend to conform to behavioral models that are acceptable to their peer groups, teenagers are particularly susceptible to this kind of influence, simply because their social consciousness emerges on the developmental timetable as a powerful inner force.

As Cooper and Anderson-Inman (1988: 239) aptly pointed out in a key classic study, this is really a manifestation of strategic interaction: "Gaining control over marked linguistic features shows a growing competence in the use of communicative strategies that both realize and regulate behavior and speech patterns appropriate to gender and peer group membership." Teenagers achieve relative status in the fluctuating hierarchy of their communities by learning how to advantageously manipulate their verbal interactions strategically. Another classic study by Maltz and Borker (1982) demonstrated that teenage boys are more inclined than girls to test the verbal skills of one another in staged "verbal duels" in order to gain the upper hand. Those with ineffectual verbal skills will either become clique outcasts or be compelled to accept lower status within the clique hierarchy.

The strategic use of aggressive and obscene language in verbal duels shows up constantly in adolescent discourse. Both the males and the females with the greatest ability to "outtalk" the others are the ones who assert a leadership role within their cliques. Eder (1990: 67) has labeled this form of verbal dueling *ritual conflict*:

> Ritual conflict typically involves the exchange of insults between two peers, often in the presence of other peers who serve as an audience. This activity is usually competitive in nature, in that each male tries to top the previous insult with one that is more clever, outrageous, or elaborate.

The goal during ritual exchanges is to "keep one's cool" by not letting the opponent realize that one is wavering. Eder (1990: 74) pointed out that "the ability to respond to even personal insults in a non-serious manner is a critical skill needed for successful participation in ritual insulting." Verbal conflict skills are developed through frequent participation in dueling exchanges. It is for this reason that those individuals who hang out more with the group seem to get a firmer command of the conflict techniques needed to succeed at verbal duels (Labov 1972: 258). The peer audience participating in this activity acts as a kind of critic. If the exchange ends with someone verbally destroying the other, the audience will invariably proceed to ridicule and defame the loser. In many cases, this post-defeat mockery unfolds in terms of a stage-like scornful scenario.

As this brief excursion into adolescent talk shows, language, age and the construction of identity are interrelated. As teenagers grow older the linguistic habits will change as well. Age, like gender, race, and ethnicity is reflected in one's L-profile. A model that would help explain the role of language for age-appropriate delivery is the one put forward by Erving Goffman (1974), which he called *frame analysis*, or the technique of dividing human interaction into separate frames of behavior that can then be analyzed in terms of constituent units of Self-portrayal, recognizable by others intuitively as part of personality. Taking his cue from Gregory Bateson (1936), he called the sequence of actions that identify a person's behavioral characteristics a "strip" (an obvious reference to the comic strip as conspicuously exemplifying a structured sequence of actions). The method of frame analysis consists in: (1) describing the strip (the actual behavioral scene); (2) reducing it to a basic typology (actions, language forms, and so on); and (3) interpreting the strategies deployed by the characters in the strip. In effect, Goffman drew attention to the implicit fact that everyday life unfolds very much like a cartoon theatrical performance, because people seek to skillfully stage their character according to social context. People are "character actors" who employ gestures, props, and conversation to impress or influence each other for specific reasons. The Latin term for "cast of characters" is *dramatis personae*, literally, "the persons of the drama," a term betraying the theatrical origin of our concept of personhood. Persona was the "mask" in Greek theater. We seem, in a phrase, to perceive life as a stage and our role in it as "character." Bateson also understood that any form of human interaction operates in terms of contrasting levels above and beyond the exchange of information; he called those levels *metacommunicative*. Metacommunication occurs all the time and is a hidden agent in determining personal success in social interactions.

Goffman actually defined the frame space as if it were a real theater, with a front region in which the "actors" perform their scripts, and the background of others as constituting an audience situation. Goffman introduced such notions as "context," "situational effects," and "role-playing" as basic sociological concepts. These have been adopted and adapted by sociolinguists broadly to describe how face-to-face verbal communication unfolds.

5.1.2 Cognition

Bilinguals and multilinguals commonly report "feeling" or "thinking" differently when they speak their different languages. Do bilinguals have a "split personality," in the non-technical sense of having two personalities inside that speak different languages according to situation? Bilinguals may unconsciously change their personality when they switch languages. It is known that people in general can switch between different ways of interpreting events and feelings—a phenomenon known as *frame shifting*. But it might well be that bilinguals who are active in two different cultures do it more readily, and that language is the trigger.

This brings us back to the Whorfian Hypothesis (discussed briefly in the opening chapter). Benjamin Lee Whorf (1956) held that a particular language influences how its speakers classify, perceive, and understand the world. This influence may show up in bilingual speech patterns, in the form of differential vocabulary, grammar, and especially in code-switching. But bilingualism, as we saw, has various forms (primary, secondary, passive, and so on). Typically, people are not symmetrically bilingual. Many have learned one language at home from parents, and another later in life, usually at school. So bilinguals usually have different competencies in their different languages and they code-switch in certain situations, for various reasons. But what about bilinguals raised in two languages? Even if they do not usually have perfectly symmetrical competence, they do use both languages functionally, as is the case among Hispanic speakers in many parts of the US. Is there something intrinsic to the different languages that encourages bilinguals to code-switch or talk differentially? In other words, are cognition and language interrelated? Do separate languages guide behaviors differentially? In Greek, for example, the verb typically comes first in a sentence, thus carrying a lot of information. This makes it easier to interrupt than when the verb is elsewhere in the syntax of a language (as studies have shown). The problem is that unrelated languages around the world also put the verb in front and similar interruption patterns have not been documented. It would be a striking finding indeed if unrelated languages had speakers more prone to interrupting each other and that this could be located in some aspect of syntax.

One of the bilingual speech communities studied in some depth by sociolinguists is the Hispanic one in the US. As we have seen in various parts of previous chapters, Spanglish is often used as a marker of identity through code-switching and code-mixing. The question arises if Spanglish has an effect on Hispanics' cognition vis-à-vis other Spanish-speaking communities such as those in Spain itself. Rothman and Rell (2005) argue that Spanglish is synonymous with identity and thus with the development of personality and cognitive traits that, say, American Mexicans are expected to display as they speak Spanglish. Thus, it is not a simple matter of a specific language affecting cognition, but of social expectations connected with speaking that language. Hence, when someone who is a "Chicano" (someone of Mexican extraction) speaks Spanish, we tend to expect in his or her L-profile differences that other Hispanics do not have. In speaking Spanglish, they do not change their ethnicity as a matter of fashion, but they may emphasize different aspects of their personality. A person who identifies himself or herself as Mexican among relatives might identify himself or herself as Hispanic at work and as American when away from the US. The same type of argument can, of course, be applied to African-American identity and personality through the use of AAVE and other sociolects.

If race and ethnicity were purely social and cultural phenomena, we would expect the long-term outcome of immigration to be the gradual weakening and eventual disappearance of racial and ethnic categories and of speech communities as distinct groups. When it does it is called *acculturation*, and this happens several generations after the first group of immigrants. This then leads to an "Americanization" of identity. Recent immigrants, by contrast, are more likely to claim national-origin identities, although there is a process of emerging Americanized identity-formation among the native-born in their communities. Some researchers believe that Spanglish does not exist as such because a way of speaking cannot be named; others consider it a dialectal or sociolectal variety often used as a marker of ancestral origin or of bilingual competence and not as a sign of insufficient knowledge of Spanish or English. Spanglish was created by the contact (or clash) between two communities developing into a sign, for some, of a new hybrid identity, in addition to a specific way of life. Clearly, the question of language, personality, and cognition is a complex one and ongoing research continues to be ambiguous in its findings. Nevertheless, it is interesting and an important issue for sociolinguists to research, especially in an ever-expanding multilingual world.

5.2 Identity

The foregoing discussion leads directly to the topic of linguistic identity. In an in-depth study of linguistic identity (henceforth LI), John Edwards (2009) argues that the language we are born into and which we use routinely imparts an intuitive sense of who we are. In a phrase, LI is forged both individually through our upbringing and as members of groups who use the same language or its varieties for daily interaction. LI affects our concept of social identity, since it allows us to build a model of ourselves, albeit a *distant* one, as Ochs (1993: 288) calls it, because it is not necessarily rendered obvious in language forms themselves:

> Linguistic constructions at all levels of grammar and discourse are crucial indicators of social identity for members as they regularly interact with one another; complementarily, social identity is a crucial dimension of the social meaning of particular linguistic constructions. But no matter how crucial language is for understanding social identity and social identity for understanding the social meaning of language, social identity is rarely grammaticized or otherwise explicitly encoded across the world's languages. In other words, the relation between language and social identity is predominantly a sociolinguistically *distant* one.

Hyperreal

The term *hyperreal* is associated with the late Jean Baudrillard (1983), who used it to claim that contemporary people can no longer distinguish, or want to distinguish, between reality and fantasy, having become so accustomed to watching television and going to the movies. As a consequence, the content produced by the media is perceived as *hyperreal*, that is, as more real than real.

Baudrillard extended the notion to include fictional or cultural ideas, events, and spectacles. An example he liked to use was that of Disney's Fantasyland and Magic Kingdom, which are copies of other fictional worlds. They are copies of copies and, yet, people appear to experience them as more real than real, indicating that simulated worlds are more desirable than real ones.

One thus constructs his or her identity in this simulated world. Eventually, as people engage constantly with the hyperreal, everything, from politics to art, becomes governed by simulation.

The concept of sociolinguistic distance is an appropriate one, or more correctly *was* in the pre-internet age, when speakers absorbed the linguistic categories of their native languages and came to the realization that these had meaning in specific social ways. To put it in more concrete terms, an individual who speaks Italian as a native language tends to experience an ethnic allegiance to Italian culture and society. But the allegiance can be easily detached from the use of the language in situations of migration or change of social status. But in cyberspace the sociolinguistic rules of the game seem to be changing, as LIs are being constructed not only through the traditional "real" structures of the world (including rearing and upbringing), but through the "hyperreal" dimensions of CMC (Baudrillard 1983). While we continue to forge and negotiate our social identity in the ways we relate to others, even in cyberspace, we now have a more flexible grasp of both our social and linguistic identities as we manage them on a daily basis through social networking sites. In the past, social relations, enduring cultural traditions, and stable patterns of work, life, and leisure assured people that fixed patterns of linguistic meaning united them in real space. The internet has shattered this assurance, forcing individuals to develop new strategies to manage their LIs for presentation in everyday life.

The question now becomes: Is the traditional notion of LI changing in an age when device-to-device communication is as dominant as face-to-face (F2F) communication, and in some ways even more so? In other words, does the sociolinguistic notion of *distance* still apply? This question will be investigated later in this chapter. Dialects and sociolects reflect the various components of LI. The sociolinguistic literature has always argued that it is the desire for new forms of identity that gives rise to linguistic change (Ochs's *distance hypothesis*). In a CMC world changes in LI are no longer distant, but *proximate* (literally on the screen) and seem themselves to be engendering a new sense of LI. This can be called the *proximate hypothesis*, which implies that immediate contact with people in online contexts, without the physical boundaries and socially contextualizing conditions of the real world, is the conduit through which LIs are being shaped.

5.2.1 Theories

As mentioned, LI is one dimension of overall identity, albeit a crucial one. One of the ways in which it is constructed is, of course, through daily linguistic interaction with others who share the same social and cultural space. The Self–Other dynamic inherent in everyday F2F communication is the frame through which we develop our LI, as Russian scholar Mikhail Bakhtin (1981) argued. Our "sense of Self" emerges primarily from this dialogical dynamic as a voice of consciousness. That voice is ensconced in the native or dominant language of upbringing.

If one sifts through the massive literature on identity in the social sciences, it becomes obvious that it evolves primarily (or becomes part of one's personality imprint) during two periods in the human life cycle—before puberty and at adolescence. In childhood, identity is a "given system," that is, it is imparted (given) to the child by and through the environment in which he or she is reared. The name, situation, language, and specific cultural codes (art, music, and so on) that the child is given (and which he or she acquires) in context make up the "native-identity" through which the child comes to develop a sense of Selfhood. This kind of process can be designated "indexical," in the sense that the child develops his or her LI in relation to social (rearing) context. Some of the features of this form of identity include the use of language to understand the immediate world. This is when language literally "refers" to things and people, without necessarily putting them in some social context. The post-pubescence form of identity, on the other hand, can be called "symbolic," since the adolescent interprets the situation more consciously and adapts to it symbolically, that is, through resources such as clothing, new forms of language and discourse, lifestyle choices, and the like. In this case, the language used is often self-reflective and at times ironic. Language becomes more displaced from the immediate environment and thus more abstract. In both cases, it is through interaction with others that the identity construction process unfolds. It is largely unconscious in childhood, since it is imparted through situational factors (given); whereas it is conscious, or at least intentional, in the coming-of-age period. The shifts in identity that come about through choices of profession, job, education level, marriage, and other aspects later in life need not concern us here. For one thing, the research shows that these are minimal; for another, the shifts remain symbolic rather than indexical.

The first attempt to understand how indexical identity evolves into a symbolic form through maturation is the one by Sigmund Freud (1905, 1913, 1923). Although many now discard Freud's basic theory of development, it nevertheless continues to have many implications and applications, despite the criticism. Essentially, Freud saw the passage from childhood to adolescence as a period of difficult emotional adjustment because the passage may or may not be successful and, when it is not, it tends to lead to traumatic results. Known as *repression theory*, the claim is that the passage is anchored in repressive experiences suffered in childhood. So, identity-formation during adolescence becomes a highly emotional event. At puberty, the repressed individual must come to grips with his or her sexual identity and body image at a symbolic level, given the hormonal and physical changes that surface during this critical time period. As a result, adolescents feel that they are inhabiting a strange new sexual body, which might make them feel awkward, anxious, guilty, or afraid of the desires and feelings that it generates. To repress these further, the adolescent seeks out peers and peer groups, which serve as kinds of sheltering social enclaves, whereby the adolescent can immerse himself or herself to gain emotional comfort. It is in these enclaves that the adolescent seeks to forge a new symbolic identity—an identity negotiated in large part through group membership. The manifestations of this identity can be seen in clothing preferences, hairstyle, and various bodily decorations, and above all else in a new sense of LI. Speaking a language at the symbolic stage of development implies that its meanings are socially focused. Ironic uses of language emerge at this stage of development for this very reason, since irony is a linguistic defense mechanism.

The psychologist who explored the emergence of symbolic identity as a crucial stage was the American Erik Erikson (1950, 1968). Though schooled in Freudian theory, Erikson developed the non-Freudian concept of *identity construction*. He defined it as the model of oneself that the adolescent starts to develop as a whole person and which he or she uses to fashion his or her personality accordingly. Erikson stressed the continual development of human beings throughout the life-cycle. At adolescence, the individual experiences an "identity crisis" because of inner conflicts related to body image and social pressures, which eventually lead to a sense of self-understanding or, as Erikson called it, "ego identity." The Russian psychologist Vygotsky (1962, 1978) similarly saw the advent of adolescence as a period of identity formation, with language playing a major role in fixing one's ego identity.

The question of what language was spoken in childhood (as a given) becomes a dominant one in adolescence. Language is no longer a tool of understanding one's world, but a means (and even a weapon) for acting upon that world. In terms of the distance hypothesis, the social and the linguistic dimensions now merge unconsciously. They can be separated, of course, and kept distant if the case arose to necessitate this (such as in social upheavals), but by and large the distance between the two becomes minimal, but is still there. In the era of CMC that distance seems to be eroding even more, as contact through digital media is bringing about a more proximate response to the conditions of social interaction.

5.2.2 Linguistic Identity

In previous rural societies, and even in many urban speech communities, LI tends to be based on dialect or regional speech, rather than on a standardized norm. The change in LI in upward mobility situations, as shown by Labov (1972), is more of a modification of identity rather than construction of it. The distance hypothesis can be seen to have historical validity, since the variation is based on the social variable of location (or geography). For example, in Italy, speakers of dialects have in the past forged their LIs on the basis of the dialects. This is why sociolinguistic studies in Italy have focused on how dialectally-based LI contrasted with a standardized sense of Italian as a national language. In a phrase, LIs were negotiated in dialectal contexts and then mitigated or adapted in contact with the structures (such as school) for imparting a standardized LI. The indexical identity was dialectal; the symbolic one became the standardized form in situations of contact (at school, in society, and so on). The factors for generating such a dichotomy are well-known and include: (1) geographical isolation; (2) patterns of cultural independence; and (3) continuous contact with standard Italian in various situations.

Research on LI encompasses not just the LI of the individual, but also of entire groups. Don Kulick (1992), for example, conducted ethnographic work in a village in Papua New Guinea called Gapun, which spoke Taiap, a language known only to the villagers. He was able to document how that language, although spoken by a small group of people, constituted a source of pride, constituting an index (a key) to identity and thus allowing the villagers to feel and claim autonomy from Tok Pisin speakers (the pidgin language spoken by others). Taiap allowed the villagers to express shared values, especially during ritualistic verbal performances that garnered a high level of emotional resonance.

Language is, as this example shows, a socializing agent. Prominent in this subfield is the work of Elinor Ochs and Bambi Schieffelin (Ochs and Schieffelin 1984; Ochs 1988; Schieffelin 1990, 1995, 2000, 2002; Ochs and Taylor 2001), who have looked extensively at how individuals participate in a community and its culture in a meaningful way through language. Children are socialized into belief systems and historical content through oral narratives. In one study, it was shown that the narratives told at dinner time in white middle-class households in southern California typically presented role structures, gender distinctions, and other socializing and enculturation themes to family members.

Worthy of mention here is also Michael Silverstein's work on the role of language in the formation and expression of ideologies (Silverstein 1976, 1979, 1985; Rumsey 1990; Kroskrity 1998). Silverstein defines *ideology* as a shared body of commonsensical notions about the nature of the world. He rejects the Marxist view that ideologies create "false consciousness" deriving from the perception in capitalist societies that material objects and institutions induce people to experience social relations in terms of the amount of capital they possess and the things they wish to purchase. Silverstein argues that, on the contrary, the form of language used by a society has more impact on ideological formations than does the socioeconomic system in place. Ideology is really "ideation" or the formation of ideas connected to language. The evolution of this system is not directly tied to political or economic forces but mirrors them, encodes them, and then filters perceptions about them. In a similar vein, Alessandro Duranti (2003) has argued that language creates an "exemplary center" or "social space" of political and ritualistic power, not a hegemonic one. This space constrains the type of speech and relations that are relevant to a specific group. In it, refined speech, for example, is hardly part of political and economic ideology, but rather a tool in a broader system of socialization.

5.3 Names

One of the most basic aspects of indexical identity-formation is name-giving. A name transforms a human being into a person, providing him or her with an identity, a link to a kinship unit, and a passage rite into a specific society. The study of names falls under the branch of linguistics called *onomastics* (from Greek *onoma* "name"). Across cultures, a neonate is not considered a full-fledged member of society until he or she is given a name. The act of naming a newborn infant is, in effect, his or her first rite of passage in society. If a child is not given a name by his or her family, then society will step in to do so. A person taken into a family, by marriage, adoption, or for some other reason, is also typically assigned the family's name. In Inuit cultures, an individual is perceived to have a body, a soul, and a name; a person is not seen as complete without all three. Generally, aboriginals have a birth name, a family name, and an adult name. Another name may be connected with the person's occupation.

5.3.1 The Social Functions of Names

In Western culture, name-giving is a largely unregulated process. But even so, it is shaped by several customs and trends, many of them implicit or even unconscious. Most of the common names come from Hebrew, Greek, Latin, or Teutonic languages. Hebrew names, such as *John* and *Michael*, have traditionally provided the most important source of names.

Names

Hebrew Names

David ("beloved")

Elizabeth ("oath of God")

Hannah ("God has favored me")

James ("may God protect")

John ("gracious gift of God")

Joseph ("the Lord shall add")

Mary ("wished for")

Michael ("who is like God")

Samuel ("God has heard")

Greek and Latin Names:

Alexander ("helper of humanity")

Barbara ("stranger")

Clarence ("famous")

Emily ("flattering")

George ("farmer")

Helen ("light")

Margaret ("pearl")

Patricia ("of noble birth")

Philip ("lover of horses")

Stephen ("crown" or "garland")

Victor ("conqueror")

Virginia ("maidenly")

Old Germanic Names:

Albert ("noble," "bright")

Arnold ("eagle power")

Edward ("rich guardian")

Richard ("brave power")

William ("will," "helmet")

Greek and Latin names, such as *Alexander* and *Emily*, are also common, reflecting the importance of these two civilizations in the history of the western world. Strangely, Teutonic (Old Germanic) names in English, such as *Richard* and *Frederick*, are rather infrequent, showing again the larger role played in English-speaking culture by classical antiquity. Teutonic names usually consist of two elements joined together. For example, *William* is composed of *Wille* ("will," "resolution") and *helm* ("helmet"). Some of these morphemes may be found at the beginning, such as *ead* ("rich") in *Edwin* and *Edmund*, or at the end, such as *weard* ("guardian") in *Howard* and *Edward*. As the foregoing discussion illustrates, naming practices have come down to us from classical languages or older forms of a language. But these are not the only sources for names in English.

Name-giving can also be tied to the circumstances of birth, such as the time of birth, the birth order, or the parents' emotional reaction to the birth itself. In Yoruba, names such as *Mwanajuma* (Friday), *Esi* (Sunday), *Khamisi* (Thursday), and *Wekesa* (harvest time) refer to the day when the child was born. Names reflecting birth order include *Mosi* (first born), *Kunto* (third born), *Nsonowa* (seventh born), and *Wasswa* (first of twins). *Yejide* (image of the mother) and *Dada* (curly hair) are examples of names indicating reaction to the birth. Analogous names in English include *June* (time of birth), *James the Second* (birth order), and *Felicity* (happy reaction).

Until the late Middle Ages, one personal name was generally sufficient as an identifier. Duplications, however, began to occur so often that additional identification became necessary. Hence, *surnames* were given to individuals (literally "names on top of a name"). These were designed to provide identification on the basis of such features as place (where the individual was from), parentage (to which family or kinship group the individual belonged), or occupation. For example, in England a person living near or at a place where apple trees grew might be called "John where-the-apples-grow," hence, *John Appleby*. Such place names (known as *toponyms*) constitute a large number of surnames—*Wood* or *Woods*, *Moore*, *Church*, or *Hill*. Descendant surnames, or names indicating parentage, were constructed typically with prefixes and suffixes—*McMichael* ("of Michael"), *Johnson* ("son of John"), *Maryson* ("son of Mary"). Surnames reflecting medieval life and occupations include *Smith*, *Farmer*, *Carpenter*, *Tailor*, and *Weaver*.

The Chinese were the first known people to use more than one name. The Emperor Fuxi is said to have decreed the use of family names about 2850 BCE. The Chinese customarily have three names. The family name, placed first, comes from one of the 438 words in the Chinese sacred poem *Baijia Xing* (also spelled *Po-Chia Hsing*). It is followed by a generation name, taken from a poem of 20 to 30 characters adopted by each family, and a given name (corresponding to a Christian name). The Romans had at first only one name, but later they also started using three names: (1) the *praenomen* stood first as the person's given name; (2) next came the *nomen*, which indicated the *gens*, or clan, to which the person belonged; (3) finally came the *cognomen*, which designated the family. For example, Caesar's full name was *Gaius Julius Caesar*. A person sometimes added a fourth name, the *agnomen*, to commemorate an illustrious action or remarkable event. Family names became confused with other aspects of naming by the fall of the Roman Empire, and single names once again became customary.

Family names came into some use again in Europe in the latter part of the tenth century, becoming common by the thirteenth. Nobles first adopted family names to set themselves apart from common people. The nobles made these family names hereditary, passing them on from father to children. As a consequence, the use of a family name became the mark of a well-bred person. Throughout Europe, wealthy and noble families adopted the practice of using family names. At first, these were not hereditary, but merely described a person. For example, the "son of Robert" might be known as *Henry Robertson*, or *Henry, son of Robert*. At times, someone might be given a descriptive surname for some reason. Someone named *Robert* might be called *Robert, the small*, because of his height, shortened eventually to *Robert Small*. In such cases the "nickname" became the surname. Many surnames were formed in this way—names like *Reid, Reed*, and *Read*, for instance, are early spellings of *red*, referring to a man with red hair.

Names are perceived throughout the world to be much more than simple identifiers. They are laden with all kinds of symbolic and social meanings. The ancient Egyptians believed that a name was a living part of an individual, shaping him or her throughout the life on Earth and even beyond. They also believed that if an individual's name was forgotten on Earth, the deceased would have to undergo a second death. To avoid this danger, names were written multiple times on walls, tombs, and papyri. Political rulers would sometimes erase the names of previous monarchs as a means of rewriting history in their favor, since removal of a person's name meant the extinction of the person from memory. In Hebrew culture, the ancient art of *gematria* was based on the belief that the letters of any name could be interpreted as digits and rearranged to form a number that contained secret messages encoded in it. Numerologists in various parts of the ancient Middle East believed that a person's name was an important clue to his or her character. Typically, they changed letters in the name to a number using a system based on the ancient Greek and Hebrew alphabets. The digits of the number were added together to produce a "personality number" from one to nine. The Romans, too, thought names were prophetic, believing that *nomen est omen*—a "name is an omen." Would the Roman view explain names such as Cecil Fielder who was a fielder in baseball, Rollie Fingers who was a pitcher, William Wordsworth who was a poet, Francine Prose who was a novelist, and Mickey Bass who was a musician? Perhaps such occurrences simply indicate that some people are inspired subliminally by their names to gravitate towards occupations suggested by them.

In a controversial 2002 study, Pelham, Mirenberg, and Jones found that individuals were more likely to choose jobs, careers, and professions with names that were similar to their own names. Similarly, in 2010, Abel and Kruger found that doctors and lawyers were more likely to have surnames that referred to their professions: people with the surname *Doctor* were more likely to be doctors than lawyers, whereas those with the surname *Lawyer* were more likely to be actual lawyers. They also found that doctors and lawyers whose first or last names began with three-letter combinations alluding to their professions ("doc," "law") also showed a significant relationship between name and profession. And they found, remarkably, that the initial letters of doctors' last names were significantly related to their subspecialty: for instance, someone named *Raymond* was more likely to be a radiologist than a dermatologist. Frank Nuessel, a professor of linguistics at the University of Louisville has coined the tongue-in-cheek term *aptonym* to refer to names that mirror the name-holder's profession, although he claims that aptonyms are more coincidental than psychologically motivated (Silverman and Light 2011).

In fact, to claim that a name impacts on life decisions is an extraordinary claim that will require extraordinary evidence. Nevertheless, we seem to feel intuitively that there is a grain of truth in aptonyms. I have actually known a number of people who have told me that they were inclined towards a particular profession because of their names. Whatever the truth, it is clear that names, identity, and social behaviors are intrinsically intertwined.

Naming trends, actually, are remarkably stable in most societies. This is because, as mentioned, names link people to culture and tradition. According to the United States' Social Security Administration, one-fourth of the top twenty names given in 2004 in America were the same as those given way back in 1880. The top five names for girls and boys in the two eras, according to that governmental agency, are as follows:

Table 5.1 Naming Patterns in America

1880	2004
Girls	
Mary	Emily
Anna	Emma
Emma	Madison
Elizabeth	Olivia
Minnie	Hannah
Boys	
John	Jacob
William	Michael
James	Joshua
Charles	Matthew
George	Ethan

In 1880, the top twenty boys' names were given to more than half of all the boys born in that year; in 2004 they were given to around 20 percent. The top twenty girls' names were given to around 34 percent of all girls born in 1880; in 2004, they were given to 14 percent. Among the ostensible reasons for this differential pattern is the fact that families are smaller today. Nevertheless, the names given today, even in a highly trendy pop culture milieu such as ours, tend, in the end, to be those that are consistent with tradition. This does not mean that people do not break away from tradition. In our celebrity culture, it is not unusual for children to be named in non-traditional ways. The late rock musician and composer Frank Zappa (1940–1993), for instance, named his daughter *Moon Unit* and his son *Dweezil*. Recently, Gwyneth Paltrow called her child *Apple*. Although this is somewhat consistent with the tradition of naming children after flowers (*Daisy, Lily, Rose*), it is rare (to the best of my knowledge) that a child would be named after a fruit. Perhaps Paltrow's intention was to connect her child to the many symbolic connotations built into the apple.

5.3.2 Nicknames

Nicknames are memorable and more likely to stand out than real names because they are more colorful and vivid. For criminals, they are part of how they define themselves, alluding to something in a gangster's character, appearance, or background that is thought to have import or significance. Lucky Luciano, born Salvatore Lucania, was called "Lucky" because of the noticeable large scars around his neck that permanently recorded his fortuitous escape from death after being slashed and left for dead by criminal rivals. The nickname of "Scarface" was given to Al Capone because he was involved in a fight that left him with three noticeable scars on his face. The nicknames became personal brands, emphasizing toughness and fierceness. In actual fact, Mafiosi have been long aware of the brand value of names. Frank Costello, known as the "Prime Minister" of Cosa Nostra in the 1930s and 1940s in the US, was quoted by *Time* magazine, as follows (*Time*, November 28, 1949, p. 16):

> I'm like Coca-Cola. There are lots of drinks as good as Coca-Cola. Pepsi-Cola is a good drink. But Pepsi-Cola never got the advertising Coca-Cola got. I'm not Pepsi-Cola. I'm Coca-Cola because I got so much advertising.

Luciano Leggio was a ruthless gangster who put on a good show for the cameras. The nickname of *La Primula Rossa* ("Scarlet Pimpernel"), by which he was known, probably comes from the 1935 movie of that name, a remake of an early silent version, which revolves around an aristocratic hero during the French Revolution, who hides his identity as an idle, useless person, but masquerades as the mysterious hero Scarlet Pimpernel, who gallantly rescues aristocrats sentenced to death. Leggio was certainly gallant in appearance, but vicious in his life. Leggio was also nicknamed "The Professor," probably because of his inclinations to pontificate to other clan members. A gangster is a nobody until he is given a nickname. As Nicaso and Lamothe (2005: 41) aptly observe, all thieves have nicknames, as part of the remaking of their identity. Made men are re-named men:

> Those who are brought into the formal underworld may have had nicknames in their former lives; however, when initiated they're given new names or allowed to choose one. Some names describe a physical characteristic—Vyacheslav Ivankov, for example, was called Yaponchik because of the Asiatic cast to his eyes. Others might be for a thief's attitude: Tank or Dashing. A home invader might be called Madhouse because of his single-minded wrecking of a victim's house.

Nicknames are essentially character profiles. An example is the one given to Michele Greco, born in Palermo in 1924 into a family with strong Mafia ties. He came to be known as *Il Papa* ("The Pope") because of the power he wielded as head of a prominent clan known appropriately with the religious epithet of *La Cupola* ("The Cupola"). Incidentally, his brother, Salvatore, was known as "Ciaschiteddu" ("Little Bird") Greco, because he was raised on a citrus fruit grove where birds would flock. Appearance, character, and affiliation are the main semantic features used in the creation of many nicknames. Antonino "Manuzza (Little Hand)" Giuffrè, for instance, the acting head of the Caccamo *mandamento* (territory), got his nickname because of his deformed right hand, mangled on account of a hunting accident. The vicious Totò Riina was also nicknamed "U curtu (Shorty)" for the self-explanatory reason that he was a short man. Pino "Scarpuzzedda (Little Shoe)" Greco was an underboss of the Ciaculli Family, and a leading hitman for the clan. His Mafioso father was nicknamed "Scarpa" ("Shoe")—hence his nickname. In a similar vein, American racketeer Joseph Lanza was nicknamed "Socks" because of his tendency to settle disputes with his fists (as in *to sock someone*).

Hip-hop culture introduced the practice of using nicknames, known as *tags*, as part of a new form of identity-construction among followers. For a few years, these were commonly etched on the urban landscape—on bus shelters, buses, subways, signs, walls, freeway overpasses, mailboxes—with markers, spray paint, or shoe polish (*Futura 2000, Phase 2, Zephyr, Crash*). In this way, hip-hop teens advertised their new identity to everyone. To symbolize the event, the tag was decorated with crowns, stars, arrows, underlines, halos, and other pictures. There were two main forms of decoration—*throw-ups* and *pieces*. The former consisted in spray-painting one's new name in bubble, block, or some other expansive style; the latter in decorating it with characters from cartoons or with proverbs. In such cities as Los Angeles and New York hip-hop teens made thousands of murals.

Actually, the history of nicknaming is highly interconnected to various emphases in a society. The Vikings have nicknames to celebrate someone's achievements; Indonesians use nicknames as forms of politeness; in Indian society, people have at least one nickname as part of a system of affection (showing some interesting thing about the person); and the list could go on and on. Clearly, they form an unofficial, yet powerful, form of LI. Among the motivating factors in nicknaming, the following are the main ones:

- *Appearance*: As we saw, the nickname "Scarface" alluded to an aspect of Al Capone's appearance. Often, these are given offensively or ironically, but this is not always the case. Among the categories are: (a) weight ("Skinny," "Fatso"); (b) height ("Shorty," "Flagpole"); (c) hair ("Blondie," "Curly"); (d) complexion ("Zit Face," "Pinky"); (e) other ("Metal mouth," "Four-eyes").
- *Character and personality*: Some nicknames are descriptors of character or personality: "Chatterbox" (talkative person), "Sleepy" (tired person), "Brainiac" (smart person), "Sherlock" (logical thinking person), and so on.
- *Lifestyle:* Lifestyle is also a source of nicknaming practices: "Jock" (sports enthusiast), "Hot Lips" (promiscuous person), "Nerd" (odd lifestyle).
- *Abbreviation or modification:* Shortening of a name can be a source of nicknaming, adding nuances to a name: "Maggie" (friendliness), "Bobbie" (cuteness or shortness), "Ed" (familiarity). Initials are sometimes used for distinctiveness purposes: "JJ," "JR," and so on. Suffixes are sometimes descriptors: "Danny" (little Daniel); "Jeannie" (little Jean).

As can be seen, nicknames have a plethora of functions—they can express irony, affection, description, and so on and so forth. These are not the official names given at birth, they are the names developed by others in social contexts. Nicknames select and amplify some aspect of personality, appearance, or behavior. They are clearly part of one's LI, whether desired or not.

5.4 e-LIs

The internet encourages self-styled constructions of identity. The coinage of handles—the names that users create for themselves in order to enter and interact in chatroom situations and in cyber communications generally—and hashtags are cases-in-point. These are essentially nicknames. But while in the past nicknames were given to people by others, in cyberspace individuals rename themselves. Handles are personal brands that seemingly empower individuals to construct their LI on their own terms. In effect, the internet is changing not only language itself in specific ways, but also assigning linguistic authority to people in truly radical ways that have obvious implications beyond language.

This has, of course, implications for identity theory. Recall from above that it was Erik Erikson, following on the coattails of Sigmund Freud, who emphasized the importance of identity-construction at adolescence. He claimed that an identity crisis would occur when an adolescent struggled with inner conflicts before gaining a sense of purpose and moving into adulthood. But in the past the sense of identity was shaped by adolescents in response to peer models of identity. Today, the identity has a much more narrative autobiographical aspect to it, as can be seen by visiting profiles online. In other words, the new social media are allowing adolescents (and others) to stay connected with their past, even if in an interpretive way.

5.4.1 Online Identities

Some young people want to efface their birth persona and L-profiles, "trying on" a different identity in a perilous fashion. This was the theme, actually, of a PBS documentary (January 22, 2008) called *Growing up Online*. The filmmakers spoke to a number of teenagers about their online habits. One girl nicknamed "Autumn" was a fourteen-year-old who felt that she "never fit the mold" in her New Jersey town, and was horribly teased about it as a result. So, she reinvented herself online as Autumn Edows, a sexy model and creative artist. She took scantily clad photos of herself and posted them on her personal blog. She began to enjoy all the attention she was receiving, having attracted many new friends through her online persona and compiled hundreds of comments telling her she was beautiful, sexy, and artistic. She was constantly on her computer, and her parents had absolutely no knowledge of her online social life. She herself was somewhat unsure of her new identity, although she did feel empowerment: "I didn't feel like myself, but I liked that I didn't feel like myself." When the school principal found out and deemed her photographs pornographic, her mother intervened and forced her to delete every single file. Her popularity disappeared and she fell back into a depressive state. Autumn responded by saying that such intervention devastated her: "If you have something that is that meaningful to you, to have it taken away is like your worst nightmare."

The filmmakers also spoke to a group of girls who, in the fall of 2006, began trading insults on MySpace. They would post comments on their profiles, and verbally fight for no reason, displaying their conflict publically on the site. In reality, however, there was no real turbulence, until "they had left a comment on one of their friends' page talking about her," and she blurted out: "You can't say it to my face. I'm right here," which resulted in a brawl. The school principal later reported having seen students videotaping the fight, which was posted on YouTube. Afterward, both groups of girls reported feeling "famous."

If L-profiles and LIs are embedded in specific linguistic structures, then the implications of these tendencies in CMC are obvious. As Marshall McLuhan (1964) claimed, before the advent of the internet age, the constant leveling off of group differences through the influence of the media would actually produce a negative reaction, at least temporarily, leading to new forms of allegiance to the group. This may explain why dialect speech in some parts of the world is, paradoxically, undergoing a type of resurgence through the digital media. It is doing so in three main ways: (1) as a complete adoption of the local dialect for inter-group communication in online groups; (2) as an occasional option for a similar purpose; (3) as part of a code-switching system to convey a new sense of regional group identity.

Given that social media are fast becoming spaces where identity is forged through writing (profiles) and multimodality (photos, videos, and so on), how is the identity-construction process unfolding and, indeed, does LI still matter? Because of the predominance of online communication, it comes as little surprise to see the study of this question burgeoning. Eckert and McConnell-Ginet (1999: 185) characterize online speech communities as groups "whose joint engagement in some activity or enterprise is sufficiently intensive to give rise over time to a repertoire of shared practices," among which emerging linguistic practices are dominant. This involves control over content and register depending on situation. In other words, language practices dovetail almost perfectly with new identity practices (Bucholtz 1999). As Spolsky (1999) suggests, language is not only a means for us to present our own notion of who we are, but it is also a way for others to project onto us their own suppositions of the way we must be. An overview of the work conducted on language and identity online can be found in Barton and Lee (2013). Generally, it shows that people are indeed renegotiating their identities in new ways and that these are more and more influencing the very sense of LI. Interestingly, and more to the point of the present discussion, online LIs are born proximately, not distantly (see above). LI is therefore highly variable and this means that the F2F version of LI and the CMC version are now co-existent, as surveys point out—people are aware of the linguistic differences and assume that possessing two LIs—an online and offline one—is a fact of contemporary life. The former can be called an e-LI (electronically-forged LI) and the latter r-LI (real-world LI).

In a study of South Korean youth, Kyongwon Yoon (2003) found that there were three kinds of relationships teens maintained via a blend of e-LIs and r-LIs. The first was to connect primarily with those who were a part of their daily lives; for example, to keep in touch with school companions and friends in their immediate environments. The second was to maintain relationships with those who were a part of a broader social network, such as friends who attended other schools. The third was to develop and acquire new friendships and to strengthen initial F2F encounters. In effect, Yoon concludes, the new technology has allowed young people to become more and more united to each other. A perusal of Facebook sites not only confirms this finding, it also shows that the identity profile posted online reflects diversity in relationships. So on the same profile one would find an identity system that reflected relationships with close friends that was different with presentations of oneself that were directed at others.

All this has clear implications for traditional LI theories. In the past the sense of Self was negotiated by people through interaction with others in real space. Today, identity has a much more virtual–pliable aspect to it. There is an inherent r-LI-versus-e-LI blending at work in the constitution of identity today. Social networking sites are appealing to people not because they are virtual, but because they are self-constructed.

Online nicknames are mainly self-established, not given (as mentioned). They are essentially pseudonyms (in the traditional literary sense of the word), which reveal varying amounts of personal information. Not all nicknames are determined in this way; gamers (previous chapter) typically negotiate their online nicknames with others in a specific gaming community—a pattern that clearly breaks from previous nicknaming traditions. In such a community, the avatar becomes the identity of the user. The avatar then acquires a reputation, which assigns to it social nuances such as trustworthiness or its opposite. Incidentally, the use of online pseudonyms has raised social concerns. The term *nymwars* refers to these concerns and the movement to mandate the use of legal names in online contexts. As this shows, the name continues to have great social significance and, while the internet is changing many things in terms of one's LI, it is not altering how we view names legally and historically.

5.4.2 Constructing e-LIs

As e-LIs and r-LIs become more and more systematic aspects of overall LI, traditional notions of dialect, speech communities and the like are changing in tandem. Distance theory is merging with proximate theory to produce what may be called hybridization theory, or the view that two identities will co-exist (Rushkoff 1996; Tapscott 1998; Prensky 2001). As e-identities and r-identities continue to merge there will be little awareness of the difference and an amalgam will result that will define the future course of identity-formation. As Gelder (2007: 143) has aptly put it, the internet offers people "a realm where one's yearnings for community can at last find their realization." In a sense the internet has provided the perfect medium for people to write themselves into existence, not take their identities from others.

E-LIs allow social media users to manage impressions and relationships through strategic uses of naming styles (Bazarova, Taft, and Choi 2013). This is due to the merging of audiences in social media and the variety of participation structures they present, including different audience sizes and interaction targets. The researchers examined self-presentational and relational concerns through the analysis of language styles on Facebook. They collected a corpus of status updates, wall posts, and private messages from 79 participants. The messages varied in certain characteristics of language style, revealing differences in underlying self-presentational and relational concerns based on the publicness and directedness of the interaction. Positive emotion words correlated with self-presentational concerns in status updates, suggesting a

Five-Factor Model of Personality

A model used in psychology and sometimes in sociolinguistics that uses five broad domains to define personality.

1 Openness to experience: the degree of intellectual curiosity, creativity and a preference for novelty and variety.

2 Conscientiousness: tendency to be organized and dependable and to show self-discipline.

3 Extraversion: outgoing, energetic, positive with a tendency to seek the company of others.

4 Agreeableness: friendly, with a tendency to be compassionate and cooperative.

5 Neuroticism: sensitive, nervous, with a tendency to experience unpleasant emotions easily.

strategic use of positive language in public and nondirected communication via status updates. Verbal immediacy correlated with partner familiarity in wall posts but not in private messages, suggesting that verbal immediacy cues serve as markers to differentiate between more and less familiar partners in public wall posts. In other words, self-presentation on Facebook involves language manipulation with online language style.

Studies such as this one are giving rise to the idea of hybrid or blended LIs (e-LIs blended with r-LIs). Gruzd, Wellman, and Takhteyev (2011) found that this dualism can be related to the fact that communication on some social media, such as Twitter, is asymmetrical—"If you follow me, I do not have to follow you." This means that there is less in-person contact among the followers, but, nevertheless personal communities coalesce in Twitter where identities are negotiated in similar ways to how they are in loose social networks offline. Ross, Orr, Sisic, Arsenault, Simmering, and Orr (2009) used a Five-Factor Model of personality with Facebook friends who generally met offline as well as on the social medium. They found that personality was not affected by the online medium as previous work had claimed. They suggest that Facebook may promote the fashioning of identity, but that it has so many uses that the issue of personality and identity is not as crucial as, for instance, the need to stay in contact with friends.

They found that individuals who were high on the trait of "extraversion" belonged to significantly more Facebook groups; but surprisingly levels of extraversion did not correlate with number of friends. This suggests that extraverts may use Facebook as a social tool, but that they do not use it as an alternative to social activities offline. Overall, the researchers found that personality factors were not as crucial in Facebook contexts, with users maintaining their profiles to match their offline personalities and identities. This study has obvious importance for sociolinguistics generally since it seems to affirm that LIs are still negotiated in real spaces and blended with online LIs. The issue is still an open one. Maybe Facebook is not as important as it was as an online social site when it first appeared. Perhaps it is now an offline-to-online social networking system that carries with it the same patterns that apply to LI specifically in F2F contexts.

In contrast to these findings, Nakardni and Hofmann (2012) discovered that Facebook is not only a social site (allowing people to belong to some community), but also a power venue for self-presentation. Using the same Five-factor model, they found that those who are neurotic, narcissistic, shy, have low self-esteem and self-worth tend to be heavy Facebook users and reshape their identity through the site. They also found, however, that the utilization of Facebook according to personality varied according to cultural and social variables. In effect, the study showed that the same factors that influenced LI in F2F contexts played the same roles in social media.

Page (2012) found that Twitter, like Facebook, is a "self-branding" marketplace. She discovered that hashtags play a key role in this process, since they promote updates, and thus by implication, authorship, through a visual channel. Analyzing approximately 92,000 tweets and comparing the discourse styles of corporations, celebrity practitioners, and ordinary users, she found that self-branding practices correlate with social and economic hierarchies that exist in offline contexts. In other words, the offline world has simply been translated into the Twitterverse, with very few, if any, adjustments. Self-branding exists in offline contexts but, it would seem, that Twitter and other social media continue the process, just diffusing it more broadly.

The ambiguous findings of such studies suggest that identity-construction patterns will vary according to community (real or virtual) but that they resemble each other in the final product. Research on this question is ongoing. As Walther (2012: 397) puts it, this whole area of research involves "the expression of affect and immediacy online, the virtual presentation of self and gender, the management of online conversations, adaptation via visual grounding in electronic collaboration, and the employment of online interaction technology to reduce intergroup prejudice." In effect, the social world is changing because of social media and, although some of these issues cross virtual and real spaces, there are now new cues to study them across these spaces.

The four main areas of e-sociolinguistic research in this thematic area are as follows:

1   *Impression management* or personal identity formation through the information internet users provide on sites such as Facebook. To what degree can this information be used to glean insights on LI?

2 *Friendship management* or the use of the profiles of others in order to decide whom they want to follow or to join others; users look at the identity markers of others for establishing criteria of social interaction.
3 *Network structure* or the roles that users play in their particular virtual communities.
4 *Bridging* of online and offline social networks in order to determine to what extent the real and the hyperreal have merged.

Terminology Review

Define or explain in your own words the following terms introduced or elaborated upon in this chapter.

frame analysis	hyperreal
idiolect	indexical identity
linguistic identity	linguistic profile
name	nickname
ritual conflict	surname
symbolic identity	verbal duel
Whorfian Hypothesis	

Exercises and Discussion

1 Read the following excerpt from K. Gibson (English Only Court Cases Involving the U.S. Workplace: The Myths of Language Use and the Homogenization of Bilingual Workers' Identities, 2004):

> *Language—both code and content—is a complicated dance between internal and external interpretations of our identity. Within each community of practice, defined by Eckert and McConnell-Ginet (1999, p. 185) as groups "whose joint engagement in some activity of enterprise is sufficiently intensive to give rise over time to a repertoire of shared practices," certain linguistic (among other) practices are understood by the members to be more appropriate than others. While monolingual speakers are restricted to altering the content and register of their speech, bilingual speakers are able to alter the code, as well as content and register, of their language dependent upon the situation. Speakers who embrace the identity of a particular community will engage in positive identity practices, while those who reject the identity will use negative identity practices to distance themselves from it (Bucholtz, 1999). However, this framework only takes into account the intentions of the speaker, and neglects the role of the hearer. Conflict arises when the hearer has a different understanding of the speaker's identity than the one the speaker desires. The tension is further compounded when the hearer is in a position of power and can not only misinterpret the desires of the speaker, but can actively thwart*

this expression, forcing the speaker into an entirely different, perhaps unwanted, identity. This plays out daily in the workplaces of America, where English Only policies are enforced to maintain the powerful hearers' view that good workers speak English among themselves and refrain from other, inappropriate, languages.

If you speak another language and consider yourself to be a bilingual, do you sense a shift in personality when you switch languages? Explain.

2   Read the following excerpt from A. Patel (Slang Words: What Are Young People Saying These Days? 2012):

"Moss," "merked," "reach" and "dip." If you have no idea what those words mean, don't beat yourself up too much—this is just everyday teenage lingo. Teens tend to have a language of their own, but if you feel like infiltrating the crowd (or even just trying to understand some tweets), we have a guide to help you sort through the jargon. And with the holidays just around the corner, it could be useful to pick up a few key phrases to blend in with the younger folks at your holiday dinner—without looking completely out of place. Last year, our teenage slang list included words and phrases like "epic fail," "photobomb" and "lipdub," which just goes to show that some things never change—they just get reused over and over again. But 2012 also brought about mainstream recognition for a few words, like "f-bomb," "sexting," "bucket list" and the Oprah-inspired "aha moment," which were all added to the Merriam-Webster Dictionary's 2012 list.

Do you know any of the slang items mentioned? If so, explain them in your own words.

3   Identify the source language or strategy and original meaning from which the following names are derived.

name	Source	Meaning
Christopher		
Danielle		
Alexander		
Sarah		
Mark		
Lucy		
Sunny		
Violet		
Laura		
Blanche		
Hugh		

4   Identify the source and meanings of the following surnames.

Surname	Source	Meaning
Rivers		
Singer		
Cardinal		
Dickenson		
Woods		
Fox		
Clinton		
Bush		
Eliot		
Hill		
Bergman		

5   What aspects of contemporary English speech (words, phrases, mannerisms, protocols) would you consider to be part of hip talk? Do you think they are part of identity? Explain why.

6   Read the following excerpt from F. Grosjean (From: Life as a Bilingual: Living with Two Languages, 2011):

> *Bilingual 1:* "*When I'm around Anglo-Americans, I find myself awkward and unable to choose my words quickly enough … When I'm amongst Latinos/Spanish-speakers, I don't feel shy at all. I'm witty, friendly, and … I become very out-going.*"
>
> *Bilingual 2:* "*In English, my speech is very polite, with a relaxed tone, always saying "please" and "excuse me." When I speak Greek, I start talking more rapidly, with a tone of anxiety and in a kind of rude way…*"
>
> *Bilingual 3:* "*I find when I'm speaking Russian I feel like a much more gentle, "softer" person. In English, I feel more "harsh," "businesslike."*"
>
> *Could it be that bilinguals who speak two (or more) languages change their personality when they change language? After all, the Czech proverb does say, "Learn a new language and get a new soul."*

Do you think that speaking a particular language makes a bilingual feel differently? Explain why you think so.

7   Read the following excerpt from M. Warschauer (Language, Identity and the Internet, 2000):

> *As it turns out, though, the fears of an English-dominated Internet were premature. Recent analysis indicates that the number of non-English websites*

*is growing rapidly and that many of the more newly active Internet newsgroups
(e.g., soc.culture.vietnamese) extensively use the national language
(Graddol 1997, 61). Indeed, by one account the proportion of English in
computer-based communication is expected to fall from its high of 80 percent
to approximately 40 percent within the next decade (Graddol 1997).
Underlying this change of direction is a more general shift from globalization
to relocalization. The first wave of globalization – whether in economics or in
media – witnessed vertical control from international centers, as witnessed
for example by the rise of media giants such as CNN and MTV. But in more
recent waves, a process of relocalization is occurring, as corporations seek to
maximize their market share by shaping their products for local conditions.
Thus, while CNN and MTV originally broadcast around the world in
English, they are now producing editions in Hindi, Spanish, and other
languages in order to compete with other international and regional media
outlets.*

Do you think that the use of English on the internet has diminished, as the
author maintains? If so, what language do you think would be used in the
two following situations?

(a) CMC between an English speaker and a speaker of another language
who knows English; and the English speaker also knows the other's
language.
(b) CMC between speakers of different languages, but who know English
to some degree.

8   Read the following excerpt from T. Grant (The Linguistic Cues That
Reveal Your True Twitter Identity, 2013):

*Twitter is awash with trolls, spammers and misanthropes, all keen to ruin
your day with a mean-spirited message or even a threat that can cause you
genuine fear. It seems all too easy to set up an account and cause trouble
anonymously, but an emerging field of research is making it easier to track
perpetrators by looking at the way they use language when they chat. The first
Twitter criminal? The #TwitterJokeTrial was an early, if unfortunate,
example of an apparent Twitter crime. Paul Chambers, frustrated at being
prevented from visiting his girlfriend when snow disrupted transport, tweeted:
"Crap! Robin Hood airport is closed. You've got a week and a bit to get your
shit together otherwise I'm blowing the airport sky high!!" Chambers was at
first prosecuted for sending a message of "menacing character", but he later
raised a successful appeal against his conviction. The message was nevertheless
clear: be careful what you write, either be nice or be anonymous. Anonymous
virtue? We've learned from these incidents that if you want to say something
controversial or aggressive on Twitter, you'd probably better do it from an
account not tied to your real name. The perceived anonymity of Twitter
trolls seemed to facilitate the trolling attacks experienced by Caroline*

Criado-Perez and Stella Creasy MP this summer. Criado-Perez and Creasy had been running a campaign to have a woman represented on UK bank notes, and so became subject to a vitriolic misogynist attack, all via the medium of Twitter. In this case, policing has led to arrests, despite the fact that trolls opened multiple accounts to hide their identities when conducting their attacks.

If you are on Twitter, what linguistic cues do you use to identify yourself?

9   Do you think that linguistic identity is being recast in virtual spaces or is it the same identity that is being managed for specific social (rather than just virtual) reasons?

10   After having read the chapter and the texts, how would you characterize your own linguistic identity? If you have acquired a language other than English in childhood, point out some of its characteristics that make it unique and thus "personal" for you. Does this make up part of your identity?

References

Abel, E. L. and Kruger, M. L. (2010). Athletes, Doctors, and Lawyers with First Names Beginning with "D" Die Sooner. *Death Studies* 34: 71–81.

Bakhtin, M. M. (1981). *The Dialogic Imagination*. Trans. C. Emerson and M. Holquist. Austin: University Press.

Baldwin, J. (1985). *The Price of the Ticket*. New York: St. Martin's.

Barton, D. and Lee, C. (2013). *Language Online: Investigating Digital Texts and Practices*. London: Routledge.

Bateson, G. (1936). *Naven: A Survey of the Problems Suggested by a Composite Picture of the Culture of a New Guinea tribe Drawn from Three Points of View*. Stanford: Stanford University Press.

Baudrillard, J. (1983). *Simulations*. New York: Semiotexte.

Bazarova, N., Taft, J., and Choi, Y. (2013). Managing Impressions and Relationships on Facebook: Self-presentational and Relational Concerns Revealed through the Analysis of Language Style. *Journal of Language and Social Psychology* 32: 121–141.

Bucholtz, M. (1999). Why Be Normal? Language and Identity Practices in a Community of Nerd Girls. *Language in Society* 28: 203–225.

Bucholtz, M. and Hall, K. (2005). Identity and Interaction: A Sociocultural Linguistic Approach. *Discourse Studies* 7: 585–614.

Cooper, D. and Anderson-Inman, L. (1988). Language and Socialization. In: M. Nippold (ed.), *Later Language Development*, pp. 225–245. Boston: Little, Brown and Company.

Danesi, M. (1994). *Cool: The Signs and Meanings of Adolescence*. Toronto: University of Toronto Press.

Duranti, A. (2003). Language as Culture in U.S. Anthropology: Three Paradigms. *Current Anthropology* 44(3): 323–348.

Eble, C. (1989). *College Slang 101*. Georgetown, Conn.: Spectacle Lane Press.

Eble, C. (1996). *Slang and Sociability*. Chapel Hill: University of North Carolina Press.

Eckert, P. and McConnell-Ginet, S. (1999). New Generalizations and Explanations in Language and Gender Research. *Language in Society* 28: 185–201.

Eder, D. (1990). Serious and Playful Disputes: Variation on Conflict Talk Among Female Adolescents. In: D. Grimshaw (ed.), *Conflict Talk*, pp. 67–84. Cambridge: Cambridge University Press.

Edwards, J. (2009). *Language and Identity*. Cambridge: Cambridge University Press.

Erikson, E. H. (1950). *Childhood and Society*. New York: Norton.

Erikson, E. H. (1968). *Identity: Youth and Crisis*. New York: Norton.

Firth, J. R. (1950). Personality and Language in Society. *The Sociological Review* 42: 37–52.

Freud, S. (1905). *Drei Abhandlungen zur Sexualtheorie*. Frankfurt am Main: Fischer.

Freud, S. (1913). *Totem and Taboo*. New York: Norton.

Freud, S. (1923). *The Ego and the Id*. New York: Norton.

Gelder, K. (2007). *Subcultures: Cultural Histories and Social Practice*. London: Routledge.

Gibson, K. (2004). English Only Court Cases Involving the U.S. Workplace: The Myths of Language Use and the Homogenization of Bilingual Workers' Identities. *Second Language Studies* 22: 1–60.

Goffman, E. (1974). *Frame Analysis*. New York: Harper and Row.

Grant, T. (2013). The Linguistic Cues That Reveal Your True Twitter Identity. *Pandodaily*, http://pando.com/2013/11/21/the-linguistic-clues-that-reveal-your-true-twitter-identity/ (accessed 6 May 2015).

Grosjean, F. (2011). Life as a Bilingual: Life with two Languages. *Psychology Today*, www.psychologytoday.com/blog/life-bilingual/201111/ (accessed 6 May 2015).

Gruzd, A., Wellman, B., and Takhteyev, Y. (2011). Imagining Twitter as an Imagined Community. *American Behavioral Scientist* 55 (10): 1294–1318.

Gusdorf, G. (1965). *Speaking*. Evanston: Northwestern University Press.

Hudson, R. (1984) *Invitation to Linguistics*. Oxford: Robinson.

Kroskrity, P. V. (1998). Arizona Tewa Kiva Speech as a Manifestation of Linguistic Ideology. In: B. B. Schieffelin, K. A. Woolard, and P. Kroskrity (eds.), *Language Ideologies: Practice and Theory*, pp. 103–122. New York: Oxford University Press.

Kulick, D. (1992). *Language Shift and Cultural Reproduction: Socialization, Self and Syncretism in a Papua New Guinea Village*. Cambridge: Cambridge University Press.

Labov, W. (1972). *Language in the Inner City*. Philadelphia: University of Pennsylvania Press.

Maltz, D. and Borker, R. (1982). A Cultural Approach to Male-Female Communication. In: J. Gumperz (ed.), *Language and Social Identity*, pp. 196–216. Cambridge: Cambridge University Press.

McLuhan, M. (1964). *Understanding Media: The Extensions of Man*. London: Routledge.

Nakardni, A. and Hofmann, S. G. (2012). Why Do People Use Facebook? *Personality and Individual Differences* 52: 243–249.

Nicaso, A. and Lamothe, L. (2005). *Angels, Mobsters & NarcoTerrorists: The Rising Menace of Global Criminal Empires*. Toronto: John Wiley Canada.

Ochs, E. (1988). *Culture and Language Development: Language Acquisition and Language Socialization in a Samoan Village*. Cambridge: Cambridge University.

Ochs, E. (1993). Constructing a Social Identity: A Language Socialization Perspective. *Research on Language and Social Interaction* 26: 287–306.

Ochs, E. and Schieffelin, B. B. (1984). Language Acquisition and Socialization: Three Developmental Stories and Their Implications. In: R. Shweder and R. A. LeVine (eds.), *Culture Theory: Essays on Mind, Self, and Emotion*, pp. 276–320. New York: Cambridge University Press.

Ochs, E. and Taylor, C. (2001). The Father Knows Best Dynamic in Dinnertime Narratives. In: A. Duranti (ed.), *Linguistic Anthropology: A Reader*, pp. 431–449. Oxford: Blackwell.

Page, R. (2012). The Linguistics of Self-Branding and Micro-Celebrity in Twitter: The Role of Hashtags. *Discourse & Communication* 6: 181–201.

Patel, A. (2012). Slang Words What Are Young People Saying These Days? *Huffington Post*, www.huffingtonpost.ca/2012/12/19/slang-words (accessed 12 May 2014).

Pelham, B. W., Mirenberg, M. C., and Jones, J. T. (2002). Why Susie Sells Seashells by the Seashore: Implicit Egotism and Major Life Decisions. *Journal of Personality and Social Psychology* 82: 469–487.

Pennebaker, J. W. (2011). *The Secret Life of Pronouns*. London: Bloomsbury Press.

Prensky, M. (2001). Digital Natives, Digital Immigrants, www.marcprensky.com/writing (accessed 23 June 2014).

Rampton, B. (1995). *Crossing: Language and Ethnicity Among Adolescents*. London: Longmans.

Ross, C., Orr, E. S., Sisic, M., Arsenault, J. M., Simmering, M., and Orr, R. (2009). Personality and Motivations Associated with Facebook Use. *Computers in Human Behavior* 25: 578–586.

Rothman, J. and Rell, A. B. (2005). A Linguistic Analysis of Spanglish: Relating Language to Identity. *Linguistics and the Human Sciences* 1: 513–536.

Rumsey, A. (1990). Word, Meaning, and Linguistic Ideology. *American Anthropologist* 92(2): 346–361.

Rushkoff, D. (1996). *Playing the Future: How Kids' Culture Can Teach Us to Thrive in an Age of Chaos*. New York: Harper-Collins.

Schieffelin, B. B. (1990). *The Give and Take of Everyday Life: Language Socialization of Kaluli Children*. Cambridge: Cambridge University Press.

Schieffelin, B. B. (1995). Creating Evidence: Making Sense of Written Words in Bosavi. *Pragmatics* 5(2): 225–244.

Schieffelin, B. B. (2000). Introducing Kaluli Literacy: A Chronology of Influences. In: P. Kroskrity (ed.), *Regimes of Language*, pp. 293–327. Santa Fe: School of American Research Press.

Schieffelin, B. B. (2002). Marking Time: The Dichotomizing Discourse of Multiple Temporalities. *Current Anthropology* 43: 5–17.

Silverman, R. E. and Light, J. (2011). Dr, Chopp, Meet Congressman Weiner: What's in a Name? *The Wall Street Journal* (2011): http://online.wsj.com/article.

Silverstein, M. (1976). Shifters, Linguistic Categories, and Cultural Description. In: K. Basso and H. A. Selby (eds.), *Meaning in Anthropology*, pp. 11–56. Albuquerque: University of New Mexico Press.

Silverstein, M. (1979). Language Structure and Linguistic Ideology. In: R. Cline, W. Hanks, and C. Hofbauer (eds.), *The Elements: A Parasession on Linguistic Units and Levels*, pp. 193–247. Chicago: Chicago Linguistic Society.

Silverstein, M. (1985). Language and the Culture of Gender: At the Intersection of Structure, Usage, and Ideology. In: E. Mertz and R. Parmentier (eds.), *Semiotic Mediation: Sociocultural and Psychological Perspectives*, pp. 219–259. Orlando: Academic Press.

Spolsky, B. (1999). Second-Language Learning. In: J. Fishman (ed.), *Handbook of Language and Ethnic Identity*, pp. 181–192. Oxford: Oxford University Press.

Tapscott, D. (1998). *Growing Up Digital: The Rise of the Net Generation*. New York: McGraw-Hill.

Vygotsky, L. S. (1962). *Thought and Language*. Cambridge, Mass.: MIT Press.

Vygotsky, L. S. (1978). *Mind in Society*. Cambridge, Mass.: Cambridge University Press.

Walther, J. B. (2012). Interaction through Technological Lenses: Computer-Mediated Communication and Language. *Journal of Language and Social Psychology* 31: 397–414.

Warschauer, M. (2000). Language, Identity and the Internet. In: B. Kolko, L. Nakamura and G. Rodman (eds.), pp. 151–170. *Race in Cyberspace*. New York: Routledge.

Whorf, B. L. (1956). *Language, Thought, and Reality*, J. B. Carroll (ed.). Cambridge, Mass. MIT Press.

Yoon, K. (2003). Retraditonalizing the Mobile: Young People's Sociality and Mobile Phone Use in Seoul, South Korea. *European Journal of Cultural Studies* 6: 328–343.

6   Conversation and Discourse

You can stroke people with words.

F. Scott Fitzgerald (1896–1940)

Consider the kinds of answers given typically during normal conversations to questions of the following type:

Question: What does your sister love?
Answer: Hamburgers.

Question: Is it true that your sister loves hamburgers?
Answer: Yes, it is.

Question: Who loves hamburgers, you or your sister?
Answer: My sister.

The use of the single word "Hamburgers" in the first Q&A sequence is sufficient to give the required information asked by the questioner. In this case, it is unnecessary to utter an entire sentence ("My sister loves hamburgers"). The answer in the second sequence uses a different type of response—a response intended to confirm (or deny) what the questioner asks. And the answer in the third sequence identifies which of the two alternatives is the appropriate one.

The nature and content of the responses are determined by what linguists call *pragmatic* structure. The term *pragmatics* was coined by the American philosopher, Charles S. Peirce (1931). But it was in the 1930s that another American philosopher, Charles Morris (1938), started applying the term to aspects of language behavior. The term is now used primarily to indicate the study of the meanings and uses of linguistic forms in their communicative and interactional contexts of use. In the 1960s, British philosopher Paul Grice (see Grice 1975) added the notion of *maxims* as the basis for the study of conversational pragmatics. Grice claimed, for instance, that there is an implicit maxim of *relevance* during conversation, by which interlocutors assume that anything spoken about is intended to be relevant (whether it is true or not). It is the expectation of relevance that is at play here. When we hear someone utter that she or he is not going to be doing the driving after a party because she or he intends to drink alcohol, we presume that the utterance is relevant to what we are talking about in the conversation. If it is not connected to it, as in a conversation about upcoming tests at school, then we map its irrelevance to the situation (it could be that the interlocutor misunderstood the conversation or that he or she may be having an off day). Grice also maintained that conversations are assumed to show the maxims of *quality* and *quantity*. If someone says, "I have three grandchildren," his or her interlocutor would not conclude that the speaker does not have *any* grandchildren or just, say, *one* grandchild. Otherwise, the interlocutor would perceive the statement as a lie. In terms of the quantity maxim, the interlocutor would infer that the speaker has exactly *three* grandchildren, not four or five.

The answers in the Q&A sequences above reveal that grammatical and lexical choices in conversations are not governed strictly by rules of grammar, but by rules of communication and by maxims. One of these is, clearly, that complete sentences are not necessary in such situations. In other words, conversations are not guided solely by *linguistic competence* but also, and more pointedly, by *communicative competence*.

In the previous chapters the focus was on how the internal bits and pieces of a language system (phonemes, morphemes, and so on) crystallize in speech (in dialects, sociolects, and so on) that mirrors social phenomena such as identity, gender, class distinctions, age, regional origin, and other such variables. However, the sociolinguistic analysis of language would not be complete if we stopped at this point. Language is a highly adaptive and context-sensitive instrument that is shaped by its uses in conversations and by the implicit rules of interaction that these entail. The internal structures of language are pliable entities that are responsive to external social situations. The ways we use language in conversations constitute primary vehicles for establishing, maintaining, defining, and cueing social relations, roles, categories, and so on. This chapter will look at these ways.

6.1 Conversation

The responses used in the Q&A in each case are not interchangeable. This simple, yet instructive, example shows that the choice of words and the types of structures that are utilized in conversations will vary systematically and are, therefore, rule-governed. This kind of practical knowledge is different from the knowledge of word-formation or sentence structure in themselves. It constitutes a pragmatic form of knowledge known as communicative competence. The term was coined by American linguist Dell Hymes (1971), as stated previously. His notion brought about an intense interest in pragmatics, which soon after started accumulating data showing that the ability to use a language appropriately in specific interactive settings was adaptive. Hymes even claimed that it had an effect in shaping and even changing linguistic competence. A simple protocol such as making contact with someone, for instance, requires a detailed knowledge of the appropriate words and nonverbal cues that will enable a speaker to be successful. It requires, in other words, both *communicative* and *linguistic* knowledge. An infringement of any of the procedural details of the communication might lead to a breakdown in a conversation.

In the 1980s and 1990s the serious study of conversations led to many new ideas about the relation between language use and social variables. The goal of such study, called conversation analysis (CA), is to document how people understand and respond to each other in conversations. Some of the findings of CA are consistent with the work on *speech acts* (also mentioned earlier), which started in the early 1960s, after British philosopher John L. Austin (1961) suggested that by speaking a person performs an *act* (such as stating, predicting, or warning), and that the meaning of the act is to be found in what it brings about. CA and speech act analysis share a lot of the same theoretical and research territories.

6.1.1 Conversation Analysis

The founding aim of CA is to show that how people talk not only taps into a system of implicit social rules and patterns, but also shapes and changes the formal language system itself. Hutchby and Wooffitt (1998: 14) delimit the goal of CA as follows:

> CA is the study of recorded, naturally occurring talk-in-interaction. Principally, it is to discover how participants understand and respond to one another in their turns at talk, with a central focus being on how sequences of interaction are generated. To put it another way, the objective of CA is to uncover the tacit reasoning procedures and sociolinguistic competencies underlying the production and interpretation of talk in organized sequences of interaction.

The tacit reasoning procedures to which Hutchby and Wooffitt refer are manifestations of communicative competence, suggesting that knowing how to use language during conversation is as systematic as knowing the grammar of the language being employed. Since then, the study of communicative competence has fallen into the subfield of pragmatics, which, as Morris (1938) claimed already in the 1930s, should actually be a branch of semiotics aiming to study how form and meaning in language and other codes vary according to situational and contextual factors. After the early work on CA in the 1980s, communicative competence became a major area of interest within sociolinguistics. By recording naturally occurring conversations in context, many facts emerge, such as how participants understand and respond to one another in socially significant ways.

In CA lexemes, morphemes, and sentences are studied as units within conversational texts. Personal pronouns, for example, are viewed not as part of a grammatical system, but as trace devices, serving conversational needs, which maintain the smooth flow of conversation by connecting its parts like an electrical network of wires. Consider, for instance, the following two texts, which tell the same story in different ways:

1   Sophia went to the mall a few days ago. Sophia ran into an old friend at the mall. Sophia hadn't seen the friend in a while. Sophia and the friend were thrilled.
2   Sophia went to the mall a few days ago. *She* ran into an old friend *there*. Sophia hadn't seen *her* in a while. *They* were thrilled.

The first text is perceived as stilted and odd, even though each sentence in it is well-formed when considered in isolation. The second text reads more like ordinary conversation because in English, as in other languages, repetition is perceived as hampering the communicative flow. For this reason, the language makes available several devices that allow for the same information to be conveyed without the repetition and thus to preserve the flow. Devices that refer back to some word or syntactic category are called *anaphoric*. In (2) above, *she* refers back to *Sophia*, *there* to *the mall*, *her* to *the friend*, and *they* to *Sophia and the friend*. Anaphora is a "repetition-eliminating" conversational strategy that is part of communicative competence. The converse of anaphora is *cataphora*.

Review of Some Relevant Grammatical Terms

Pronoun: Any word that can replace a noun or noun phrase, such as *you*, *he*, *him*, *mine*, and so on.

Subject pronoun: A pronoun that functions as the subject of a sentence. Its form often indicates this function: *I*, *you*, *he*, *she*, *they*, and so on.

Object pronoun: A pronoun that functions as the object of a sentence. Its form often indicates this function as well: *me*, *him*, *her*, *them*, and so on.

Locative: Any word that refers to place or location: *here*, *there*, *up*, *down*, and so on.

Demonstrative: A word that specifies whether something or someone is relatively near or far: *this car*, *that car*, *these ideas*, *those ideas*.

Adverb: A word that indicates the manner, time, or location connected with some action: *often*, *slowly*, *clearly*, *there*, and so on.

This involves the use of a lexeme, morpheme, and so on that anticipates some other unit. For example, in the sentence "Even though she will deny it, I tell you that Mary did it," the pronoun *she* refers ahead to *Mary*. Subject and object pronouns, locative particles, demonstratives, adverbs, and other kinds of morphemes, often function as anaphoric and cataphoric devices in conversations.

This type of analysis highlights the fact that the sentences in conversations have a different composition and even structure than if they were considered in isolation. In CA sentences are studied as text-governed forms, that is, as part of the logical structure of the text which includes keeping the flow of the conversation smooth and economical. In this view of language, it is obvious that sentence-based grammar is seen as telling only a small part of the story. In a pragmatic approach to grammar, therefore, personal pronouns are seen as trace devices and repetition-reducing strategies, not only as grammatical forms. They are designed, as mentioned, to keep a conversation flowing smoothly with minimal effort. The choice of pronouns is thus not due to rules of syntax; but to rules of *parole*—a realization that led to the formation of a branch of linguistics called *systemic linguistics* or *functional grammar*, headed in the 1970s and 1980s by Michael A. Halliday (1985). Although there is much leeway in the grammatical and lexical choices that can be made to carry out a conversation successfully, the research in systemic linguistics has shown that these choices are nonetheless constrained by factors such as situation, social rules, and style. By the 1990s, text linguistics based on corpus structure, came forward to lead the way in the study of the *langue–parole* interplay.

Sometimes the term *gambit* is used to refer to devices that cohere in various ways within a conversation. Gambits are used to open a conversation, to keep it going, to repair any anomaly within it, and so on. The following are common English gambits:

1   Uh huh… yeah… hmm… aha…
2   It's, like, she never meant it, you know, …
3   You like this, don't you?
4   May I ask you something?
5   She arrived a few hours ago; sorry, I meant a few minutes ago.

The grunt-like expressions uttered in (1) are hedges; they are devices that allow a listener to make it known to a speaker that he or she is in fact listening, especially on the phone. The word "like" and the phrase "you know" in (2) are fillers; they allow a speaker to gather his or her thoughts before proceeding to the next part of an utterance, thus maintaining the ground in a communication situation, rather than conceding it to an interlocutor. Total silence is not a hedge or filler gambit in English, although it may be in other languages. The gambit in (3) is a tag question—a strategy that is designed to seek approval, agreement, consent, not an answer. Utterance (4) is an opening gambit for starting a conversation, taking a turn within a conversation, or entering into a conversation. In English, expressions such as "May I?" "Sorry, but could you tell me…?" "Excuse me?" are all opening or interceding gambits. Utterance (5) is a repair. When there is a minor breakdown in a conversation, or something is not explained properly, repairs allow the speaker to solve the problem. Expressions such as "sorry" and "I meant" are examples of repair gambits.

The work of Sacks, Jefferson, and Schegloff (1995) has revealed that gambits allow for a conversation to unfold in a sequential fashion with implicit structure—that is, as a set of rules that speakers intuitively utilize as they speak. The utterances of interlocutors are thus said to form *adjacency pairs*. So when someone asks something, the interlocutor knows that an answer is the appropriate follow-up in the sequence. If someone intervenes with an opening gambit, the interlocutor understands that the speaker wants to enter into the conversation. These are all adjacency pairs. The three Q&A's with which we started off this chapter form adjacency pairs with the questions used.

Overall, the study of conversations has subsequently led to the study of texts as units of linguistic analysis, rather than compositions of sentences. Sociolinguists started finding by the 1970s that when they are used in conversations words and grammatical forms cohere systematically. Consider the following stretch of conversation, which lacks anaphoric or cataphoric structure:

Speaker A: Jasmine is a lawyer.
Speaker B: Yes, Jasmine is a lawyer.
Speaker A: Jasmine always likes to talk about Jasmine.
Speaker B: Yes, Jasmine sure does like to talk about Jasmine.

Each sentence, when considered individually, is well-formed grammatically, but the conversational text as a whole is perceived as awkward. It does not lack sentence structure; it lacks "text structure." An appropriate version of the same text is the one where pronouns are used as traces to the nouns (see above):

Speaker A: Jasmine is a lawyer.
Speaker B: Yes, *she* is.
Speaker A: *She* always likes to talk about *herself*.
Speaker B: Yes, Jasmine sure does like to talk about *herself*.

Conversational texts show that we are sensitive to *sequence* structure. We anticipate how the forms in a text relate to each other and cohere sequentially into a message-making system.

Another area of interest in pragmatics concerns what is called the social framing of speech. Conversations can be aggressive or subdued, competitive or cooperative, depending on situation. In the case of competitive speech, the language used is typically adversarial, whereas in the case of cooperative speech, the language used indicates that the speakers are inclined to work together to produce shared meanings. In other words, competitive or cooperative speech acts have identifiable characteristics. Cooperative speech, for instance, is marked by features such as the following:

1 Speakers tend to build upon each others' comments ("That's true," "I agree").
2 They tend to use well-placed hedges to indicate consent ("Uh-huh," "Yeah," "Sure," "Right").
3 Disagreement is rare, and when it surfaces, a difference of opinion is negotiated with various hedges ("Yeah, but, maybe...").
4 Tag questions are used often to ensure consent ("You agree, don't you?").

This behavior imparts a sense of togetherness among speakers. As Robin Lakoff (1975) has observed, speakers regularly refrain from saying what they mean in many situations in the service of the higher goal of politeness or cooperation in its broadest sense, that is, to fulfill one of the primary social functions of conversation, which has been called the phatic function (see also Watts 2003). Competitive or conflictual conversations are marked just as saliently by specific strategies that stand in direct opposition to the ones above:

1 Speakers tend to contradict one another's comments ("That's really not true," "I wouldn't say that").
2 They tend to use hedges to indicate dissent ("No-no," "No way," "Not true").
3 Difference of opinion is indicated with different kinds of hedges or fillers ("Sure, but, maybe...").
4 Tag questions are used to challenge ("You don't mean that, do you?").

6.1.2 Grice's Maxims

As stated briefly above, one of the notions used in CA is that of maxims. It was Herbert Paul Grice (1975, 1989), a British philosopher, who came up with this notion after studying the logical structure of arguments during conversations and the implications this had for human interaction. His definition of conversational maxims is an implicit set of principles of human interaction that make people enter into conversations in the first place. Without these principles we hardly would want to engage in conversation, although it happens all the time, as in court cross-examinations, police interrogations, and so on where people know from the outset that they may not apply. Grice's maxims are as follows:

1 *Maxim of quantity*: (i) this asserts the interlocutors tend to make their message as informative as required for the purposes of the exchange; and (ii) that they generally do not make it more informative than required.

2   *Maxim of quality*: this asserts that interlocutors expect the contents of an utterance to be true, because (i) people tend not to say what they believe to be false, and (ii) they will likely not say something for which they lack adequate evidence.

3   *Maxim of relation or relevance*: this asserts that interlocutors enter into a conversation because they believe that it will be relevant.

4   *Maxim of manner*: this asserts that interlocutors will tend to be perspicuous by (i) avoiding obscurity of expression, (ii) avoiding ambiguity, (iii) being brief, and (iv) being orderly.

These maxims remind us that we tend to perceive communications as part of ethical behavior. When a conversation turns out to violate the maxims we actually react negatively to the speaker. In effect, conversations are fraught with danger and thus require a lot of strategic interaction to keep them "honest," or at least seemingly so. It is the expectation that is at play here, not necessarily the reality, since people break the maxims all the time for various reasons. Grice also pointed out that most of the meanings that are built into utterances are implicit, rather than explicit. He called the process *conversational implication*. He illustrated it as follows (Grice 1989: 306):

A: How is John getting on with his new job at the bank?
B: Oh, quite well I think; he likes his colleagues, and he hasn't been in prison yet.

B's answer seems to contain an irrelevant remark about John having not been in prison yet. A, however, likely infers that B was implying something more, such as, for instance, that John "is the sort of person likely to yield to the temptations provided by his occupation" (Grice 1975: 306). How does A arrive at this conclusion? Grice proposed that it occurred through a cooperation on the part of the interlocutors reflecting a "common purpose, or set of purposes" upholding the reason behind the conversation. The interlocutors want to be cooperative, contributing meaningfully to the purpose of the exchange. So, A extracts from B's utterance that B wanted to communicate more than what he actually said. It is this pattern of inferential reasoning that characterizes utterance meaning and which, obviously, can be a source of misunderstanding in many conversations.

6.1.3 Speech Acts

The notion of *speech act* has become a central one for CA, since it provides a taxonomy for pigeonholing utterances in terms of their social functions. A speech act is an utterance that aims to bring about, modify, curtail, or inhibit some real action. The utterance "Be careful!," for instance, would have the same effect as putting a hand in front of someone to block him or her from crossing the road carelessly. The statement "I sentence you to life imprisonment" uttered by a judge has the same effect as marching the accused directly to prison and locking him or her up. The interesting thing about speech acts is that they influence the composition and flow of sentences, showing again that linguistic and communicative competencies intersect constantly.

There are various versions of speech act theory. The central idea in all of these is that linguistic structures are sensitive to situations, including the social status of the speakers, their ages, the intent of each one, the goal of the conversation, and so on and so forth. In other words, speech acts allow people to carry out social functions. The main ones are:

1   *Locutionary*, the act itself of saying something and in which things are said with a specific sense ("The moon is a sphere;" "My name is Mark;" "She said, 'You can't go out tonight. It's my birthday'.").
2   *Illocutionary*, an utterance that indicates the speaker's purpose in saying something—asking and answering questions, giving information, assurance, identifying, promising, ordering, and so on ("I'll do it, sooner or later;" "Come here!" "She protested against what I said").
3   *Perlocutionary*, an utterance that produces sequential effects on the feelings, thoughts, or the actions of interlocutors or else conveys a speaker's own emotional state ("I'm sorry;" "Don't worry;" "Go ahead, tell me everything;" "She stopped me, bringing me around").

Each of these acts can be broken down further as follows (Searle 1969; Nastri, Pena, and Hancock 2006):

1   *Representatives*, utterances that commit the speaker to something: stating, concluding, representing, deducing ("I will do it for you").
2   *Assertives*, statements of fact so as to get an interlocutor to form or attend to a belief ("What the President said is a fact").
3   *Effectives*, statements designed to change something ("You're fired").
4   *Directives*, attempts by the speaker to get an interlocutor to do something: command, offer, invite, ask, request, beg, permit, dare, challenge ("Just do it").
5   *Commissives*, utterances committing the speaker to some future course of action: promise, pledge, threaten ("Only a few days to go").
6   *Expressives*, utterances revealing the psychological state of the speaker toward something: thank, congratulate, apologize, condole, deplore, welcome ("Your music is amazing").
7   *Declarations*, utterances connecting propositional content (assumptions in the utterance) to reality: appoint, resign, nominate, pronounce ("I am leaving this job because of what I said to you").
8   *Quotations*, utterances reporting someone else's speech ("She said that she was coming too").

Speech acts are units of conversation providing a connection to social life. Many of these are used in overlapping and complementary ways. They do not explain conversations; rather, they allow us to refer to their functions or their intents in specific ways. Searle characterized a speech act as language that both describes and is the action. Through speech acts an individual not only "acts" within the world but also "interacts" with the world around him or her. The individual thus influences the attitudes and actions of everyone involved in the act. Speech act analyses have taken many forms across multiple media. Cultural differences between interlocutors can often be traced to differences in the forms of the acts themselves, since it is assumed that, regardless of language background, communication is designed to create meaning and purpose through the speech act.

6.2 Communicative Variables

Sometimes, speakers may refrain from saying what they desire for reasons of politeness or cooperation in its broadest sense, that is, to fulfill one of the primary social functions of conversation, which has been called the *phatic* function. The following excerpt of conversation is typical of how we make phatic contact using words and expressions as politeness-bearing forms, rather than literally:

A: Hi, how's it going?
B: Great. See ya' later.
A: OK!

Speaker A's question "How's it going?" has no literal meaning. It is used simply as a polite form of contact, with a well-wishing subtext built into it. This fact is clearly understood by B, whose adjacency answer ignores the literal meaning. Indeed, if B had said something different, such as "It is not going well," then the conversation would have taken a completely different turn. Clearly, knowing how to frame speech in conversation entails an awful lot of knowledge of how language and situation intersect. The sequences that occur in conversations are thus strategies that "provide participants with resources for displaying evaluations of events and people in ways that are relevant to larger projects that they are engaged in" (Goodwin and Goodwin 1992: 181). As Goffman (1978: 814) perceptively remarked, our utterances often make "a claim of sorts on the attention of everyone in the social situation," and that each situation is grounded in cultural presuppositions that reveal themselves through the language used. In effect, most conversations are grounded in unstated knowledge.

Dell Hymes (1971) identified eight basic variables that shape communicative competence. He cleverly named each variable so that its initial letter would be a letter in the word *speaking*:

S   = *setting* and *scene*: the time, place, and psychological setting of a conversation

P   = *participants*: the speaker, listener, audience involved in a conversation

E   = *ends*: the desired or expected outcome of the interaction

A   = *act sequence*: the sequence in which the parts of a conversation unfold

K   = *key*: the mood or spirit (serious, ironic, jocular, etc.) of the speech act

I   = *instrumentalities*: the dialect or linguistic variety used

N   = *norms*: conventions or expectations about volume, tone, rate of delivery

G   = *genres*: different types of performance (joke, formal speech, sermon).

These are the main components of communicative competence. Note that it relates to how language forms are incorporated into usage, suggesting that it may be more crucial than linguistic competence. This is a controversial issue, though, and need not be discussed here. Suffice it to say that abstract knowledge of language structures forms in the mind of the child, as Hymes argued, only as these are used in actual communication.

6.2.1 Modeling Communication

The work on speech acts is really one possible way to simply model communicative competence. Another often-cited model is the one put forward by the Moscow-born American linguist Roman Jakobson (1960). The model identifies the main functions and constituents of communicative competence in a comprehensive way, allowing the sociolinguist to examine these in contexts and with the usual research tools of the field. First, there are six main constituents that make up verbal communication:

1   an *addresser* who starts (or addresses) a communication; the addresser can be a single person, an organization, or any other entity capable of communicating something;

2   a *message* that he, she, or it constructs for some reason or in response to something;

3   an *addressee* to whom the message is addressed; the addressee can be a single person (as in a conversation), an audience, and so on;

4   a *context* in which the message is constructed and which gives it overall meaning; for example, the utterance "Help me" would have a different meaning depending on whether it was spoken by someone lying motionless on the ground or by a student in a classroom working on a difficult math problem;

5   a mode of *contact* by which a message is delivered; this involves the social and psychological connections that exist or are established between the

addresser and addressee; it could be face to face, through a chatroom, on Facebook, and so on; the mode can thus be synchronous, occurring at the same time (as in oral conversation or through devices such as instant-messaging devices); or asynchronous, occurring in a delayed fashion (as in e-mails);

6   a *code* providing the expressive forms or resources (language, gesture, facial expressions, and so on) for constructing and deciphering messages meaningfully and efficiently.

Each of these constituents determines or involves a different communicative function:

1   *emotive*, which comprises the addresser's emotions, attitudes, social status; emotivity here refers to the addresser's intent, which, no matter how literal his or her message might be, will invariably reveal the reason why he or she entered into a speech act in the first place;

2   *conative*, which is the effect (physical, psychological, social) that the message has or is expected to have on the addressee;

3   *referential*, which is a message constructed to carry information unambiguously; it is also the term indicating that any message is perceived as referring to something other than itself;

4   *poetic*, which is a message constructed with poetic style; this can be found, for instance, in the love messages given at Valentine's Day ("You are my sweetheart;" "I give you my heart and soul"); but it also occurs in other contexts for effect;

5   *phatic*, which is a message designed to establish or ensure continuous social contact ("Hi, how's it going?");

6   *metalingual*, which is a message referring to the code being used ("The word I just used is a foreign word").

This model suggests that ordinary conversations go well beyond situations of simple information transfer. They involve determining and comprehending who says what to whom; where and when it is said; and how and why it is said. These are determined by knowledge of how the code, contact, emotivity, and other factors involved produce sense and meaning.

The notions of phatic function and context require further commentary. At a pure contact level, the phatic function ensures fluid social continuity. So, for example, when two office workers pass each other in the morning and say, "Hi, how's it going?" "Not bad, and you?" they are not literally inquiring about each other's health. The adjacency pairs are part of phatic speech and are intended solely for making contact and keeping the social relation going. All kinds of rituals and social practices are based on phatic communication, which is not intended to create new meanings but to reinforce ritualistic ones and, thus, to ensure social cohesion. The term context is not a synonym for setting. The words used in communication point to the place (here, there), time (now, then), and specificity (this, that) of a communication event. In other words, language tells us where something is going on, how it is going on, what is going on, and so forth

6.2.2 Speech Functions

Long before the work on speech acts and CA, already in the early 1920s, anthropologist Bronislaw Malinowski (1922) saw language as fulfilling and serving specific functions. For example, he was the one who coined the term *phatic communion*, as the exchange of words and phrases that are important less for their dictionary meanings than for establishing social contact. From Malinowski's work came the notion of *speech function*, which was taken up in the 1920s and early 1930s by several linguists, including Sapir (1921) and Whorf (1956). Essentially it implies that speech mirrors social functions, from classification of the environment to making contact ritualistically.

Various typologies have been put forward as frameworks for studying speech functions. Some of these are summarized below:

1 *Instrumental*, the use of language to satisfy material needs: "May I have some water please? I'm thirsty."
2 *Regulatory*, the utilization of language to control others: "Please shut the door."
3 *Interactional*, the exercise of speaking with no actual meanings as such, but simply to maintain social ties and relations, filling in blanks in a conversation, making contact, and so on: "Hi, how's it going?"; also called *phatic* (as we have seen above).
4 *Personal*, using language as a means to express oneself emotionally: "Ouch!" "Hey, leave me alone!"
5 *Heuristic*, employing language to gain information: "What's that?" "Can you explain the Pythagorean theorem to me?"
6 *Imaginative*, the use of language to convey unique ideas creatively: "I wonder why time flies?"
7 *Representational*, using language to represent things, that is, to classify the world in specific ways.
8 *Performative*, the use of language in rituals and performances (magic, prayers).
9 *Socialization*, utilizing language to indicate a connection to a society, community, or group.

Most of these functions show that language is, as Blot (2003: 3) aptly puts it, "a badge of identity." Speaking in certain ways provides access to specific groups or communities in a society or else enacts expected social events and actions. Individuals seek entry into groups to order their social lives, to reduce the complexities of the world, or simply to show allegiance to a certain lifestyle or worldview. Belonging implies controlling specific linguistic cues.

6.2.3 Politeness: A Case-In-Point

The topic of politeness puts on display how communicative competence unfolds in the enactment of a specific speech function. We all use politeness cues unconsciously. Using the *tu* (familiar) forms to a stranger in France, rather than the *vous* (polite) forms, will be considered impolite or rude, unless the speaker is conspicuously a foreigner. Saying *ciao* ("hi"), rather than *scusi* ("excuse me") to a stranger in Italy in order to get his or her attention will similarly be perceived as rude, unless the speaker is a foreigner. Such linguistic forms are perceived as breaks in social manners, not a lack of linguistic knowledge.

Politeness is constrained by culture, and therefore what is considered polite in one society can sometimes be perceived as being rude or eccentric in another. Penelope Brown and Stephen Levinson (1987) have argued that politeness is related to *face*, or the public self-image that we want to claim for ourselves (Goffman 1955: 213).

In English this is conveyed with speech protocols such as "If it's OK,..." "I really hope you don't mind,..." and so on. These are indirect speech acts that are designed to show or convey deference. As such, they allow us to present, in effect a "face," which in this case conveys a sense of respect for one's interlocutor. Politeness is also intended to display a positive relationship with an interlocutor and thus is grounded in direct speech acts, such as "Could you please pass the salt?" "Excuse me, do you know where this building is?"

Politeness Strategies

"If you don't mind..."

"If it's no bother,..."

"I hope this isn't too much trouble..."

"Glad to make your acquaintance..."

"Sir, you are right..."

"Dr. Smith, my apologies..."

"Please, can you help me out?"

"Excuse me, do you know where this street is?"

Politeness strategies include juxtaposing criticism with compliments, establishing common ground through humor, tag questions and other markers of group solidarity, such as code-switches, jargon, and the like. Common ground is the term used to refer to information that interlocutors perceive to be shared. Brown and Levinson argue that it is a major strategy of politeness, which unfolds as a series of conversational tactics that are designed to recognize the partner's needs and wants in a way that shows they represent a commonality of knowledge, attitudes, interests, goals, and so on.

Research on politeness and gender shows that women generally use more polite speech than men. This often occurs in societies where, historically, women have had a secondary role in society vis-à-vis the men. Therefore, it is expected in such societies that women show more politeness. The same has been shown for class differences. Meyerhoff (2006), for example, found that those who were reared in speech communities that are more oriented towards negative face will tend to employ negative politeness strategies. They may be perceived as aloof or rude in communities where positive politeness is the norm. Conversely, people reared in communities where positive face is an attribute, tend to use positive politeness and interpret those who do not as boorish or vulgar.

Overall, Brown and Levinson identified three sociological variables that guide the choice of politeness strategies in specific situations: (1) the social distance of the interlocutors; (2) the relative power of one interlocutor over the other; and (3) the absolute ranking of impositions in the culture. The greater the social distance between the interlocutors, the more the use of positive politeness in interaction. Analogously, the greater the relative power of one interlocutor over another, the more expectation of politeness on the part of the lower-ranking interlocutor. And the heavier the imposition made on an interlocutor (the more his or her time is required, or the greater the favor asked), the more the politeness level of speech.

6.3 Discourse and Dialogue

Terms such as conversation, dialogue, and discourse are used interchangeably both in society and, often, by language experts. This is likely because they are perceived to be different facets of the same communicative competence. But there are differences. Superficially, the main difference between *conversation* and *dialogue* is one of intentionality. Conversations are adaptive to situation— they guarantee social cohesion (Grice's maxims), they allow for speech acts to fit into life agendas (Jakobson), and so on. The *dialogue*, on the other hand, has traditionally served different functions, even though it involves interlocutors. Above all else, it is a teaching tool and a means for achieving self-understanding. The dialogue was used by the Greek philosopher Socrates as a kind of question-and-answer exchange that his pupil Plato later called "dialectic reasoning."

The so-called "Socratic method" is still used in pedagogy in order to impart knowledge and skill to learners.

Discourse refers to a broader social use of language. The importance of discourse in social theories was put forward as early as the 1920s by the Russian literary critic Mikhail M. Bakhtin (1981), who anticipated many key notions of current discourse theories. He was the first to use the term to denote the particular way in which language is used by specific groups for social or ideological purposes. This is why one can talk about "political discourse" or "sports discourse," in reference to the kinds of language used by certain people or groups to reveal shared values, worldviews, beliefs, biases, and so on. These "discourses" are typically characterized by keywords that appear frequently in speech acts (Stubbs 2008). As Scollon and Wong Scollon (2001) have amply documented, discourses are characterized by a jargon, register, style, and coded structures shared by the members of the group, and especially by specific ways of communicating that in their subtexts imply a particular ideology.

6.3.1 Discourse

Discourse is found in most social situations—families, schools, corporations, universities, the media, and other groups that develop styles which determine how people speak both within and outside the group. Some of Bakhtin's more important ideas include the notion that discourse is context-based involving: (1) the specific physical place or physical medium in which speech is used; (2) a shared knowledge system based on cultural presuppositions; and (3) a shared evaluation of the meaning of a context. In essence, discourse style makes sense only in a context and this means different things to different groups of speakers. It is implanted in human activities that assign recurrent and recognizable roles to participants and greatly constrain the kind of utterances that can be exchanged. This implies that discourses are grounded in *genres*. These can be written or spoken, dialogic or monologic (internal speech). Genres include such speech acts as speeches, job interviews, university lectures, medical consultations, courtroom interactions.

Discourses are connected to previous speech acts, assuring sense and coherence to the individual speech acts, allowing them to be perceived as being connected to each other in an unbroken discourse chain. This means that discourse is *intertextual* and *interdiscursive*, directly or indirectly citing or alluding to previous meaningful speech through some specific strategy (imitation, presupposition, rejoinder, critique, parody, and so on). Intertextuality is the term used to refer to speech that brings into it various important texts for the group. For example, the Bible figures prominently in Christian discourse. Some texts are *canonical* for a certain discourse community: for example, the Bible, Shakespeare, Martin Luther King's speeches, and the like are canonical for, say, religious groups, English scholars, and politicians respectively.

Discourse Glossary

Common ground:

the sense among interlocutors participating in a discourse style that they share common beliefs.

Genres:

types of discourses reflecting specific styles of delivery—speeches, interviews, and so on.

Intertexuality:

allusion to cultural texts (the Bible, Shakespeare, and so on) during discourse ensuring the common ground.

Interdiscursivity:

connection of one particular discourse event to others that are well-known to the group.

Interdiscursivity refers to the connections that are made in group speech acts to other speech events that are meaningful to the group. For example, a university professor interacting with a colleague might refer to something that was said recently at a conference they both attended in order to discuss its implications.

Overall, discourse analysis involves figuring out why people speak the way they do, not just how. Discourse allows speakers to insert their intentions and worldviews into speech acts, which reveal ideological orientations. Discourse can also be subdivided into *specialized* and *common*. The former is the type of discourse that is used by specialized groups—doctors, lawyers, mechanics, and the like. The latter is the type that emerges from a setting and is incorporated into the speech habits of people in that setting. The speech styles that are promulgated by media events fall under this rubric. In other words, there is a "media discourse" or a "pop culture discourse," to which most people have access.

Common discourse, like all discourses, is recognizable through so-called *keywords*. Take, for example, the word *cool* used to describe attractive lifestyles. This comes out of pop culture and is now an intrinsic part of common discourse. It refers by suggestion to a stylish and smart mode of dressing, acting, and talking that is in synch with the times. Flappers in the 1920s were cool; rock stars are cool; rappers are cool; celebrities are cool; and so on. Synonyms for *cool* have cropped up in modern media and pop culture history. They include *hip*, *groovy*, and *hot*. The last word is now a common keyword to indicate that someone or something is sexy (including morphemic variants such as *hottie*). The word was used in the 1920s to describe the New Orleans style of jazz, with its syncopated rhythms and fast tempi, as exemplified by Louis Armstrong's performances. A 1933 film named *Hot Pepper*, with Lupe Vélez playing a sexy siren, epitomized, and probably ensconced, the use of *hot* as a code word for "sexual allure." From the 1930s to the 1960s the expression *hot pants* emerged as a "slang term" for sexy men and women. So, the use today of *hottie* in a sexual sense has really been a part of common discourse for a long time.

In a phrase, common discourse emerges from trends in culture. It is highly intertextual and interdiscursive. *Animal House* (1978) introduced slang terms still used today, such as *wimp*, which is a commonly-used term for someone who is scared or has no courage, and *brew* which means getting a beer. *Clueless* (1995) introduced keywords such as *As if*, an exclamation of disbelief, and *whatever* to convey disinterest in what another person is saying. In 2004, the film *Mean Girls* helped spread a new form of discourse used by young females across North America, with words such as *plastic*, meaning fake girls who look like Barbie dolls, and *fetch* which is an abbreviation of fetching to describe something cool and trendy.

The foregoing discussion is meant to emphasize how strongly the modern media have influenced common discourse styles. The term *pop language* was introduced by journalist Leslie Savan in the book, *Slam Dunks and No-Brainers* (2005) to refer to this type of discourse. Throughout contemporary society, Savan notes, people are using a style, which seems to carry with it a built-in applause sign or laugh track. Phrases such as "That is so last year," "Don't go there," "Get a life," "I hate it when that happens," "It doesn't get any better than this," come from television sitcoms and popular movies. This type of discourse is used by ordinary people, claims Savan, because it emanates from popular media and is thus perceived to be contemporary and meaningful.

Savan decries the abuse of language in common discourse. Her point seems to be that in the past, the primary conduits of new language were writers. Shakespeare, for instance, brought into acceptable usage such terms as *hubbub*, *to bump*, and *to dwindle*. But not before the twentieth century did it become routine for the conduits to be pop culture and the media. The number of keywords that have entered the communal lexicon since the 1960s is truly mind-boggling, constituting strong evidence that pop culture in all domains of modern-day life has become a major social force.

6.3.2 Ritualistic Discourse

In addition to specialized and common discourses, the term ritualistic discourse is used to designate the kinds of speech forms that characterize rituals and rites. Ceremonies, rallies, debates, university lectures, and the like revolve around ritualistic discourse, either frozen (formulaic) or created on purpose. Ann Gill (1994: 106) describes the power of such discourse as follows:

By portraying experience in a particular way, words work their unconscious magic on humans, making them see, for example, products as necessary for success or creating distinctions between better or worse—be it body shape, hair style, or brand of blue jeans. Words create belief in religions, governments, and art forms; they create allegiances to football teams, politicians, movie stars, and certain brands of beer. Words are the windows of our own souls and to the world beyond our fingertips. Their essential persuasive efficacy works its magic on every person in every society.

In various ancient societies, knowing or using the name of a god was believed to bestow great power on someone—as mentioned previously, in Egyptian mythology, Isis tricked Ra into revealing his name, thus gaining power over him and other gods. In some cultures, the ritual of bestowing an ancestral name to a newly-born is perceived to bring with it all the qualities of the ancestor, weaving a sort of magical protective aura on the individual so named. The Inuit, for instance, believe that a newborn baby cries because it wants its name, and will not be complete until it gets it. In some traditional Inuit tribes, an individual will not pronounce his or her name, fearing that this senseless act could break the magical spell of protection that it brings with it. As Espes Brown (1992: 13) puts it: "the fact that when we create words we use our breath, and for these people and these traditions breath is associated with the principle of life; breath is life itself. And so if a word is born from this sacred principle of breath, this lends an added sacred dimension to the spoken word."

Linguistic rituals do not create new meanings; rather, they have a phatic function, ensuring cultural cohesion. Ritualistic speeches (homilies, prep rallies, and so on) tap into the shared beliefs of groups and are thus intended to unite members in a common worldview or cause. These create a "word magic" that keeps people bound to each other literally through the power of performed words in rituals.

6.3.3 Critical Discourse

An important area of analysis is so-called *critical discourse analysis* (CDA), which aims to describe and interpret discourses in social contexts and to offer explanations of why and how they work. In CDA, the term *critical* is applied to the power relations that exist in discourse situations among the interlocutors. A common example used by CDA to show how power is embedded in language is the difference between *this* and *that*. When a speaker says "This is true" it foregrounds the topic to a level of importance, while "That is true" backgrounds it, thus taking away its power and also showing a differential power relation among speakers. CDA aims to show that discourses are formed historically to enact power relations. The dominant discourses are those associated with education, the law, the government, and other authoritative agencies. These are reproduced and reinforced constantly.

CDA views discourse as social practice, focusing on how power and political domination are embedded in texts and discourses of various kinds. Fairclough (1992) developed a three-pronged approach to CDA, so as to be able to separate critical discourse from other types:

1   The analysis of texts (spoken or written) in order to glean from them presuppositions and cues that signal differential relations.
2   The analysis of discourse practices themselves, such as text production, distribution, and consumption (that is, who decides which texts get out there and have influence).
3   The analysis of events that certain discourses bring about (such as at pep rallies).

For critical discourses to be effective they must be intertextual and interdiscursive, that is allude to other canonical texts (see above) and to form a chain of texts that people perceive as giving them coherence. This chain creates belief by virtue of the fact that it resounds with authority. The assumption of CDA is that social structures, power structures, and discourse are intertwined.

6.3.4 Dialogue

Dialogue involves specific or skilled uses of language. It is found in all kinds of social spaces, from the theatrical and narrative arts, to education and courtroom interactions. Dialogue can be defined as a purposeful use of speech to achieve knowledge, understanding, or to impart sense (as in a play) to something. It was Plato who introduced the systematic use of dialogue as a distinctive form of philosophical inquiry. Except for the *Apology*, many of Plato's major writings are constructed in dialogical form. After Plato, the dialogue was relegated primarily to the literary theatrical domain, although it is said that Aristotle (Plato's pupil) wrote several philosophical treatises in dialogical style, none of which, however, has survived. The dialogue was revived somewhat by early Christian writers, especially St. Augustine, Boethius, and somewhat later by Peter Abelard. However, under the powerful influence of Scholasticism, the dialogue was replaced by the more formal and concise genre of the *summa*, or synthetic treatise, of which the most emblematic is the one written by medieval theologian St. Thomas Aquinas.

The dialogue was reintroduced into scientific and philosophical inquiry by various European thinkers starting in the late seventeenth century. For example, in 1688, the French philosopher Nicolas Malebranche published his *Dialogues on Metaphysics and Religion*, contributing to the genre's revival. The Irish prelate George Berkeley employed it as well in his 1713 work, *Three Dialogues between Hylas and Philonous*. But perhaps the most well-known use of the dialogue was by Galileo in his *Dialogue Concerning the Two Chief World Systems* of 1632.

One of the most common uses of dialogue today is in psychotherapy. This involves entering into a dialogue on the part of the therapist with the patient and asking specific questions in order to unravel some mental issue. The questions used by the therapist are obviously aimed at detecting some factor in the patient's life that is causing problems. The trained analyst can thus use the responses to determine what the problems are. Many other settings involve this kind of dialogue (community centers, classrooms, help agencies of various kinds) in order to enable people to share their experiences about difficult problems and build an understanding of such problems. True dialogue is thus non-judgmental; it seeks to determine something.

Contrary to this type of dialogue, courtroom interrogations are often designed to get a witness or an accused person to reveal something, which may not even be connected to the truth of the matter, but is usable by the interrogator to argue for or against the innocence of an accused person. In cross-examinations this kind of dialogue can be called simply conflictual. An obvious objective of such dialogue is to obtain information. Unlike a speech (monologue), cross-examinations can proceed only with the interaction of both parties, who make agreements during the course of dialogue which facilitate the process of interrogation and reply. The idea is to get the respondent to commit to a particular position. The questioner then has the option of using the answer as the basis of further argumentation. Here is a hypothetical example:

> *Prosecutor*: Did you see the victim the day before?
> *Accused*: No, I didn't.
> *Prosecutor*: But then why did you say that you met often on that day.
> *Accused*: Something happened on that day.
> *Prosecutor*: Can you explain?

The prosecutor uses the "No" answer to connect something said previously to the situation. At this point the dialogue can take a different course, allowing the prosecutor to extract statements that he or she will need for subsequent interrogation. If the evidence has no bearing on the case, then the lawyer can still use the Q&A to cast doubt on the veracity of the accused person. By arranging the content of questions strategically, damaging admissions can be obtained. These lines of questioning are used typically to get someone to commit himself or herself to some situation: (1) "How do you know that?" (2) "What do you mean by that?" and (3) "Doesn't this contradict your previous statement?" Obtaining information and agreements, however, is not the sole purpose of cross-examinations. Of great importance is the impression made by the questioners and respondents on the judge or the jury. Because cross-examination is so revealing, it can become a basis for determining the human character of the participants. Needless to say, the assessment is not always accurate, but it is always affected in some way by the cross-examination itself.

Among the dialogical strategies used in successful cross-examination, the following main ones are highly relevant:

- The questioner should avoid appearing crafty or adversarial at first, so that the witness may let down his or her defensive mechanisms.
- The questions should be clear and comprehensible.
- The questioner should not stray from a particular line of questioning.
- The respondent must not be allowed to take over the cross-examination. This can be done by interrupting long-winded and circuitous responses. This is done typically with a simple "OK" or "Thank you."
- There may be situations in which politeness is paramount, in order to get the respondent to be compliant. This is sometimes called "playing possum," whereby the intention is to lure the respondent into admitting something he or she wants to hide.

6.4 e-Conversations

Conversations that take place in online contexts can be called, simply, e-conversations. The use of such terminology throughout this book is not to claim that online and offline speech are radically different or serve differential social functions. Rather, it is intended to emphasize that the medium in which a speech act occurs has an effect on the act and on how people perceive communication. The idea is thus to assess any differential patterns that may emerge. Text messaging (TM), for example, is constructed in real time, since both users can conduct a back-and-forth exchange, but since it involves a different medium of delivery various linguistic features emerge that apply to TM in contrast to F2F conversations. Some of these have already been discussed previously. In this section we will now look at some further research in this area and derive some general implications for sociolinguistics.

The question that is relevant in this case is the following one: Are online conversations serving the same kinds of functions as offline ones? This question, in its various facets, is something that sociolinguists have started to investigate a lot. Some of the results of the investigation are reported in this section.

Textspeak, as we have seen, is a form of shorthand that allows text message conversations (TMCs) to unfold quickly and effectively. Even the term *text messaging* is now written as *txt msg*. Textspeak developed originally in bulletin board systems and chatrooms so that users could type more quickly, relying on the redundancy features built into language: vowels, for instance, are largely predictable in written words and thus can be eliminated. For example, one can easily reconstruct the sequence *W r cmng tnght t th prty* as *We are coming tonight to the party*, even though all vowels have been removed from it.

CA applied to online contexts, such as Twitter (Gillena and Merchant 2013), has shown that the medium does not affect the functions and patterns of F2F communication to any significant degree. However, some research has found that some functions, such as politeness, are being negotiated and verbalized in new ways (Foxtree, Mayer, and Betts 2011; Carr, Schrock, and Dauterman 2012). Carr, Schrock, and Dauterman (2012) examined speech acts on Facebook. They compiled a total of 204 status messages created by 46 participants, captured 3 times daily over 14 consecutive days. A content analysis of the data revealed that status messages were most frequently constructed with expressive speech acts, followed by assertives (see above). Additionally, humor was integrated into almost 20 percent of the messages.

Members of networks can see messages posted in public areas, even if messages are developed and presented for a specific recipient in the user's network. This changes the "sentiment" that undergirds communication, making users more sensitive to messages themselves. Such conversations are both public and personal. Expressive speech acts tend therefore to emerge as prevalent, as the Carr, Schrock, and Dauterman (2012) study showed. These are based on emotional reactions to situations and used to convey feelings and are the most frequently used speech acts in social network site status update messages. The study also revealed that Facebook users are aware of the public aspects of the internet. By constructing primarily expressive and assertive messages, in tandem with often humorous overtones, users are presenting themselves in a manner that encodes personal concepts at the same time that they show sensitivity to the public forum. In other words, the conversation is aimed not only at an interlocutor but at an audience as well. It is this duality that differentiates many e-conversations from F2F ones.

One interesting aspect of e-conversations is how ironic statements are encoded and negotiated. Reyes, Rosso, and Veale (2013) found that irony is a pervasive aspect of CMC, even though it is made more difficult by the absence of F2F contact and vocal intonation. There are two broad categories of irony: verbal irony itself and verbal reports of irony (also known as situational irony). The former is a playful use of language in which a speaker implies the opposite of what is literally said; or expresses a sentiment in direct opposition to what is actually believed. Using Grice (1975), it can be said that an utterance is ironic if it violates various conversational maxims. Situational irony, in contrast, is an unexpected or incongruous quality in a situation or event that stands out conspicuously, such as a no-smoking sign in the foyer of a tobacco company, or a vegetarian having a heart attack outside a McDonald's.

The researchers found that irony is detected in several ways in tweets and text messages—through *signatures* ("you're loving person" after a bitter text), *unexpectedness* (such as throwing in a satirical comment when unexpected ("she said that she was coming, as she always does, btw"), *style* (as in F2F ironic statements, "That is so yesterday"), and *emotivity* (such as using !!!!!! after an assertive, indicating that the assertive was meant ironically). With a corpus of

40,000 tweets, automatically harvested from Twitter, the researchers found that users do not have a single, precise notion of irony; rather, they seem to possess a diffuse understanding of what it means for a text to be ironic. In other words, irony is difficult to convey in cyberspace, but it is there nonetheless; it is much more subtle.

Overall, e-conversations seem to be very much like F2F conversations, but also different. In other words, it is becoming evident that the social rules themselves for carrying out conversations are adaptive to medium of communication. As the medium changes so too does the conduct and flow of that interaction.

Terminology Review

Define or explain in your own words the following terms introduced in this chapter. Some of these have already been introduced but are elaborated upon here.

adjacency pair	anaphora
cataphora	communication maxims
communicative competence	conversation
conversation analysis	dialogue
discourse	filler
gambit	hedge
illocutionary	locutionary
perlocutionary	speech act
tag question	

Exercises and Discussion

1 Identify what is conversationally anomalous in each statement.

   Example: Greetings mother, see you later.
   Greetings normally indicates the act of making contact, not of leave-taking. It is thus anomalous in the above utterance, unless of course it is intended to be facetious or to produce a particular kind of ironic, sarcastic, or satirical effect.

   (a) Madam, I gotta split!
   (b) Gina, I wish to inform you that I am in love with you.
   (c) Little girl, could you indicate to me what your name is?
   (d) Hey little doggie, would you mind coming over here?

2 Identify each utterance as locutionary, illocutionary, or perlocutionary.

   (a) Really?

(b) It's not true.
(c) My friend lives in Italy.
(d) Tell me all that you know.
(e) Quiet!
(f) What time is it?
(g) My name is Alexander.

3 How would a 17-year-old say hello to the following today?

(a) a peer
(b) a teacher
(c) his or her mother or father.

4 Underline and identify the anaphoric and cataphoric devices in each of the following.

(a) Claudia likes the album I bought her yesterday.
(b) I gave it to Sarah, that is, the cup.
(c) Who ate the slice? I ate it.
(d) When did you go to Venice? I went there five years ago.

5 Change the following utterances, making them more appropriate conversationally by using anaphoric and cataphoric devices.

(a) My sister went downtown yesterday. My sister ran into a teacher of my sister at one of the stores that my sister went to. My sister greeted the teacher and the teacher greeted my sister. My sister had not expected to see the teacher downtown, because my sister thought that the teacher never went downtown.
(b) Even though my brother will deny it, my brother is in love with Victoria. Victoria is also in love with my brother. But Victoria does not know yet that she is in love with my brother. My brother and Victoria go to the same school. Victoria wants to become a doctor; and my brother, even though my brother is good at math, wants to become a lawyer.
(c) Mack loves Julie. Yesterday Mack saw Julie, as Julie was walking on the street. Mack has known Julie for four years, and now Mack is in love with Julie. Mack called out to Julie, and then Mack gave Julie a kiss. Mack gave Julie a kiss because Mack loves Julie. But Julie doesn't love Mack, so Julie did not appreciate the kiss.

6 Read the following excerpts as one text.
P. ten Have from Conversational Analysis Versus Other Approaches to Discourse, 2006:

> The term "conversation analysis" (CA) is by now quite firmly established as the name for a particular paradigm in the study of verbal interaction that was initiated in the 1960s by Harvey Sacks, in collaboration with Emanuel

Schegloff and Gail Jefferson. In CA the focus is on the procedural analysis of talk-in-interaction, how participants systematically organize their interactions to solve a range of organizational problems, such as the distribution of turns at talking, the collaborative production of particular actions, or problems of understanding. The analysis is always based on audio or visual recordings of interaction, which are carefully transcribed in detail.

R. Wooffitt from *Conversation Analysis and Discourse Analysis*, 2005:

Discourse analysis emerged in the sociology of scientific knowledge. It established a departure from realist accounts of scientists' actions to a study of scientists' accounting practices. It proposes that language is used variably. Accounts are constructed from a range of descriptive possibilities, and are intimately tied to the context in which they are produced and the functions they perform.

P. ten Have from *Conversational Analysis Versus Other Approaches to Discourse*, 2006:

The DA story, however, is completely different. In the larger sense of the term, there is an enormous variety of approaches, but not a relatively stable core set of ideas and methods. For DA, in the restricted sense as used by Wooffitt, the core idea is the intention to shift focus from the referents of discourse, (for instance, a mental state such as cognition), to the discursive practices through which such referents are invoked.

A. Gentle, *Twitter and Conversation Analysis—Who's Here?* 2009:

I believe that phone conversations for customer support have been studied quite a bit—looking for phrases that sound like triggers for anger, avoiding long pauses, and when one party overtakes a phone conversation, it's relatively easy to detect when that's happening. But with Twitter, you could have long pauses intentionally as asynchronous, IM-like conversations happen when someone gets up from their desk and returns after a business meeting, for example. Neither party is angry about that long pause, it's just an understood agreement in the Twitter medium that you may or may not be immediately responsive. How does that time factor change the "agreement" for a support exchange? Is Twitter reserved for the narcissistic whiners? Or are true relationships happening and caring, meaningful attention being paid to customers on Twitter?

Discuss the following:

(a) How is CA different from DA (discourse analysis)?
(b) What features of CA regard the study of communicative competence?
(c) What features of tweets are particularly interesting from a CA/DA perspective?

7   How would you rephrase the following utterances in a formal (polite) way?

Example: Come here and hurry up!
Would you mind coming here quickly?

(a) Get your butt over here!
(b) Get lost!
(c) Give me a cup of coffee right away!
(d) You stink at telling jokes.
(e) You are rude. Cut it out!
(f) Leave me alone!

8   Identify the type of gambit used in the following utterances, along with its function.

(a) Yeah…yeah…
(b) I get it, you know?
(c) You agree, don't you?
(d) Allow me…

9   Identify the communicative function(s) of each utterance. Use Jakobson's typology.

(a) Hi, Claudia. How are you?
(b) I've got a headache!
(c) See you tomorrow!
(d) Good morning.
(e) Good night.
(f) I don't like opera.
(g) Do you like Ike, as they used to say?
(h) The meaning of that word is "loving."
(i) Bloor Street is two blocks north of here.

10 Give examples of utterances that might be used for the following functions.

functions	Illustrative Utterances
Instrumental	
Regulatory	
Interactional	
Personal	
Heuristic	
Imaginative	
Representational	
Performative	
Socialization	

References

Austin, J. L. (1961). *How to Do Things with Words*. Cambridge, MA: Harvard University Press.

Bakhtin, M. M. (1981). *The Dialogic Imagination*. Trans. C. Emerson and M. Holquist. Austin: University of Texas Press.

Blot, R. K. (ed.) (2003). *Language and Social Identity*. Westport: Praeger.

Brown, P. and Levinson, S. C. (1987). *Politeness: Some Universals in Language Usage*. Cambridge: Cambridge University Press.

Carr, C., Schrock, D. and Dauterman, P. (2012). Speech Acts within Facebook Status Messages. *Journal of Language and Social Psychology* 31: 176–196.

Espes Brown, J. (1992). Becoming Part of It. In: D. M. Dooling and P. Jordan-Smith (eds.), *I Become Part of It: Sacred Dimensions in Native American Life*, pp. 1–15. New York: Harper Collins.

Fairclough, N. (1992). *Discourse and Social Change*. London: Blackwell.

Foxtree, J., Mayer, S., and Betts, T. (2011). Grounding in Instant-Messaging. *Journal of Educational Computing Research* 45: 455–475.

Gentle, A. (2009). Twitter and Conversation Analysis—Who's Here? Notes from the Webworks RoundUp 2009. (http://justwriteclick.com/2009/10/26/twitter-and-converation-analysis-whos-here/)

Gill, A. (1994). *Rhetoric and Human Understanding*. Prospect Heights, Ill.: Waveland.

Gillena, J. and Merchant, G. (2013). Contact Calls: Twitter as a Dialogic Social and Linguistic Practice. *Language Science* 35: 47–58.

Goffman, E. (1955). On Face-Work: An Analysis of Ritual Elements in Social Interaction. *Psychiatry: Journal for the Study of International Processes* 18: 213–231.

Goffman, E. (1978). Response Cries. *Language* 54: 787–815.

Goodwin, C. and Goodwin, M. H. (1992). Assessments and the Construction of Context. In: A. Duranti and C. Goodwin (eds.), *Rethinking Context: Language as an Interactive Phenomenon*. Cambridge: Cambridge University Press.

Grice, H. P. (1975). Logic and Conversation. In: P. Cole and J. Morgan (eds.), *Syntax and Semantics*, Vol. 3, pp. 41–58. New York: Academic.

Grice, H. P. (1989). *Studies in the Way of Words*. Cambridge: Harvard University Press.

Halliday, M. A. K. (1985). *Introduction to Functional Grammar*. London: Arnold.

Hutchby, I. and Wooffitt, R. (1998). *Conversation Analysis*. Cambridge: Polity Press.

Hymes, D. (1971). *On Communicative Competence*. Philadelphia: University of Pennsylvania Press.

Jakobson, R. (1960). Linguistics and Poetics. In: T. Sebeok (ed.), *Style and Language*. Cambridge, Mass.: MIT Press.

Lakoff, R. (1975). *Language and Woman's Place*. New York: Harper and Row.

Malinowski, B. (1922). *Argonauts of the Western Pacific*. New York: Dutton.

Meyerhoff, M. (2006). *Introducing Sociolinguistics*. London: Routledge.

Morris, C. W. (1938). *Foundations of the Theory of Signs*. Chicago: University of Chicago Press.

Nastri, J., Pena, J., and Hancock, J. T. (2006). The Construction of Away Messages: A Speech Act Analysis. *Journal of Computer-Mediated Communication* 11: 1025–1045.

Peirce, C. S. (1931–1958). *Collected Papers*. Cambridge, Mass.: Harvard University Press.

Reyes, A., Rosso, P., and Veale, T. (2013). A Multidimensional Approach for Detecting Irony in Twitter. *Language Resources & Evaluation* 47: 239–268.

Sacks, H., Jefferson, G. and Schegloff, E. A. (1995). *Lectures on Conversation*. Oxford: Blackwell.

Sapir, E. (1921). *Language*. New York: Harcourt, Brace, and World.

Savan, L. (2005). *Slam Dunks and No-Brainers: Language in Your Life, the Media, Business, Politics, and, Like, Whatever*. New York: Alfred A. Knopf.

Scollon, R. and Wong Scollon, S. (2001). *Intercultural Communication*. 2nd edn. Oxford: Blackwell.

Searle, J. R. (1969). *Speech Acts: An Essay in the Philosophy of Language*. Cambridge: Cambridge University Press.

Stubbs, M. (2008). Three Concepts of Keywords. Paper presented to the conference on Keyness in Text, University of Siena.

Ten Have, P. (2006). Conversation Analysis Versus Other Approaches to Discourse. *Forum: Qualitative Social Research* 7, www.qualitative-research.net/index.php/fqs/article/view/100/209 (accessed 6 May 2015).

Watts, R. (2003). *Politeness*. Cambridge: Cambridge University Press.

Whorf, B. L. (1956). *Language, Thought, and Reality*, J. B. Carroll (ed.). Cambridge, Mass.: MIT Press.

Wooffitt, R. (2005). *Conversation Analysis and Discourse Analysis: A Comparative and Critical Introduction*. London: Sage Publications.

7 Writing and Society

The writer who neglects punctuation, or mispunctuates, is liable to be misunderstood. For the want of merely a comma, it often occurs that an axiom appears a paradox, or that a sarcasm is converted into a sermonoid.

Edgar Allan Poe (1809–1845)

The relation between language and society can also be sought in the nature and function of the writing system(s) used for both official and informal purposes. Before the advent of alphabets, people communicated and passed on their knowledge through the spoken word. But even in early cultures, tools had been invented for recording and preserving ideas in pictographic form. So instinctive is pictography as a mode of writing that it comes as little surprise to find that it has not disappeared from our own modern world, even though most of our written communication is based on the alphabet. The figures designating *men* and *women* on washrooms found in public buildings, to mention but two common examples, are modern-day pictographs:

Figure 7.1 Public Washroom Signs

Writing serves a host of functions. Just think of the books, magazines, and all the other materials that are based on writing and that we use on a daily basis for a host of functions, from information-gathering to entertainment. Some of the written texts of a society, such as sacred texts, are preserved and revered everlastingly. The purpose of this chapter is to take a schematic look at the social functions of writing, as well as at the kinds of changes it is undergoing today in cyberspace.

7.1 Writing Systems

The earliest pictographs so far discovered were unearthed in western Asia, dating from the Neolithic era (eighth millennium to fourth millennium BCE). They were made by means of elemental shapes on clay tokens that were used as image-making forms or molds (Schmandt-Besserat 1978, 1992). They are, in effect, the first writing tools of history. Writing is often considered to be foundational for human civilizations, since it provides a means to preserve ideas by transferring them onto some surface (a cave wall, a rock or stone, a tablet, a piece of papyrus, and today computer screens) and thus transmitted to subsequent generations, thus creating continuity of knowledge and the possibility for discovery (Gelb 1963; Harris 1986; Coulmas 1989; Daniels and Bright 1995).

One of the first civilizations to utilize pictographic writing as a means of recording ideas, keeping track of business transactions, and transmitting knowledge was ancient China. According to some archeological estimates, Chinese pictography may date as far back as the fifteenth century BCE. Here are examples of two early Chinese pictographs (pictograms). Each one is self-explanatory. The basic principle evident in their construction is to let the pictorial sign stand directly for its referent through some form of imitation, resemblance, or simulation. Over time, this representation becomes more and more stylized, that is, rendered much more simple and thus not accurate or precise:

Figure 7.2 Chinese Pictograms

Abstract pictographic signs are called, more specifically, *ideographs* or *ideograms*. These also bear resemblance to their referents, but assume much more of a conventional knowledge of the relation between picture and referent on the part of the user. International symbols for such things as public telephones and washrooms today are examples of ideographs. Increasingly abstract pictographs are known as *logographs* or *logograms*. These combine elements of basic pictography and ideography. For example, the Chinese logograph for *east* is a combination of the pictographs for *sun* and *tree* (Billeter 1990).

A pictographic–ideographic–logographic system was also used by the ancient Sumerian civilization that emerged nearly five thousand years ago. Called *cuneiform*, because it consisted of wedge-shaped picture symbols, the Sumerians recorded their symbols on clay tablets, making it a very expensive and impracticable means of communication (Walker 1987). In the illustration below, the progression from pure pictography to stylized symbols is shown in various stages of early civilizations:

MEANING	OUTLINE CHARACTER, BC 3500	ARCHAIC CUNEIFORM, BC 2500	ASSYRIAN, BC 700	LATE BABYLONIAN, BC 500
1. The sun				
2. God, heaven				
3. Mountain				
4. Man				
5. Ox				
6. Fish				

Figure 7.3 Cuneiform Writing

Writing Terms

Pictograph/pictogram: picture symbol for a referent, for example the picture of an eye standing for an eye:

Ideograph/ideogram: picture or combination of pictures or visual forms standing for something. An ideograph sign for *No smoking* might look like this:

Logograph/logogram: symbol that stands for a morpheme. The & sign is an example; it stands for "and."

Phonograph/phonogram: symbol designed to approximate how a morpheme or phoneme is pronounced. For example, the pronunciation of Italian *sociale* (social) can be approximated with English letters as follows: *sohchahleh*.

Alphabet: system of characters (known as letters) that stand for phonemes (by and large).

From about 2700 to 2500 BCE another type of pictographic script, called *hieroglyphic*, was invented in Egypt. The signs that referred to concrete referents (*eye, giraffe, sandal, reed, bread, flute*) are the ones that show the greatest degree of resemblance. Those that refer to abstract referents, on the other hand, involve a more ideographic style of representation (*beat, cry, walk, break, bind*). Interestingly, there seems to be a connection between parts of speech and style of representation. Concrete nouns are typically portrayed with straightforward pictographs, whereas verbs are almost always represented with ideographs (Goldwasser 1995). This might be a hidden clue with regard to the origins of language. Early pictographic systems have an abundance of signs for concrete nouns, seemingly suggesting that nouns are more rudimentary than are other parts, and this is perhaps why they make up the largest component of core vocabularies (and of vocabularies generally). The pictographic record provides, in other words, a means of possibly inferring how the parts of speech evolved and how they are connected with seeing and with abstraction.

The hieroglyphic system eventually developed *phonographic* elements within it—*phonographs (phonograms)* are forms standing for parts of words, such as syllables or individual sounds. The first true *syllabaries*—systems of signs for representing syllables—were developed by the Semitic peoples of Palestine and Syria from the Egyptian hieroglyphs during the last half of the second millennium BCE. Syllabaries are still used in some cultures. Japanese, for example, is still written with two complete syllabaries—the *hiragana* and the *katakana*—devised to supplement the characters originally taken over from Chinese.

A complete phonographic system for representing single sounds is called *alphabetic*. The first alphabetic system emerged in the Middle East, and was transported by the Phoenicians (a people from a territory on the eastern coast of the Mediterranean, located largely in modern-day Lebanon) to Greece. It contained symbols for consonant sounds only. When it reached Greece, symbols for vowel sounds were added to it, making the Greek system the first full-fledged alphabetic one.

Pictography gave way to alphabetic writing in the marketplaces of the ancient world because it made the writing of transactions rapid and efficient. The transition was evolutionary, however, not revolutionary. Every alphabet character is the symbolic residue of a stylistic alteration to some earlier pictograph. Take, for example, the emergence of the alphabet character **A**. It started out as a pictograph of the head of an ox in Egypt (and other parts of the Middle East). The full head of the ox came at some point to be drawn only in its bare outline, especially in Semitic cultures. It was this outline that came eventually to stand for the word for ox (*aleph*). Around 1000 BCE Phoenician scribes, who wrote from right to left, drew the ox outline sideways (probably because it was quicker and "more natural" for them to do so). The slanted Phoenician figure came to stand just for the first sound in the word (*a* for *aleph*), because it became very familiar. The Greeks, who wrote from left to right, took the Phoenician figure and stylized it further. Around 500 BCE, as such "abbreviated picture writing" became more standardized and letters stopped changing directions, the **A** assumed the upright position it has today in Roman script—the ox had finally settled on its horns! The history of **A** can be shown schematically as follows:

	The ancient Egyptians
	The Semites
	The Phoenicians
	The Greeks
	The Romans

Figure 7.4 The Evolution of "A"

When the Greeks started the practice of naming each symbol by such words as *alpha, beta, gamma,* and so on, which were imitations of Phoenician words (*aleph* "ox," *beth* "house," *gimel* "camel"), it was evidence that the concept of "alphabet" had been established. Incidentally, the idea of an alphabetic order was derived from the fact that the sequence of letters was used to count the numbers in order—**A** stood for 1, **B** for 2, **C** for 3, and so on.

7.1.1 Writing and Society

Because writing takes time and effort and because it is more durable than oral language, it has played a special role in the evolution of civilizations, allowing humans to encode knowledge, transmit it, and thus give a shape to history. In fact, history is something written or narrated; it is not inherent in the physical world. Alphabetic writing has become the norm in many societies, although pictography has not disappeared. As mentioned, it is found on common signs in public spaces. We even use letters themselves in a pictographic or ideographic way. Take for example, phonograms which are the graphic counterpart to onomatopoeia, as a technique for representing sounds in letters. Here are some examples:

- Braaannnngggg! (graphic form for the noise of an alarm)
- Aaaahhhhh! (graphic form for the sound of gulping for air)
- Hehheheh (graphic form for the belly sound associated with laughter)
- Booooo! (graphic form for a sound made to evoke fear)

Phonogram writing brings out the fact that alphabet characters were born as pictographs. Moreover, pictography continues to serve a vast array of functions, even in an alphabet-using society like ours. One of these is in the domain of computers, where the term *icon* is used to designate any tiny picture on a computer screen. Each icon represents a command. Users can usually tell by the icons how to get the computer to do what they want. There is little doubt that they contributed to the early rise of the personal computer in the mid-1980s, starting in 1984 when the Apple Computer Company introduced the Macintosh, the first personal computer to include icons. Because they make computers easy to use, icons quickly became standard throughout the computer industry.

Alphabets brought about a cognitive revolution, as McLuhan (1964) wrote, because the alphabet "shapes and controls the scale and form of human association and action" (McLuhan 1964: 9). McLuhan put forward four "laws" to which all human artifacts (including writing) are subject: amplification, obsolescence, reversal, and retrieval. These laws imply that a new invention or technology will at first amplify some sensory, intellectual, or other faculty of the user; but, while one area is amplified, another is lessened or eventually rendered obsolete, until the artifact is used to maximum capacity and must reverse its characteristics until it is retrieved in another medium. As we have seen in this book the digital media have indeed amplified the scope and reach of daily communications, at first rendering print media obsolescent. But, today, print and other media of representation have merged on the internet (that is, they have been retrieved) as multimodality integrates previous print forms with nonverbal ones.

The sociolinguistic study of writing involves the use of other disciplines, including literary studies, semiotics, genre studies, stylistics and rhetoric (Lillis 2013). Writing practices are social practices. The two mirror each other (Derrida 1976, 1978). Derrida believed that written discourse has misguided us in answering profound existential questions by creating linguistic categories, and precise definitions, for this task, etching them into the alphabet characters of texts. The assumption that language is a tool that encodes ideas without distortion is rendered useless when one looks at the history of writing and all the changes it has undergone. Derrida analyzed philosophical discourse and found it to be highly entangled, circular, and serving the particular interests of the philosopher. It was hardly a tool for gaining truth about reality, which is elusive by its very nature.

Derrida's main contention was that the meaning of a written text cannot be determined in any absolute way because it shifts according to who reads it, when it is read, how it is read, and so on. Thus authorship is a myth, and only the reader can determine meaning. He rejected the traditional way scholars interpreted literary works as reflecting the author's views. A narrative text has no unchanging, unified meaning, because the author's intentions cannot be unconditionally accepted. There are an infinite number of legitimate interpretations of a text that are beyond what the author intends. Hence, the text "deconstructs" itself over time. By their very nature, writing practices are self-referential. Thus, what appears true in a text turns out to be only a specific opinion. In a sense, Derrida is correct. Society is a fiction, created by humans to carry out activities in an orderly and structured way, with writing a means by which these can be recorded for reproduction. Although sociolinguistics has by and large ignored the role of writing in the constitution of societies (Sebba 2009; Lillis 2013), this has changed in the internet age, as we have seen throughout.

7.1.2 Writing, Literacy, and Power

As discussed briefly in Chapter 3, literacy equals social power. Those who are literate—that is, those who can read and write—are those who have always wielded authority and influence throughout history. Before the late 1400s, the vast majority of people throughout the world were illiterate. Most had never had an opportunity to learn to read and write because there were few schools, and books were scarce and often expensive. Although some people at every level of society could read and write, most literate people belonged to the upper classes. Illiterate people relied on literate people to read and write for them. They were powerless and, to this day, illiteracy implies powerlessness and socioeconomic travail.

Literacy spread at an uneven rate until the invention of the printing press in the late 1400s. Social class often determined who became literate. Literacy levels varied widely from region to region, even within one country. But the printing press changed all that. McLuhan characterized the new world shaped by the advent of the printing press, in fact, as the Gutenberg Galaxy, as we saw in the third chapter (see 3.4.3). Through books, newspapers, pamphlets, and posters, the printed word became, after the fifteenth century, the primary means for the propagation of knowledge and ideas. More importantly, given the fact that books could cross political boundaries, the printing press set in motion the globalization of culture. It also encouraged the gaining of literacy across the world, paving the way for the European Renaissance, the Protestant Reformation, and the Enlightenment (as mentioned in chapter 3, section 3.4.3).

With the spread of commerce and industry during the eighteenth and nineteenth centuries, large numbers of people migrated to cities where they were forced to learn how to read instructions and perform tasks that required literacy. Governments began to value educated citizens, and systems of public schooling expanded. By the late 1800s, formal education had become common and mainly obligatory. As a result, more people had the opportunity and motivation to learn to read and write, causing the literacy rate to rise rapidly.

Literacy is required today in most societies for all kinds of social reasons. This is why most regions of the world now impose obligatory education. There are, moreover, levels of literacy established within each society, and these are generally associated with higher levels of education. There are also many types of specialized literacies given the nature of the modern-day workplace, whereby certain people are required to have expertise in some technical area, which entails its own form of literacy. But such expertise still implies the more general ability to read texts so as to be able to glean from them the relevant information. Throughout the world, there is also the concept of a "common literacy," which implies knowledge of certain key texts, such as for example religious, literary, and philosophical texts. Many social critics today decry the fact that common literacy is being marginalized in favor of the specialized literacies. We will return to this issue below.

The notion of critical literacy (sometimes called functional literacy) has now become a target of sociolinguistic interest (Gee 1996). Critical literacy is the process of extracting meaning from print and putting meaning into print. This process is developed through formal schooling and beyond, being reinforced by the social order in which literacy plays a dominant role. Critical literacy is shaped by the personality preferences of individuals and may develop further in later life. But there are also broader social functions of critical literacies that have shaped writing practices in the evolution of a society. There is, in other words, a power ideology behind literacy. Those with the highest levels of literacy tend to be power brokers with the ability to make themselves heard and noticed (Schuster 1990). Illiteracy generally assigns people to ghettoized communities. Cynthia Selfe (1999) argues that today the notion of critical literacy has little relevance unless it is related to computer and technological literacies, since the power paradigm has shifted to online contexts. As discussed already, there is in fact a new form of literacy emerging online. The question is whether there are now two forms of literacy—an online and an offline one. This topic will be discussed below.

7.2 Abbreviated Writing

As discussed, the more frequently a word or expression is used the more likely it will be replaced by a shorter equivalent. More generally, this suggests that language forms are being constantly condensed, abbreviated, reduced, or eliminated in order to minimize the effort expended to produce and use them. We abbreviate the names of friends and family members (*Alex* for *Alexander*, *Bob* for *Robert*, *Cathy* for *Catharine*, *Debbie* for *Deborah*), of common phrases (*TGIF* for *Thank God it's Friday*), and of anything else that refers to something common or familiar. Abbreviation is also a common writing technique, which includes acronymy, that is, abbreviation of phrases with the first letters of separate words.

Abbreviated writing was used even by the ancients as archeological analyses of ancient manuscripts reveal. Writing on walls or on valuable materials such as papyri is conducive to finding shortcuts. But there is more to it than this. It

Common Abbreviated Forms

English

- 24/7 (24 hours a day, seven days a week)
- aka (also known as)
- ad (advertisement)
- ATM (automated teller machine)
- CD (compact disc)
- CEO (chief executive officer)
- DNA (deoxyribonucleic acid)
- ETA (estimated time of arrival)
- GNP (gross national product)
- IQ (intelligence quotient)
- PC (personal computer)
- PIN (personal identification number)
- TGIF (Thank God it's Friday)
- VIP (very important person)

French

- BP (*boîte postale* = post office box)
- H (*heure* = o'clock)
- HS (*hors service* = out of order)
- PDG (*président-directeur general* = CEO)
- RN (*revenu national* = GNP)

Spanish

- CÍA (*compañía* = company)
- LIC (*licenciado* = attorney)
- SL (*Sociedad Anónima* = LTD)
- WC (*water closet* = bathroom)
- TEL (*teléfono* = telephone)
- UD (*usted* = you)

seems to suggest that what undergoes abbreviation is either very common or else very important. In other words, abbreviation is tied to social processes and perceptions of various kinds. This is perhaps why so many institutions use abbreviations to represent themselves. These seem to imbue them with a symbolic status all its own, especially since the abbreviations are constructed with capital letters, which suggest importance. Here are a few common ones: A.A. (Alcoholics Anonymous), AMA (American Medical Association), AP (Associated Press), CIA (Central Intelligence Agency), EPA (Environmental Protection Agency), ERA (Equal Rights Amendment), EU (European Union), FBI (Federal Bureau of Investigation), IBM (International Business Machines Corporation), NATO (North Atlantic Treaty Organization), PBS (Public Broadcasting System), UN (United Nations). It is unlikely that those who wield very little power or have low social salience would abbreviate their institutions in this way. For one thing, they would not be recognized as easily as, say, CIA or NATO. In effect, abbreviation is tied, in many ways, to social power.

7.2.1 Social Functions

Abbreviations have always been used by people in positions of authority or importance. They suggest a high level of literacy. They are used commonly, in fact, in technical and scientific material (in indexes, in footnotes, in bibliographies). Many Latin abbreviations are still used in academic and scientific writing to this day. Here are a few of them:

- ad lib (*ad libitum*) = as one pleases
- e.g. (*exempli gratia*) = for example
- et al. (*et alii*) = and others
- etc. (*et cetera*) = and so forth
- ibid. (*ibidem*) = in the same place
- id. (*idem*) = the same
- loc. cit. (*loco citato*) = in the place cited
- N.B. (*nota bene*) = note well
- op. cit. (*opere citato*) = in the work cited
- Q.E.D. (*quod erat demonstrandum*) = which was to be shown or proved
- q.v. (*quod vide*) = which see
- i.e. (*id est*) = that is
- v. (*vide*) = see
- vs. (*versus*) = against.

As Nida (1992) has written, this kind of writing is used so that only specialists are able to understand the unnecessarily complex features of the textual contents. It is a form of code that keeps outsiders out, and insiders in the know.

Not all abbreviation is tied of course to writing of this type. For most intents and purposes, it is used simply to make writing rapid and efficient. However, it should be noted that it often happens that the abbreviated forms have replaced the original forms so completely that people no longer read them as abbreviations. This is the case of words such as *laser* and *radio*, which are no longer perceived as convenient acronyms (*laser* = light amplification by stimulated emission of radiation; *radio* = radiotelegraphy). This can be seen especially in the contraction or blending of separate words into common single forms such as *sexpert* (*sex* + *expert*), *motel* (*motor* + *hotel*), *brunch* (*breakfast* + *lunch*), and *guestimate* (*guess* + *estimate*), which people no longer read as blends.

Alphabetic symbols, moreover, have many symbolic values and uses. In a fascinating book titled *Sign after the* X (2000), Marina Roy has traced the history of the **X** sign, showing that it has had very little to do with phonetics at any period of its history, but everything to do with symbolism. Here are a few of its traditional meanings:

- any unknown or unnamed factor, thing, or person;
- the signature of any illiterate person;
- the sign for mistake;
- cancellation;
- the unknown, especially in mathematics;
- the multiplication symbol;
- the Roman numeral ten;
- a mechanical defect;
- on a map a location;
- choice on a ballot;
- a motion picture rating;
- a symbol for Christ;
- the symbol for a kiss;
- the symbol for Chronos, the Greek god of Time; and
- the symbol for the planet Saturn in Greek and Roman mythology.

Today it seems to stand for youth culture (Xbox), adventure comic heroes (X-Men), and erotic movies (X-rated). It is little wonder to find that this very symbol is now found throughout the advertising and brand-naming world, reverberating with its many meanings latently. As this example shows, single letters are just as often symbols as they are alphabet characters.

For most of its history, linguistics has taken spoken language as its primary object of study. Writing has been seen as a vocal speech substitute, defined as "merely a way of recording language by means of visible marks" (Bloomfield 1933: 21). But a growing number of linguists and sociolinguists in particular are beginning to note the relation between writing and social power structures as well as social variables. The new emphasis on literacies, online and offline, has made writing a major topic of investigation.

7.2.2 Abbreviation and Meaning

Alphabet characters, as we have seen, are essentially abbreviated pictographs. Abbreviated writing brings out a communication principle—the reason why speakers minimize communicative effort by shortening the length of words and utterances is to save on time and space. At the same time, people want to be able to interpret the meaning of shortened forms unambiguously and with little effort. Frequency of usage correlates typically with the abbreviation and compression of writing. As Zipf (1932) demonstrated, in fact, there exists an intrinsic interdependence between the length of a specific word (in number of phonemes) and its rank order in the language (its position in order of its frequency of occurrence in texts of all kinds). The higher the rank order of a word (the more frequent it is in actual usage), the more it tends to be shorter (made up with fewer phonemes). For example, articles (*a, the*), conjunctions (*and, or*), and other function words (*to, it*), which have a high rank order in English (and in any other language for that matter), are typically monosyllabic, consisting of one to three phonemes. This phenomenon does not stop at the level of function words, however. It can be seen to manifest itself in the tendency for phrases that come into popular use to become abbreviated (*FYO, UNESCO, Hi, Bye, ad, photo, Mr., Mrs., Dry, 24/7,* and so on).

Blending, or the creation of a new (shorter) word that combines two other words, is a product of the same tendency. *Fanzine,* for instance, is a blend of *fan* and *magazine.* Similarly *sitcom* is a blend of *situation* and *comedy, sportscast* of *sports* and *broadcast,* and *chexting* of *cheating* and *texting.* Alphabets result from this tendency (as mentioned), making it possible for writing to become the foundation for efficient knowledge storage. Before alphabets, people passed on knowledge primarily through the spoken word and pictography. In 1958, psycholinguist Roger Brown subsequently claimed that abbreviation tendencies are associated with meaning patterns in a general way. Language users encode the concepts that they need. And this determines the size of their vocabularies and of the lexemes in them. If speakers of a language are involved in using colors a lot, then they will develop more words for color concepts than do other languages; and these words will be shorter than others, which is the case: *red* (three letters), *green* (five letters), *blue* (four letters), and so on. Brown (1958: 235) put it as follows:

> Suppose we generalize the finding beyond Zipf's formulation and propose that the length of a verbal expression (*codability*) provides an index of its frequency in speech, and that this, in turn, is an index of the frequency with which the relevant judgments of difference and equivalence are made. If this is true, it would follow that the Eskimo distinguishes his three kinds of snow more often than Americans do. Such conclusions are, of course, supported by extralinguistic cultural analysis, which reveals the importance of snow in the Eskimo life, of palm trees and parrots to Brazilian Indians, cattle to the Wintu, and automobiles to the American.

This interpretation has been critiqued in the relevant literature. The linguist George Miller (1981: 107) dismisses such work abruptly as follows: "Zipf's Law was once thought to reflect some deep psychobiological principle peculiar to the human mind. It has since been proved, however, that completely random processes can also show this statistical regularity." But a resurgence of interest in writing in the internet age suggests something very different—namely, that the relation between form and meaning is not arbitrary. In human affairs there are always two forces at work: a social force (the need to be understood), and the efficiency force or the desire to be brief. These forces imply a relation between form and meaning—a relation that generates linguistic change.

7.2.3 Stylometry and Corpus Linguistics

The empirical study of writing phenomena comes under the categories of stylometry and corpus linguistics, both involving the direct use of statistical-quantitative techniques. The features that are most commonly studied by stylometrists, and which have had the greatest practical value, are the relative frequencies of such units as phonemes, syllables, words, and syntactic constructions that can be associated with a certain literary genre or a specific author, or an individual's style (idiolect). Relevant data is collected and analyzed statistically to reveal various things—including the stylistic features inherent in a text, the sources of texts, the meaning of historical writings. To establish relationships between the data and the style, stylometry employs simple inferential statistics (Chapter 1), which allow analysts to explore the probabilistic properties of various subsystems—phonological, morphological, syntactic, semantic. Stylometric linguistics conceptualizes categories as normal probability distributions and views the structure of language not as a minimal set of discrete categories but as a set of gradient rules that may be characterized by such distributions.

Individuals use certain words, phrases, and other linguistic forms consistently as part of their discourse style, but are barely conscious of so doing. Given this tendency, the stylometrist uses the statistical analysis of these forms as a means of establishing the identity of the author of some text. The assumption is that each individual has a unique set of habits. An interfering factor is the fact that an individual's style is always susceptible to variation from environmental influences, including other speakers, the media, and changes in language itself. Nevertheless, stylometric research has shown that grammatical and vocabulary styles tend to be fairly stable and immune from outside influences even as people age. A written text can thus be examined for lexical and grammatical patterns within it by classifying these in specific ways and then measuring them statistically against known style features of the author. The analysis may be adequate to eliminate an individual as an author or narrow down an author from a small group of subjects.

Perhaps the earliest example of the analysis of a text to determine its authenticity based on a stylistic analysis is that of Lorenzo Valla's 1439 proof that the fourth-century document, *Donation of Constantine*, was a forgery. Valla based his argument in part on the fact that the Latin used in the text was not consistent with the language as it was written in fourth-century documents. One of the features that indicated forgery is the fact that some of the words could not have been written in the fourth century. For example, Valla remarked, correctly, that the term *fief* "an estate of land associated with the feudal system" emerged much later.

The principles of modern-day stylometric analysis were laid out by Polish philosopher Wincenty Lutosławski in 1890. Today, computer databases and algorithms are used to carry out basically the same kinds of analytical stylistic procedures. Much suspicion about the validity of stylometry existed until Donald Foster brought the field into the scientific domain with his 1996 study that correctly identified the author of the pseudonymously authored book, *Primary Colors*, as Joe Klein (Foster 2001). Modern stylometry has thus made it possible to determine authorship and to detect forgeries. It suggests that we all have linguistic habits and that we reveal these constantly in our conversations and writings. Like a musician who espouses a specific style, so too each one of us has a stylistic repertoire which we utilize all the time unconsciously. With the growing corpus of texts on the internet, stylometry is being used more and more to refine its methods. The main concept is that of *writer invariant*—a property of a text that is invariant in the author's idiolect. To identify this feature, the 50 most common words are identified and the text is then broken into word chunks of 5,000 items. Each is analyzed to determine the frequency of the 50 words. This generates a unique 50-word identifier for each chunk.

Another common technique is called the *artificial neural network* (ANN) (Tweedie, Singh, and Holmes 1996). The ANN can be used to carry out a nonlinear regression analysis so as to generalize the recognition patterns detected in a text. ANNs are special kinds of algorithms that are modeled after the structure of the mammalian brain. A large ANN might have hundreds or thousands of processor units, simulating functions such as those of the retina and the eye. ANNs do not carry out programmed instructions; rather, they respond in parallel (either simulated or actual) to the pattern of inputs involved. There are also no separate memory addresses for storing data in ANNs. Instead, information is contained in the overall activation state of the network. ANNs work well in capturing regularities in data where the diversity and volume is very great. A related approach, known as the *genetic algorithm*, comes up with similar extractions of recurrence. It works somewhat like this: "If *well* occurs more than two times in every thousand words, then the text is authored by X."

Perhaps the best-known use of stylometric techniques is in the area of forensic science and archeological–philological investigations of various kinds. Within these fields the cognate technique of *lexicometry* is often used, which is simply the measurement of the frequency of words within a text and then plotting the frequency distribution of a given word in the speech of an individual, a specific genre of text, and so on. This allows the analyst to determine how a lexical item is used and who the probable user might be. Thus, lexicometry, like stylometry in general, is used both as proof and as a heuristic tool.

Stylometry is part of a general quantitative branch of linguistics called *corpus linguistics*, or the study of language as expressed in real-world texts known as *corpora*. The objective is to derive a set of general rules of vocabulary use, sentence formation and text-construction on the basis of the automated analyses of language samples collected in natural speech environments. Quirk's 1960 survey of English usage and Kucera and Francis's 1967 computational analysis of a carefully chosen corpus of American English, consisting of nearly one million words, are early examples of corpus linguistic analysis. The idea is to collect all the common forms used in a language at a specific point in time. One of the offshoots of this type of work has been the preparation of dictionaries combining prescriptive information (how language should be used) and descriptive information (how it is actually used). Examples of prescriptive versus descriptive forms include the following. Note that the term "descriptive" here refers to the actual form as it is used:

Table 7.1 Descriptive versus Prescriptive Entries

Actual Form (Descriptive)	Prescribed Form
ain't	am not, is not, are not
gonna	going to
yeah	yes
outta here	out of here
goin	going

Corpus Linguistics has produced several research methods allowing for theoretical generalizations to be made on the basis of actual corpora of data. Wallis and Nelson (2001) summarize the principles of corpus linguistics in terms of what they call the 3A perspective: Annotation, Abstraction and Analysis. Annotation is the application of a scheme to texts, such as a structural mark-up, parsing, and other such rule-based frames; abstraction involves generating a mapping of the data against the model or scheme used; and analysis is the statistical generalization of the data in order to determine what models work best. In effect, corpus linguistics has become an important branch of linguistics for validating if certain features or patterns in speech samples are relevant to explicating structural and semantic aspects of a language, in addition to idiolectal characteristics. This adds a significant empirical or data-based component to linguistic theories and models.

7.3 Literary Practices

The topic of writing invariably leads to the topic of literature and literary practices generally. The formal study of literature falls under the rubric of *literary studies*, but the sociological study of literature is, clearly, a topic of sociolinguistic relevance. Two areas of investigation consist of the study of the social functions of the original myths of a society and the uses of narrative. They constitute practices of cultures (oral and literate) that connect texts to social situations. As social practice, myths and canonical stories (literary works that everybody cites, such as Shakespeare in English) structure the lives of communities and groups and are shared by and relevant to many of their members. They are significant because they reaffirm the identity of those who practice (read) them as a group or a society.

Some critics, like Michel Foucault (1971) actually see literary practices as a tool to discipline and thus subordinate various targeted groups, since literature "from high to low, from epic poems to Sunday-school prize books, played a key role in shaping and effecting transformations in schooling and in the social function of reading" (Foucault 1971: xiv); and "literary texts help constitute the educational discourses and practices of their time as well as critically addressing them" (Foucault 1971: 32). Whether representing new views of childhood, endorsing innovative educational methods or appealing to female and lower-class reading publics, literature was increasingly enlisted in a project of social control. In the past this may have been a valid interpretation, since the field of literary practices was primarily male-biased, with only a few exceptions of female writers and publishers. That has changed today, especially on the internet. But it is true that whoever gets published and read with a degree of interest will yield authority and even control over people's minds through his or her written text. But literary practices are not just instruments of social control. Myths, for example, are founding social narratives and many fictional narratives reflect common people's ideas, not those of the people in power.

7.3.1 Myth

In all early societies, myth and sacred rituals are linked. The word *myth* derives from the Greek *mythos* "word," "speech," "divine tale." An originary myth (called "cosmogonic") is a narrative in which the main characters are gods, superhuman heroes, mystical beings, and various supernatural creatures who interact with humans; the plots revolve around the origin of the world, humans, and the natural phenomena of the universe; and the setting juxtaposes the real world against a metaphysical backdrop.

The Zuñi people of North America, for instance, claim to have emerged from a hole in the earth, thus establishing their kinship with the land. Their language uses many metaphors related to the earth, farming, and the power of nature to both bless and destroy human life. Rome was said to have been founded by Romulus, who as an infant had to be suckled by a wolf, thus alluding to a supposed fierceness of the Roman people. The vocabulary regarding war in Latin attests indirectly to this emphasis. English words such as *bellicose, battle, assault, antebellum, ally,* and others derive from Latin. Although this kind of evidence is anecdotal, it does suggest that by studying the language of myths, we might be able to learn how different societies have answered basic questions about the world and the role of language in constituting early customs, ways of life, and the values that bind members of a collectivity together.

The words in myths are little theories of the world attempting to explain natural processes or events. The society of the Trobriand Islands in the Pacific Ocean believed that people were immortal when the world originated. When they began to age, they swam in a certain lagoon and shed their skin. They quickly grew new skin, renewing their youth. One day, a mother returned from the lagoon with her new skin. But her unexpected youthful appearance frightened her little daughter. To calm the child, the mother returned to the lagoon, found her old skin, and put it back on. From then on, according to this myth, death could not be avoided. The lexicon of the Trobriand language is replete with metaphors relating age to physical appearance and death to changes in physical appearance. These are used to evaluate everyday occurrences in that language to this day.

We get the concept that "up" is where good things are (such as heaven) and "down" where bad things are (such as hell) from many ancient myths. Most of the sacred places were thought to be in the sky, on top of mountains, or, on the contrary, below the earth. The most sacred place in Japanese mythology is Mount Fuji, the tallest mountain in Japan. During part of their history, the Greeks believed their divinities lived on a mythical mountain called Olympus that was later identified as Mount Olympus in northern Greece. The Greeks also believed in mythical places beneath the ground, such as Hades, where the souls of the dead lived. The Norse believed in Hel, an underground home for the souls of all dead persons, except those killed in battle. The souls of slain warriors went to Valhalla, which was a great hall in the sky.

Myths are thus sources of early vocabularies. The Greeks symbolized the sun as the god Helios driving a flaming chariot across the sky. The scientific word *helium* is a residue of this notion. Words for natural phenomena, animals, and plants have stood as symbols for ideas, historical events, and human personalities in myths. From the Germanic and Roman myths we have inherited the names of most of the days of the week and months of the year: Tuesday is the day dedicated to the Germanic war god Tiu; Wednesday to the chief god Wotan, Thursday to Thor, Friday to the goddess of beauty Frigga; and Saturday is dedicated to the Roman god Saturn, January to Janus, and so on. Our planets bear a similar pattern of nomenclature: Mars is named after the Roman god of war, Venus after the Roman god of love, and so on.

The French anthropologist Claude Lévi-Strauss (1978) saw myth as the original source for the development of languages, which are built from the vocabularies constituting early myths. And, he claimed, mythic language is an "instinctual" language, as can be seen from the fact that in childhood we respond to mythic stories, such as Santa Claus and the Tooth Fairy, with no hesitation in accepting them as true. Religious rites, sermons, pep rallies, political debates, and other ceremonial gatherings are anchored in mythic language.

A particularly interesting modern example of the latent mythic function of language is oath-taking. An oath is a pledge or promise. The language used in oaths is highly formulaic. The judicial oath, for example, is used by a witness in a court of law who swears that all of his or her statements are true. Often the person must lay a hand on a religious text while taking the oath. This gesture means that the person is making a declaration that is binding. A person swearing to the truth of an affidavit may be given the following oath: "You do solemnly swear that the contents of this affidavit by you subscribed are true, so help you God." Societies throughout the world have similar oaths. They reveal a deeply-entrenched and unconscious belief that language and truth are intertwined. And any infringement of this belief is seen as a dishonest act. A person who takes an oath in court and then makes a dishonest statement while under oath is guilty of perjury—perceived universally as a serious crime.

7.3.2 Narrative and Literacy

The term *narrative* refers to anything that has a recognizable story structure, not just stories in themselves. It is often distinguished from myth in various ways. For the present purposes, one of the most important ways is that narratives are by and large written, rather than just spoken. The widespread development of literacy in Western culture can arguably be traced to the rise of fictional narratives. Gaining literacy meant being able to read stories and this implied, in turn, that literacy became the basis for cultural changes (Hodges and Davies 2013). To this day, we present written stories to children not only for entertainment and engagement, but also so that they can initiate the literacy-gaining process. The term *emergent literacy* is often used to refer to the child's knowledge of what reading and writing imply before he or she gains literacy—a knowledge that is picked up in social rearing contexts. The main aspects of emergent literacy are the following ones:

- *Print motivation.* This refers to the fact that children will become interested in story books if these play a role in the rearing process.
- *Print awareness.* As a consequence of this motivation, children may become aware early on of the nature of books and of reading; that is, they learn how to handle books (turn pages, for example) and how to follow words on a page.

- *Symbol awareness.* As children follow along they become aware of the phonic connection between written symbols and content, starting to recognize them as they start to read on their own.
- *Vocabulary.* Knowing the names of things emerges from this assisted reading process (a caregiver reading to a child as he or she follows along).
- *Narrative skills.* This implies that the child can reiterate plot lines and character descriptions meaningfully, connecting them to the printed words.

The concept of emergent literacy was introduced by Marie Clay in 1966 so as to describe how children become engaged with written narratives, even though they lacked literacy. Since then, work on emergent literacy has shown that literacy develops before school through the narrative frame, but that success involves interactions with adults, degree of exposure to literary materials, and the use of follow-up activities.

Today, literacy is used as a synonym for competencies in various domains of knowledge—hence, media literacy, technological literacy, math literacy, arts literacy, and so on. The use of this term implies that such competencies are tied to reading and writing language. And indeed, such competencies would not emerge on their own without resource to relevant written texts. The Russian scholar Vladimir Propp (1928) also argued, in a similar vein, that ordinary discourse was connected to narrative structure. The themes, concepts, and turns of phrase that become standardized in narrative literacy are embedded in discourses of all types. Intertexuality means exactly this (as we saw previously).

7.4 e-Literacy

Abbreviated writing as discussed above, has spread to all areas of society. But nowhere has it become such a characteristic feature of communication as it has in online writing. This type of literacy can be called, again for the sake of convenience, e-literacy (see section 3.5.1). As Pérez-Sabater (2012) found in her study of writing practices on Facebook, e-literacy is spreading to all social domains, including technical writing practices among academics.

David Crystal (2011) has claimed that studying how society views the new e-literacy, or more accurately, the two new literacies (online and offline), each one contextualized according to space, is having an impact on all kinds of social processes. In schools, it is not uncommon for educators and students to be given the choice to move back and forth between these literacies. Also, through online discussions, students and instructors have become participants in the use of new literacy practices. These forms of academic social networking are on the rise as educators from all over the world continue to seek new ways to better engage students and to tap into new literacy patterns.

E-literacy also involves the influence of global forces that have become intrinsic to everyday communication and literacy practices online. These include:

1   *Multilingualism*, the prevalence of various languages on the internet and thus of different literacy practices.
2   *Technology*, the influence of new media on the globalization of literacy and other social practices.
3   *Online communication*, which, as already discussed is both extending and altering the nature of written language.
4   *Stylistic diffusion*, or the spread of slangs and jargons from online culture to various e-literacy practices.

The internet has had direct impacts on traditional school literacy. These include an increasing use of informal registers, inconsistency in writing patterns, and a rise in abbreviated writing. Naomi Baron (2008) claims, however, that online literacy practices have little effect on offline ones, since the two now exist as a dichotomy, producing what can be called a new kind of diglossia, with online writing being assigned an L value and offline formal writing an H value (as discussed, see 3.5.1 and 3.5.2). Others claim instead that online language is a pidginized form that may eventually develop into a global Creole that will indeed signal a new literacy.

Actually, given the fact that CMC is writing-based, it may have actually increased sensitivity to writing itself, thus producing a kind of "meta-literacy" awareness. Online writing is a hybrid of phonetic writing (imitating sounds), pictographic writing, and compressed alphabetic writing. Traditional writing is static, but e-writing is dynamic both in how words are spelled and how they are supported visually and audio-orally. This new mode of writing has implications for how written communications are conducted. The concept of framing found in e-mails and discussion forums, for example, is unlike anything in traditional writing practices. In replying to e-mails, people generally use the sender's message as a frame to write their own messages, choosing to respond to certain parts while leaving others out. Studies of children and adolescents in school have shown that this is indeed leading to what Baron called a literacy dichotomy:

1   Knowledge of when to use textisms (abbreviations, slang, and so on) in formal versus informal communications.
2   Knowing how to translate textisms to Standard English in certain situations.
3   Sensitivity to the two literacies and the ability to distinguish between them.

E-literacy also implies the development of different subliteracies and knowledge of new textual practices, such as those below:

- *Mobile literacy:* This refers to the kinds of texts written on mobile devices, which appear to have different characteristics according to medium—Twitter or Facebook, for instance. There are now text messaging poetry competitions, with the mobile system producing a channel for exploiting one's linguistic creativity. The cellphone has actually generated a new literary genre—"cellphone novels" consisting of chapters that readers download in short installments. They are novels in the traditional sense, but without editing or rewriting.
- *Blogs:* Blogs have brought about new forms of writing, including photoblogs, videoblogs, audioblogs, and moblogs. These have encouraged new linguistic and stylistic conventions and might continue to change literacy in the future.
- *Virtual worlds:* These include role-playing games and virtual spaces such as Second Life. They have led to new slangs or dialects within virtual communities, such as *pwn* and *noob*. *Pwn* is a "leetspeak" slang term derived from the verb *own*, meaning to gain ownership, implying the domination or humiliation of a rival in the internet-based video game culture to taunt an opponent who has just been soundly defeated. *Noob* or *noobish* is a raw variant of hacker language.
- *E-mail:* This is the medium that is closest to traditional print literacy practices. It is the medium used by businesses, schools, and other institutions and thus more sensitive to formal registers than other types of CMC.
- *Instant messaging:* which has developed its own form of informal language, although with corrective devices such as those in iPhones that make spelling more complete, it is evolving more and more into a spelling system that is similar to the offline one.

In cyberspace there are ever-growing intertextualities that cut across modes and genres, with an emphasis on collaborative creativity and re-mixing. As Halliday (1985: 82) predicted a while back: "When new demands are made on language, it changes in response to them… We are making language work for us in ways it never had to do before, it will have to become a different language in order to cope." E-literacy also entails vernacular literacy—knowledge of how different languages or jargons now interact online—and information literacy—knowledge of how to mine information from the internet and appropriate it for communicative practices. Overall, e-literacy can be defined as the ability to extract and use relevant information in multiple formats from a wide range of sources via digital devices. E-literacy thus encompasses other literacies, such as technological and information literacies, that go beyond traditional reading and writing skills.

7.4.1 The Wikis

Today, "looking up something" means either consulting a wiki or Google, rather than a print dictionary or encyclopedia. These are thus becoming major sources of literacy and knowledge spread. The term *wiki* refers to any website that provides information of a specific kind—*Wikipedia* (encyclopedic), *Wiktionary* (dictionary), and so on. The difference between these texts and the print ones is that they allow visitors to edit and change content, sometimes without the need for registration—a situation that obviously has implications for what literacy is. The first software to be named a *wiki* was WikiWikiWeb, named by its maker, computer programmer Ward Cunningham, who apparently took it from the name of a Hawaiian airport shuttle.

Wikipedia is arguably the most popular and influential of all the wikis. It was launched on 15 January 2002 by Larry Sanger and Ben Kovitz, who wanted, at first, to create an English-language encyclopedia similar to Nupedia (founded in 2000), to be written by expert contributors, in line with the internet-based encyclopedia project called the Interpedia (launched in 1993). But they soon made the decision to have it written and edited collaboratively by volunteers and visitors to the site. Needless to say, there has been controversy over Wikipedia's accuracy and overall reliability, since it is susceptible to the whims of users. The encyclopedia has remedied this situation somewhat (especially with "warning" annotations), but it still remains a kind of marketplace reference source, where knowledge, like commercial products, can be negotiated, tailored, and discarded as the values of that marketplace change. The main idea behind Wikipedia is to bring the domain of knowledge and functional literacy within everyone's reach. The founders describe it as "an effort to create and distribute a multilingual free encyclopedia of the highest quality to every single person on the planet in his or her own language." It makes further research efficient by providing hyperlinks in each entry and other cross-referencing tools that facilitate the search for specific information. The articles are now also linked to other digital forms (such as dictionaries provided by computer programs). Wikipedia is thus not a rigidly created text, impervious to change without authoritative consent (as is the case in traditional encyclopedias). It allows anyone to be involved in knowledge-construction in a continuing process of creation, reconstruction, and collaboration, thus ensuring that the knowledge source is constantly evolving and up to date. Critiques of Wikipedia are that it is inaccurate and poorly edited. This may be true, but the Wikipedians have started to turn it more and more into a traditional, quality-controlled online reference tool. Moreover, it seems that its infelicities soon get noticed and eliminated. Wikipedia is a self-organizing reference system. It has turned functional literacy into a descriptive rather than prescriptive form of knowledge.

7.4.2 Google

The shift from print-based literacy to digitally-based forms is nowhere more evident than in the social power that Google itself has attained over a relatively short period of time. The company's declared goal is to organize information from around the world and make it accessible to anyone through the World Wide Web. Google was established in 1995 by Larry Page and Sergey Brin, graduate students in computer science at Stanford University. At first they created a search engine that they called BackRub, running the business from their dormitories. The name they finally chose, Google, is derived from the mathematical term *googol* (the number represented by 1 followed by 100 zeros), which itself was coined by mathematicians Kasner and Newman in a 1940 book, *Mathematics and the Imagination*. The term indicates the vast amount of information that is available on the World Wide Web. Google was launched officially in 1998.

The advent of Google elicits philosophical and sociological concerns. One of these involves copyright, authorship, and the public domain. When works fall into the public domain, anyone can use them as they wish without having to pay royalties and without being subject to any liability. Copyrighted material enters the public domain when the copyright expires. The advent of Google has also led to a debate about what constitutes functional literacy. Millions of books are now available online. This has had a profound effect on the book publishing world and on print culture generally. The noble idea of opening up all books and libraries to everyone via Google is highly idealistic, but it remains to be seen if it is practicable. In the United States, copyright was included in the Constitution (Article 1, Section 8) for "limited times" and only to promote "the progress of science and useful arts." In effect, the Constitution put the public's right to access information before private profit. Google sees its mission as putting library collections online as a means of encouraging universal literacy—the ultimate goal of enlightened democracies as it has constantly asserted.

While this is admirable, there are also some drawbacks. The main one is that knowledge is now in the hands of the digitizers, who will choose what to make available, even though Google has claimed that it will try to make "everything possible" available. There is also great danger in giving one particular company, Google, enormous power. Another major issue with respect to the Google universe is the effects it might have on cognition, identity, socializing, and communication (among other things). Does Google make us more intelligent than in the past (since it purportedly entices more people to read) or more passive, since it seems to stress the use of information without reflection? Suffice it to say that the reading and writing tools and rules we use to understand the world contribute to shaping how we form our thoughts and how we perceive the world. And thus Google will unquestionably have effects on all of us—what these are still remain to be seen.

Google provides an increased capacity for people to do what they used to do offline, but in a more efficient way. However, it also encourages ephemerality or short-lived faddishness. It does so by making "viral events" the criteria by which we perceive something as important. A new band, for instance, can be discovered and become a celebrity over night after appearing on YouTube. But, as it all too often turns out, it then quickly fades from public favor. The term nano-celebrity is now used to describe this type of celebrity. Critical studies are beginning to show that Google is bringing about a new form of culture and literacy (Auletta 2008; Carr 2008). Statistics and popularity rule the Google universe. Using the algorithm called PageRank, Google can easily determine the relevancy of sites and thus, by implication, assign value to information through measurement. Rather than just ranking sites according to the number of times a particular searchword is used, Google ranks them on the basis of the number of links the sites have. If a popular site is linked to a page, then that link is given even greater relevancy. Relevancy is thus tied to statistically determined popularity. As Carr (2008) argues, this meaning of relevancy is based on a science of measurement, not around any assessment of the intrinsic value of information. As a result, Carr believes, Google has conditioned us to process information efficiently and statistically, not in terms of understanding. So, rather than encourage reading in the reflective sense of the word, Google is leading to selective and superficial browsing, guided by the criterion of popularity. As Vaidhyanathan (2011: 89) has put it, "We are not Google's customers: we are its product. We—our fancies, fetishes, predilections, and preferences—are what Google sells to advertisers." The questions raised by the advent of Google are now the substance of debates across the social sciences and philosophy.

Terminology Review

Define or explain in your own words the following terms introduced in this chapter. Some of these have been introduced before but are elaborated upon here.

alphabet	corpus linguistics
cuneiform	emergent literacy
functional literacy	hieroglyphic
ideography	literacy
logography	myth
narrative	phonogram
phonography	pictography
stylometry	syllabary
writing	

Exercises and Discussion

1   Can you identify any modern-day pictographs, ideographs, or logographs? Explain what they mean and, more importantly, how they represent their meanings.

2   Pictographs stand, by and large, for concrete things and ideas (*cat, house, sun, moon*, etc.). Ideographs stand instead, again by and large, for abstractions (*love, justice,* and so on). Create your own pictographs or ideographs (as appropriate) for each of the following things. Explain your techniques.

   (a) sky
   (b) child
   (c) love
   (d) justice.

3   Trace the pictographic origins of the following alphabet characters, providing a possible explanation for how each pictograph became an alphabet character.

   (a) B
   (b) C
   (c) D
   (d) I
   (e) S.

4   Below are some abbreviations. Do you know what they stand for? If so, explain the technique used in each case (acronymy, syllable reduction, and so on).

abbreviation	Full Form	Technique
AM		
AC		
ad		
aka		
BBQ		
DVD		
e-mail		
FAQ		
n/a		
UN		

5   Many contemporary brands use names imitating online style to increase their appeal. How many brand names do you know that use such a style? For each one indicate what aspect of online style has been utilized.

6   The following words referring to months and days of the week have a mythic origin. Using an etymological dictionary, give the mythical source for each one.

Words	Mythic Sources
January	
February	
Monday	
Tuesday	
Wednesday	
Thursday	
Friday	
Saturday	

7   Read the following excerpt from F. de Saussure (*Course in General Linguistics*, 1916):

> *Nearly all institutions, it might be said, are based on signs, but these signs do not directly evoke things. In all societies we find this phenomenon: that for various purposes systems of signs are established that directly evoke the ideas one wishes; it is obvious that a language is one such system, and that it is the most important of them all; but it is not the only one, and consequently we cannot leave the others out of account. A language must thus be classed among semiological institutions; for example, ships' signals (visual signs), army bugle calls, the sign language of the deaf-and-dumb [now "hearing-impaired"], etc. Writing is likewise a vast system of signs. Any psychology of sign systems will be part of social psychology, that is to say, will be exclusively social; it will involve the same psychology as is applicable in the case of languages. The laws governing changes in these systems of signs will often be significantly similar to laws of linguistic change. This can easily be seen in the case of writing although the signs are visual signs which undergo alterations comparable to phonetic phenomena.*

Saussure discusses signs as part of *semiology* (also called *semiotics*). Do you know what this discipline is? How is it related to linguistics? Would you say that the sociolinguistic study of writing and literacy is really a semiotic enterprise, or not?

8.   Read the following excerpt from A. Hudson (Outline of a Theory of Diglossia, 2002):

> *Gumperz's intermediate societies resemble quite closely Sjoberg's "preindustrialized civilized societies," in which the bulk of the written tradition consists mainly of the society's sacred writings, and where writing is restricted to, and is perpetuated by, a small, educated, priestly group (Sjoberg 1964:*

892). As a result, "the upper status, educated group typically employs at least two speech styles, in some cases more," all of which "differ from the speech of the common man—in the lexicon and often the phonology and grammar" (Sjoberg 1964: 893). Furthermore, the formal speech style "tends to be perpetuated over centuries with relatively little change, a phenomenon that results from the high prestige accorded it and its close tie with the written language" (Sjoberg 1964: 893).

Hudson suggests that literacy was once connected with sacredness and authority figures. Would you say that it has retained this function somewhat today, living in a secular world? Who are the authority figures today that espouse a form of literacy that we might want to emulate?

9　Would you say that processes of modernization have changed perceptions of literacy from the past? How so?

10　Read the following excerpt from S. Ali Dansieh (SMS Texting and Its Potential Impacts on Students' Written Communication Skills, 2011).

> *As more and more students worldwide acquire and use mobile phones, so are they immersing themselves in text messaging. Such is the situation that some teachers, parents and students themselves are expressing concerns that student writing skills stand the risk of being sacrificed on the altar of text messaging. In view of the attested addictive effects of text messaging (Nokia, 2002), caution must be exercised in encouraging students in its use. If not checked, students are likely to get so used to it that they may no longer realise the need for Standard English constructions even in writings that are supposed to be formal, a phenomenon O'Connor (2005) describes as "saturation." Be that as it may, it is important to eschew complacency and rather adopt conscious and pragmatic measures now so as to prevent the phenomenon from further worsening students' writing skills. All efforts must therefore be made to help students write good English whether on phone or paper.*

The author takes a negative view of textspeak, backing it up with his own empirical findings. What is your take on the debate? Is texting changing literacy for the worse, or is it just another form of literacy?

References

Auletta, K. (2008). *Googled: The End of the World as We Know It*. New York: Penguin.

Baron, N. S. (2008). *Always On*. Oxford: Oxford University Press.

Billeter, J. F. (1990). *The Chinese Art of Writing*. New York: Rizzoli.

Bloomfield, L. (1933). *Language*. New York: Holt.

Brown, R. (1958). *Words and Things: An Introduction to Language*. New York: The Free Press.

Carr, N. (2008). *The Shallows: What the Internet is Doing to our Brains*. New York: Norton.

Clay, M. (1966). *Reading: The Patterning of Complex Behaviour*. Auckland, New Zealand: Heinemann.

Coulmas, F. (1989). *The Writing Systems of the World*. Oxford: Blackwell.

Crystal, D. (2011). *Internet Linguistics: A Student Guide*. New York: Routledge.

Daniels, P. T. and Bright, W. (eds.) (1995). *The World's Writing Systems*. Oxford: Oxford University Press.

Dansieh, S. Ali (2011). SMS Texting and Its Potential Impacts on Students' Written Communication Skills. *International Journal of English Linguistics* 1: 222–229.

Derrida, J. (1976). *Of Grammatology*, trans. by G. C. Spivak. Baltimore: Johns Hopkins Press.

Derrida, J. (1978). *Writing and Difference*. Chicago: University of Chicago Press.

Foster, D. (2001). *Author Unknown: Tales of a Literary Detective*. New York: Holt.

Foucault, M. (1971). *The Archeology of Knowledge*, trans. by A. M. Sheridan Smith. New York: Pantheon.

Gee, J. P. (1996). *Social Linguistics and Literacies: Ideology in Discourses*. London: Taylor & Francis.

Gelb, I. J. (1963). *A Study of Writing*. Chicago: University of Chicago Press.

Goldwasser, O. (1995). *From Icon to Metaphor: Studies in the Semiotics of the Hieroglyphs*. Freiburg: Universtätsverlag.

Halliday, M. A. K. (1985). *Introduction to Functional Grammar*. London: Arnold.

Harris, R. (1986). *The Origin of Writing*. London: Duckworth.

Hodges, G. and Davies, B. (eds.) (2013). *Narrative and Literacy*. Special Issue of *Literacy*, 47, April 2013.

Hudson, A. (2002). Outline of a Theory of Diglossia. *International Journal of the Sociology of Language* 157: 1–48.

Kucera, H. and Nelson Francis, W. (1967). *Computational Analysis of Present-Day American English*. Providence: Brown University Press.

Lévi-Strauss, C. (1978). *Myth and Meaning: Cracking the Code of Culture*. Toronto: University of Toronto Press.

Lillis, T. (2013). *The Sociolinguistics of Writing*. Edinburgh: Edinburgh University Press.

McLuhan, M. (1964). *Understanding Media: The Extensions of Man*. London: Routledge.

Miller, G. A. (1981). *Language and Speech*. New York: W. H. Freeman.

Nida, E. A. (1992). Sociolinguistic Implications of Academic Writing. *Language in Society* 21: 477–485.

Pérez-Sabater, C. (2012). The Linguistics of Social Networking: A Study of Writing Conventions on Facebook. *Linguistik Online* 56, www.linguistik-online.de/56_12/perez-sabater.html (accessed 6 May 2015).

Propp, V. J. (1928). *Morphology of the Folktale*. Austin: University of Texas Press.

Quirk, R. (1960). Towards a Description of English Usage. *Transactions of the Philological Society*: 40–61.

Roy, M. (2000). *Sign After the X*. Vancouver: Advance Artspeak.

Saussure, F. de (1916). *Cours de linguistique générale*. Paris: Payot.

Schmandt-Besserat, D. (1978). The Earliest Precursor of Writing. *Scientific American* 238: 50–59.

Schmandt-Besserat, D. (1992). *Before Writing*, 2 vols. Austin: University of Texas Press.

Schuster, C. (1990). The Ideology of Literacy: A Bakhtinian Perspective. In: E. A. Lunsford, H. Moglen, and J. Slevin (eds.), *The Right to Literacy*. New York: MLA.

Sebba, M. (2009) Sociolinguistic Approaches to Writing Systems Research. *Writing Systems Research* 1: 35–49, DOI: 10.1093/wsr/wsp002

Selfe, C. (1999). *Technology and Literacy in the Twenty-First Century: The Importance of Paying Attention*. Carbondale: Southern Illinois University Press.

Tweedie, Fiona J., Singh, S. and Holmes, D. I. (1996). Neural Network Applications in Stylometry: The Federalist Papers. *Computers and the Humanities* 30: 1–10.

Vaidhyanathan, S. (2011). *The Googlization of Everything (and Why We Should Worry)*. Berkeley: University of California Press.

Walker, C. B. F. (1987). *Cuneiform*. Berkeley: University of California Press.

Wallis, S. and Nelson, G. (2001). Knowledge Discovery in Grammatically Analysed Corpora. *Data Mining and Knowledge Discovery* 5: 307–340.

Zipf, G. K. (1932). *Selected Studies of the Principle of Relative Frequency in Language*. Cambridge, MA: Harvard University Press.

8 Language, Mind, and Culture

All objects, all phases of culture are alive. They have voices. They speak of their history and interrelatedness. And they are all talking at once!

Camille Paglia (1947–)

As discussed in the opening chapter, linguistic anthropology and sociolinguistics share a large territory of research, theoretical interests, and overall objectives. The difference is really one of emphasis and, in part, of methodology. Linguistic anthropology focuses on the relation between language, mind, and culture, sociolinguistics more on the social structures mirrored in, and shaped by, language and its attendant conceptual structures. Clearly, the dividing line between the two is a thin one indeed.

The research agenda in "linguistic anthropology amalgamated with sociolinguistics" is a vast and varied one. What ties the work together between the two disciplines is the focus on the language–culture relation and the many ways that it manifests itself in everyday communicative phenomena such as vocabulary choices and conversations. In the earliest research efforts, the focus was on how cultural classification and language were intertwined because, as Sapir (1921: 75) wrote, the specific categories of the language that speakers are familiar with allow them to understand the real world:

> Human beings do not live in the object world alone, nor alone in the world of social activity as ordinarily understood, but are very much at the mercy of the particular language system which has become the medium of expression for their society. It is quite an illusion to imagine that one adjusts to reality essentially without the use of language and that language is merely an incidental means of solving specific problems of communication or reflection. The fact of the matter is that the "real world" is to a large extent unconsciously built up on the language habits of the group.

With different kinds of research techniques, work in this area, known more specifically as *ethnosemantics*, continues to this day. For instance, John Lucy

(1996) studied the effect of grammar on memory tasks in English and Yucatec (a Mayan language) speakers, focusing on the presence of a dichotomy between the two languages: English requires a plural marker for count nouns (*dog–dogs*); Yucatec does not, except for a small number of nouns. Lucy presented pictures of Yucatec village scenes to both speakers and asked them to perform recall tasks. He found that English speakers paid attention to the number of animate beings and objects, but ignored number for substances; Yucatec speakers paid attention to number only for animate beings. The experiment showed that grammatical categories did indeed condition how people recalled the world.

Overall, this line of inquiry has showed that, once classified, "reality" is a linguistic code. Of course, people can change their views of the world any time they want, by simply inventing new words for new realities that are meaningful to them. This chapter will look at the relation of language to culture and cognition, with a view towards related social effects. In other words, it will integrate sociolinguistics with linguistic anthropology in a general schematic, but hopefully insightful, way.

8.1 Language and Social Classification

In his study of American aboriginal languages, Boas (1940) discovered features that suggested to him that languages served people and societies, above all else, as classificatory systems for coming to grips with their particular environmental and social realities. For example, he noted that the Inuit language had devised various terms for the animal we call simply a *seal* in English:

- one is the general term for "seal";
- another renders the idea of "seal basking in the sun"; and
- a third refers to a "seal floating on a piece of ice."

This *specialized vocabulary*, as it is called, for referring to this particular animal is necessitated by the vital role that seals play (or have historically played) in Inuit life. Inuit vocabulary also has individual lexemes for referring to the different types of seals. In English, we must instead use descriptive terms (usually adjectives, metaphors, and the like) for referring to them: for example, *bull seal* and *elephant seal*, which are analogies to other animals that the seals appear to resemble. The study of the relation between language, mind, and culture starts with the study of specialized vocabularies.

8.1.1 Specialized Vocabularies

Specialized vocabularies serve classificatory functions across societies, encoding realities that are perceived to be critical by particular people. In contemporary technological culture, specialized terms to name new devices (*iPod*, *iPhone*, and so on) are being devised on a regular basis, bearing witness to the importance of digital devices and technologies in our culture. Not too long ago, we possessed a sophisticated terminology for referring to typewriters. Most of the terms have disappeared, for the simple reason that we no longer need them, unless of course we are a collector of antique typewriters. In a phrase, changes in language mirror changes in society and culture. Vocabulary also shapes how we come to perceive and understand that world, since the words we use guide everyday tasks of referring to the world. The ways in which language and cognition are intertwined—a topic that has ancient origins—is part of the broader scope of sociolinguistics as well as linguistic anthropology. The paraphrases used above to convey the various meanings of the terms used by the Inuit language to refer to seals show that there are always ways in which the resources of any language can be used for the purpose of cross-cultural communication.

Naming the objects, events, things, plants, flowers, animals, beings, ideas, and so on that make up human experience allows people to organize the world conceptually. Words allow us to remember those parts of the world that are considered meaningful in the society in which we are reared. Without names the world would not have parts to it that can be recalled at will through language; the world would remain a flux of impressions based on our senses and instinct.

Inuit Specialized Vocabulary

Seals

    natsiq (ringed seal)

    netsilak (adult seal)

    otok (basking seal)

    tiggak (breeding male)

    ugjuk (bearded seal)

Snow

    aputi (snow on the ground)

    siku (ice in general)

    aniu (snow used for water)

    pukak (crystalline snow)

    qanik (snow falling)

Some of the ways in which seals and snow are named, and thus classified, by Inuit speakers of central Canada show, as mentioned, that these two referents play a crucial role in their society. When a word is coined for a specific reason it automatically classifies something as part of a category, culling it into mental awareness. Consider the word *cat*. By naming this type of animal, we have *ipso facto* differentiated it conceptually from other animals. At the point of naming, the world is divided into animals that are *cats* and all the other animals, perceived provisionally as *non-cats*. Now, having distinguished cats from non-cats bears consequences—by having the word *cat* in our lexicon we are predisposed to attend to the presence of this creature in the world as unique. Armed with that word, we now turn our attention to the world of *non-cats*. Within that larger domain, we start to perceive the existence of creatures that have physical affinities to *cats*. Features such as whiskers, tails, and retractile claws, for instance, seem to associate the cat conceptually to other animals. This suggests a larger category. In English, the name for that is *feline*. The world of animals can now be divided into *felines* and *non-felines*. In the feline part, we can now devise further differentiations of cat-like creatures, naming them *lions*, *tigers*, *cougars*, *jaguars*. We might then consider further distinctions as being useful. The words *Siamese* and *Persian* (indicating the origin of the cat) are two such distinctions. At that point, we stop classifying the feline world and consider the *non-feline* one. And the whole differentiation process starts over. Cultures stop their classificatory decision-making when they no longer see differentiations as useful or necessary.

The word *feline* encodes what is known today in psychology as a *superordinate* concept. Such a word has a general classificatory function. The word *cat* encodes instead a *basic* or *prototypical* concept. *Lions*, *cougars*, *jaguars*, and *tigers* also belong to this level of classification. Finally, the word *Siamese* encodes a subordinate concept. It indicates a type of *cat*. The reason for making such fine distinctions has some social or cultural reason behind it. Classifying felines in the way just described is just that—one way. We could easily have classified cats in some other category, along with *dogs* and *horses*, given that they are all four-legged creatures.

Because of the inbuilt relativity of specialized vocabularies, biologists decided early on to establish universal criteria for classification, so that they could communicate with each other unambiguously, regardless of language. But deciding what criteria are critical in science has always been a difficult problem. The scientific classification of animals depends largely on the features the animals are perceived to share. In general, the more features they share, the more closely they are seen to be related. The largest group is the kingdom *Animalia* itself, which includes all animals. Next, each animal is placed in a group called a *phylum*. Each phylum is divided into groups called *classes*. The classes are broken down into *orders*, and the orders into *families*. The families are split into *genera*, and the genera into *species*.

Such schemas are called *taxonomies* (the word comes from the Greek for "naming arrangements"). Taxonomies have always existed, even in pre-scientific eras. Early human beings divided all organisms into two groups—useful and harmful, as archeological research has revealed. As people began to recognize more kinds of living things, they developed new ways to classify them. One of the most useful schemes was suggested by Aristotle, who classified animals as those having red blood (animals with backbones) and those without red blood (animals without backbones). He divided plants by size and appearance as herbs, shrubs, or trees. Aristotle's scheme served as the basis for classification for almost 2,000 years. During the seventeenth century, the English biologist John Ray (1627–1705) first suggested the idea of species in classification. But the basic system for modern classification began with the work of the Swedish naturalist Carolus Linnaeus (1707–1778) in the subsequent eighteenth century. Linnaeus classified organisms according to their physical structure and gave distinctive two-word names to each species. Modern classifications are based on microscopic structural and biochemical characteristics, as well as on presumed evolutionary relationships among organisms.

8.1.2 Words and Concepts

Conceptual knowledge is not an innate feature of the mind. Like other animals, human infants come to understand the world at first with their senses. When they grasp objects, for instance, they are discovering the tactile properties of things; when they put objects in their mouths, they are probing their gustatory properties; and so on. However, in a remarkably short period of time, they start replacing sensory knowledge with conceptual knowledge—that is, with words, pictures, and other sign-forms that stand for things. This event is extraordinary—all children require is simple exposure to words and symbols in social context for concepts to form. From that point on, they require their sensory apparatus less and less to gain knowledge, becoming more and more dependent on words and symbols to learn about the world.

The question now becomes: How do we shift from sensory to conceptual modes of knowledge? Take the word *blue* in English. As a concrete concept, *blue* was probably motivated from observing a pattern of hue found in natural phenomena such as the sky and the sea, and then by noting the occurrence of the same hue in other things. The specific concept that *blue* elicits in the mind will, of course, be different from individual to individual. But all variants will fall within a certain hue range on the light spectrum. In a phrase, the word *blue* allows speakers of English to talk and think about the occurrence of a specific hue in the world. But that is not all it does. Speakers use the very same word to characterize emotions, morals, and other abstractions. Consider, for instance, the two sentences below:

1   Today I've got the *blues*.
2   That piece of information hit me right out of the *blue*.

The use of *blue* in (1) to mean "sad" or "gloomy" is the result of a culture-specific process, coming out of the tradition of "blues" music, which is perceived typically to evoke sadness or melancholy through its melodies, harmonies, rhythms, and lyrics. The use of *blue* in (2) to render the concept of "unexpectedness" comes, instead, out of the tradition of ascribing unpredictability to the weather. In other words, the category encoded by *blue* is expanded in culture-specific ways through a system of associations. In the nineteenth century, the early psychologists, guided by the principles enunciated by James Mill (1773–1836) in his *Analysis of the Phenomena of the Human Mind* (1829), studied experimentally how subjects made associations. They found that factors such as intensity, inseparability, and repetition played a role in associative processes: for example, arms are associated with bodies because they are inseparable from them; rainbows are associated with rain because of repeated observations of the two as co-occurring phenomena; and so on.

8.2 The Whorfian Hypothesis

The presence of specialized vocabularies in the world's languages suggests that early cultures did not coin words arbitrarily, but on the basis of need. This suggests, in turn, that languages that are used habitually, rather than reflectively, shape perception. This is commonly called the *relativity principle*, or the Whorfian Hypothesis (WH), as pointed out several times. The workings of this principle can be seen even in the use of an apparently simple particle of speech such as a preposition. In English we read something *in a newspaper*, implying through that preposition that we have learned to perceive the newspaper as a container of information into which we must go to seek it out. That is why we also say that *we got a lot out of the newspaper*, or that there *was nothing in it*. On the other hand, Italian speakers use the preposition *su* (on), implying that the information is impressed on the surface of the pages through its words. In Italian, therefore, there are no expressions similar to *we got a lot out of the newspaper* and *there was nothing in it*.

The WH is connected intrinsically with specialized vocabulary formations. If someone were to utter the word *hand* in English, the image that comes to our mind is that of the lower appendage of the arm; if someone says *ruká* in Russian, then the image that comes to mind is that of the whole appendage, from shoulder to fingers. One should read no more into the WH than this. It simply asserts that the way we classify the world, or talk about it, with our specific languages evokes images in our minds that other languages do not. For sociolinguistics it means that the words we use to refer to certain social phenomena carry with them social concepts that are implicit in the world we live in. The use of the title *Mrs.* indicates that we see women as married or not, whereas *Mr.* for men implies no such association, as we saw. The question of which came first, the word or the thought is a moot point; it is sufficient to say that the two are interconnected.

8.2.1 Language and Thought

The idea that language shapes people's perception of reality caught the attention of the Gestalt psychologists in the 1930s. Gestalt psychology is a school that aims to discover the extent to which forms influence perception. They found, for example, that when they showed subjects a picture and then asked them later to reproduce it, the reproductions were influenced by the verbal label assigned to the picture. The drawing of two circles joined by a straight line, for instance, would generally be reproduced as something resembling "eyeglasses" by those subjects who were shown the *eyeglasses* label. On the other hand, those who were shown the *dumbbells* label tended to reproduce it as something resembling "dumbbells."

There is no other way to explain the results, other than by the fact that language conditions the way we see things. The Navajo language of Arizona is rich with words referring to lines of various shapes, colors, and configurations. The language has around 100 words for this purpose (much more than English). Among the words are the following three:

1   *Adziisgai*, a word referring to "parallel white lines running off into the distance."
2   *Ahééhesgai*, a word referring to "more than two white lines forming concentric circles."
3   *Álhch'inidzigai*, a word designating to "two white lines coming together at a point."

Although the word *angle* is used in English for (3), it refers to the space between the lines, not the lines themselves. There are no equivalent words for these figures in English. The gist is that Navajo speakers have a more sophisticated vocabulary for discussing geometrical arrangements than do speakers of English, who must use lengthier descriptions to achieve the same result. Nevertheless, English speakers (or speakers of any other language) can come up with ways of describing the figures encoded by the Navajo words. The Navajo classificatory system suggests that the geometry of basic shapes has cultural value. It thus comes as little surprise that Navajo toponyms (place names) are overwhelmingly geometrical. For example, the term *Tse Áh˝ii'áhá* is used to describe "two rocks standing vertically parallel to each other." Does this mean that Navajo speakers perceive the world differently from English speakers? It might. Once classified, the world is passed on through language forms to subsequent generations who acquire knowledge of the world through those very forms. Of course, subsequent generations can change their views of the world any time they want, by simply inventing new words.

Examples of perceptual differences shaped by language differences abound. In English, when we say that something is *in front of us* or *ahead*, we imply that it will occur in the future; while something which is *behind us* is perceived as having occurred in the past.

1   Your whole life lies *in front* of you.
2   Do you know what lies *ahead*?
3   Just put all that *behind* you. It's ancient history.
4   I have fallen *behind* in my work.

These expressions seem so natural to us that we rarely stop to consider what it implies. We tend to perceive time as standing still while people travel through it, from left to right. The lexicon of the English language presents us with ways to articulate this. Greek speakers, on the other hand, perceive people as standing still while time overtakes them from behind. The future is still behind, and not yet visible, while the past is already in front, and thus visible. The Greek lexicon presents comparable ways to articulate this.

The language with which Whorf became fascinated was Hopi, an American aboriginal language spoken in the southwest region of the US (Whorf 1956). Today there are only about 11,000 Hopi people, half of whom live on the Hopi reservation in Arizona. They live in 11 villages on or near three high mesas (tablelands). One village, Oraibi, is one of the oldest continuously inhabited villages in America. It was founded about 800 years ago. Two things in particular about the language spoken by the Hopi caught Whorf's attention (SAE = Standard Average European):

1   *Plurality and Numeration.* SAE languages form both real and imaginary plurals—"four people," "ten days." The latter is considered to be imaginary because it cannot be objectively experienced as an aggregate. SAE tends to objectify time, treating it as a measurable object ("two days, four months," etc.). Hopi, on the other hand, does not have imaginary plurals, since only objective aggregates can be counted. Moreover, it treats units of time as cyclic events, not as measurable ones.
2   *Verb Tense.* SAE languages have three basic tense categories that predispose speakers to view time sequences as occurring in the present, in the past, and in the future. Hopi verbs, on the other hand, are marked by validity forms, which indicate whether the speaker reports, anticipates, or speaks from previous experience, and by aspectual forms, which indicate duration and other characteristics of an action.

These two aspects of Hopi grammar, Whorf claimed, mirror their philosophy of the world and, thus, how they organize their lives. By not seeing time as an objectifiable phenomenon, Hopi people are less dependent on devices such as watches, timetables, and the like to carry out their daily affairs. Their philosophy of how things work in the world is mirrored in their verb tense system.

The WH has been a topic of fierce debate among linguists, ever since Whorf articulated it in the 1940s. Those opposed to the WH allege that it implies that we are prisoners of the languages we speak. But there is no such implication in the WH, at least as I understand it. It simply states that language and thought are intertwined. The WH certainly does not claim that the languages of other cultures cannot be learned. This happens every time someone learns a foreign language, as a classic study of Navajo children dramatically showed (Kramsch 1998: 13–14). Navajo children speak a language that encodes the actions of "picking up a round object," such as a ball, and "picking up a long, thin flexible object," such as a rope, as obligatory categories. When presented with a blue rope, a yellow rope, and a blue stick, and asked to choose which object goes best with the blue rope, Navajo children tend to choose the yellow rope, associating the objects on the basis of their shapes, whereas English-speaking children almost always choose the blue stick, associating the objects on the basis of color, even though both groups of children are perfectly able to distinguish colors and shapes. In effect, the speakers tend to sort out and distinguish things according to the categories provided by their languages. Interestingly, Navajo children who had studied English chose the blue stick and yellow rope in a fairly equal way.

In a truly fascinating study, a government survey-taker, named Alfred Bloom, reported what he found during one of his surveys just before Hong Kong was to become part of China in the early 1980s, gaining autonomy from its British past (Bloom 1981). He did so because he found the answer to one of his questions rather extraordinary, given its Whorfian implications. The question was (paraphrased): *If the government were to take away your freedom, what would you do?* Bloom found that native speakers of English responded, as anticipated, with answers such as the following (paraphrased again here for convenience):

A: I would leave.
B: I'm not sure what I would do.
C: I probably wouldn't do anything.
D: I would organize a protest.
E: What could I do? Probably nothing.

The verbal structure *If… were to* is an example of a counterfactual, a syntactic form that is intended to convey the concept of "contrary to given facts." In all responses by native speakers he got a type of response that follows logically from the counterfactual: *I would…*, *What could I…*. However, when he asked the same question to speakers who had learned English in school and for whom it was not a native language, he got the following typical response:

Question: If the government were to take away your freedom, what would you do?
Response: It hasn't.

Bloom explained the differential pattern of responses in Whorfian terms by suggesting that the non-native speakers had not developed a functional knowledge of counterfactuals and thus answered in factual terms. Bloom's study created a fuss, with many claiming that it was biased against speakers of Chinese. But what the critics missed is that Chinese has other ways to convey counter-to-fact ideas. They are different but just as effective as English.

Take, as another example, the verb system of Navajo. In that language, the categorization of motion is a major conceptual focus of its verb system. Many verbs designate specific aspects of motion and of objects affected by motion. For this reason, Navajo uses metaphors of motion in its verb system, which manifest a specific kind of understanding and experience of the world that contrasts conspicuously with English, as the following examples show:

Table 8.1 Navajo Concepts

English Concept	Navajo Concept Translated Literally
one dresses	one moves into clothing
one lives	one moves about here and there
one is young	one moves about newly
to sing	to move words out of an enclosed space
to greet someone	to move a round solid object to meet someone

Comparisons such as this provide concrete insights into how cultural perceptions of reality are reflected in the structure of grammars. Differences in grammar end up being, essentially, differences in worldview. They are neither better nor worse, just different, encoding the specific needs of the people that created them.

The American linguist Ronald Langacker (1987, 1990, 1999) is well known for his study of language and thought. Nouns, he claims, elicit images of referents that appear to trace a "region" in mind-space—for example a count noun is imagined as referring to something that encircles a bounded region, whereas a mass noun is visualized as designating a non-bounded region. The noun *water* elicits an image of a non-bounded region, whereas the noun *leaf* evokes an image of bounded region. This conceptual dichotomy produces grammatical effects—*leaves* can be counted, *water* cannot; *leaf* has a plural form (*leaves*), *water* does not (unless the referential domain is metaphorical); *leaf* can be preceded by an indefinite article (*a leaf*), *water* cannot; and so on. These grammatical features encode different perceptions of things, as can be seen by examining the same referential domains in other languages. In Italian, for

> ### Grammar terms
>
> *Mass (Noncount) Noun:*
>
> - a noun referring to something that cannot be counted, such as a substance or quality; in English a mass noun lacks a plural in ordinary usage and is not used with the indefinite article: *rice, baggage, ice*
>
> - it will have a plural form when it refers to different units or types: *sugars, breads, meats.*
>
> *Count Noun:*
>
> - a noun referring to something than can be counted: *book, leaf*
>
> - it will thus have a plural form and, in the singular, can be used with the indefinite article (*books, a book, leaves, a leaf*).

instance, the concept of *grapes* is assigned to the mass noun category (*uva*). As a consequence there is no plural form for *uva*.

In reviewing relevant studies, Deutscher (2005) came to the conclusion that the grammatical gender of a noun influences the way we think about the object it names. This occurs on a subconscious level, suggesting that language plays a role in the formation of memory and implicit thoughts.

There is another side to the debate, however (Martin 1986; Pullum 1991). The often-cited example of the many words for snow in the Inuit dialects has been challenged on several counts. Laura Martin, for instance, argued that it was a specious claim, since it depends on what we mean by lexeme. In the Inuit language it is obvious that there are different lexemic resources from those in English. The former prefers individual lexemes, the latter phrases and expressions to refer to snow patterns. But the results are the same. Geoffrey Pullum (1991) concurred, calling the whole situation a hoax. The problem lies in the definition of "word." Pullum argued that the number of word roots used for "snow"—which is thought by some to have as many as 30 to 40 separate words for different referents of what we call simply "snow" in English—is not extensive and parallel to the number of words in English: *qani-* for "snowflake," *apu-* for "snow lying on the ground or covering things up," which is similar to English "slush." But this misses the point that different lexicalizations involve different needs and thus emphases. The debate cannot be resolved, of course. What is of relevance here is that the WH raises specific and intriguing questions that can be researched empirically and debated theoretically. And that is what sociolinguistics and linguistic anthropology are essentially about.

8.2.2 Specialized Needs

As mentioned several times, every culture develops specialized vocabularies over time according to need. In other words, specialized vocabularies emerge to serve specialized needs. In Shinzwani (a language spoken in the Comoro Islands of the western Indian Ocean), the word *mama* refers to both *mother* and *aunt*. The reason for this is that the two individuals perform similar kinship duties. As this simple, albeit key, example shows, naming mirrors specific kinds of social concepts. In English, the primary kinship relations are encoded by the words *mother*, *father*, *brother*, *sister*, *grandmother*, *grandfather*, *grandson*, *granddaughter*, *niece*, *nephew*, *mother-in-law*, *father-in-law*, *sister-in-law*, and *brother-in-law*. English vocabulary also distinguishes between *first* and *second cousins* and *great-aunts*, *great-uncles*, and so on. However, it does not distinguish lexically between younger and older siblings. Moreover, English distinguishes a *nephew/niece* from a *grandchild*. But the latter distinction is not encoded in other languages. In Italian, for example, *nipote* refers to both "nephew/niece" and "grandchild."

Kinship terms reveal how the family is perceived in a given culture, what relationships are considered to be especially important, and what attitudes towards specific kin may exist. Take, as another example, the Hawaiian kinship system, where all relatives of the same generation and sex are referred to with the same term—the term used to refer to *father* is used as well for the father's brother and the mother's brother (for which we use *uncle*). Similarly, the mother, her sister, and the father's sister (for which we use *aunt*) are all classified together under a single term. Essentially, kinship reckoning in Hawaiian culture involves putting relatives of the same sex and age into the same category. On the other hand, in the Sudanese system, the mother's brother is distinguished from the father, and mother's sister is distinguished from the mother, as well as from the father's sister. Each cousin is distinguished from all others, as well as from siblings. This system is one of the most precise ones in existence. In few societies are all aunts, uncles, cousins, and siblings named and treated as equals in the kinship line.

Color terminologies are similarly specialized, as already discussed (Chapter 2). Potentially, we can perceive perhaps as many as 10 million hues. Our names for these are, thus, far too limited to cover them all. As a result, we often have difficulty trying to describe or match a certain color, showing that we have named those hues that are common and necessary in our world. A classic study of color terminology is the 1953 one by linguist Verne Ray. Ray interviewed the speakers of 60 different languages spoken in the southwestern part of the US. He showed them colored cards under uniform conditions of lighting, asking the speakers to name them. The colors denoted by *black*, *white* and *gray* were not included in the study.

Ray was able to show how the color terms overlapped, contrasted, and coincided with each other. In Tenino and Chilcotin, for example, a part of the range of English *green* is covered by a term that includes *yellow*. In Wishram and Takelma, on the other hand, there are as many terms as in English, but the boundaries are different. In still other cases, there are more distinctions than in English. Ray (1953: 59) concluded as follows: "Color systems serve to bring the world of color sensation into order so that perception may be relatively simple and behavioral response, particularly verbal response and communication, may be meaningful."

Shortly after, in 1955, Harold Conklin examined the four-term color system of the Hanunóo of the Philippines. He found that the four categories into which the Hanunóo grouped colors were interconnected with light and the plant world (the prefix *ma-* means "having" or "exhibiting"):

ma-biru ("darkness, blackness")
ma-lagti ("lightness, whiteness")
ma-rara ("redness, presence of red")
ma-latuy ("greenness, presence of green").

The *ma-biru* category implies absence of light, and thus includes not only *black* but also many deep shades—*dark blue, violet, green, gray,* and so on. The *ma-lagti* category implies instead the presence of light, and thus includes *white* and many lightly pigmented shades. The other two terms derive from an opposition of freshness and dryness in plants—*ma-rara* includes *red, orange,* and *yellow,* and ma-*latuy* includes *light green* and *brown.* The Hanunóo language can, of course, refer to color gradations more specifically than this, if the need should arise. But its basic system encodes a "color reality" that is specific to the Hanunóo's environment.

Specialized vocabularies bring out how language serves specific human needs and then doubles back on humans to guide their view of the world. Consider bodies of water. In English, we classify them as *lakes, oceans, rivers, streams, seas, creeks,* and so on. Clearly, bodies of water are important in English, perhaps because of the importance of such bodies in the original English-speaking world. People living in the desert have very few words for bodies of water, for obvious reasons. Because of their importance, criteria such as size enter the classificatory picture—*ocean* versus *lake*—as does width and length—*river* versus *stream*—among other features.

As another example, consider sitting objects, which are also important to English speakers, probably because of the extensive industry developed over time to produce such objects. Here are a few examples of how English vocabulary is specialized in this domain:

Table 8.2 Sitting Objects in English

Object	Distinguishing Features (Among Others)
chair	sits one person, with a back
stool	sits one person, without a back
sofa	sits more than one person, with a back, soft
bench	sits more than one person, with a back, hard
lawn chair	sits one person, with a back that can be reclined
armchair	sits one person, with a back, soft

These words are said to constitute a *lexical field* (as mentioned). This is defined as a set of concepts that share some basic property (in this case "designed for sitting"). Color concepts, kinship terms, and the like all form lexical fields. These show how language serves needs and how the two evolve in tandem.

8.3 Ethnosemantics

The discussion of specialized vocabularies falls under the category of *ethnosemantics*, or the study of semantic systems in terms of their culture-specific implications. Through the study of specialized vocabularies, lexical fields, and the like, ethnosemantics attempts to understand the relation between language and specific forms of knowledge. It was Franz Boas (Chapter 1) who established the principles of ethnosemantic research, emphasizing the study of language as a product of historical and geographical conditions.

Data is gathered by fieldwork and basic ethnographic method (Chapter 1). This implies that the analyst has to enter into the mindset of a specific culture and how the language used allows the culture to understand and interpret its particular reality. Ethnosemantics developed the technique of componential analysis that is now used broadly within linguistics—the technique involves decomposing meaning into constituent elements.

8.3.1 Componential Analysis

Consider the word sets below:

1   father, mother, son, daughter
2   bull, cow, calf (male), heifer
3   dog (male), dog (female), pup (male), pup (female).

If we contrast the items in these sets with words such as *bread, milk, sword, car*, and so on we can easily see that they all share the property of animacy (that is, they refer to living referents). Hence, the feature [±animate] would appear to be a basic component of the meaning of the items in all three sets. Now, comparing the items in set (1) with those in (2) and (3) it is easy to see that they are kept distinct by the feature [±human]; and comparing the items in (2) and (3) it is obvious that the distinctions [±bovine] and [±canine] are needed. Within each set, what keeps the first two items separate from the second two is the feature [±adult]. Finally, [±male] and [±female] are needed to ensure that all items contrast by at least one feature. We can draw up a table to show which distinctive semantic features (or components) are possessed by each word as follows:

Table 8.3 Componential Analysis

	animate	human	bovine	canine	adult	male	female
father	+	+	-	-	+	+	-
mother	+	+	-	-	+	-	+
son	+	+	-	-	-	+	-
daughter	+	+	-	-	-	-	+
bull	+	-	+	-	+	+	-
cow	+	-	+	-	+	-	+
calf (male)	+	-	+	-	-	+	-
heifer	+	-	+	-	-	-	+
dog (male)	+	-	-	+	+	+	-
dog (female)	+	-	-	+	+	-	+
pup (male)	+	-	-	+	-	+	-
pup (female)	+	-	-	+	-	-	+

This type of table makes it possible to show what differentiates, say, *mother* from *daughter* or *heifer* from *dog (female)* in a precise manner. Although this is a useful way of establishing the differential meanings of lexical items, it can produce anomalous results. The difference above between *heifer* and *dog (female)* can be given as either [+bovine] versus [-bovine] or as [-canine] versus [+canine]. There really is no way to establish which one is, conceptually, the actual trigger in the opposition. Moreover, when certain words are defined in terms of features, it becomes obvious that to keep them distinct one will need quite a vast array of semantic features. The whole exercise would thus become artificial and convoluted. One might need as many features as words.

But this approach is still useful in studying different feature arrays for different languages, which will reveal which distinctions are meaningful. Thus, componential analysis can be used simply as an organizing grid to understand the data collected at "face value." It is a starting point in ethnosemantic analysis. Obviously, the larger "meaning picture" will subsequently become dominant in refining the overall analysis of meaning. In English, generational differences in kinship systems are distinguished lexically. Take, for instance, the [female] gender component in descending order (from the oldest to the youngest):

1   grandmother
2   mother
3   daughter
4   granddaughter.

Logically, there are other critical features in English, such as the distinction between this set and the correlative [male] set, *mother–father, sister–brother*, and the set of [lineal, collateral relations], *mother–aunt, daughter–niece*. In Iroquois dialects the system shares some components with the English one, in the area of generational and sex distinctions, but it is also different. For example, it uses separate terms for older and younger siblings: older sister–younger sister; older brother–younger brother. And it groups together lineal categories: father–father's brother; mother–mother's sister.

Ethnosemantic research has shown that classification systems share various componential properties, but also are adaptive to the specific environment and situation in which a language develops. The language spoken by the Papago people of Arizona has a sophisticated vocabulary for referring to plants. It has five classes that reflect the environment in which the Papago live and economy connected to it:

- trees = stick things
- cacti = stickers
- cultivated seasonals = things planted from seeds
- wild seasonals = growing by itself
- unlabeled = wild perennials that are neither cacti, trees, nor bushes.

These show that the features [±stick figure] and [±planting] are essential in how the Papago speak about and perceive plants. Similar analyses throughout the world have shown that lexical fields form componential systems. We saw above that sitting objects in English are distinguished by features such as [±back], [±more than person], and so on.

8.3.2 Cultural Schemas

Another ethnosemantic notion is that of *cultural schema* (CS) (Nishida 1999), which is basically a unit of pre-established cultural knowledge about some familiar situation. CS theory proposes that when we interact with members of the same society in certain situations and talk about certain topics with them many times, cultural schemas are involved in guiding conversations and discourses.

CSs include categories of color, images of abstractions such as love, and other schemas that emerge from a society's collective knowledge (Malcolm and Sharafian 2002). CSs are structures of information derived from cultural experiences that allow people to interpret the world in specific ways. In a fundamental sense, each word is a CS, since it is a capsule of information about the world, coded in a specific way and thus interpreted each time it is used.

The main types of CSs for social interaction, according to Nishida (1999), are as follows:

1   *Fact-and-concept schemas*: These are knowledge units framed with specific lexemes that refer to general facts about the world, such as the fact that New York is a city in America, or the fact that automobiles are vehicles with (generally) four wheels and a motor. These schemas typically involve denotative concepts.

2   *Person schemas*: These refer to different types of people or personality traits. They are typically encoded by adjectives and other qualitative structures: *shy, outgoing, cute, intelligent*. They are portrayals of personality features that are steeped in cultural experiences and formulations.

3   *Self schemas*: These refer to how people see themselves, and thus to how they expect others to see them. Personal pronouns (*I, you*) and other forms allow people to juxtapose themselves against others through the relational functions of schemas of this type.

4   *Role schemas*: These refer to social roles that condition sets of behaviors in given situations. These are encoded by gendered language, class-based language, and the like. For example, the use of registers involves role schemas, as do honorifics.

5   *Context schemas*: These refer to how certain contexts can change meanings and how it is possible to adapt to these.

6   *Procedure schemas*: These refer to the relevant sequence of events that apply in common situations. At a restaurant, the order of speech mirrors the order in which dishes are served.

7   *Strategy schemas*: These involve language used to solve problems. The language of teachers is full of strategy schemas. For instance, a music teacher will say "bring this up" in order to get a student to solve the problem of wrong dynamics.

8   *Emotion schemas*: These are schemas that contain affective information. Expressions such as *I love you with all my heart* reveals that we locate some emotions in an organ.

CS theory is closely linked to the ideas put forward by Lakoff and others in the conceptual metaphor movement (discussed previously). Recall that the metaphorical statement "That person is a snake" connects two referents: (1) "that person" and (2) "a snake." The linkage of the two is guided by a mental schema that infers similarities between the two referents. It is a schema for evaluating personality encoded in the formula *people are animals*, which is the conceptual metaphor. The schema engenders a perspective of personality that literal language cannot possible convey—a perspective that is sensory and based on cultural experiences and representations of snakes as dangerous reptiles. The reason why we speak this way, claims Lakoff (1987), is because we unconsciously perceive qualities in one domain (the animal kingdom) as coexistent in another domain (human personality). Take, for example, linguistic metaphors such as the ones below:

1   Your ideas are circular, leading us nowhere.
2   I never saw the point of that idea.
3   Those are central to the entire discussion.
4   Our ideas are diametrically opposite.

The conceptual metaphor is: *ideas are geometrical figures/relations*. The origin of this conceptual metaphor is traceable, in all likelihood, to the tradition of using geometry for abstract discourse. Lakoff and Johnson (1980) trace the cognitive source of such language, as mentioned, to image schemas—mental outlines or images that are produced by our sensory experiences of locations, movements, shapes, substances, and so forth, as well as our experiences of social events in general.

Schema theories in general are now used broadly in anthropology and sociolinguistics to explain the link between language, mind, and culture. Like other theories they provide a basis on which to design studies and conduct research. Whether they are "true" or not in any sense is a moot point. The real point is that they allow for investigations to take place in a structured way. Sometimes researchers end up finding the opposite of what they were looking for. That is how all science works.

8.4 The Whorfian Hypothesis Online

If different languages encode different cultural and cognitive categories, which may affect the way people think, then the online changes that are taking place should have an impact on people's worldviews. Only a handful of studies exist on the relation of e-language on cognition. Lanchantin, Simoës-Perlant, and Largy (2012) examined the instant messages of 32 French-speaking students around the age of 13. They found that the digital writers used a form of "graphemic cognition" that translates sounds into letters and expressions. Tagliamonte and Denis (2008) collected data from traditional and digital writing texts of English-speaking adolescents between the ages of 15 and 20, noting that there were no differences in how the languages were used to talk about the same referents. But Baron (2010) contested this pattern of findings suggesting that the use of words is reduced as much as possible in digital writing, making it vastly different. Users write their instant messages by breaking sentences down in ways that were different in F2F conversations.

Huang, Yen, and Zhang (2008) looked at the effects of emoticons on users of instant messages (IMs). Since many people maintain constant contact with multiple friends and relations via IMs simultaneously whenever they are online, whether working on other applications or not, the potential effect of IM style on cognition is probable. The researchers explored the effects of emoticon use on cognition and emotional states. The results showed that the user of emoticons felt a positive effect on enjoyment, personal interaction, perceived information richness, and perceived usefulness. The results suggested, therefore, that emoticons were not just enjoyable to use, but also a way of involving people cognitively and emotionally that may have little or no corresponding features in F2F contexts.

Zappavigna (2011) explored how language is used to build community with Twitter. A corpus of 45,000 tweets was collected in the 24 hours after the announcement of Barak Obama's victory in the 2008 US presidential elections. Zappavigna looked at the evaluative language used to affiliate in tweets. She found that the hashtag had extended its meaning potential to operate as a linguistic marker referencing the target of evaluation in a tweet (#Obama). That fact both rendered the language searchable and used to upscale the call to affiliate with values expressed in the tweet. Zappavigna concluded that there is now a cultural shift in electronic discourse from online conversation to such "searchable talk." In this case the subtext is: "Search for me and affiliate with my value!"

Much work needs to be done in this domain of research. The basic assumption is that if we change the form of language, or invent new forms, then cognition is altered. If this is so, then the study of the Whorfian Hypothesis online is an important aspect of general sociolinguistic and anthropological research. Cyberspace is a new field laboratory to test out this hypothesis.

Terminology Review

Define or explain in your own words the following terms introduced in this chapter. Some have already been introduced but are elaborated upon here.

componential analysis	cultural schema
ethnosemantics	semantic feature
specialized vocabulary	Whorfian Hypothesis

Exercises and Discussion

1   How many names do you know for dogs? In effect, these are ways of classifying the different breeds. Give the social meaning that each one elicits.

2   Make a list of the emotion(s) designated by the given color terms in English, giving a probable reason why the terms and the emotions were linked in the first place.

Example: green = envy (*You're green with envy*).
Possible reason: Green is the color of grass and an associated English expression, *The grass is greener on the other side*, may indicate that one envies that "grass," metaphorically speaking. This is, of course, just a guess.

(a) red
(b) green
(c) yellow
(d) blue
(e) pink.

3   Go through a dictionary of a language other than English. Set up the following categories of vocabulary, translating the words that illustrate them and thus comparing them to English. What patterns, if any, do you notice?

(a) kinship
(b) occupations
(c) plants
(d) animal
(e) spatial terms.

4   Using componential analysis, establish the least number of features that will be needed to keep each set of words distinct.

(a)	Distinctive Feature
mouth	_____
arm	_____
hair (on the head)	_____
neck	_____
body	_____
finger	_____
face	_____
forehead	_____
leg	_____
knee	_____
elbow	_____
cheek	_____
lip	_____

tongue   _____
hand   _____
nose   _____
eye   _____
ear   _____
chest   _____
foot   _____
shoulder   _____
head   _____
fingernail   _____
(b)
mother   _____
father   _____
son   _____
daughter   _____
brother   _____
sister   _____
grandfather   _____
grandmother   _____
uncle   _____
aunt   _____
cousin   _____

5   Read the following excerpt from B. L. Whorf's *Language, Thought, and Reality*, 1956:

> *When linguists became able to examine critically and scientifically a large number of languages of widely different patterns, their base of reference was expanded; they experienced an interruption of phenomena hitherto held universal, and a whole new order of significances came into their ken. It was found that the background linguistic system (in other words, the grammar) of each language is not merely a reproducing instrument for voicing ideas but rather is itself the shaper of ideas, the program and guide for people's mental activity, for their analysis of impressions, for their synthesis of their mental stock in trade. Formulation of ideas is not an independent process, strictly rational in the old sense, but is part of a particular grammar and differs, from slightly to greatly, among different grammars. We dissect nature along lines laid down by our native languages. The categories and types that we isolate from the world of phenomena we do not find there because they stare every observer in the face; on the contrary, the world is presented in a kaleidoscopic flux of impressions which has to be organized by our minds— and this means largely by the linguistic systems in our minds. We cut nature up, organize it into concepts, and ascribe significances as we do, largely because we are parties to an agreement to organize it in this way—an agreement that holds throughout our speech community and is codified in the*

patterns of our language. The agreement is, of course, an implicit and unstated one, but its terms are absolutely obligatory; we cannot talk at all except by subscribing to the organization and classification of data which the agreement decrees.

Summarize Whorf's ideas in your own words. Do you agree?

6   Can you give examples of words in other languages that cannot be translated into English and are thus borrowed? One example would be the French word *naïve*.

7   Give examples of specialized vocabularies in English that reflect modern-day living, as for example the vocabulary associated with computers, fashion, and cars. Do these vocabularies have exact counterparts in other cultures? Which do and which do not? Why?

8   Read the following excerpt from G. Wrisley's, Rules, Language, and Reality, 2014:

> *Language plays an enormously important role in our interaction with other people and with the world. We employ various words and concepts to talk about objects (tables and flowers), properties (colors and shapes), and relations (the flower is on the table, the pain is in my arm). We express feelings, ask questions, give commands, tell jokes, tell stories, sing songs, and so on. So let's return to our initial questions: How is it that we're able to do all of these things with language? How is it that certain signs, symbols, and sounds are meaningful, and what exactly is their meaning? Is the word 'cat' meaningful because of what it refers to—namely, those furry, meowing fleabags many of us have as pets? Is the meaning of 'cat' just those animals themselves? Further, does the world determine what our concepts are to be? That is, with language do we simply try to mirror the various kinds of objects, properties, and relations that exist, or is the world 'open' to different ways of conceptualizing it?*

Do you think reality is filtered by the categories of language? How so?

9   The counterargument to the Whorfian Hypothesis is that each language encodes the same reality with different forms, but in effect refers to the same world. Do you agree with this side of the debate? Why?

10   Read the following excerpt from F. Wei, W. K. Wang, and M. Klausner's, Rethinking College Students' Self-Regulation and Sustained Attention: Does Text Messaging During Class Influence Cognitive Learning? 2012:

> *Students' texting during class emerged as a partial mediator of the effect of self-regulation on sustained attention. The results showed that college students' self-regulation was negatively related to their text messaging use during class, which in turn was negatively related to their sustained attention*

to classroom learning, meaning that college students who possess a high level of self-regulation are less likely to text during class and are more likely to sustain their attention to classroom learning.

Do you think that text messaging in class affects your thought processes?

References

Baron, N. S. (2010). Discourse Structures in Instant Messaging: The Case of Utterance Breaks. Language@Internet 7. www.languageatinternet.org/articles/2010/2651/Baron (accessed 5 June 2014).

Bloom, A. (1981). *The Linguistic Shaping of Thought: A Study in the Impact of Language on Thinking in China and the West*. Hillsdale, N. J.: Lawrence Erlbaum Associates.

Boas, F. (1940). *Race, Language, and Culture*. New York: Free Press.

Conklin, H. (1955). Hanonóo Color Categories. *Southwestern Journal of Anthropology* 11: 339–344.

Deutscher, G. (2005). *Why the World Looks Different in Other Languages*. New York: Henry Holt.

Huang, A. H., Yen, D. C., and Zhang, X. (2008). Exploring the Potential Effects of Emoticons. *Information & Management* 45: 466–473.

Kramsch, C. (1998). *Language and Culture*. Oxford: Oxford University Press.

Lakoff, G. (1987). *Women, Fire, and Dangerous Things: What Categories Reveal about the Mind*. Chicago: University of Chicago Press.

Lakoff, G. and Johnson, M. (1980). *Metaphors We Live By*. Chicago: Chicago University Press.

Lanchantin, T., Simoës-Perlant, A., and Largy, P. (2012). The Case of Digital Writing in Instant Messaging: When Cyber Written Productions are Closer to the Oral Code Than the Written Code. *Psychology Journal* 10: 187–214.

Langacker, R. W. (1987). *Foundations of Cognitive Grammar*. Stanford: Stanford University Press.

Langacker, R. W. (1990). *Concept, Image, and Symbol: The Cognitive Basis of Grammar*. Berlin: Mouton de Gruyter.

Langacker, R. W. (1999). *Grammar and Conceptualization*. Berlin: Mouton de Gruyter.

Lucy, J. (1996). The Scope of Linguistic Relativity: An Analysis and Review of Empirical Research. In: J. Gumperz and S. Levinson (eds.), *Rethinking Linguistic Relativity*, pp. 37–70, New York: Cambridge University Press.

Malcolm, I. G. and Sharafian, F. (2002). Aspects of Aboriginal English Oral Discourse: An Application of Cultural Schema Theory. *Discourse Studies* 4: 169–181.

Martin, L. (1986). Eskimo Words for Snow: A Case Study in the Genesis and Decay of an Anthropological Example. *American Anthropologist* 88: 418–423.

Nishida, H. (1999). Cultural Schema Theory: In: W. B. Gudykunst (ed.), *Theorizing About Intercultural Communication*, pp. 401–418. Thousand Oaks: Sage Publications.

Pullum, G. (1991). *The Great Eskimo Vocabulary Hoax and other Irreverent Essays on the Study of Language*. Chicago: University of Chicago Press.

Ray, V. (1953). Human Color Perception and Behavioral Response. *Transactions of the New York Academy of Sciences*, Volume 16.

Sapir, E. (1921). *Language*. New York: Harcourt, Brace, and World.

Tagliamonte, S. A. and Denis, D. (2008). Linguistic Ruin? Lol! Instant Messaging and Teen Language. *American Speech* 83: 3–34.

Wei, F., Wang, W. K., and Klausner, M. (2012). Rethinking College Students' Self-Regulation and Sustained Attention: Does Text Messaging During Class Influence Cognitive Learning? *Communication Education* 61: 185–204.

Whorf, B. L. (1956). *Language, Thought, and Reality*, J. B. Carroll (ed.). Cambridge, Mass.: MIT Press.

Wrisley, G. (2014). Rules, Language, and Reality. *Philosophy Now* 58. http://philosophynow.org/issues/58/Rules_Language_and_Reality.

Zappavigna, M. (2011). Ambient Affiliation: A Linguistic Perspective on Twitter. *New Media & Society* 135: 788–806.

9 Overview

Words convey the mental treasures of one period to the generations that follow; and laden with this, their precious freight, they sail safely across gulfs of time in which empires have suffered shipwreck and the languages of common life have sunk into oblivion.

Anonymous

Sociolinguistics studies the interconnection between language, society and verbal communication. Everything from conversations, titles, slang, and text messaging to bilingualism and language maintenance in ethnic communities and borrowing among languages can be looked at with sociolinguistic eyes, so to speak, because they lead to an understanding of how this interconnection unfolds. The application of sociolinguistic methods to new media, as a consequence, is leading to new insights between language and the medium used to interact with it. Take, for example, blogs. Blogging is now a major form of writing, replacing, in some cases, the traditional print article. The earliest blogs originated in the online discussion of chat groups of the early internet, some of which reach as far back as the 1970s (including such online services as bulletin board systems). Some blogs resemble magazines, complete with graphics, photos, audiovisual supports, and so on. Others are simple textual compositions. It is estimated that today there are more than 100 million blogs worldwide. They cover the entire gamut of human interest, from politics to cartoons.

Blogs have several advantages over print articles. First and foremost, they reach a broad (and potentially international) audience instantaneously and cheaply, whereas print articles take more time to release and entail many more costs to publish. Blogs can be edited online and thus can be updated continuously, while print articles need to be revised and republished over a period of time. Blogs can be maintained permanently on websites and indexed in any way one wishes (in the order in which they were written, according to themes, and so on). They can easily include visual and audio material, and feedback is rapid and far-reaching, since most blogs allow for readers to respond and leave comments on the site, to which the blogger can reply. This has led to the formation of blogging communities. A collection of "local blogs" is sometimes called a bloghood. Comments are the basis for the trackback feature, which transmits alerts to previous commentators. In addition, permalinks allow users to comment on specific posts rather than on entire blogs, and this, in turn, allows the blog to create an archive of past posts.

Blogs have impacted significantly on the conduct of journalism and on writing traditions generally. One no longer has to submit a piece of writing to an editorial process based on selection and preference variables, as is typically the case in the world of traditional print culture. This means that there is likely to be very little prepublication quality control. The value of a blog is assessed by the inhabitants of the blogosphere, not by some editor or evaluator in advance. In other words, it is up to the user, not a filtering agent or agency, to decide if a blog has merit or not. In a way, this has put the onus on writers to write honestly and accurately, since their opinions and facts can easily be checked on the internet and discussed throughout the blogosphere (Rodzvilla 2009).

Blogs have also changed many social rules and systems. The rise of the political blog to social importance is evidenced by various events in the early 2000s. In one 2002 case, bloggers critiqued comments made by US Senate majority leader Trent Lott at a party in honor of Senator Strom Thurmond. Lott suggested that Thurmond would have made the ideal president. The bloggers portrayed this as implicit approval of racial segregation, since Thurmond had seemingly promoted segregation in his 1948 presidential campaign, as documents recovered by the bloggers showed. The mainstream media never reported on this story until after the bloggers broke it. The end result was that Lott stepped down as majority leader.

Given the increasing power of the blogosphere, it should come as no surprise to find that by 2004 politicians, governments, and other social groups joined the blogosphere. Many claim that US President Barack Obama's 2008 victory was largely fuelled by enthusiastic bloggers constantly putting forward his message about the need for change.

Blogging has also made it possible for those who previously would not have been noticed by the mainstream media to garner attention. Authors of books now have blogs to inform their readership about various aspects of their writing. A novelist, for example, might maintain a blog to inform readers about the background to the novel as well as to field questions from readers. Some have even used the blog format to publish their books, without going through a traditional publishing house. There are now prizes for the best blog-based book. The story of blogs can be reiterated throughout the CMC universe. It is showing that medium, channel, and mode of communication do indeed alter language and the social patterns its encodes.

In this final chapter, we will take an overview of sociolinguistic method today, especially as it applies to the new media of communication. Many of the ideas introduced earlier are repeated here for the sake of summary and integration and in order to tie a few loose strings together.

9.1 Computer-Mediated Communication

In a series of books, the sociologist Manuel Castells (1989, 1996, 2001) warned everyone, before the advent of Web 2.0 technologies, of the economic and social transformations that the information technology revolution was bringing about. His main argument was that a new type of human communication and interaction had emerged that was more variable and more global than ever before in human history, repeatedly facing worldwide (rather than nationalistic) challenges.

CMC has indeed changed the world. Mathematician Norbert Wiener (1948) was among the first to realize that, because of science and technology, one could not only draw analogies between machines (robots and computers) and humans, but also study the psychological and social consequences of human and machine interfaces and interactions. CMC is a product of these, bringing about a new and multifaceted form of communicative competence, which can be defined as the ability of internet citizens to use language in different digital media and alter it to fit the physical and conceptual features of the media involved. As Androutsopoulos (2006) has aptly argued, CMC provides a new empirical venue for studying communicative competence and sociolinguistic variation.

9.1.1 Linguistic Features

The starting point, as we have seen several times already, is to look at various forms and structures in language that can be connected to social and communicative structures. In the case of CMC, the main patterns include:

1   The use of functionally distinct features (hashtags, for example) that make it recognizable from other forms.
2   Attenuation of the formal-versus-informal register option, with a growing admixture of formal and informal traits.
3   The abundant use of abbreviated writing.
4   The breaking down of various writing and grammatical conventions.
5   The use of personalized language forms as part of a construction of identity.

It is interesting to note, that at the start of Web 2.0, abbreviations were capitalized, but now they are generally not; *lol* (or *haha*) is also often used in place of punctuation; a function also taken on by smileys or <3 [All examples taken from University of Toronto student messages enrolled in a sociolinguistics class and offered to the instructor as part of research for this book]:

"I'm utterly disturbed… lol"

"Walking for 20 minutes a day will prevent my depression… except my 20 minute walk is me walking to class lol not exactly uplifting"

"Except now I really need cider <3 I apparently really like drinks"

"My prof would trip over his mic in my smallest class and look at me as I'm trying to contain myself haha wouldn't have gotten caught in con hall"

The compacting of phrases and sentences is now also a standard form of syntax:

"i'll facebook her" = I'll send her a Facebook message

"i tumbled it" = I posted it on Tumblr

"i pinned it" = I posted it on Pinterest

A message in all caps signifies high degrees of emotivity, as does the abundant use of punctuation marks and the repetition of letters:

"WHY IS THERE NO MORE SUN IN MY LIFE"

"I'M FREE ON SATURDAYYY"

"omg and IT'S TRANSPARENT"

"?!" (disbelief)

"I'm sorry, did we just fast forward to winter?! Soooo cold"

"What happened?! I didn't think it was serious

"i am soooooooooo bored"

"Can you pleeeeeeaseeeee help me?"

"Ahhahaha!! I've never seen that one, I dunno but they're hilarious, such great gifts :)"

Hashtags have also emerged to signify searchable talk, altering somewhat their initial function of indexing, categorizing and the searching of tweets. They are now placed within a sentence, or at the end:

"Nothing says fall like a sweater for #PSL. Cooler weather is definitely here. (Starbucks FB ad)"

"To cover the #eyes. To be emotionally #anonymous. Is that #freedom"

When placed at the end of the sentence, the hashtag seems to force tweeters to draw a certain conclusion:

"Just paid $17 for 12 books at the Vic College Book Sale #noregrets"

"Paper due Tuesday... time to paint my nails! #procrastination #favecolour"

"Preparing for the hurricane #hunters #obvs"

"First quasi road trip under my belt. Drove straight from Ithaca to Newark, non-stop. At night. #driversdiary #driving #love @kristness"

"Dose of cuteness from meinen Deutscher schäferhund. #hund #love #german#cute"

"Fun in the sun #unigames #unimelb #gold coast"

It is also used broadly to convey sarcasm or mockery:

"Selfie saturdayyyzzzz xoxo #noshame"

"Ahhh another beautiful morning in Kensington... #sarcasm #graffiti#no filtercouldsavethis"

"#BESTROOMMATEEVER #WHATWOULDIDOWITHOUTHIM

"#IDBEHAPPIER"

As mentioned previously (section 5.4.2, Chapter 5) Ruth Page (2012) has shown how hashtags are now part of self-branding. She portrays Twitter as a marketplace where self-branding and micro-celebrities are made or at least presented. Hashtags are a powerful resource within this system, varying according to discourse styles, from those adopted by corporations to everyday Twitter users. Hashtags are thus a new form of discourse, exhibiting many of the same features of media talk and hype as found in advertising contexts.

CMC has also introduced new styles and practices in protocols, thus changing the perception of registers and sociolects. On Facebook posts it is standard practice to not use any greeting formula or sign-off cue:

"Just finished that assignment a full week in advance in a totally unprecedented outburst of preparedness – thought you'd be proud of me"

"electro swing is having another thing on nov 8"

"I just went back through all our camping photos and have a sudden urge to go canoeing with you"

However, there are gender-based and age-based differences in the use of protocols. Older people tend to sign off regularly:

"looking forward to you coming, love grandad and nanni"

"When is the play? In the fall? Have a nice weekend, Mamie"

Females often sign off to other females with "love you" (and similar affection expressions):

"bahaha oh yeahhhh. LOVE YOUU"

"you were really awesome this weekend. love you!"

"Internet was being stupid, can we try calling another time? Love you!"

"SO DRUNK LOVE YOUUUU"

The research on CMC language has also made it obvious that some of the older linguistic categories, email-versus-textspeak, may be breaking down as CMC language gradually develops standardized forms and uses.

Is this new language affecting language overall and having a deleterious effect on traditions of writing and literacy? In a comprehensive study, Varnhagen et al. (2010) collected instant messaging conversations over a one-week period from adolescents to develop a taxonomy of new language use. Then they gave the subjects a writing task and found that the short-cuts, abbreviations, acronyms, and unique spellings that were most prevalent in the instant message conversations, along with pragmatic signals, such as emoticons and emotion words, were relatively uncommon in the written assignment. With rare exceptions, notably true spelling errors, spelling ability was not related to use of instant messaging. They concluded that CMC does not have a harmful effect on conventional written language.

With regard to other sociolinguistic phenomena, it seems that the literature is equivocal in terms of gender differences. Females tend to use more emoticons in instant messaging than do males, but it has also been found, paradoxically, that males also use more emotional markers in online communication than they seemingly do in offline contexts.

Paralinguistic

This term is used by linguists to refer to features that accompany vocal speech and are superimposed on speech simultaneously. Paralanguage includes all noises and sounds that are extra-speech sounds, such as hissing, shushing, whistling, and imitation sounds, as well as a large variety of speech modifications, such as quality of voice, pitch, tone, hesitations, and speed in talking.

Paralinguistic features also include nonverbal cues such as gestures and facial expressions that accompany vocal speech.

The emoticon is a paralinguistic feature. In oral speech a listener may understand whether a message is a question or a statement based on the speaker's tone of voice or even facial expression, conveying a sense of surprise about the situation or statement. Emoticons are, at one level, an attempt to compensate for the lack of paralinguistic features in written language. Emoticons thus represent facial cues that in F2F talk indicate the mood and/or attitude of the user. But there is much more to the emoticon than paralinguistics. Emoticons often have pragmatic function, especially when they appear strategically in an entire utterance. Consider the following examples of a text message:

((BrknHeartd) :-)

Wanna watch a program? / lol:-) / or are you too busy?]

(:-D juuuuuuuuuuuuuust joking around

:-) :-) :-) let me say :-) :-) that I really like u

OK!

In each instance, the emoticons serve to elicit a response from the interlocutor in the conversation. The "BrknHeartd's" smile indicates a need to change the topic of the conversation taking place, constituting an entreaty to continue sympathetically. In this instance, "BrknHeartd" functions as a rhetorical device that allows for a turn-taking shift in the conversation. The emoticon smiley (as opposed to any other kind of cue, such as "haha" or "lol" or "<smile>") demonstrates sophisticated pragmatic knowledge of how to use the symbol. Essentially, the smiling visual icon stands not only for the face, but also for a shift in the conversation. Because the invitation appears to have been rejected, as can be seen by the interlocutor's expression of regret, the other interlocutor alters the response ("just joking around") to attenuate the situation. The repeated emoticons suggest a pause in the utterance, much like hedges, so that ideas can be elaborated along the path of the utterance.

9.1.2 Sociolinguistic Aspects

The traditional sociolinguistic patterns are etching themselves into online contexts and morphing somewhat. This has brought about new forms of the traditional discourse structures that involve new modes of communication involving turn-taking and sequencing, thus altering register and sociolectal structure.

As we have seen throughout, variables such as age, gender, and class are involved in shaping speech, and they are producing new patterns in online speech. Tossell et al. (2012) studied the use of emoticons in text messages from smart phones aiming to determine how the genders differed in the frequency and variety of emoticons used. Previous research had found small and sundry differences in emotive expression online suggesting that technology had closed the gender gap. However, their data, based on private communications data over a six-month period, discovered that emoticon use had indeed diminished considerably but significantly that differences between the genders continued to manifest themselves in the amount and variety of emoticons used. Females sent more messages with emoticons; however, the surprising finding was that males used a more diverse range of emoticons. A related study by Derks, Bos, and Grumbkow (2007) suggested that social context (task-oriented versus socio-emotional), rather than gender, influenced the use of emoticons in CMC. When compared to the work on facial expression in F2F, the researchers claim that the online mode corresponds to the offline one. A similar pattern of findings emerged from the study conducted by Ilona Vandergriff in 2013. So, it would seem that some of the factors that made communication gender-distinct are breaking down, while other remain.

9.2 Virtual Communities

One of the basic notions of sociolinguistics is that of speech community, as we have seen, since it is within communities that speech characteristics develop to unite members producing specific kinds of linguistic practices. The concept of *virtual community*, however, implies a greater reach in terms of members of a community and in terms of the fact that people now may belong to many virtual communities, each with different forms of communication, registers, and discourse styles. Finding a definition for virtual communities (VCs) that can be used universally by sociolinguists to conduct research with the standard tools of the discipline is proving to be elusive. An early definition by Rheingold (1993: 5) is still a useful one: "social aggregations that emerge from the Net when enough people carry on public discussions long enough, with sufficient human feeling, to form webs of personal relationships in cyberspace."

Added to this is the fact that VCs are vastly different social structures because they do not provide physical contact and proximity and they lack the stable membership, commitment, longevity, and accountability that would make them qualify as communities in the traditional sense. So, VCs require a different purview of this basic sociolinguistic concept. As Castells (2000: 389) has put it, VCs "do not follow the same patterns of communication and interaction as physical communities do. But they are not 'unreal,' they work in a different plane of reality." Currently, e-sociolinguistics has identified features that would allow for a definition of VC with respect to the traditional speech community. These include (Preece, Maloney-Krichmar and Abras 2003: 1023):

1   regular communication around a shared purpose or interest

2   the development of linguistic and social practices based on this interest, including specialized vocabulary encoding group-specific meanings
3   the negotiation of social and linguistic identities within the virtual community
4   the creation of linguistic norms that allow members to organize interactions and to make conversation and dialogue fluid and efficient
5   the development of rituals and politeness strategies that maintain hierarchies of various kinds (not necessarily based on class and background)
6   development of conversation gambits designed to maintain harmony and thus to resolve conflicts and rivalries.

VCs thus seem to blend online and offline community practices. Some VCs, like Twitter communities, are based around "a shared, negotiated, and fairly specific enterprise" (Meyerhoff 2006), and thus occasional users of the site may not truly be part of the communities.

The question of linguistic identity is also a critical one for defining VCs, since it is typically formed within speech communities. Given the individual freedom granted by the anonymity of VCs, virtual identities are now being forged that are different from offline ones. Personal homepages are reflections of such identities, since these allow for the construction of multiple personae through a blending of word and image (Miller and Arnold 2001). Internet users have a variety of resources to "interactively create identifiable personalities for themselves," including the choice of online names and signatures, new in-group language, explicit forms of self-disclosure, and the assumption of a particular role within the group (Baym 1998, 2000). The construction of linguistic and social identities online is now a major area of interest within e-sociolinguistics.

VCs are best described as imagined communities. In a study of Twitter communities Gruzd, Wellman, and Takhteyev (2011) describe the characteristics that make up such communities as follows:

1   A common language. Twitterspeak, for example, is based on a set of linguistic conventions constructed by Twitter participants, including the use of hashtags to identify intrinsic topics. The hashtag is thus part of a "folksonomy," a user-created naming system, which is quite distinct from a taxonomy, a centrally created naming system.
2   A dual-faceted community structure. It is at once both collective and personal. It is collective because tweeps belong to the worldwide group of tweeps who understand Twitter's common language and its norms. Moreover, almost all tweeps' pages and messages are reachable—and hence readable—except for a small number of partially locked private pages. Yet community on Twitter is also personal because tweeps imagine they are following and talking to specific other tweeps.

3   There is a sense of belonging and thus the belief that members have the ability to influence others in the network through their replies and retweeting.

Twitter is a good case-in-point to understand how people integrate information and communication technologies to form new social connections or maintain existing ones. Such communities are more successful than real-world ones because they are open to newcomers. Any tweep can start following any other tweep without requiring the other tweep to follow them back. And no initiation rites or rituals are involved. In this community, tweets from newcomers are often responded to, making it easier for them to get connected.

9.2.1 Ethnography

As mentioned at the beginning of this book, in addition to quantitative research methods, sociolinguists employ ethnography, which entails (usually) living among the subjects studied. In VCs this has obvious different implications than it does in traditional speech communities.

As E. Gabriella Coleman (2010: 488) has aptly put it, "digital artifacts have helped engender new collectivities: Web-cam girls, gamers, hackers, and others, whose senses of self, vocation, and group sociabilities are shaped significantly, although not exclusively nor deterministically, by digital technologies." She goes on to argue that a new form of ethnography is needed to study the new VCs and their characteristics, because of the synergy that online culture is having on offline society: "digital media feed into, reflect, and shape other kinds of social practices, like economic exchange, financial markets, and religious worship. Attention to these rituals, broad contexts, and the material infrastructures and social protocols that enable them illuminates how the use and production of digital media have become integrated into everyday cultural, linguistic, and economic life." Clearly, she goes on to argue, a new ethnography is needed—a cyberspace ethnography—that can study these linkages with new tools, including software algorithms, data mining techniques, and the like. All of these have been made possible because of the World Wide Web.

Not everyone agrees, of course, casting doubt on the autonomous power of technology to engender change and arguing that, far from stimulating breakdowns of the old rigorous social order, digital technologies in many instances have facilitated social reproduction. Clearly, a new empirical approach to ethnography, integrating it with quantitative methods, is now a crucial aspect of research methodology. It would take VCs and their discourse practices as a starting point to gain access into the nature of all the other variables, modes, and features of language in cyberspace, and to map these against the offline world. An ethnographic approach that is consistent with the shift of perspective, emphasizing the local and situated character of internet community practices is now of vital importance.

One of the implicit findings of the research studies (a number of which have been discussed in previous chapters) is that the internet is no longer a monolithic structure, but rather an interconnected system of separate communities and practices that involve different technologies, norms, and rituals. As with F2F studies of community and identity, there are various versions of cyberspace ethnography, which can be subdivided into several main approaches:

1   The systematic observation of sites, venues, and devices to document discourse and conversations in cyberspace, complementing this with actual F2F interviews with the participants (Hine 2000), and with the goal of determining if participants form a true community.
2   The researcher may or may not become involved as a member of a community (or communities), unlike F2F ethnographic methods where such choice does not exist.
3   A blending of offline and online ethnographies, with an amalgamation of F2F interviews, questionnaires, and online methods of data-mining.

It is now impossible to not account for CMC as part of sociolinguistic analysis, given the increase in CMC today. The analysis of users in a 2009 study by Hoadley, Heng Xu and Rosson showed that Facebook has taken over many of the functions of F2F communication. More generally, internet use by all kinds of individuals, regardless of gender, class, ethnicity, and so on, indicates that virtually everyone now uses it to communicate on a daily basis, as user frequency studies now point out (Lenhart et al. 2010).

9.2.2 Some General Patterns

Data-mining is the term used by computer scientists to refer to the techniques of extracting relevant information from a set of raw data. The techniques include the automatic grouping of documents or files, categorizing them into directories, and analyzing patterns and interrelationships within them. One particular technique, called filtering, involves making profiles of people's interests and then comparing these against related information from various sources. The breadth and scope of the data-mining techniques available with the new technologies are mind-boggling, since it is now possible to collate disparate facts about individuals and generate profiles of various kinds (psychographic, sociographic, and so on) about them based on those facts in a matter of seconds. In this way, dialect usage, sociolectal variation, and various other parameters can now be compiled and examined in ways that were not possible in the past.

The World Wide Web

The World Wide Web is a system of computer files linked together on the internet. The first web software was invented by Tim Berners-Lee, a computer scientist at the European Organization for Nuclear Research (CERN) physics laboratory near Geneva, Switzerland.

It became part of the internet in 1991.

Web 1.0

A website is a site (location) on the World Wide Web. Each website contains a home page, which is the first document users see when they enter the site. The site might also contain additional documents and files. Each site is owned and managed by an individual, company or organization.

Browsers are software applications which allow Web users to surf the Web and to access web pages by interpreting HTML files and other languages used on the Web. The first popular web browser was NCSA Mosaic, whose version 1.0 was released in September 1993 (its development was discontinued in 1997).

Web 2.0

The term *Web 2.0* refers to the second generation of the World Wide Web that is focused on the ability for people to collaborate and share information online. Web 2.0 basically refers to the transition from static HTML Web pages to a more dynamic system.

The term was proposed for the first time in 2004 as a provocative suggestion, and has since then garnered great attention. Web 2.0 is a new way of using the Web itself, whose key components are *user-generated contents* (UGC).

Besides expanding the group of online publishers—hence moving from "passive"/"read only" competence to "active"/"read and write" competence—Web 2.0 also supports a different metaphor of the web itself, not only conceived as an expanding library (where you can go and pull as much information as you like), but also as a public place, where people go to meet other people and have shared experiences.

The services that Web 2.0 makes available are: *Social networks* (Twitter, Facebook, YouTube) which are services that support social exchanges within given groups, allowing members to share data and knowledge or find the right people; and *Wikis*, which are websites that support collaborative document editing, such as Wikipedia.

Some of the general patterns derived from virtual ethnographies (many of which are based on data-mining) can be summarized as follows:

- Sociophonology is harder to examine in online contexts, although phonemic patterns can be both inferred from writing (as we saw) and collected through follow-up interviews, phone calls, and other audio-oral media.
- Gender and age can often be inferred from screen names and member profiles, while participant status (core versus peripheral users) is determinable using discourse register and style criteria.
- Members of VCs generally make their social profile explicit in terms of age, geographical location, ethnicity, in combination with various social categories. The traditional notions of politeness, honorific protocols, bilingual code-switching can now be accessed through this indirect process.
- Research on the relationship between language and identity in CMC and on language and gender has been discussed several times already. Overall, while there is some ambiguity in the findings, by and large, the F2F dichotomies have surfaced in cyberspace ethnographies. There continue to be systematic differences in style between males and females, older and younger, higher and lower classes, and so on and so forth.
- In asynchronous CMC, male users tend to write more and longer messages; male discourse style is characterized by strong assertions, disagreement and less politeness than female style, which is characterized by affective speech patterns and the expression of feelings. In synchronous CMC, males use more profanity and slang styles than females, who use more emoticons and laughter, as well as neutral verbs. In sharp contrast to the illusion of egalitarian discourse on the internet, gender asymmetries and male dominance seem to persist.
- However, Huffaker and Calvert (2005: 19) found that "blogs operated by young males and females are more alike than different" and that male adolescent bloggers use more emoticons than females, while the latter "are not using language that is more passive, accommodating, or cooperative." The assumptions that gender bias exists in all spaces is breaking down with cyberspace ethnographies, which now show that there is a performance of

gender in virtual interaction rather than a habitual response to social role perceptions.

- A growing body of research examining multilingualism on the internet is showing two contrasting trends: the dominance of English as a lingua franca and the emergence of a new type of linguistic diversity online. English dominated the cyberspace landscape of the 1990s in terms of both users and the language used on available websites. Since then there has been an increase in linguistic diversity, with many users and websites today using a language other than English.
- Therefore, the internet is contributing to the preservation of endangered languages and dialects, providing a space for different literacies using variants. However, the success of these utilizations ultimately depends on the active participation of the population concerned.

9.3 Communicative Competence Again

Sociolinguistics deals essentially with communicative competence, in one form or other—either as a means for accessing the social processes that communicative events imply or else as a database for examining linguistic variation in all its forms. Perhaps never before in the history of sociolinguistics has it been possible to study the structure, strategies, and various other features of conversations than it is today in cyberspace, where Web 2.0 technologies have made conversational data available to anyone who seeks it. Here previous messages provide the datasets required to analyze conversations in all CMC contexts. As Gillen and Merchant (2013) have argued, perhaps the notion of communicative competence, as online research is now showing, needs to be refashioned as part of a more generic competence, that involves technological savvy.

For example, an important feature of Twitter is the fact that the individual user can choose who to attend to—whose tweets to read and whose to filter out. An individual Twitter account allows people to search for and select others to follow, and this selection determines whose tweets show up on one's own page. This gives the individual a personal point of view and a social network that is not possible in real space. This entails a different form of communicative competence that is based on the technological aspects of a VC, rather than on speech patterns in themselves. To participate in Twitter is to enter into a discursive relationship with others and to expect more flexibility in style and procedures than in F2F contexts.

There actually may be two competencies, real-world communicative competence (RCC) and digital communicative competence (DCC), with the two often blending into a general form of communicative competence, especially in proficient uses of both forms of language. There is some evidence that DCC is weaker in older netizens. A study by Stapa (2012), for example, investigating the language features and patterns of online communicative language among Malaysian Facebook users found that there is an age gap or linguistic disparity that differentiates the young online users from the older generations who are not used to online communication environments. After examining Facebook conversations among 120 young Malaysians from different ethnic groups, mother tongues, and cultural background, the study found that DCC involves a new sense of linguistic identity that is not found among older users. Needless to say, as young netizens age, it will be interesting to see how many of the characteristics that now define DCC will be carried over into subsequent life and transmitted to subsequent generations.

9.3.1 Online–Offline Synergies

Conversational analysis, as we saw, is a means used by sociolinguistics to penetrate social roles and relations. So, what has the research based on virtual ethnography revealed overall? CMC is an all-encompassing term for a wide range of writing options, since it both resembles offline texts and oral speech. We also have different expectations of CMC messages—we expect a web page to be more of a finished product and instant messages as part of ongoing conversations. But nowadays, websites are becoming increasingly interactive, and thus taking on the same patterns of text messages and F2F talk. Stepping back from individual modes of CMC, the research shows that conversation varies according to the: (1) function of the communication; (2) device constraints and features; (3) special linguistic forms (discussed above and elsewhere); and (4) profile of participants.

When linguists set about to write the "grammar" of a language, they presuppose the existence of a stable set of linguistic elements, combination rules, and usage conventions that characterize the knowledge that users of the linguistic system have. The problem with attempting to write grammars characterizing CMC is that CMC tends to be at once a diffuse and a moving target. Some people have suggested that use of written CMC will be replaced altogether by audio transmission of messages (perhaps complete with web cams). However, written CMC has a number of clear advantages over receiving audio signals: production of a durable record; potential to conceal age, gender, physical condition, or ethnic or linguistic background; relative privacy in public places; and the ability to multitask (compose and receive IM while speaking on the phone). Consequently, those who study the internet generally doubt that written CMC will disappear, regardless of technologically available alternatives. Since CMC is a written language, it is not surprising that some of the linguistic conventions common in more informal types of CMC are spreading to various other writing situations. Abbreviations and acronyms, random spellings, and haphazard grammar—all of which are generally accepted in the world of CMC—are increasingly showing up in informal print texts generally (notes, memos, and so on). But as mentioned in Chapter 7, the research is showing that CMC users are aware of the differences between registers and literacy levels nonetheless. A more subtle effect of CMC on traditional written language may be on text length. Historically, the emergence of telegraphy at the end of the nineteenth century helped shape a writing style that was more direct and used shorter sentences than usual writing style, given the physical constraints and related cost issues of the new technology. While it may be too soon to tell what effects the brevity of IM and SMS messages may have on writing in general, there are already signs that the internet is fostering different types of writing practices that may have some lasting effects on all forms of writing.

9.3.2 Motivations

In a relevant study, Pampek, Yermolayeva, and Calvert (2009) found that people used Facebook as part of a daily routine and that they communicated on Facebook using a one-to-many style, in which they were the creators disseminating content to their friends. Even so, they spent more time observing content on Facebook than actually posting content. As this study suggests, the motivations for communicating in digital venues is the same as the motivation for communicating, period—to socialize, to present oneself to others, and to gain understanding of things. The forms of communication may have changed, but the motivations seem to be the same ones.

The study of motivations has traditionally fallen outside the purview of traditional sociolinguistics, being considered more of a topic within psychology and psycholinguistics, since it is part of individual rather than social phenomena. But the research is telling a different story. For example, a study out of the University of Kansas, posting a video on YouTube asking the question "Why do you use YouTube?" received 370 video responses (Wesch 2007). The top ten answers as to why people use YouTube are shown below:

1. 61 percent—to connect with others or to be social.
2. 43 percent—for fun or entertainment.
3. 41 percent—simply because they like it.
4. 33 percent—to express their opinions.
5. 25 percent—to be creative.
6. 19 percent—because they are bored ("nothing better to do").
7. 17 percent—because it is more "real" or authentic than commercial productions.
8. 16 percent—hoping they might become famous.
9. 5 percent—to see what other people think of them.
10. 12 percent—because they are addicted.

The results were significant in attenuating some common assumptions about YouTube as a site simply for viral video watching. Most people go on YouTube to socialize. All this suggests that the main motivation in digital spaces is to socialize and the nature of the motivation may influence the type of language used. YouTube also creates its own VCs. YouTube has also educational uses, since many schools are now using it to deliver classes, lectures, and the like. Online learning communities have been called "adhocracies," or forms of organization with few fixed structures or established relationships between interlocutors. In other words, an adhocracy is the polar opposite of the contemporary university (which preserves rigid territories between disciplines and departments). McKinney (2006) argues that YouTube is an example of how VCs emerge spontaneously, without connection to historical in-group associations.

9.4 e-Sociolinguistics

The world has become smaller as a result of the emergence of internet technologies permitting communication across distances and independently of time constraints. It is now routine to communicate with people across the globe almost instantaneously, regardless of their national origins. This has changed the rules of social interaction and communication to varying degrees. The goal of e-sociolinguistics is to document this paradigm shift in human interaction.

As discussed throughout this book, the findings in F2F sociolinguistics and e-sociolinguistics are shedding light on the phenomenon of language variation as one governed not only by real space conditions, but also technology and modes of text-making. Unlike the traditional speech communities, VCs are not constrained to a specific geographic location or nation. They are interpersonal and increasingly intercultural ones, with members of diverse social, cultural, gender, racial, ethnic, class, and linguistic backgrounds sharing scattered sets of "virtual norms" regarding the use of language, which shape emerging styles within each VC. Seargeant and Tagg (2011) use the idea of hybrid languages, examining the mixture of English and Thai Facebook forms as typical of the new paradigm. Most hybrid languages involve English mixed with other languages, indicating the continuing hegemonic force of Anglo-American culture. People instinctively and habitually add English words or expressions to their native languages, reflecting transnational cultural flows that are different than the lingua franca flows of the past (Pennycook 2007). As e-sociolinguistic studies have shown, internet-facilitated globalization of English unnecessarily elicits the fear that English will assimilate or dominate all other languages. But the reality is a different one, since other languages are now influencing English.

One of the more important findings pertains to register. As discussed previously, Halliday and Hasan (1976: 22) define register as "the linguistic features, which are typically associated with a configuration of situational features—with particular values of the field, mode and tenor." The tendency in early work has been to categorize linguistic practices online as constituting distinct registers (Squires 2010). Some researchers argue that netspeak is neither a spoken nor written language, according to the conventional definitions of these two modes (Savas 2011). It cannot be categorized as a spoken mode because in CMC people cannot hear or talk to each other and the amount of information they exchange is far less than that in F2F communication. In this sense, online language is delivered primarily as a written language, unless technologies such as Skype are used instead. Online written communication, as we have seen, has many features of orality. Therefore, online language usually presents itself as incomplete or grammatically improper (lacking punctuation marks and capitalization), in ways that parallel spoken language. It is informal and may be synchronous and ephemeral like vocal speech, while it is also editable, text-based and asynchronous, like writing (Squires 2010). It belongs to both the spoken and written modes. Research is showing that grammatical change is coming through this hybrid mode, whereby "literary vocabulary, prepositions, conjoining, participles, the locative adverbials, and second person pronouns" are disappearing at the same time as it is changing the "coordination and the use of third person pronouns" (Freiermuth 2001: 23).

Al Sa' di and Hamdan (2005) compare spoken and written English to internet English (netspeak) and find attributes that align both the spoken and the written with internet English even though these do not align with each other in offline contexts. For example, in online chats, one expects immediate replies from one's interlocutor, which is similar to using language in F2F communication. But different from the spoken form, CMC can be edited and polished somewhat before the text is sent off, like the written mode of offline language. Internet language thus provides the sender far more opportunities to monitor the reader's feedback and effect repair than offline written language. Consequently, internet language is defined as "a distinct form" and "a new mode of language" (Freiermuth 2001; Savas 2011).

Tenor refers to "the type of role interaction, the set of relevant social relations, permanent and temporary, among the participants involved" (Halliday and Hasan 1976: 22). In communicative activities, the social status and roles of the participants are realized by diverse tenors, which are directly related to five levels of formality: frozen (static register), formal, consultative, casual, intimate (Joos 1967). As the research has shown, digital communication has reduced disparities of status, and made people communicate equally (at least in routine situations). Therefore, the linguistic styles on the internet tend to be casual and intimate, occasionally consultative, seldom frozen or formal, unless the situation requires it (such as e-mails to prospective employers). The ways to begin and end an online chat shows this: "Hi/hello", "ok?", "free?" or "chat?" which are common opening gambits, while "bye" or "88" without any further explanation are typical ending gambits.

Field is the total event "together with the purposive activity of the speaker or writer; and includes subject-matter as one of the elements" (Halliday and Hasan 1976: 22). Technical or non-technical speech is now leveled, given that online jargon is purposive allowing all classes of people to participate in it. But due to diverse nationalities, classes, and backgrounds, netizens who communicate online hardly share technical subject matter, being more inclined to engage in a casual chat about the immediacy of everyday life. In this sense, CMC is usually non-technical and without specific specialized purpose, unless the communication is intended to be so, as in scholarly online publishing and communication between professionals, which continues to be jargon-based.

Another general pattern pertains to politeness. In real space, politeness strategies are conditioned by three socio-interpersonal variables in a given context, which Brown and Levinson (1987) list as power, distance, and imposition. When the social distance between the interlocutors is great (for example, if they are strangers or know little about each other), the politeness strategies employed meets the expectation by showing deference, but if the speaker and listener have a close relation, then the ones used will convey solidarity. As Vinagre (2008) showed, in e-mail exchanges the participants are willing to ignore the convention of employing formulaic politeness strategies while using implicit ones to express their solidarity and friendliness, no matter what the social relation of the interlocutors.

The topic of languages in contact has been a major one in offline sociolinguistic research. In a relevant study Gao (2006) looked at language contact in CMC using data from Chinese internet chat, internet novels, personal e-mails, and various websites. From these he concludes that Chinese internet language is changing drastically and identifies English-based influences of syntactic adaptation in Chinese CMC including word order and word categorization. An example of this change is: "In (the sentence)- *Wo chi wufan zai jia li* [I eat lunch home inside] the prepositional phrase *zai jia li* (at home) was moved from before the verb phrase *chi wufan* (to have lunch) to after it" (Gao 2006: 301) due to English influence. Gao (2006) suggests that cross-modal linguistic influence in online communication could ultimately extend to the realm of non-electronic communication, which could lead to more permanent changes in language generally. However, not everyone would agree. Soffer (2012) suggests that online linguistic patterns are a reflection of current sociolinguistic tendencies and thus will not replace language use offline, just alternate with it.

Sociolinguistics is a thriving and adaptive field of research. A final cautionary comment is, however, in order. No matter how scientific, fact-based, or theoretically sound an account of the connection between language and society might appear or might be purported to be, no science can ever truly account for the remarkable phenomenon that we call language. We might be able to describe what the bits and pieces are like and how they mesh together; but we will never be able to put into a theory or model all there is to know about language. The goal of the linguist is to figure out how the pieces of the language puzzle fit together to produce meaning. But this tells us nothing about why meaning is needed in the first place, nor what relevance its encoding in language has to human survival. The research in sociolinguistics has shown that diversity is the norm, but that diversity reflects differentiated attempts to solve similar problems across the world. It shows how we come up with different solutions according to situation, time, and place. The fact that we can understand each other shows how much we are really all one race, equal and seeking similar objectives and outcomes to the experience of existence.

Terminology Review

Define or explain in your own words the following terms introduced in this chapter. Some of these have been already introduced but are elaborated upon here.

CMC   emoticon

ethnography   hashtag

paralinguistic   virtual community

Exercises and Discussion

1   Design a study of your own, using any technique you think is appropriate, to gather data on online language and its uses. For example, you may simply want to list all the abbreviations found across several Facebook pages and then extract general patterns from them.

2   Do you think that ethnography needs to change even more to study the languages used in various online venues, such as Facebook and Twitter?

3   Design a study to see how Twitter is used by specific Twitter communities.

4   What social practices do you think Twitter allows people to carry out?

5   Do you think that social media are replacing all other kinds of media for daily interaction?

6   Make a list of expressions that you use in online conversations and explain what each one means and why you use it.

7   Do you think that digital forms of language are affecting literacy negatively? If so, how so? If not, why not?

8   How would you explain the difference between sociolinguistics and e-sociolinguistics?

9   Do you believe that there is a synergy between online and offline communication? How do they affect each other?

10 Now that you have gone through the course, give ways that you can envision for using your new knowledge constructively and for helping others.

References

Al Sa' di, R. A. and Hamdan, J. M. (2005). Synchronous Online Chat English: Computer-Mediated Communication. *World Englishes* 24: 409–424.

Androutsopoulos, J. (2006). Sociolinguistics and Computer-Mediated Communication. *Journal of Sociolinguistics* 10: 419–438.

Baym, N. K. (1998). The Emergence of On-line Community. In: S. Jones (ed.), *CyberSociety 2.0: Revisiting Computer-Mediated Communication and Community*, pp. 35–68. London: Sage.

Baym, Nancy K. (2000). *Tune In, Log On: Soaps, Fandom, and On-Line Community*. Thousand Oaks, California: Sage.

Brown, P. and Levinson, S. C. (1987). *Politeness: Some Universals in Language Usage*. Cambridge: Cambridge University Press.

Castells, M. (1989). *The Informational City: Information Technology, Economic Restructuring, and the Urban Regional Process*. Oxford: Blackwell.

Castells, M. (1996). *The Information Age: Economy, Society, and Culture*. Oxford: Blackwell.

Castells, M. (2000). *The Internet Galaxy*. Oxford: Oxford University Press.

Coleman, E. C. (2010). Ethnographic Approaches to Digital Media. *Annual Review of Anthropology* 39: 487–505.

Derks, D., Bos, A. E. R., and Grumbkow, J. von (2007). Emoticons and Social Interaction on the Internet: The Importance of Social Context. *Computers in Human Behavior* 23: 842–849.

Freiermuth, M. R. (2001). *Features of Electronic Synchronous Communication: A Comparison of Online Chat, Spoken and Written Texts*. Stillwater: Oklahoma State University.

Gao, L. (2006). Language Contact and Convergence in Computer-Mediated Communication. *World English* 25: 299–308.

Gillen, J. and Merchant, G. (2013). Contact Calls: Twitter as a Dialogic Social and Linguistic Practice. *Language Sciences* 35: 47–58.

Gruzd, A., Wellman, B., and Takhteyev, Y. (2011). Imagining Twitter as an Imagined Community. *American Behavioral Scientist* 55 (10): 1294–1318.

Halliday, M. A. K. and Hasan, R. (1976). *Cohesion in English*. London: Longman.

Hine, C. (2000). *Virtual Ethnography*. London: Sage.

Hoadley, C. M., Heng Xu, J. J., and Rosson, M. B. (2009). Privacy as Information Access and Illusory Control: The Case of the Facebook News Feed Privacy Outcry. *Electronic Commerce Research and Applications* 9: 50–60.

Huffaker, D. A. and Calvert, S. L. (2005). Gender, Identity, and Language Use in Teenage Blogs. *Journal of Computer-Mediated Communication* 10: 2. http://jcmc.indiana.edu/vol10/issue2/huffaker.html .

Joos, M. (1967). *The Five Clocks*. New York: Harcourt, Brace and World.

Lenhart, A., Purcell, K., Smith, A., and Zickuhr, K. (2010). Social Media and Mobile Internet Use Among Teens and Young Adults. www.pewinternet.org/2010/02/03/social-media-and-young-adults (accessed 6 May 2015).

McKinney, J. (2006). Why YouTube Works. Unsought Input. www.unsoughtinput.com/index.php/2006/08/21/ (accessed 15 May 2014).

Meyerhoff, M. (2006). *Introducing Sociolinguistics*. London: Routledge.

Miller, H. and Arnold, J. (2001). Self in Web Home Pages: Gender, Identity and Power in Cyberspace. In: G. Riva and C. Galimberti (eds.), *Towards Cyberpsychology: Mind, Cognition and Society in the Internet Age*, pp. 74–93. Amsterdam: IOS Press.

Page, R. (2012). The Linguistics of Self-Branding and Micro-Celebrity in Twitter: The Role of Hashtags. *Discourse & Communication* 6: 181–201.

Pampek, T. A., Yermolayeva, Y. A., and Calvert, S. A. (2009). College Students' Social Networking Experiences on Facebook. *Journal of Applied Developmental Psychology* 30: 227–238.

Pennycook, A. (2007). *Global Englishes and Transcultural Flows*. London: Routledge.

Preece, J., Maloney-Krichmar, D., and Abras, C. (2003). History of Online Communities. In: K. Christiansen and D. Levinson (eds.), *Encyclopedia of Community*, pp. 1023–1027. Thousand Oaks: Sage.

Rheingold, H. (1993). *The Virtual Community*. Cambridge, Mass.: MIT Press.

Rodzvilla, J. (ed.) (2009). *We've Got Blog: How Weblogs Are Changing Our Culture*. New York: Basic Books.

Savas, P. (2011). A Case Study of Contextual and Individual Factors that Shape Linguistic Variation in Synchronous Text-Based Computer-Mediated Communication. *Journal of Pragmatics* 43: 298–313.

Seargeant, P. and Tagg, C. (2011). English on the Internet and a 'Post-Varieties' Approach to Language. *World Englishes* 30: 496–514.

Soffer, O. (2012). Liquid Language? On the Personalization of Discourse in the Digital Era. *New Media & Society* 14: 1092–1110.

Squires, L. (2010). Enregistering Internet Language. *Language in Society* 39: 457–492.

Stapa, S. H. (2012). Understanding Online Communicative Language Features In Social Networking Environment. *GEMA Online Journal of Linguistic Studies* 12: 817–830.

Tossell, C. C., Kortum, P., Shepard, C., Barg-Walkow, L. H., Rahmati, A., and Zhong, L. (2012). A Longitudinal Study of Emoticon Use in Text Messaging from Smartphones. *Computers in Human Behavior* 28: 659–663.

Vandergriff, I. (2013). Emotive Communication Online: A Contextual Analysis of Computer-Mediated Communication (CMC) Cues. *Journal of Pragmatics* 51: 1–12.

Varnhagen, C., McFall, P., Pugh, N., Routledge, L., Sumida-MacDonald, H., and Kwong, T. E. (2010). lol: New Language and Spelling in Instant Messaging. *Reading and Writing* 23(6): 719–733.

Vinagre, M. (2008). Politeness Strategies in Collaborative E-mail Exchanges. *Computers & Education*. 50: 1022–1036.

Wesch, P. (2007). Why do You Tube?—Video Response Analysis Digital. *Ethnography*. http://mediatedcultures.net/ksudigg/?p=82.

Wiener, N. (1948). *Cybernetics, or Control and Communication in the Animal and the Machine*. Cambridge, Mass.: MIT Press.

Glossary

accommodation theory	in communication theory, the idea that people adapt their speech characteristics to the situation at hand
acronym	word created from the first letters of other words: *NATO* is an acronym for *North Atlantic Treaty Organization*
addressee	initiator of a verbal interaction
addresser	intended receiver of a verbal message
adjacency pair	expressions that are often found together in conversations as part of turn-taking: *What's your name?* is normally followed by *My name is…*
affix	morpheme that is added to another lexeme or morpheme, such as the *ir-* in *irregular* and the *-al* in *national*
affricate	composite speech sound produced by a stop immediately followed by a fricative: the *ch* in *church* and the *j* in *junk*
allomorph	variant of a morpheme, that is, the actual form that a morpheme takes in a phrase: *a* and *an* are allomorphs of the same indefinite article morpheme, with *a* used before forms beginning with a consonant (*a boy, a girl*) and *an* before forms beginning with a vowel (*an egg, an apple*)
allophone	variant of a phoneme, that is, the actual form that a phoneme takes in a word: the [l] and [ɫ] sounds are allophones of /l/: the latter occurs at the end of syllables and words (*will, bill*), the former occurs elsewhere (*love, life*)

alphabet	system of symbols, known as letters or characters, whereby each symbol stands for a sound (or sounds) in words
alveolar	sound produced when the tongue touches the area just above the upper teeth
alveopalatal	sound produced when the tongue touches the area above the upper teeth where the hard palate begins
anaphoric device	word or particle that refers back to a word uttered or written previously in a sentence or a discourse: *he* in *Alex says that he likes baseball*
ANOVA	statistical method for analyzing variance in data
antonym	word with the opposite meaning of another word: *night* vs. *day*
argot	slang of specialized groups, especially criminal ones
asynchronous communication	communication that takes place over time (not simultaneously)
bilabial	sound produced by bringing both lips into contact with each other
bilingualism	the use of two languages by an individual, social group, or nation
borrowing	process of adopting a word from another language, for general use: Italian has borrowed the word *sport* from English
bound morpheme	morpheme that must be attached to another morpheme: *un-* and *-ly* in *unlikely*
calque	word-by-word translation of a foreign phrase or expression: the title *The Brothers Karamazov* is a calque of the corresponding Russian phrase (the word order in English should be *The Karamazov Brothers*)
cant	type of secretive slang used especially by criminal organizations
case	form of a noun, pronoun or adjective that indicates its syntactic relation to other words in a sentence
case study	study that examines a particular manifestation of a phenomenon
cataphoric device	word or particle that anticipates a word in a sentence or paragraph: *he* in *Although he likes Italy, Alex is not going this year*
central tendency	the main characteristic of a set of data
Chi-square test	measure of how closely the frequency distribution of actual data matches that expected in theory

code-mixing	mixing two or more languages during conversation
code-switching	alternating between two or more languages or varieties of language in conversation
cognates	words in different languages that are derived from the same source: Latin *pater* and English *father*
colloquialism	word or expression that is not formal but used in ordinary conversation
communicative competence	ability to use a language appropriately in social contexts
community of practice	group of people who share a common goal or outlook
commutation test	test comparing two forms that are alike in all respects except one, in order to see if a difference in meaning results: *pill* vs. *bill*
comparative grammar	early school of the language sciences based on comparing forms in languages to see if they are related historically
complementary distribution	process whereby allophones of the same phoneme occur in different environments: in English [pʰ] occurs in word-initial position followed by a vowel (*pin, pill*), whereas [p] occurs in all other positions (*spin, spill, prize, cap*)
componential analysis	breaking down the meaning of words into smaller components of meaning: for example, *man* is [+male, +human], *lion* is [+male, -human]
conative function	effect a message has or is intended to have on its receiver
conceptual metaphor	generalized metaphorical formula: *people are animals* underlies *He's a dog, She's a tiger*, and so on
connotation	extensional meaning of a word: the meaning of *cool* as "attractive"
consonant	sound produced by means of some obstruction to the airstream emanating from the lungs
contact	physical situation in which discourse occurs
context	psychological, social, and emotional relations people assume during discourse
contrast	minimal difference between two elements
conversation analysis	study of how conversations unfold
core vocabulary	basic vocabulary of a language, containing items such as *mother, father, son, daughter*, etc.

Creole	language that has developed from the mixture of two or more languages, becoming the first language of a group
critical period	period of childhood during which language is learned
cryptolect	language used for secretive purposes
cuneiform	wedge-shaped writing that makes it possible to inscribe symbols on hard materials (such as stone)
data mining	extracting data from the internet with appropriate algorithms
deixis	language form that points out or indicates something: *up, down, here, there*
demotic	type of ancient writing that reflected everyday speech
denotation	basic meaning of a word
dental	sound produced when the tongue touches the teeth
derivational morpheme	morpheme that is derived from some other morpheme: *emailing* is derived from *email*
diachronic analysis	analysis of change in language
dialect	regional or social variant of a language
dialect atlas	atlas of maps showing language forms in specific regions
dialect continuum	range of dialects spoken over a given region
dialectology	study of dialects
dialogue	conversation between people with a specific intent
différence	minimal feature that distinguishes the meaning of forms, such as *pin* versus *bin*, whereby a single sound changes the meaning
diglossia	the study of prestige in language forms
diphthong	syllable containing two vowels pronounced as one segment: *quick, tweak*
discourse	specific use of language in social ideological ways
displacement	feature of language whereby a word evokes what it stands for even if it is not present for the senses to process
distinctive feature	minimal trait in a form that serves to keep it distinct from other forms
double articulation	the notion that with a relatively small number of units (sounds) one can make forms and meanings ad infinitum
doublet	pairs of morphemes or lexemes that are associated with differential gender or class use

e-sociolinguistics	term used here for the study of language and society in online contexts
elaborated code	notion that formal language is an elaborated social code
emotive function	speaker's intent during discourse
empiricism	view that we learn language from scratch, so to speak, as if the mind were an empty slate
ethnography	method of collecting data by living among the subject group or by interacting with the group in some direct way
ethnology	alternative for *ethnography*
ethnosemantics	study of the relation between specific categories of language and cultural worldviews
Eye and Ear-to-Eye and Ear	type of communication involving the eyes and the ears
Face-to-Face (F2F)	communication in offline contexts
field	the total event of communication
fieldwork	research whereby the analyst lives among the subjects
filler	linguistic unit that serves a communicative function: for example, *Uhm, you know*
Finger-to-Keyboard (F2K)	communication involving a writing device
flap	sound produced by briefly striking the roof of the mouth: the *r* in *carrot*
FOXP2	gene that might be linked to a specific language impairment involving word inflections and complex syntax
frame analysis	study of how communication involves certain modes of presenting oneself strategically
free morpheme	morpheme that can exist on its own: *cautious* in *cautiously*
free variation	existence of two variant forms: the pronunciation of the /o/ in *tomato* as either open or close
frequency distribution	the number of instances that variables take in a set of data
fricative	sound produced by forcing the airstream through a narrow opening in the mouth: the *f* in *fish*, the *v* in *vine*
function word	word such as *the* or *and* that has grammatical function

gambit	verbal strategy for initiating or maintaining discourse flow
generative grammar	analysis of language based on examining the types of rules and rule-making principles by which sentences are generated
genre	type of speech act (speech, lecture, and so on)
gesticulant	gesture that accompanies vocal speech
gesture	communication involving hand movement
glide	sound produced by moving from one point of articulation to the next: the /w/ sound in *going* = /gowing/
glottal	sound produced by completely or partially closing the glottis
grammar	system of rules for the formation of words and sentences
ground	meaning of a metaphor; situation or conditions that affect communicative interaction
hedge	a type of speech strategy that has various communicative functions (*like, uhm, er*)
hieroglyph	form of Egyptian pictographic writing
homograph	word that is spelled the same as another but with a different meaning: *port* as in *The ship arrived at the post* vs. *Portuguese port is excellent wine*
homonym	word that is pronounced or spelled the same as another but with a different meaning: *play* as in *I like to play baseball* vs. *I didn't like that new play*
homophone	word that is pronounced the same as another but with a different meaning: *aunt* vs. *ant*
honorific	a word or expression indicating respect or class status (such as a title)
hypermedia	media involving multimodality and multimediality
hypertext	software system that links topics
hyponym	word that is inclusive of another: *flower* vs. *rose*
iconic gesture	gesture accompanying discourse that aims to actually show the shape of something mentioned in the utterance
idealized cognitive model (ICM)	amalgam of source domains used to deliver a cultural concept
ideograph	pictographic form that expresses an idea
idiolect	personal style of speech

illocutionary act	type of speech act that specifies a call to action: *Come here!*
index	form or unit that relates someone or something to something else in time, space, and the like
infix	affix added internally in a morpheme: *-li-* in *friendliness*
inflection	change in the form of a word: the *-s* in *plays*
inflectional morpheme	morpheme that produces inflection
innatism	view that we are born with a blueprint for language
interdental	sound produced by putting the tongue between the teeth: *th* in *thing*
interdiscursivity	discourses that build upon each other
International Phonetic Alphabet	abbreviated as IPA, is the standard system of symbols used by linguists to transcribe sounds
intertextuality	texts that refer to other texts during conversation
interview	questioning subjects for experimental purposes
intonation	pitch and tone in language
irony	word or statement used in such a way that it means the opposite of what it denotes: *What a beautiful day!* uttered on a stormy day
jargon	language of specialized groups (lawyers, doctors, etc.)
labiodental	sound produced by placing the upper teeth on the inside lower lip: *f* in *funny*
language maintenance	process of preserving a language or dialect
language planning	legislation and official policies aimed at language
language shift	movement away from one language to another
language spread	the diffusion of one particular variant of a language over regions
langue	theoretical knowledge of a language (its rules, its structure, etc.)
lateral	sound produced by letting the tip of the tongue touch the alveolar ridge so that air can escape on the sides: *l* in *love*
lexeme	morpheme with lexical meaning: *logic* in *logical*
lexical field	collection of lexemes that are interrelated thematically, such as sports vocabulary
lexicography	craft or science of dictionary-making
lexicon	set of morphemes in a language
lexicostatistics	mathematical study of time depth, the length of time since two related languages became separated

lingua franca	language adopted as a common language among speakers of different languages
linguistic competence	abstract knowledge of a language
linguistic performance	knowledge of how to use a language
linguistic profiling	use of linguistic features to identify the racial, ethnic, or other characteristics of speakers
linguistic relativity	view that languages influence how people come to perceive the world
liquid	consonant pronounced without friction: *l* in *love*, *r* in *right*
literacy	ability to read and write a language and to use it for formal purposes
loanword	word borrowed from another language: *cipher* was borrowed from the Arabic language
locutionary act	speech act that entails making a direct statement: *Her blouse is green*
manner of articulation	how a sound is articulated
marked category	form that is specific and not representative of an entire category
markedness	theory that certain forms in language are basic and others derived from them
mean	average in a set of data
median	mid point in a set of data
message	information or intent of a communication
metalingual function	referring to the forms of language used in discourse: *The word noun is a noun*
metaphor	process by which something abstract is rendered understandable by reference to something concrete: *Love is sweet*
metonymy	process whereby the part stands for the whole: *the White House* for "the American government"
minimal pair	pair like *pill* vs. *bill* which differ by only one sound in the same position
mode	way in which language is used
morpheme	minimal unit of meaning: in *cautiously* there are two morphemes *cautious* and *-ly*
morphology	level of language where words are formed
multilingualism	the presence of various languages in a collectivity
multimedia	use of more than one medium to create a message (text, video, audio, and so on)

multimodality	use of various modes to create messages
mutual intelligibility	the ability of speakers to understand each other—criterion used to establish dialects
myth	narrative recounting origins of cultures in some metaphysical way
name	word that identifies a person (and by extension animals, products, etc.)
nasal	sound produced by expelling the airstream partially through the nasal passage: *n* in *near*
nativization	process whereby a loanword is reshaped phonetically to become indistinguishable from a native word
netlingo (netspeak)	online language with its particular compressed forms
noncontinuant	consonant that is produced through complete blockage of the air stream
nonsegmental feature	feature that is not vocalic or consonantal
obstruent	sound produced with a degree of obstruction
occlusive	(also **stop** or **plosive**) sound produced by closure of the vocal tract: *p* in *pop* and *t* in *tight*
onomastics	study of names
opposition	difference that keeps units distinct, such as the opposition between *night* and *day*
palatal	sound produced when the tongue touches the hard palate: *ch* in *chin*
palatalization	process by which a sound becomes a palatal, or more like a palatal
parameter	feature of a specific language that manifests a more general innate principle
parole	knowledge of how to use a language
Pen-to-Ear (P2E)	communication involving writing and listening
Pen-to-Paper (P2P)	communication involving writing alone
perlocutionary act	speech act that entails a request for some action: *Can you call me?*
phatic function	use of language to make or maintain social contact: *How's it going?*
phone	technical name for speech sound
phoneme	minimal unit of sound that distinguishes meaning
phonemics	study of the phonemic system of a language
phonetics	description of how sounds are articulated
phonograph	writing symbol that approximates the pronunciation of a referent

phonology	sound system of a language
phrase structure	basic type of word arrangement in the construction of sentences
pictography	use of pictures to represent things, ideas, actions, and so on
pidgin	simplified language made up of elements of two or more languages
plosive	another name for *occlusive*
poetic function	language that possesses poetic features, such as repeating sounds: *no-no, pitter-patter*
point of articulation	place in the mouth where a sound is articulated
pop language	language spoken in the media that has spread to society at large
poverty of stimulus	notion that children must already know a lot about language to create meanings given that they are exposed to so little input
pragmatics	general analysis of language use
prefix	affix that is added before another morpheme: the *il-* in *illogical*
prosody	set of tones, intonations, etc. used in language
protolanguage	undocumented language that has been reconstructed
prototypical concept	basic member of a category: *cat* is a prototypical member of the *feline* category
qualitative analysis	research based on observation
quantitative analysis	research based on statistical analysis
referent	what a word refers to
referential function	use of words to refer to something other than the words themselves
register	style of language used in social situations
repair	strategy for correcting a misused language form
restricted code	code (usually dialectal) restricted to in-group use
root morpheme	morpheme with lexical meaning: the form *logic* in *logically*
segmental	any vowel or consonant sound
segmentation	decomposing a form or a phrase into its minimal elements: the word *illogically* can be segmented into *il-*, *logic*, *-al*, and *-ly*
semantics	study of meaning in language
sentence	minimal syntactic unit
sibilant	a consonant that is produced as a hiss, such as the *s* in *sister*

sign	something that stands for something other than itself
slang	socially-based variant of a language used by specific groups
sociolect	social dialect
sonorant	voiced sound
sound symbolism	use of sounds to construct words in such a way that they resemble the sound properties of their referents or to bring out some sound-based perception of meaning
source domain	concrete part of a conceptual metaphor: the *sweet* in *love is sweet*
specialized vocabulary	vocabulary used to describe specific things as collectivities: color terms, sitting devices, and so on
speech	language as it is used vocally or in writing
speech act	specific use of language to imply an action
speech community	group of speakers of a language
speech network	group of speakers who relate to each other in interconnected ways
standard deviation	degree to which data cluster around the average
standard language	language that societies agree to use for formal purposes
standardization	process whereby a dialect or variant is turned into a standard language
stop	another name for *occlusive*
stress	degree of force used to pronounce a vowel
structuralism	type of linguistic analysis aiming to study language as a system of structures
style	distinctive form of language connected to some social or individual usage
subordinate concept	concept that provides detail: for example, *Siamese* details a type of cat
suffix	affix added to the end of a morpheme: *-ly* in *logically*
suprasegmental	feature used with a segment (vowel or consonant), such as tone or accent
syllabary	list of symbols representing syllables
syllable	minimal breath group in the pronunciation of words
synchronic analysis	study of language at a particular point in time, usually the present
synchronous communication	communication that occurs in real time

synecdoche	figure of speech in which a part is made to represent the whole: *Milwaukee won the World Series* (*Milwaukee* = Milwaukee's baseball team)
synonym	word that has the same (approximate) meaning as another word: *happy–content*
syntax	study of how phrases, clauses, sentences, and entire texts are organized
t-test	statistical test used to determine if the data has significance
tag	word or phrase added to the end of a sentence to secure consent or something similar: *You agree, don't you?*
target domain	topic of a conceptual metaphor: the *love* in *love is sweet*
tenor	term referring to the participants in a conversation and their relationships
text	the term refers to the ways in which forms of language are combined in a coherent way to produce a message or some meaning
text message	type of message created by some mobile device
textspeak	language used in text messaging
topic	what the metaphor is about: the *love* in *love is sweet*
toponym	place name
tweet	message on Twitter
Universal Grammar	set of rule-making principles present in the brain at birth that make up the language faculty
unmarked category	default form in a class of forms
uvular	sound produced in the area of the uvula (at the back of the throat)
variation	process whereby forms vary according to geography, social class, etc.
vehicle	concrete part of a metaphor: the *sweet* in *love is sweet*
velar	sound produced with the back of the tongue close to or in contact with the soft palate: *k* in *kitchen*
vocabulary	set of morphemes in a language or in some discourse, conversation, etc.
vocalization	process by which a consonant is changed to a vowel
voiced	sound produced by vibrating the vocal cords in the larynx: *z* in *zip*
voiceless	sound produced by not vibrating the vocal cords in the larynx: *s* in *sip*

voicing	process whereby a voiceless consonant is voiced
vowel	sound produced with no significant obstruction to the airstream
Whorfian Hypothesis	theory which posits that a language predisposes its speakers to attend to certain aspects of reality as necessary
Zipf's Law	theory which claims that language forms are condensed, abbreviated, reduced, or eliminated to minimize the effort expended in producing and using them

Index